Cordelia Harris Turner

Cyclopedia of Practical Floriculture

Cordelia Harris Turner

Cyclopedia of Practical Floriculture

ISBN/EAN: 9783337222390

Printed in Europe, USA, Canada, Australia, Japan

Cover: Foto ©Andreas Hilbeck / pixelio.de

More available books at **www.hansebooks.com**

CYCLOPEDIA
— OF —
PRACTICAL FLORICULTURE,

EDITED BY

Mrs. C. H. Turner.

NEW YORK:
TOWNSEND MAC COUN.
1884.

Preface

THE love of flowers having become so nearly universal, it seems almost superfluous for an author to attempt any explanation in placing a work at all pertaining to the subject before the public, as every work, either elaborate or simple, must awaken a response in some heart where nature has placed her shrine. To those endowed with keen perceptions, the magnificent, intricate and wonderful handiwork of the All-wise is daily manifested, and always new, in the infinite variety of the floral world.

A number of years ago, the writer, being interested in the mythological legends of the Greeks and Romans, was frequently struck with the number of fabled gods and goddesses, and the various rural nymphs who attended them, that were transformed into a tree, shrub or flower, either to mitigate some sorrow, gratify revenge, or as a punishment for some breach of the laws supposed to govern the deities of that time.

Having made numerous memoranda of such legends, the love of flowers was sufficient to interest one in the general history of plants, their nativity, uses, the chief events in the history of each species, its cultivation and introduction into America. The "FLORAL KINGDOM"

PREFACE.

is the mature outgrowth of such notes. In order to make the book pleasing to the general reader, it has been the endeavor to exclude all technical terms pertaining to the science of botany, except the mere classification of plants into families to show the relation of one plant to another.

This arrangement has been made according to what is called the Natural System, it being the one most in use in the various books on botany, as more philosophical than the Linnaean System.

The sentiment or language assigned to each flower has been the result of an extended search through various works both ancient and modern, the most ancient being the richest, however, in material and in poetic ideas. The sentiments attached to flowers originating in the imaginative minds of the people, served as a means of communication at a time when the art of writing was known only to the few, these being mostly learned men and professional scribes. As the well known disagreements of authors in attributing different languages to the same plant often make it difficult to determine which to choose, it is proper to state that the sentiments here given have been preferred because of the weight of authority in their favor.

Having led the reader into the bowers of nature, what more natural than that many paths should be found leading into the garden of the poets, where rich intellectual blossoms are scattered with an unsparing hand? The love of poetry elevates the soul and makes it more susceptible to those delicate, spiritual and subtle influences that are found in other souls; it gives it a more rare appreciation of those higher beauties that are daily seen both in nature and art; it awakens a depth of feeling that almost entirely obliterates selfishness, and opens the heart to generous sympathies and warm impulses. The selections made for this work are numerous, and are the result of a very prolonged and laborious quest. They have been culled from many sources and various authors, foreign and native, and comprehend many of the choicest gems from the works of the best poets of all ages.   C. H. T.

Contents

ALPHABETICAL LIST OF AUTHORS QUOTED, . . . pages x - xi
AUTOGRAPH LETTER AND POEM, by William Cullen Bryant, . . " xii - xiii
HYMN TO THE FLOWERS, by Horace Smith, . . . " xiv - xv

PART I.—Description, Language and Poetry of Flowers.

	PAGE.		PAGE.
ACACIA (ROSE)—Friendship,	1	ASPHODEL—Remembered beyond the tomb,	31
ADDER'S TONGUE—Deceit,	2	ASTER—Cheerfulness in old age,	32
ADONIS—Sorrowful remembrances,	3	AURICULA—Painting,	33
AGERATUM—Politeness,	4	AZALEA—Temperance,	34
AGRIMONY—Thankfulness,	5	BACCHARIS—Intoxication,	35
AILANTUS—Lofty aspirations,	6	BACHELOR'S BUTTON—Single blessedness,	36
ALMOND—Despair,	7	BALM (MOLUCCA)—You excite my curiosity,	37
ALOE—Grief,	8	BALM (SWEET)—Charms,	38
ALOYSIA—Forgiveness,	9	BALM (WILD)—I value your sympathy,	39
ALYSSUM—Merit before beauty,	10	BALM OF GILEAD—Sympathetic feeling,	40
AMARANTH—Immortality,	11	BALSAMINE—Impatience,	41
AMARANTH (GLOBE)—I change not,	12	BARTONIA (GOLDEN)—Does he possess riches?	42
AMARYLLIS—Pride,	13	BASIL (SWEET)—Good wishes,	43
AMERICAN ARBOR VITÆ—Thine till death,	14	BAYBERRY—I respect thy tears,	44
AMERICAN ELM—Patriotism,	15	BEECH—Lovers' tryst,	45
AMERICAN LINDEN—Matrimony,	16	BEGONIA—Deformity,	46
ANDROMEDA (MARSH)—Bound by fate,	17	BELLFLOWER—A constant heart,	47
ANEMONE—Anticipation,	18	BERBERRY—A sour disposition,	48
ANGELICA—Inspiration,	19	BIRCH—Elegance,	49
APOCYNUM—Falsehood,	20	BLACK HOARHOUND—I reject you,	50
APPLE BLOSSOM—Preference,	21	BLADDERNUT—A trifling character,	51
APRICOT—Temptation,	22	BORAGE—Abruptness,	52
ARBUTUS—Simplicity,	23	BOUNCING BESS—Intrusion,	53
ARETHUSA—Fear,	24	BOX—Stoicism,	54
ARISTOLOCHIA—Prodigality,	25	BROOM—Humility,	55
ARNICA—Let me heal thy grief,	26	BROOM CORN—Labor,	56
ASCLEPIAS—Conquer your love,	27	BROWALLIA—Can you bear poverty?	57
ASH—Grandeur,	28	BUGLOSS—Hypocrisy,	58
ASPARAGUS—Emulation,	29	BULRUSH—Indecision,	59
ASPEN—Excessive sensibility,	30	BURDOCK—Proximity undesirable,	60

CONTENTS.

	PAGE		PAGE
BUTTERCUP—Distrust,	61	DARNEL—Vice,	112
BUTTERFLY ORCHIS—Gaiety,	62	DAY LILY—Coquetry,	113
CACALIA—Adulation,	63	DEADLY NIGHTSHADE—Death,	114
CACTUS (NIGHT-BLOOMING)—Transient beauty	64	DODDER—Baseness,	115
CACTUS (SNAKE)—You terrify me,	65	DOGWOOD—Honesty, true nobility,	116
CALCEOLARIA—Novelty,	66	DRAGON'S CLAW—Danger,	117
CALLA LILY—Feminine beauty,	67	DWARF PINK—Innocence,	118
CALYCANTHUS—Benevolence,	68	DYER'S WEED—Design,	119
CAMELLIA—Perfect loveliness,	69	EBENASTER—Night,	120
CANARY GRASS—Perseverance,	70	EGLANTINE—Home,	121
CANDYTUFT—Architecture,	71	ELDER—Zeal,	122
CANTERBURY BELLS—Gratitude,	72	ENCHANTER'S NIGHTSHADE—Sorcery,	123
CARDAMINE—Infatuation,	73	ENDIVE—Medicine,	124
CARDINAL FLOWER—Preferment,	74	ENGLISH MOSS—Fortitude,	125
CARNATION—Contempt,	75	ESCALLONIA—Opinion,	126
CATCHFLY—I am thy prisoner,	76	ETERNAL FLOWER—Eternity,	127
CEDAR (RED)—I live for thee,	77	EUPATORIUM—Delay,	128
CELANDINE—Future happiness,	78	EUPHORBIA—Reproof,	129
CHAMOMILE—Mercy,	79	EUTOCA—A Gift,	130
CHESTNUT—Deceptive appearances,	80	EYEBRIGHT—Your eyes are bewitching,	131
CHICKWEED—Star of my existence,	81	FENNEL—Worthy all praise,	132
CHICORY—Prudent economy,	82	FENNEL FLOWER—Artifice,	133
CHINA ASTER (DOUBLE)—Bounty,	83	FERN (WALKING)—Curiosity,	134
CHINA ASTER (SINGLE)—I will think of it,	84	FEVERFEW—Beneficence,	135
CHRYSANTHEMUM—Slighted affections,	85	FIR BALSAM—Health,	136
CINERARIA—Always delightful,	86	FLAX—Domestic industry,	137
CITRON—Marriage,	87	FLOWER-OF-AN-HOUR—Trifling beauty,	138
CLIANTHUS—Glorious beauty,	88	FOUR-O'CLOCK—Time,	139
CLOTBUR—Detraction,	89	FOXGLOVE—Delirium,	140
CLOVER—Industry,	90	FRITILLARIA—Persecution,	141
COBÆA—Gossip,	91	FUCHSIA—Grace,	142
COCKSCOMB—Foppery,	92	GENTIAN—Intrinsic worth,	143
COLUMBINE—Folly,	93	GERANIUM—Confidence,	144
COREOPSIS—Happy at all times,	94	GLADIOLUS—Ready armed,	145
CORIANDER—Merit,	95	GLOBE FLOWER—Fancy,	146
CORN COCKLE—Worth above beauty,	96	GOURD—Extent,	147
CORONILLA—Success crown your wishes,	97	GRASS—Utility,	148
COTTON PLANT—Greatness,	98	GROUND IVY—Enjoyment,	149
CRANBERRY—Hardihood,	99	GROUND PINE—Complaint,	150
CRAPE MYRTLE—Eloquence,	100	GUM TREE—Enthusiasm,	151
CROCUS (SPRING)—Cheerfulness,	101	HAWKWEED—Quick-sightedness,	152
CROWN IMPERIAL—Imperial power,	102	HEATH—Solitude,	153
CUPHEA—Impatience,	103	HELENIUM—Tears,	154
CURRANT—You please all,	104	HELIOTROPE—Devotion,	155
CYCLAMEN—Diffidence,	105	HELLEBORE—Calumny,	156
CYPRESS—Sorrow,	106	HEMP—Fate,	157
DAFFODIL—Chivalry,	107	HOLLYHOCK—Ambition,	158
DAHLIA—Dignity,	108	HOLLY—Foresight,	159
DAISY—Innocence and beauty,	109	HONESTY—Honesty,	160
DANDELION—Youthful recollections,	110	HONEYSUCKLE—Bonds of love,	161
DAPHNE—Sweets to the sweet,	111	HOP—Injustice,	162

CONTENTS.

	PAGE		PAGE
HORSE CHESTNUT—Luxury,	163	MOURNING BRIDE—Unfortunate attachment,	213
HOUSELEEK—Vivacity,	164	MULLEIN—Good nature,	214
HOYA—Sculpture,	165	MUSK PLANT—A meeting,	215
HYACINTH—Jealousy,	166	MUSTARD—Indifference,	216
HYDRANGEA—Boasting,	167	MYRTLE—Love,	217
HYSSOP—Purification,	168	NASTURTIUM—Heroism,	218
ICE PLANT—Formality,	169	NEMOPHILA—Prosperity,	219
INDIAN MALLOW—Estimation,	170	NETTLE—Slander,	220
IPOMŒA—Attachment,	171	OAK—Honor,	221
IPOMOPSIS—Suspense,	172	OATS—Country life,	222
IRIS—A messenger,	173	OLEANDER—Beware,	223
IVY—Lasting friendship,	174	OLEASTER—Providence,	224
JASMINE (WHITE)—Amiability,	175	OLIVE—Peace,	225
JUNIPER—Asylum,	176	ORANGE—Chastity,	226
JUSTICIA—Female loveliness,	177	ORCHIS—A belle,	227
KENNEDYA—Mental beauty,	178	OSIER (BASKET)—Frankness,	228
LADY'S SLIPPER—Fickleness,	179	OSMUNDA—Dreams,	229
LAKE-FLOWER—Retirement,	180	OXALIS—Parental affection,	230
LANTANA—Rigor,	181	PÆONY—Shame,	231
LARKSPUR—Levity,	182	PARSLEY—Festivity,	232
LAUREL—Glory,	183	PASSION FLOWER—Holy love,	233
LAURESTINE—I die if neglected,	184	PEA (SWEET)—Departure,	234
LAVENDER—Confession,	185	PEACH BLOSSOM—I am your captive,	235
LEMON BLOSSOM—Discretion,	186	PENTSTEMON—High-bred,	236
LETTUCE—Cold-hearted,	187	PERIWINKLE—Early friendship,	237
LILAC—Awakening love,	188	PERSIMMON—Amid nature's beauties,	238
LILY—Purity,	189	PETUNIA—Keep your promises,	239
LILY OF THE VALLEY—Return of happiness,	190	PHASEOLUS—Opportunity,	240
LION'S HEART—Bravery,	191	PHLOX—Unanimity,	241
LOASA—Pleasure,	192	PIMPERNEL—Mirth,	242
LOBELIA—Malevolence,	193	PINE—Philosophy,	243
LOCUST—Vicissitude,	194	PITCHER PLANT—Instinct,	244
LOPHOSPERMUM—Ecstasy,	195	PLUMBAGO—Meekness with dignity,	245
LUPINE—Voraciousness,	196	POINSETTIA—Brilliancy,	246
MAGNOLIA—Love of nature,	197	POMEGRANATE—Lightning,	247
MALLOW—Goodness,	198	POPPY (OPIUM)—Sleep,	248
MAPLE (ROCK)—Reserve,	199	PORTULACA—Variety,	249
MARIGOLD—Cruelty,	200	POTENTILLA—Beloved daughter,	250
MARJORAM (SWEET)—Blushes,	201	PRIMROSE—Youth,	251
MATTHIOLA—Promptitude,	202	PRIVET—Defense,	252
MAURANDIA—Courtesy,	203	QUEEN OF THE MEADOW—Praise,	253
MAYWEED—Rumor,	204	QUEEN OF THE PRAIRIE—Nobility,	254
MEDICK—Agriculture,	205	QUINCE—Allurement,	255
MELILOT—Philanthropy,	206	RAGGED ROBIN—Wit,	256
MERMAID WEED—Necessity,	207	RANUNCULUS—Ingratitude,	257
MIGNONETTE—Your qualities surpass your charms,	208	RHODORA—Beauty in retirement,	258
MINT—Virtue,	209	ROCKET—Rivalry,	259
MISTLETOE—Obstacles to be overcome,	210	ROSE (AUSTRIAN)—Loveliness,	260
MONKSHOOD—Knight-errantry,	211	ROSEBAY—Talking,	261
MORNING GLORY—Repose,	212	ROSE (DAMASK)—Blushing beauty,	262
		ROSE-LEAVED RUBUS—Threats,	263

CONTENTS.

	PAGE		PAGE
ROSEMARY — Remembrance,	264	SYRINGA — Memory,	296
ROSE (MUSK) — Charms,	265	TANSY — Resistance,	297
ROSE (WHITE) — Secrecy,	266	TEASEL — Misanthropy,	298
RUDBECKIA — Justice,	267	THISTLE — Austerity,	299
RUE — Repentance,	268	THORN — Difficulty,	300
SAGE — Domestic virtue,	269	THORN APPLE — Deceitful charms,	301
SALVIA — Energy,	270	THRIFT — Sympathy,	302
SARSAPARILLA — Experience,	271	TIGER FLOWER — Pride befriend me,	303
SASSAFRAS — Favor,	272	TRUMPET FLOWER — Fame,	304
SENSITIVE PLANT — Bashful modesty,	273	TUBEROSE — Voluptuousness,	305
SHAMROCK — Light-heartedness,	274	TULIP — Declaration of love,	306
SNAPDRAGON — Presumption,	275	TUSSILAGO — Justice to you,	307
SNOWBALL — Thoughts of heaven,	276	VALERIAN — Obliging disposition,	308
SNOWDROP — Consolation,	277	VENUS'S FLY-TRAP — Deceit,	309
SNOWDROP TREE — Exhilaration,	278	VENUS'S LOOKING-GLASS — Flattery,	310
SOUTHERNWOOD — Jesting,	279	VERBENA — Sensibility,	311
SPEEDWELL — Female fidelity,	280	VIOLET — Modesty,	312
SPIDERWORT — Transient happiness,	281	VIRGIN'S BOWER — Filial affection,	313
SPIKENARD — Benefits,	282	WALLFLOWER — Fidelity in misfortune,	314
SPRUCE — Farewell,	283	WALNUT — Intellect,	315
STAPELIA — Offense,	284	WATER LILY — Eloquence,	316
STAR FLOWER — Reciprocity,	285	WEEPING WILLOW — Melancholy,	317
STAR OF BETHLEHEM — Reconciliation,	286	WHEAT — Riches,	318
STRAWBERRY — Perfect goodness,	287	WHITE WALNUT — Understanding,	319
SUMACH — Splendor,	288	WINTER CHERRY — Deception,	320
SUMMER SAVORY — Success,	289	WITCH HAZEL — Witchery,	321
SUNFLOWER — Lofty thoughts,	290	WORMWOOD — Absence,	322
SWEET FLAG — Fitness,	291	YARROW — War,	323
SWEET POTATO — Hidden qualities,	292	YEW — Sorrow,	324
SWEET SULTAN — Felicity,	293	YUCCA — Authority,	325
SWEET WILLIAM — Stratagem,	294	ZINNIA — Thoughts in absence,	326
SYCAMORE — Woodland beauty,	295		

PART II. — Cultivation and Analysis of Plants.

PRACTICAL FLORICULTURE.

	PAGE
SOILS — Loam; Sand; Leaf-mold; Turf; Peat; Manures,	330-331
FLOWER-BEDS — In Relation to Symmetry and Color; Deformities Concealed,	331-333
PROPAGATING PLANTS — Sowing Seeds; Cuttings or Slips; Layering; Offshoots; Bulbs,	333
POTTING PLANTS,	335
WATERING PLANTS,	337
PRUNING PLANTS,	338
INSECTS — *Foliage Insects;* Aphis Rosæ; Thrips; Red Spider; Mealy Bug; Coccus; Verbena Mite; Roller Caterpillar; Rose Beetle; Tobacco Worm,	338-340
Root Worms: Angleworm; Millepod; Cut-Worm; Wire Worm,	341

DISEASES OF PLANTS — Mildew; Blackrust; Damping Off,	342
PRACTICAL PRECEPTS,	342

CULTURE OF FAVORITE PLANTS.

ABUTILON,	346
ACHYRANTHUS,	347
AGAPANTHUS,	347
ALTERNANTHERAS,	348
AMARYLLIS,	349
ASTER,	349
AZALEA,	350
BALSAM,	350
BEGONIA,	351
BOUVARDIA,	352

CONTENTS.

	PAGE
Cactus,	352
Caladium,	353
Camellia,	354
Canna,	355
Carnation,	355
Coleus,	356
Crape Myrtle,	357
Crocus,	357
Cyclamen,	358
Daisy,	359
Dicentra,	360
Dracæna,	360
Echeveria,	361
Erythrina,	361
Fittonia,	362
Fuchsia,	363
Funkia,	363
Gardenia,	364
Geranium,	365
Gladiolus,	366
Heliotrope,	367
Hibiscus,	368
Hoya,	369
Hyacinth,	370
Libonia,	371
Lily,	371
Lily of the Valley,	372
Linaria,	373
Mahernia,	373
Oleander,	374
Pansy,	375
Pelargonium,	375
Peperomia,	376
Petunia,	377
Phlox,	377
Physianthus,	378
Primrose,	379
Rose,	380
Saxifrage,	382
Scilla,	382
Sedum,	383
Selaginella,	384
Smilax,	384
Stephanotis,	385
Tritoma,	386
Tropæolum,	386
Tuberose,	387
Tulip,	388
Verbena,	389
Violet,	389
Weigela,	390

NEGLECTED BEAUTIES.

	PAGE
Choice Native Wild Flowers — Anemone nemorosa; Uvularia; Erythronium; Dodecatheon meadia; Tradescantia Virginica; Coreopsis; Asclepias tuberosa; Cassia chamæcrista; Liatris; Gentiana crinita; Asters,	392
Climbing Plants — *Climbers;* Passiflora Fordii; Clematis virginiana; Clematis Sieboldii; Clematis Jackmanni; Clematis John Gould Veitch; Cobæa scandens; Eccremocarpus scaber; Cucurbitaceæ,	394
Twiners: Ipomœa; Quamoclit vulgaris; Calystegia sepium; Boussingaultia basilloides; Mikania scandens; Lonicera; Celastrus scandens; Aristolochia sipho; Lathyrus odoratus; Maurandia; Thunbergia; Menispermum Canadense; Wistaria Sinensis; Phaseolus multiflorus; Adlumia cirrhosa; Jasminum officinale; Humulus lupulus; Periploca Græca,	394-396
Creepers: Hedera helix; Ampelopsis Veitchii; Ampelopsis quinquefolia; Tecoma radicans; Ficus repens,	396-397
Trailers: Epigæa repens; Tradescantia zebrina,	397
Ferns,	398
Grasses,	399
Heaths,	400
Mosses,	401

STRUCTURE OF PLANTS.

Chemistry of Plants,	402
Tissues,	403
Roots — Annuals; Biennials; Perennials,	404
Stems — Stalks; Axil,	405
Leaves — Stipules; Bracts; Buds; Æstivation,	406
Flowers — Calyx; Corolla; Stamen; Pistil; Pericarp; Seed; Receptacle; Nectary,	408
Inflorescence,	410

DIVISIONS OF THE VEGETABLE KINGDOM.

Variety; Subspecies or Race; Species; Subgenus or Section; Genus; Tribe and Subtribe; Suborder; Order; Subclass or Alliance; Class, Series or Subkingdom, 411-412

SYSTEMS OF CLASSIFICATION.

Artificial System of Linnæus — Twenty-four Classes; Twenty-six Orders,	414-415
Natural Orders of Linnæus,	415
Natural Systems,	416-417
Influence of Floriculture,	418
Index of Sentiment,	421-424

Alphabetical List of Authors Quoted.

Abbey, Henry.
Adams, John S.
Addison.
Akenside.
Aleyn.
Alimony, Lady.
Anacreon.
Ancrum, Earl of.
Angelo, Michael.
Armstrong, Dr. John.
Ascher, Isidore G.
Aylward, James S.

Babington.
Bailey.
Baillie, Joanna.
Barrett, Miss.
Barton, Bernard.
Baxter, Sylvester.
Beattie.
Beaumont and Fletcher.
Beddoes, Thomas Lovell.
Bell, Alexander.
Bellman Carl Michael.
Benjamin, Park.
Bennett, Emily T.
Bennett, W. C.
Benton, Joel.
Bidlake.
Bird.
Bird, Robert M.
Blackmore, Sir R.
Blair.
Blessington, Countess of.
Bogart, Elizabeth.
Boker, George H.
Bowles, Miss.
Bowring, John.
Bradley, Mary E.
Brock, Sallie A.
Brome.
Brooke.
Brooke, Lord.
Brooks, James G.
Brown.
Browne.
Browne, Mary Anne.
Browne, William.
Browning, Elizabeth Barrett.
Bruce, Michael.
Bryant, William Cullen.
Brydges, Sir S. E.
Bulwer.
Burbidge, Thomas.
Burger, G. A.
Burleigh.
Burns.
Butler.
Butler, Mrs. Frances A. K.
Byron.

Campbell.
Carey, Phœbe.
Carew, Lady.

Carew, Thomas.
Cartwright.
Chandler, Mary.
Chandler, Mrs. C. N.
Chapman, George.
Churchill.
Cibber.
Clare.
Clare, John.
Clark, Willis Gaylord.
Clarke, Sara Jane.
Clason, Isaac S.
Cleveland.
Clinch.
Clinch, L. H.
Coleridge.
Collins.
Comer, Joseph.
Congreve.
Conrad, Robert T.
Cook, Eliza.
Cooper, George.
Cordner, Charlotte.
Cornwell, Barry.
Cotton.
Cowley.
Cowper.
Crabbe.
Cranch, Christopher Pearse.
Crown.
Cumberland.

Dana, R. H.
Daniel, Samuel.
Darley, George.
Darwin, Dr. E.
Davenant, Sir William.
Davenport.
Davies, Sir John.
Dawes, Rufus.
Decker.
Denham, Sir J.
Dickens, Charles.
Dinnies, Mrs. Anne Peyre.
Dobell, Sydney.
Dodge, Mary B.
Donne.
Dorr, Julia C. R.
Drayton.
Drayton, Nicholas.
Drew.
Dryden.
Dyer.

Eastburn, J. W.
Eldredge, Mrs. R. T.
Eliot, Mrs. Elizabeth F.
Ellis.
Ellis, Edward.
Embury, Mrs.
Emerson, Ralph Waldo.
Eusden.
Euphorion.
Evans.

Everest, C. W.
Everett, John.

Fairfax.
Fawcett, Edgar.
Fenton.
Fielding.
Fields, James T.
Fitts, James Franklin.
Foote.
Ford, John.
Fountain.
Franklin.
Franklin, James.
Frisbie, Levi.
Frowde.
Fuller, Frances A.

Gay.
German, from the.
Gibbs, A.
Gifford.
Gifford, Lena I.
Gilman, Caroline.
Glyndon, Howard.
Goffe.
Goldsmith.
Gould, Miss.
Granville.
Gray.
Greek, from the.
Green.
Greenwell, Dora.
Grey, Barton.

Habington, William.
Hale, Mrs. S. J.
Hall, Marcia.
Halleck.
Hamlin, G.
Harney, Will Wallace.
Harte, Walter.
Harvard.
Hay, William.
Hayne, Paul H.
Hays, Samuel.
Hayley.
Heath.
Heine.
Hemans, Mrs.
Henderson.
Herbert, George.
Herbert, William.
Herrick, Robert.
Heywood.
Hill.
Hill, Aaron.
Hill, Kate. J.
Hillhouse, James A.
Hirst, Henry B.
Hoffman, Chas. Fenno.
Holmes, Oliver Wendell.
Home, John.
Hood, Thomas.

Howard, Mrs. V. E.
Howard, Sir Robert.
Howel.
Howitt, Mary.
Howitt, William.
Hoyt, Ralph.
Hughan, O. G.
Hugo, Victor.
Hunt, Josie F.
Hunt, Leigh.
Hunt, Sir A.

Ingelow, Jean.

Jeffery.
Jenks, H. N.
Jewsbury, Miss.
Johns, H. I.
Johnson, C.
Johnson, Dr.
Jones, Sir W.
Jonson, Ben.

Keats, John.
Kemble, Frances Anne.
Kermode, Tamar Anne.
King, Dr. Henry.
Knowles.
Korner.

Labree, L.
Lake.
Landon, L. E.
Langey, W. F.
Larcom, Lucy.
Lawrence, William R.
Lee.
Lee, Mary E.
Leech, H. H.
Leggett, William.
Lewis, Anna Estelle.
Lewis, Mrs.
Leyden, Dr.
Lillo.
Locke, Jane E.
Locke, A. A.
Locke, Mrs.
Longfellow.
Lover, Samuel.
Lowell, James Russell.
Lynch, Charlotte Anne.
Lyttleton.

Macaulay, Lord.
Mahan.
Mackellar.
Madden, Dr. S.
Malcolm, Edith.
Mallet.
Mant.
Marlow.
Marmyun.
Marston.
Mason.

ALPHABETICAL LIST OF AUTHORS QUOTED.

Massey.
Massinger.
Maturin.
May, Edith.
May, Thomas.
Mayne.
Merivale.
Metastasio.
Middleton.
Miller.
Miller, Joaquin.
Milman.
Milton.
Mirror for Magistrates.
Moir.
Montgomery.
Montgomery, W. R.
Moore.
Moore, L. Bruce.
More, Hannah.
Morris, Robert.
Motherwell.
Motteux.
Munson, S. A.
Murphy.
Murray, Lindley.

Nabb.
Nancy, A. W.
Norris, John.
Norton, Andrews.
Norton, Mrs.

Ogilvie.
Old Play.
Ordway.
O'Reilly, John Boyle.
Orrery, Earl of.
Osgood, Frances Sargent.
Osgood, Kate Putnam.
Otway.
Ovid.

Paine, R. T.
Palmer, J. W.
Parnell.
Patterson.
Pattison.
Paulding.
Peerbold.
Percival.
Percival, James G.

Petrarch.
Philips, Ambrose.
Philips, John.
Philips, Katherine.
Pierpont, John.
Pierson, Mrs. Lydia Jane.
Pike, Albert.
Pindar.
Pinkney, Edward C.
Pittaeus.
Poem of 1584.
Pollock.
Pope.
Porteage.
Pratt, ct.
Prentice, G. D.
Prior.
Proctor.
Procter, Adelaide Anne.
Proctor, Bryan W.

Quarles, Francis.

Raleigh, Sir Walter.
Rand, Mrs. M. H.
Randolph.
Randolph, Mrs. Eliza S.
Read, Thomas Buchanan.
Reid, Christian.
Renaud, Edward.
Richards, W. C.
Robinson, Mary.
Robinson, Mrs.
Rochester.
Rogers.
Roscoe, William.
Rosenmmen.
Rossetti, Christina Georgina.
Rowe.
Russell, P. W.
Ryan.

Salmagundi.
Sandys.
Sanford, Lucy M.
Sappho.
Sargent, Epes.
Savage.
Saxe, John G.
Scott, Sir Walter.
Shakespeare.
Shaw.

Shelly.
Shenstone.
Sheridan.
Shirley.
Sidney, Sir Philip.
Sigourney, Mrs.
Simms, W. G.
Smith.
Smith, Horace.
Smith, Mrs. E. Oakes.
Smith, Mrs. L. P.
Smith, Mrs. Margaret.
Smith, Mrs. Seba.
Smith, William.
Smollett.
Southern.
Southey.
Southey, Mrs.
Southwell, Robert.
Spanish, from the.
Spear, Thomas G.
Spencer, Caroline.
Spenser.
Sprague, Charles.
Stapleton, Sir Robert.
Steele, Anne.
Sterling (or Stirling), Earl of.
Sterling, John.
Millingfleet.
Story, W. W.
Street.
Street, Alfred B.
Strickland.
Stuart, Carlos D.
Swain, Charles.
Swain, John.
Suckling, Sir John.
Sweeney, Robert.
Swift.
Sylvester, Joshua.
Sylvestre, L.

Tasso.
Tate.
Taylor, Bayard.
Taylor, Henry.
Tennyson.
Terry, Rose.
Thackeray, William Makepeace.
Thaxter, Celia.
Thompson.

Thomson.
Thompson, James Maurice.
Thurlow, Lord.
Tickell.
Tighe, Mrs.
Timon, The New.
Tracy.
Trapp.
Tuckerman, F. G.
Tuke.
Tosser.
Twiss, Horace.

Very, Jones.
Virgil.

Walcot, Dr.
Walker, James.
Waller.
Waller, John Francis.
Walsh, William.
Wandesford.
Wathyns.
Watson, J. T.
Webber, Fred W.
Webster.
Webster, John.
Welby, Mrs. Amelia B.
Wesley, J.
White, Henry Kirke.
Whitman, Sarah Helen.
Whittier, J. G.
Wilcox, Carlos.
Wilde, R. H.
Wilkins.
Willis, N. P.
Wilson.
Wilson, John.
Wither, George.
Woodsworth.
Wordsworth.
Wotten, Sir Henry.

Young.

INITIALS.

C. C.
C. H. T.
H. C.
J. H. S.
W. H. C.

Roslyn Long Island May 2 Oct. 1875

Dear Sir:

I find among my papers a few brief notes when my invention was more prolific than now. Many years I used, which seem at if composed for this very purpose. I send them on the other half of this sheet that the Rev. Mr. Turner's lady may make whatever she pleases of them; prefixing them to those or another, or putting them elsewhere. Please cause to her my good wishes for the success of the publication.

I am sir,
Respectfully yours,
W C Bryant

Not idly do I stray,
At prime, where far the mountain ridges run,
And note, along my way,
Each flower that opens in the early sun,
Or gather blossoms by the valley's spring
When the sun sets and dancing insects sing.

Each has her moral code,
Each of the gentle family of flowers;
And I, with patient heed,
Oft spell their lessons in my graver hours.
The faintest streak that on a petal lies
May speak instruction to initiate eyes.

Well do the poets teach
Each blossom's charming mystery; they declare
In clear melodious speech
The silent admonitions pencilled there,
And from the love of Beauty, aptly taught,
Lead to a higher good the willing thought.

Hymn to the Flowers.

DAY-STARS! that ope your frownless eyes to twinkle
    From rainbow galaxies of earth's creation,
And dew-drops on her lonely altars sprinkle
    As a libation.

Ye matin worshipers! who, bending lowly
    Before the uprisen sun, God's lidless eye,
Throw from your chalices a sweet and holy
    Incense on high.

Ye bright mosaics! that with storied beauty
    The floor of Nature's temple tessellate,
What numerous emblems of instructive duty
    Your forms create!

'Neath cloistered boughs, each floral bell that swingeth,
    And tolls its perfume on the passing air,
Makes Sabbath in the fields, and ever ringeth
    A call to prayer.

Not to the domes where crumbling arch and column
    Attest the feebleness of mortal hand,
But to that fane, most catholic and solemn,
    Which God hath planned:

To that cathedral, boundless as our wonder,
    Whose quenchless lamps the sun and moon supply;
Its choir the winds and waves, its organ thunder,
    Its dome the sky.

There, as in solitude and shade I wander
    Through the green aisles, or stretched upon the sod,
Awed by the silence, reverently ponder
    The ways of God,

HYMN TO THE FLOWERS.

Your voiceless lips, O flowers! are living preachers,
    Each cup a pulpit, every leaf a book,
Supplying to my fancy numerous teachers
        From loneliest nook.

Floral Apostles! that in dewy splendor
    "Weep without woe, and blush without crime,"
O, may I deeply learn, and ne'er surrender,
        Your love sublime!

"Thou wert not, Solomon, in all thy glory,
    Arrayed," the lilies cry, "in robes like ours!
How vain your grandeur! ah, how transitory
        Are human flowers!"

In the sweet-scented pictures, heavenly artist!
    With which thou paintest Nature's wide-spread hall,
What a delightful lesson thou impartest
        Of love to all!

Not useless are ye, flowers! though made for pleasure;
    Blooming o'er field and wave, by day and night,
From every source your sanction bids me treasure
        Harmless delight.

Ephemeral sages! what instructors hoary
    For such a world of thought could furnish scope?
Each fading calyx a *memento mori*,
        Yet fount of hope.

Posthumous glories! angel-like collection!
    Upraised from seed or bulb interred in earth,
Ye are to me a type of resurrection
        And second birth.

Were I in churchless solitudes remaining,
    Far from all voice of teachers and divines,
My soul would find, in flowers of God's ordaining,
        Priests, sermons, shrines.

—HORACE SMITH.

PART I.

Description, Language and Poetry of Flowers.

The Language of Flowers.

Their language? Prithee! why, they are themselves
  But bright thoughts syllabled to shape and hue—
The tongue that erst was spoken by the elves,
  When tenderness as yet within the world was new.

And, oh! do not their soft and starry eyes—
  Now bent to earth, to heaven now meekly pleading,
Their incense fainting as it seeks the skies, [ing—
  Yet still from earth with freshening hope reced-

Say, do not these to every heart declare,
  With all the silent eloquence of truth,
The language that they speak is Nature's prayer,
  To give her back those spotless days of youth?
              — *Charles Fenno Hoffman.*

Acacia—Rose.

Robinia hispida. NATURAL ORDER: *Leguminosæ — Pulse Family.*

THE Rose Acacia is a beautiful shrub of the locust tribe, varying in height from three to five feet, and is grown for its large clusters of rose-colored, pea-shaped flowers, which are very pleasing to the eye. The Acacias are all very handsome plants, with great diversity of foliage, and number, in all their varieties, upward of four hundred. They are found in every quarter of the globe, except Europe, and some of them are natives of our own Southern States. The flowers of the choice varieties are yellow, pale straw-color, red, or purple. They require the protection of the greenhouse to grow them in perfection.

Friendship.

SMALL service is true service while it lasts;
  Of friends however humble, scorn not one;
The daisy, by the shadow that it casts,
  Protects the ling'ring dewdrop from the sun.
      —*Wordsworth.*

OH! let my friendship in the wreath,
  Though but a bud among the flowers,
Its sweetest fragrance 'round thee breathe—
  'Twill serve to soothe thy weary hours.
      —*Mrs. Welby.*

LOVE is a sudden blaze which soon decays;
  Friendship is like the sun's eternal rays;
Not daily benefits exhaust the flame;
It still is giving, and still burns the same.
      —*Gay.*

FRIENDSHIP'S an abstract of love's noble flame,
  'Tis love refined, and purged from all its dross;
The next to angel's love, if not the same;
  As strong as passion is, though not so gross:
    It antedates a glad eternity,
  And is a heaven in epitome.   —*Katherine Phillips.*

FRIENDSHIP is a plant of heavenly birth,
  Constant its nature, and immense its worth,
Its essence virtue, and is known to rest,
And glow most warmly in the virtuous breast!
      —*Prentice.*

FRIENDSHIP is the cement of two minds,
  As of one man the soul and body is;
Of which one cannot sever but the other
Suffers a needful separation.
      —*Chapman.*

Adder's Tongue.

Ophioglossum vulgatum.   NATURAL ORDER: *Filices — Fern Family.*

A STRANGE name has this singular little plant, being derived from two Greek words, *ophis*, meaning serpent, and *glossa*, a tongue; so called from the lance-like spike on which the seeds are produced. It belongs to the beautiful family of ferns, most of which propagate themselves by seeds or spores, arranged in various ways on the back of their leaves, some being too minute to be visible to the naked eye. It is found in low grounds, with solitary fronds measuring from two to three inches in length. It has been chosen as an emblem of deceit, because those by whom we are deceived are usually compared to serpents lurking in the grass, and ready to sting us unawares.

Deceit.

AND this was he who loved me; he who came
  To whisper vows to my too willing ear
With lip of melody and heart of flame;
Vows whose glad truth I deem'd so trebly dear
To him who breathed them, that had doubt or fear
Been raised within my heart, they could not grow —
He whose bright eyes bespoke a soul sincere —
This; *this* was he who — vain remembrance now! —
He lives to scorn the past — he lives to break his vow.
        — *Mrs. Norton.*

NO man's condition is so base as his;
  None more accursed than he; for man esteems
Him hateful 'cause he seems not what he is;
God hates him 'cause he is not what he seems;
What grief is absent, or what mischief can
Be added to the hate of God and man?
        — *Francis Quarles.*

AH! that deceit should steal such gentle shapes,
  And with a virtuous visor hide deep vice!
        — *Shakespeare.*

BETTER the truth,
  Though it bring me ruth,
Than a lie as sweet as the dreams of youth.
  Better to stand
  In a lonely land,
My feet unshod in its desert sand,
  Than to blindly go
  Where cool streams flow,
And a serpent coils in the grasses low.
        — *Mary E. Bradley.*

Adonis.

Adonis autumnalis. NATURAL ORDER: *Ranunculaceæ — Crowfoot Family.*

IN the Adonis we have a fine hardy annual of European birth, which, according to ancient mythology, sprung from the blood of Adonis, one of the lovers of Venus, who while hunting was killed by a boar. Venus mourned his loss with many tears. While she was weeping over the spot, a beautiful plant came up covered with flowers like drops of blood. Thus have the fables and flowers descended to us through the mists of ages, laden with the reminiscences of vanished time.

Sorrowful Remembrances.

TEARS, idle tears,—I know not what they mean,
Tears from the depth of some divine despair
Rise in the heart, and gather in the eyes,
In looking on the happy autumn fields,
And thinking of the days that are no more.
— *Tennyson.*

THEY bid me raise my heavy eyes,
Nor mournful still in tears complain —
They bid me cease these broken sighs,
And with the happy smile again;
They say that many a form of light
Is gliding round me while I pine,
But still I weep — though fair and bright,
It is not thine. —*Mrs. Norton.*

WHEN the cold breath of sorrow is sweeping
O'er the chords of the youthful heart,
And the earnest eye, dimmed with strange weeping,
Sees the visions of fancy depart;
When the bloom of young feeling is dying,
And the heart throbs with passion's fierce strife,
When our sad days are wasted in sighing,
Who then can find sweetness in life?
—*Mrs. Embury.*

MEMORIES on memories! to my soul again
There come such dreams of vanish'd love and bliss
That my wrung heart, though long inured to pain,
Sinks with the fullness of its wretchedness.
—*Phœbe Cary.*

Ageratum.

Ageratum Mexicanum. NATURAL ORDER: *Compositæ — Aster Family.*

SCARCELY any flower is more in use among florists for grouping in bouquets than the Ageratum; its small, fringe-like heads filling in so softly around the more unyielding blossoms; toning down all harsh outlines, and harmonizing tints too antagonistic to each other, by its unobtrusive presence. There are only two varieties in color: one a most delicate blue, the other white; and two in height, a dwarf and a tall kind. It produces a fine effect when grown in masses in the garden, or is well adapted for pot culture, the dwarf having the preference, the blossoms being about the same size. It is a native of Mexico and the West Indies.

Politeness.

HER air, her manners, all who saw admired;
Courteous, though coy, and gentle though retired;
The joy of youth and health her eyes display'd,
And ease of heart her every look convey'd.
—*Crabbe.*

THE nymph did like the scene appear,
Serenely pleasant, comely fair;
Soft fell her words as blew the air.
—*Prior.*

WHAT are these wondrous civilizing arts,
This Roman polish, and this smooth behavior,
That render man thus tractable and tame?
—*Addison.*

EASE in your mien, and sweetness in your face,
You speak a siren, and you move a grace;
Nor time shall urge these beauties to decay,
While virtue gives what years shall steal away.
—*Tickell.*

IN simple manners all the secret lies:
Be kind and virtuous, you'll be blest and wise.
—*Young.*

OF softest manners, unaffected mind;
Lover of peace, and friend of human kind.
—*Pope.*

A MORAL, sensible, and well-bred man
Will not affront me, and no other can.
—*Cowper.*

Agrimony.

Agrimonia parviflora.   NATURAL ORDER: *Rosaceæ—Rose Family.*

AGRIMONY, a plant well known to the Greeks and Romans, and by them very highly esteemed for its healing properties, was at one time thought superior to all others known to science as medicinal. Some authors derive the name from the Greek "*argema*, the web or pearl of the eye, a disease of which it was supposed to cure." Several plants under this name are found throughout the United States, in the fields and woods. The flowers are small and yellow, in long, slender racemes. The plants vary in height from one to three feet, some of them being quite aromatic.

Thankfulness.

FOR she hath lived with heart and soul alive
To all that makes life beautiful and fair;
Sweet thoughts, like honey-bees, have made their hive
Of her soft bosom-cell, and cluster there.
—*Amelia B. Welby.*

THROUGH all his tuneful art how strong
The human feeling gushes!
The very moonlight of his song
Is warm with smiles and blushes.
—*J. G. Whittier.*

I UNDERSTOOD not that a grateful mind
By owing owes not, but still pays, at once
Indebted and discharg'd.
—*Milton.*

SOUL, where thoughts like to white-winged angels,
Brood in the hush of this dim, dark eve,
Whisper to me thy sweet evangels,
Whisper and sigh, but do not grieve;
Out of the depths of thy charmed chambers
Raise me a song that shall thrill afar;
Kindle thy fires, blow bright thine embers,
Gleam on *her* soul like the gleam of a star.
—*Barton Grey.*

WE owe thee much; within this wall of flesh
There is a soul counts thee her creditor,
And with advantage means to pay thy love.
—*Shakespeare.*

THANKS, thanks to thee, my worthy friend,
For the lesson thou hast taught.
—*Longfellow.*

IF you have lived, take thankfully the past;
Make, as you can, the sweet remembrance last.
—*Dryden.*

Ailantus.

Ailantus glandulosa.   NATURAL ORDER: *Rutaceæ — Rue Family.*

LUXURIANT in aspect is this Chinese tree, the botanical name of which is derived from its Malay name, *ailanto*, that is, Tree of Heaven. It grows to a great height, the trunk is usually very straight, and the leaves, a yard or more in length, are composed of smaller leaflets arranged along the central stem, with one at the tip, similar to the leaves of the butternut. They are abundant, and form a plentiful and delightful shade. The tree grows rapidly; the wood is soft and of no utility.

Lofty Aspirations.

THE planted seed, consigned to common earth,
Disdains to molder with the baser clay,
But rises up to meet the light of day,
Spreads all its leaves and flowers and tendrils forth,
And, bathed and ripened in the genial ray,
Pours out its perfume on the wandering gales,
Till in that fragrant breath its life exhales;
So this immortal germ within my breast
Would strive to pierce the dull, dark clod of sense;
With aspirations winged and intense,
Would so stretch upward, in its tireless quest
To meet the Central Soul, its source, its rest.
— *Charlotte Anne Lynch.*

A RESTLESS, strong, impetuous will,
Eager to do and dare the worst,
Emulous ever to be first,
Attaining, yet aspiring still.   — *Kate J. Hill.*

UP from its trammels the freed spirit wings,
Higher to soar;
Attar immortal a pure essence flings,
Sweet, evermore!   — *Mary B. Dodge.*

NATURE never stands still, nor souls either. They ever go up or go down;
And hers has been steadily soaring — but how has it been with your own?
She has struggled, and yearned, and aspired — grown purer and wiser each year;
The stars are not farther above you, in yon luminous atmosphere!   — *Julia C. R. Dorr.*

Almond.

Amygdalus pumila. NATURAL ORDER: *Rosaceæ—Rose Family.*

THE Almond is a beautiful little shrub, sending forth its delicate pink, crape-like blossoms early in the spring, completely covering each branch from base to apex, while the foliage is almost unseen. The ancients had a beautiful custom of wreathing poetic fables with everything, and there is scarcely a flower but what is clothed with some affecting tale of disappointed lovers. The Almond tree was said by them to have sprung from the dead body of Phyllis, princess of Thrace, who was watching for her betrothed husband's return. On the day appointed for his arrival, she watched and waited anxiously, and at last, hopeless and despairing, killed herself upon the shore, and was changed into this shrub.

Despair.

BUT dreadful is their doom whom doubt has driven
 To censure fate, and pious hope forego:
Like yonder blasted boughs by lightning riven,
 Perfection, beauty, life, they never know,
 But frown on all that pass, a monument of woe.
—Beattie.

METHINKS we stand on ruin; nature shakes
 About us; and the universal frame's
So loose, that it but wants another push
To leap from its hinges. —*Lee.*

THERE is no light shed on my way,
 Ev'n hope's pale beam has fled,
And those I loved have gone for aye
 To the cold realms of the dead.
—Marcia Hall.

HOW like gall and wormwood to the taste
 The cup that we have longed to drain may prove.
—Lydia Jane Pierson.

OH! my darling, earth is weary,
 Life, without thee, sad and dreary,
Ocean's song a *Miserere!*
And my sun is burning low,
Fainter yet life's embers glow,
Tides will ebb that cannot flow.
—James Franklin Fitts.

WHO sees laid low,
 At a single blow,
The sweetest thing in his life, may know
 What bitter ruth
For my heart, in sooth,
Was born of this naked, terrible truth.
—Mary E. Bradley.

Aloe.

Agave Americana. NATURAL ORDER: *Amaryllidaceæ—Amaryllis Family.*

THIS plant is a native of the tropical portions of America, although the same species are found in the burning sands of the Eastern Hemisphere. The leaves are thick and fleshy, tapering to a point, and dentate on the edges. They sometimes grow as much as six or eight feet in length, each leaf coming out one close above the other, with no interval on the stem. The flower-stalk rises from the center of the surrounding leaves to the height of twenty to thirty feet, bearing on the summit a pyramidal panicle of numberless yellow flowers. Formerly it was said to bloom only once in a century. It is now known to bloom from eight years upward, according to the attention given it, and the region where it grows. Another variety, with smaller leaves of almost invisible green, is completely covered with white, bead-like dots, forming a striking contrast to the color on which they rest.

Grief.

OH sorrow! where on earth hast thou not sped
   Thy fatal arrows! on what lovely head
Hast thou not poured, alas! thy bitter phial,
And cast a shadow on the spirit's dial.
              —*Anna Estelle Lewis.*

IN tears, the heart oppressed with grief,
   Gives language to its woes;
In tears its fullness finds relief,
   When rapture's tide o'erflows!
Who, then, unclouded bliss would seek
   On this terrestrial sphere,
When e'en delight can only speak,
   Like sorrow, in a tear?
        —*Metastasio.*

HALF of the ills we hoard within our hearts,
   Are ills because we hoard them. —*Proctor.*

BUT where the heart of each should beat,
   There seemed a wound instead of it,
From whence the blood dropped to their feet,
   Drop after drop—dropped heavily,
As century follows century
   Into the deep eternity. —*Elizabeth Barrett Browning.*

I AM dumb, as solemn sorrow ought to be;
Could my griefs speak, the tale would have no end.
        —*Otway.*

Aloysia.

Aloysia citriodora. NATURAL ORDER: *Verbenaceæ — Vervain Family.*

DESERVING of all praise is the Aloysia, sometimes called Lemon Verbena. It is from Paraguay, and received its name in honor of Queen Mary Louisa, of Spain, the mother of Ferdinand VII. It is cultivated as a greenhouse shrub, for the aromatic odor of its delicate leaves, the least touch of which yields the delightful fragrance of the lemon. Frequently it is placed in the ground in summer, and in a dry cellar in winter. It should be trimmed back in the spring before the leaf buds begin to start, as otherwise it is inclined to a straggling growth. The flowers are small, appearing in spikes. They seldom bloom in this latitude. The young branches are used by florists in bouquets.

Forgiveness.

SOME grave their wrongs on marble; he, more just,
Stoop'd down serene, and wrote them in the dust.
— *Dr. S. Madden.*

WHILE yet we live, scarce one short hour perhaps,
Between us two let there be peace. — *Milton.*

IF there be
One of you all that ever from my presence
I have with saddened heart unkindly sent,
I here, in meek repentance, of him crave
A brother's hand, in token of forgiveness.
— *Joanna Baillie.*

'TIS easier for the generous to forgive
Than for offense to ask it. — *Thompson.*

KNEEL not to me:
The power that I have on you, is to spare you;
The malice toward you, to forgive you; live
And deal with others better. — *Shakespeare.*

FORGIVE and forget! why the world would be lonely,
The garden a wilderness left to deform,
If the flowers but remember'd the chilling winds only,
And the fields gave no verdure for fear of the storm.
— *Charles Swain.*

IF ever any malice in your heart
Were hid against me, now forgive me frankly.
— *Shakespeare.*

THE narrow soul
Knows not the God-like glory of forgiving.
— *Rowe.*

Alyssum.

Alyssum maritimum.   NATURAL ORDER: *Cruciferæ — Mustard Family.*

AMONG the ancients the Alyssums were supposed to possess some charmed property, which had power to control and subdue violent and ungovernable paroxysms of temper, and keep the disposition mild and passive. Its name is derived from the Greek *a*, not, and *lussa*, rage. It is a perennial of easy culture, and gladdens the garden from June to October with its fine leaves, delicate white flowers and sweet perfume. The Rock (Saxatile) Alyssum is a native of Candia, and has yellow blossoms in close corymbous bunches.

Merit Before Beauty.

SAID I she was not beautiful? Her eyes upon your sight
Broke with the lambent purity of planetary light,
And as intellectual beauty, like a light within a vase,
Touch'd every line with glory of her animated face.
—*Willis.*

TELL me not that he's a poor man,
　That his dress is coarse and bare;
Tell me not his daily pittance
　Is a workman's scanty fare;
Tell me not his birth is humble,
　That his parentage is low;
Is he honest in his actions?
　This is all I want to know.
—*Joseph Comer.*

HERE only merit constant pay receives;
Is blest in what it takes, and what it gives.
—*Pope.*

OH, how much more doth beauty beauteous seem,
By that sweet ornament which truth doth give!
The rose looks fair, but fairer we it deem
For that sweet odor which doth in it live.
—*Shakespeare.*

FAR better in its place the lowliest bird
　Should sing aright to Him the lowliest song,
Than that a seraph strayed, should take the word
　And sing his glory wrong.
—*Jean Ingelow.*

Beauty provoketh thieves sooner than gold.
—*Shakespeare.*

GOOD actions crown themselves with lasting bays;
Who well deserves needs not another's praise.
—*Heath.*

IT is witness still of excellency
To put a strange face on its own perfection.
—*Shakespeare.*

Amaranth.

Gomphrena perennis.   NATURAL ORDER: *Amarantaceæ — Amaranth Family.*

SOUTH AMERICA has contributed this variety of the Amaranth to the flora of the United States. It is a plant about two feet high, with narrow, tapering leaves, and flowers similar in shape to those of the common red clover. They are crimson in color, and equally fadeless and durable as in the annual species. Because of this quality they have been the chosen emblem of immortality from the early days of Homer down to the poets of modern times.

Immortality.

A VOICE within us speaks that startling word —
"Man, thou shalt never die!" Celestial voices
Hymn it into our souls; according harps,
By angel fingers touch'd, when the mild stars
Of morning sang together, sound forth still
The song of our great Immortality.
— *R. H. Dana.*

'TIS immortality deciphers man,
And opens all the mysteries of his make,
Without it, half his instincts are a riddle,
Without it, all his virtues are a dream.
— *Young.*

IMMORTALITY o'ersweeps
All pains, all tears, all time, all fears — and peals
Like the eternal thunders of the deep
Into my ears this truth — Thou liv'st forever!
— *Byron.*

PRESS onward through each varying hour;
Let no weak fears thy course delay;
Immortal being! feel thy power,
Pursue thy bright and endless way.
— *Andrews Norton.*

ALL, to re-flourish, fades;
As in a wheel, all sinks, to reäscend,
Emblems of man, who passes, not expires.
— *Young.*

THE spirit of man
Which God inspired, cannot together perish
With this corporeal clod.
— *Milton.*

COLD in the dust this perish'd heart may lie,
But that which warm'd it once shall never die.
— *Campbell.*

Amaranth--Globe.

Gomphrena globosa.   NATURAL ORDER: *Amarantaceæ—Amaranth Family.*

THE Globe Amaranth is a tender annual from the flowery vales of India. It is valued chiefly for its heads of bright, round, purple flowers, which, if gathered when freshly blossomed, will retain their brilliancy for years. The white variety is cultivated for the same purpose, the two forming very pretty bouquets for winter. The seeds are enveloped in a cottony substance, which should be removed before planting, as it hinders the process of germination.

I Change Not.

I CHANGE but in dying, and no holier vow
  From lips mortal e'er came than I breathe to thee now;
It comes from a heart with love for thee sighing;
Believe me, 'tis true—I change but in dying.
—John S. Adams.

I WAS not false to thee, and yet
  My cheek alone look'd pale!
My weary eye was dim and wet,
  My strength began to fail;
Thou wert the same; thy looks were gay,
  Thy step was light and free;
And yet, with truth my heart can say,
  I was not false to thee.
—Mrs. Norton.

I WOULD not leave thee did I know
  That all the world's reproach were true—
That 'neath some great temptation's power
  Thy soul had lost its native hue;
Had dyed itself with darkest guilt;
  Had plunged without remorse in crime:
Not even then would I forsake—
  Thine, and thine only, for all time.
—H. C.

THE mountain rill
  Seeks with no surer flow, the far, bright sea,
Than my unchang'd affection flows to thee.
—Park Benjamin.

CHANGELESS as the greenest leaves
  Of the wreath the cypress weaves—
Hopeless often when most fond—
Without hope or fear beyond
  Its own pale fidelity.
—Miss Landon.

GO! and with all of eloquence thou hast,
  The burning story of my love discover;
And if the theme should fail, alas! to move her,
Tell her when youth's gay summer-flowers are past,
Like thee, my love will blossom till the last!
—Charles F. Hoffman.

Amaryllis.

Sprekelia formosissima. NATURAL ORDER: *Amaryllidaceæ—Amaryllis Family.*

NUMEROUS varieties of these beautiful tropical bulbs are to be found with florists and seedsmen, the most common being, perhaps, those known as the Atamasco, Belladonna, and Jacobea lilies, from their superb, lily-like flowers. There are, however, about a hundred and fifty others, differing in their coloring, time of blooming, or shape of flower, that are worthy all the enthusiasm they have inspired. The root is similar to a large onion, either tapering upward or flattened, according to the species; the leaves thick, long and narrow; the flower-stalk about a foot high. They are grown in pots, either as window or greenhouse plants. The Amaryllis receives its name from a nymph, mentioned in the Eclogues of Virgil, where Corydon thinks the cruel anger and proud disdain of Amaryllis was easier to bear than the cool indifference of Alexis, whom he so madly loved.

Pride.

PRIDE, self-adorning pride, was primal cause
Of all sin past, all pain, all woe to come.
—*Pollock.*

WAKEN, thou fair one! up, Amaryllis!
  Morning so still is;
Cool is the gale;
The rainbow of heaven,
With its hues seven,
Brightness hath given
To wood and dale;
Sweet Amaryllis, let me convey thee;
In Neptune's arms naught shall affray thee;
Sleep's god no longer power has to stay thee,
Over thy eyes and speech to prevail.
—*Carl Michael Bellman.*

HOW poor a thing is pride! when all, as slaves,
  Differ but in their fetters, not their graves.
—*Doud.*

THOUGH various foes against the truth combine,
  Pride, above all, opposes her design;
Pride, of a growth superior to the rest,
The subtlest serpent, with the loftiest crest,
Swells at the thought, and kindling into rage,
Would hiss the cherub Mercy from the stage.
—*Cowper.*

I'LL go along, no such sight to be shown,
  But to rejoice in splendor of mine own.
—*Shakespeare.*

American Arbor Vitæ.

Thuja occidentalis. NATURAL ORDER: *Coniferæ — Pine Family.*

THIS tree is almost identical with the White Cedar, and is frequently mistaken for it. It is very abundant along the rocky shores of lakes, rivers, and swamps of the northern parts of the United States and the Canadian provinces. The trunk is crooked and covered with evergreen foliage from bottom to top, the branches diminishing in length toward the apex. The wood is very light and soft, yet it is said to be durable. The classical name is derived from the Greek word *thuo*, I sacrifice, as its fragrance made it a favorite wood for sacrificial fires.

Thine till Death.

SO we grew together.
  Like to a double cherry, seeming parted,
But yet a union in partition,
Two lovely berries molded on one stem;
So with two seeming bodies, but one heart.
— Shakespeare.

IF life for me hath joy or light,
  'Tis all from thee;
My thoughts by day, my dreams by night,
  Are but of thee, of only thee;
Whate'er of hope or peace I know,
My zest in joy, my balm in woe,
To those dear eyes of thine I owe;
  'Tis all from thee.

My heart, ev'n ere I saw those eyes,
  Seem'd doom'd to thee;
Kept pure till then from other ties,
  'T was all for thee, for only thee.
Like plants that sleep till sunny May
Calls forth their life, my spirit lay,
Till touch'd by love's awak'ning ray,
  It lived for thee, it lived for thee.
— Moore.

I CHANGE but in dying! the trials of earth
  May gather around me and darken my path,
But true as the needle, which points to the pole,
Will my heart turn to thee — thou beloved of my soul.
— T. Drew.

THE task befits thee well,
  To gather firmness as the tempests swell
Around me still, companion, wife and friend,
To cling in fond endurance to the end.
— Victor Hugo.

BUT green above them
  Thy branches grow;
Like a buried love, or a vanish'd joy,
Link'd unto memories none destroy.
— Miss Jewsbury.

American Elm.

Ulmus Americana.   NATURAL ORDER: *Ulmaceæ—Elm Family.*

ONE of the most beautiful trees in the United States is the American Elm. Nothing can surpass the exquisite beauty of its long, pendulous branches, that hang from its ample crown like brown threads strung with dark-green leaves. The trunk rises erect to a considerable height, whence it stretches upward innumerable arms to sustain the wealth of foliage whose shadow lies so enticing on the grass beneath. Clusters of smaller twigs adorn the body of the tree, where they sway with all the grace of an ostrich plume, catching the slightest motion of the toying breeze, as if the sun and air filled them with an ecstatic joy. The Elm thrives best in moist lands, particularly lowland pastures, where it makes a rapid growth. It has been much used around the sequestered homes of New England, and the effect has been most picturesque.

Patriotism.

O HEAVEN, he cried, my bleeding country save!
  Is there no hand on high to shield the brave?
Yet though destruction sweep those lovely plains,
Rise, fellow-men! our country yet remains! —*Campbell.*

SNATCH from the ashes of your sires
  The embers of their former fires,
And he who in the strife expires
Will add to theirs a name of fear
That tyranny shall quake to hear.
—*Byron.*

THE sword may pierce the bearer,
  Stone walls in time may sever;
'Tis heart alone,
Worth steel and stone,
That keeps man free forever!
—*Moore.*

JUDGE me not ungentle.
  Of manners rude, and insolent of speech,
If when the public safety is in question,
My zeal flows warm and eager from my tongue.
—*Rowe.*

HE who maintains his country's laws
  Alone is great; or he who dies in the good cause.
—*Sir A. Hunt.*

American Linden.

Tilia Americana.   NATURAL ORDER: *Tiliaceæ — Linden Family.*

BASSWOOD is the common name for this forest tree in our Northern States. It grows to a great height, and abounds in a wholesome mucilaginous juice. Its tender young twigs are often pulled and eaten by school children for this property. The inner bark is sometimes manufactured into rope. The wood is very soft and white, and is used for the paneling of carriages and in cabinet work, as it is easily wrought. The celebrated Russia matting is manufactured from a species of European Linden, while the East Indians rely upon the native species for their rice bags, fishing nets and lines.

Matrimony.

WEDDED love is founded on esteem,
   Which the fair merits of the mind engage,
For those are charms which never can decay;
But time, which gives new whiteness to the swan,
Improves their luster.
                    — *Fenton.*

THOUGH fools spurn Hymen's gentle powers,
  We, who improve his golden hours,
    By sweet experience know
That marriage, rightly understood,
Gives to the tender and the good,
  A paradise below.   — *Cotton.*

HAVE I a wish? 'tis all her own:
  All hers and mine are rolled in one —
  Our hearts are so entwined,
That like the ivy round the tree,
Bound up in closest amity,
  'Tis death to be disjoined.   — *Lindley Murray.*

TEMPTING gold alone
  In this our age more marriages completes
Than virtue, merit, or the force of love.
                    — *Wandesford.*

LET still the woman take
  An elder than herself; so wears she to him,
So sways she level in her husband's heart.
                    — *Shakespeare.*

WHAT thou art is mine;
  Our state cannot be sever'd; we are one,
One flesh; to lose thee were to lose myself.
                    — *Milton.*

Andromeda—Marsh.

Andromeda hypnoides.   NATURAL ORDER: *Ericaceæ—Heath Family.*

CEPHEUS, an ancient king of Ethiopia, had a very proud and haughty wife named Cassiopeia, and a daughter Andromeda. His wife was so vain of her beauty that she contested with Juno for the supremacy. For such temerity, Jupiter issued a decree that her daughter should be bound to a rock on the coast, that she might be devoured by sea-monsters. Perseus, a son of Jupiter, and adopted son of the king of Seriphos, undertook an expedition against the Gorgon Medusa, and upon his return discovered the luckless Andromeda languishing in the cords that bound her, and after overcoming dangerous obstacles, rescued and married her. Her name was given to a constellation in the heavens, and botanists have also named this little shrub in her honor.

Bound by Fate.

LET wit her sails, her oars let wisdom lend;
   The helm let politic experience guide;
Yet cease to hope thy short-lived bark shall ride
   Down spreading fate's unnavigable tide.
— Prior.

UNWILLING I forsook your friendly state,
   Commanded by the gods and forced by fate.
— Dryden.

O THOU who freest me from my doubtful state,
   Long lost and wilder'd in the maze of fate!
Be present still.
— Pope.

SOME taste the lotus, and forget
   What life it was they lived before;
And some stray on the seas and set
   Their feet on every happy shore;
But I—I linger evermore
— James Maurice Thompson.

FATE steals along with ceaseless tread,
   And meets us oft when least we dread;
Frowns in the storm with threatening brow,
Yet in the sunshine strikes the blow.
— Cowper.

HERE I walk the sands at eve,
   Here in solitude I grieve,
Break the spells we loved to weave.
— James Franklin.

THE day too short for my distress; and night,
   Ev'n in the zenith of her dark domain,
Is sunshine to the color of my fate.
— Young.

Anemone.

Anemone coronaria. NATURAL ORDER: *Ranunculaceæ — Crowfoot Family.*

WIND FLOWER is a frequent appellation of this beautiful little plant, which comes from the countries bordering on the eastern coast of the Mediterranean, known collectively as the Levant. We find quite a beautiful fable concerning it in heathen mythology: Anemone was a nymph greatly beloved of Zephyr, and Flora, being jealous of her beauty, banished her from court, and finally transformed her into the flower that bears her name; whence it is sometimes taken to express withered hopes. It is also connected with the story (already given) of the love of Venus for Adonis, on which account the language has been made "Anticipation," as she spent one-half the year longing and watching for his return.

Anticipation.

TO the fond, doubting heart its hopes appear
  Too brightly fair, too sweet to realize;
All seem but day-dreams of delight too dear;
  Strange hopes and fears in painful contest rise,
While the scarce-trusted bliss seems but to cheat the eyes.
                              — *Mrs. Tighe.*

SHE looked from out the window
  With long and asking gaze,
From the gold-clear light of morning
To the twilight's purple haze.
Cold and pale the planets shone,
Still the girl kept gazing on.

From her white and weary forehead
  Droopeth the dark hair,
Heavy with the dews of evening,
Heavier with her care;
Falling as the shadows fall,
'Till flung 'round her like a pall.
                        — *L. E. Landon.*

IN our hearts fair hope lay smiling
  Sweet as air, and all beguiling;
And there hung a mist of bluebells on the slope and down the dell;
  And we talked of joy and splendor
  That the years unborn would render,
And the blackbirds helped us with the story, for they knew it well.
                        — *Jean Ingelow.*

Angelica.

Angelica atropurpurea. NATURAL ORDER: *Umbelliferæ — Parsley Family.*

HIS plant is the largest of the species, the stalks attaining the height of from four to six feet. It grows usually in a wild or half-naturalized state, in fields and meadows, possesses strong aromatic properties, and is sometimes used in medicine. The garden Angelica is supposed to be a native of Labrador, and is the plant cultivated and used the same as celery, the blanched stalks adding a good relish when other salads are scarce. The poets of Lapland fancied they derived inspiration from wearing it as a crown; hence its application.

Inspiration.

THE poets may of inspiration boast,
   Their rage, ill governed, in the clouds is lost;
He that proportioned wonders can disclose,
At once his fancy and his judgment shows;
Chaste moral writing we may learn from hence,
Neglect of which no wit can recompense.
The fountain which from Helicon proceeds,
That sacred stream should never water weeds,
Nor make the cup of thorns and thistles grow.
Which envy or perverted nature sow.   —*Roscommon.*

POETS are limners of another kind,
   To copy our ideas in the mind;
Words are the paint by which their tho'ts are shown,
And nature is the object to be drawn.
      —*Granville.*

EYES planet calm, with something in their vision
   That seemed not of earth's mortal mixture born;
Strange mythic faiths and fantasies Elysian,
And far, sweet dreams of "fairy lands forlorn."
      —*Sarah Helen Whitman.*

THE poet's eye, in a fine frenzy rolling,
   Doth glance from heaven to earth, from earth to heaven;
And, as imagination bodies forth
The forms of things unknown, the poet's pen
Turns them to shapes, and gives to airy nothing
A local habitation and a name.   —*Shakespeare.*

Apocynum.

Apocynum androsæmifolium.   Natural Order: *Apocynaceæ — Dogbane Family.*

AMONG our wild field-flowers we meet with this plant, sometimes called Dogbane, because, according to Pliny, some of the species were supposed to be fatal to those animals, as is, indeed, the extract of one of the genus, which is obtained from the seeds of the strychnos nux vomica of India. It is sold under the name of strychnine, and is fatal not only to the canine race, but to all animal life. This plant is about three feet high, with opposite leaves from two to three inches long, rounded at the base, and sharp at the point. The flower is small, white, striped with red, and is rather pretty.

Falsehood.

AH! doom'd indeed to worse than death,
  To teach those sweet lips hourly guile;
To breathe through life but falsehood's breath,
  And smile with falsehood's smile.
— *Mrs. Osgood.*

FIRST, I would have thee cherish truth,
  As leading star in virtue's train;
Folly may pass, nor tarnish youth,
  But falsehood leaves a poison-stain.
— *Eliza Cook.*

THE man of pure and simple heart
  Through life disdains a double part;
He never needs the screen of lies
His inward bosom to disguise.
— *Gay.*

WINNING his carriage, every look
  Employed whilst it concealed a hook;
When simple most, most to be feared;
Most crafty when no craft appeared;
His tales no man like him could tell;
His words, which melted as they fell,
Might even a hypocrite deceive,
And make an infidel believe.
— *Anon.*

AND though I stand
  In a lonely land,
Afar from the touch of a tender hand,
  Or a mouth to kiss —
  It is better this
Than to cling to a falsehood and dream it bliss.
— *Mary E. Bradley.*

NO falsehood shall defile my lips with lies
  Or with a veil of truth disguise.
— *Sandys.*

Apple Blossom.

Pyrus malus. NATURAL ORDER: *Rosaceæ — Rose Family.*

WITH lavish hand have the fruits been bestowed upon southern and tropical climates, both in regard to variety and abundance; but the apple, which is superior to them all, on account of the various ways it may be used, the length of time which it will keep in perfection, and the frequency with which it may be eaten without satiating the appetite, is a particular boon to the dwellers of cold climates, for there it obtains its greatest size and most perfect flavor. The blossom is sweet-scented, and has a delicate pink flush. An orchard in bloom is a charming sight.

Preference.

I MIND the apple blossoms, how thick they were that spring!
  Yes, and I'm likely to mind them as long as any thing.
Some of the boughs, I remember, were just a sight to see;
The buds were as red as roses, all over the top of the tree.
I held a branch while she stripped it, till, shaken out of place,
A bee from one of the broken flowers came flying into her face.
She screamed, and I — I kissed her, just for a cure, you know,
And she blushed till her cheeks were pinker than the pinkest apple blow.
                      — *Kate Putnam Osgood.*

COME, let us plant the apple tree;
  Cleave the tough greensward with the spade;
Wide let its hollow bed be made;
There gently lay the roots, and there
Sift the dark mold with kindly care,
  And press it o'er them tenderly,
As round the sleeping infant's feet
We softly fold the cradle sheet;
  So plant we the apple tree.

What plant we in this apple tree?
Buds, which the breath of summer days
Shall lengthen into leafy sprays;
Boughs where the thrush, with crimson breast,
Shall haunt, and sing, and hide her nest;
  We plant, upon the sunny lea,
A shadow for the noontide hour,
A shelter from the summer shower,
  When we plant the apple tree. — *Bryant.*

IF others be as fair,
  What are their charms to me.
I neither know nor care,
  For thou art all to me. — *Mrs. Seba Smith.*

Apricot.

Prunus Armeniaca.   NATURAL ORDER: *Rosaceæ — Rose Family.*

IN the Apricot we have a tree that is thought to have originated in Armenia, but which is also found in the countries adjacent, and as far east as the Celestial Empire and Japan. Its introduction into Europe is said to have been effected by Alexander the Great, since whose time it has been generally cultivated there. The tree is medium in size, being from fifteen to twenty feet high. The flowers are white, and make their appearance in April or May, before the putting forth of the leaves. The fruit is of a purplish-golden hue, from one to two inches in diameter, and is palatable either to be eaten in its natural state or made into a preserve or jelly. It is cultivated in some parts of the United States, and thrives best in a temperate or warm climate.

Temptation.

TO shun th' allurement is not hard
  To minds resolved, forewarn'd and well prepared;
But wondrous difficult, when once beset,
  To struggle through the straits and break th' involving net. —*Dryden.*

I PICTURE easeful moments spent
  Among broad, shadowy branches, lifting
Their gloss to some pure firmament
  Where spheres of pallid fleece are drifting;

I see the flexuous vine-coil drowse,
  The deep, dark mosses glimmer greenly,
And watch between close tangled boughs
  The clear-curved breaker flashing keenly.
  —*Edgar Fawcett.*

NO fort can be so strong,
  No fleshy breast can armed be so sound,
But will at last be won with battery long,
  Or unawares at disadvantage found;
Nothing is sure that grows on earthly ground —
  And who most trusts in arm of fleshy might,
And boasts in beauty's chain not to be bound,
  Doth soonest fall in disadventurous fight,
And yields his caitiff neck to victors most despight. —*Spenser.*

Arbutus.

Epigœa repens.   NATURAL ORDER: *Ericaceæ — Heath Family.*

NOT infrequently called Trailing Arbutus, and sometimes Mayflower, this plant is found in mountainous and hilly districts in our Northern States and British America. It is a procumbent shrub, and derives its botanical name from *epi* and *gaea*, two Greek words signifying lying on the ground, from the habit of the plant. The flowers appear in spring from April to May. They are white, frequently with a blush of red cast over them, and are very fragrant. It has been suggested that this plant be adopted, under the name of Mayflower, as the floral emblem of our country, corresponding to the Rose of England, the Fleur-de-lis of France, etc.

Simplicity.

I KNOW the wildwood haunts where thou abidest,
  And there, the mossy nooks where most thou hidest,
Arbutus, sweet and shy.
  — *W. C. Richards.*

ARBUTUS graceful trailing,
  Amid brown mosses vailing,
Thy pink-wax clusters hailing,
  Thy fragrance we adore.

Mayflower! Anew we name thee!
A nation now we claim thee —
No dastard e'er defame thee,
  Symbol forevermore!
  — *Emily T. Bennett.*

I WAS not born for courts or great affairs;
I pay my debts, believe, and say my prayers.
  — *Pope.*

DARLINGS of the forest!
  Blossoming alone,
When earth's grief is sorest
  For her jewels gone —
Ere the last snowdrift melts, your tender buds
have blown.

Tinged with color faintly,
  Like the morning sky,
Or, more pale and saintly,
  Wrapped in leaves ye lie —
Even as children sleep in faith's simplicity.
  — *Rose Terry.*

A CHARM hast thou no forest flower can boast,
  Thou little beaming herald of the spring!
How thrilled thy smile when on our rock-bound coast
  The wearied pilgrims found thee blossoming! — *H. N. Jenks.*

Arethusa.

Arethusa bulbosa. NATURAL ORDER: *Orchidaceæ—Orchis Family.*

DAMP places, such as swamps and low, marshy meadows, are the chosen retreats of this beautiful plant. Each plant bears one handsome, large, fragrant flower, of a rich purple hue. It derives its name from Arethusa, a nymph of great beauty, who served in the suit of the goddess Diana. She attracted the attention of the river-god Alpheus, while bathing in his river, the Alpheius of Arcadia. He immediately fell in love with her perfections, and she fled away abashed. To save her from his pursuit, she was changed by Diana into a fountain.

Fear.

THE clouds dispell'd, the sky resum'd her light,
And nature stood recover'd of her fright,
But fear, the last of ills, remain'd behind,
And horror heavy sat on every mind. —*Dryden.*

ARETHUSA arose
From her couch of snows,
In the Acroceraunian mountains,—
From cloud and from crag
With many a jag,
Shepherding her bright fountains.
She leapt down the rocks
With her rainbow locks
Streaming among the streams;—
Her steps paved with green
The downward ravine
Which slopes to the western gleams;
And gliding and springing,
She went ever singing
In murmurs as soft as sleep.
The earth seemed to love her,
And heaven above her,
As she lingered toward the deep.
—*Shelly.*

HIS hand did quake
And tremble like a leaf of aspen green,
And troubled blood through his pale face was seen,
As it a running messenger had been. —*Spenser.*

HIS fear was greater than his haste;
For fear, though fleeter than the wind,
Believes 'tis always left behind. —*Butler.*

THOU shalt be punish'd for thus frighting me,
For I am sick and capable of fears;
Oppress'd with wrongs, and therefore full of fears.
—*Shakespeare.*

Aristolochia.

Aristolochia sipho. NATURAL ORDER: *Aristolochiaceæ — Birthwort Family.*

HERE is a climbing shrub found in our Middle and Southern States, generally in upland woods, frequently attaining the height of thirty feet or more. The leaves are large and heart-shaped, arranged alternately on each side of the stem. The flowers are particularly striking, blooming singly, each tube being long and turned up in the form of a tobacco-pipe, and of a brownish color. Hence the shrub is frequently called Dutchman's Pipe. The Aristolochia Bonplandi, a fine plant for greenhouse culture, is a native of Patagonia, and, like some two or three others, thrives best in the warm, moist air of the hothouse. The flowers of all have the same peculiar structure; the colors are purple or a greenish brown, some of them being beautifully spotted.

Prodigality.

YOUR wisdom is most liberal, and knows
   How fond a thing it is for discreet men
To purchase with the loss of their estate
The name of one poor virtue, liberality,
And that, too, only from the mouth of beggars!
One of your judgment would not, I am sure,
Buy all the virtues at so dear a rate.   *—Randolph.*

BUT th' earth herselfe, of her owne motion,
   Out of her *fruitfull* bosome made to growe
Most daintie trees, that, shooting up anon,
Did seeme to bow their blooming heads full lowe
For homage unto her, and like a throne did show.
     —Spenser.

I HAVE spent all the wealth
   My ancestors did purchase; made others brave
In shape and riches, and myself a knave;
For tho' my wealth rais'd some to paint their door,
'Tis shut against me, saying I am poor.
     —Wilkins.

THE feast is such as earth, the general mother,
   Pours from her fairest bosom, when she smiles
In the embrace of autumn.   *—Shelly.*

Arnica.

Arnica mollis. NATURAL ORDER: *Compositæ — Aster Family.*

GROWING in the ravines of the White, Essex and other mountains in the east, and on the Rocky mountains in the west, the Arnica, an Alpine plant, is found. The flowers are yellow, and are borne on stalks from one to two feet high. When dried they form an article of commerce, being used to reduce inflammation in wounds and bruises. A tincture is usually prepared with alcohol, or spirits of some kind; or for temporary use a lotion is made by steeping them in water.

Let Me Heal Thy Grief.

> WHAT, man! ne'er pull your hat upon your brows!
>   Give sorrow words: the grief that does not speak,
> Whispers the o'er-fraught heart, and bids it break.
> — Shakespeare.

IF thou wilt ease thine heart
  Of love, and all its smart —
    Then sleep! dear, sleep!
And not a sorrow
Hang any tear on your eyelashes;
    Lie still and deep,
Sad soul, until the sea-wave washes
The rim o' the sun tomorrow,
    In eastern sky.

But wilt thou cure thine heart
  Of love, and all its smart —
    Then die! dear, die!
'Tis deeper, sweeter,
Than on a rose bank to lie dreaming
    With folded eye;
And then alone, amid the beaming
Of love's stars, thou'lt meet her
    In eastern sky.
— Thomas Lovell Beddoes.

HALF the ills we hoard within our hearts
  Are ills because we hoard them. *Proctor.*

IN sympathy, then, I give thee a hand,
  And greet thee as thus we go,
And pledge a renewal in that bright land
Where pleasures perennial grow.
— Jane E. Locke.

THO' dark the night, 'tis not forever;
  A day-beam comes, in mercy given —
Before its ray the storm-clouds sever,
The wandering soul hath rest in heaven.
— James S. Aylward.

Asclepias.

Asclepias cornuti. NATURAL ORDER: *Asclepiadaceæ — Milkweed Family.*

FROM a hoary antiquity has descended the name Æsculapius, represented as an aged man with a heavy beard, leaning upon his jointed cane, and his head adorned with a crown of laurel. He was the god of medicine, and by his wisdom and skill improved the art of healing very much. It was also believed of him that, while physician to the Argonauts, he had the power of calling the dead to life again. At last Pluto, the god of the lower world, jealous and provoked, complained that he was losing his subjects, and persuaded Jupiter to kill him, which he did with a thunderbolt. He was afterward worshiped as a god in many cities of Greece and at Rome, because he had once delivered that city from pestilence. This plant takes its name from him, and is the common inhabitant of our roadsides, known to school children as milkweed.

Conquer Your Love.

THEN crush, e'en in the hour of birth,
  The infant buds of love,
And tread the growing fire to earth
  Ere 'tis dark in clouds above. —*Halleck.*

QUIT, quit for shame! this will not move,
  This cannot take her;
If of herself she will not love,
  Nothing can make her. —*Sir John Suckling.*

O SLIPP'RY state
  Of human pleasures, fleet and volatile,
Given us and snatch'd again in one short moment,
To mortify our hopes, and edge our suff'rings.
    Trapp.

LOVE is a sickness full of woes,
  All remedies refusing;
A plant that most with cutting grows,
  Most barren with best using.
    Why so?
More we enjoy it, more it dies;
If not enjoyed, it sighing cries
    Heigh-ho! —*Samuel Daniel.*

I PRAY you do not fall in love with me,
  For I am falser than vows made in wine.
Besides, I like you not. —*Shakespeare.*

AND let the aspiring youth beware of love,
  Of the smooth glance beware; for 'tis too late,
When on his heart the torrent-softness pours.
    Thompson.

Ash.

Fraxinus Americana. NATURAL ORDER: *Oleaceæ — Olive Family.*

BEAUTIFUL is the ash, one of the most dignified denizens of the forest, rising to a height of from thirty to forty feet without branching, and then crowning itself with large, dense and handsome foliage to an extent fully equal to the growth of its stately trunk. It delights in moist locations, as the banks of rivers and marshes, and does not thrive well in barren or bleak situations. Its timber is elastic, light, tough and durable, and is much used by car-builders, carriage-makers, wheelwrights and ship-builders, as well as in the manufacture of agricultural implements.

Grandeur.

WITH goddess-like demeanor forth she went —
Not unattended, for on her as a queen
A pomp of winning graces waited still,
And from about her shot darts of desire
Into all eyes to wish her still in sight.
— *Milton.*

WHAT is grandeur? Not the sheen
Of silken robes; no, nor the mien
And haughty eye
Of old nobility —
The foolish that is not, but has been.
The noblest trophies of mankind
Are the conquests of the mind.
— *Sir A. Hunt.*

MARK her majestic fabric! She's a temple
Sacred by birth, and built by hands divine;
Her soul's the deity that lodges there;
Nor is the pile unworthy of the god.
— *Dryden.*

WHAT winning graces, what majestic mien!
She moves a goddess, and she looks a queen.
— *Pope.*

I WAS born with greatness;
I've honors, titles, power, here within:
All vain external greatness I contemn.
— *Crown.*

I KNOW an ash
Named Ygg-drasill;
A stately tree,
With white dust strewed.

Thence come the dews
That wet the dales.
It stands aye green
O'er Urda's well.
— *Henderson's Iceland.*

Asparagus.

Asparagus officinalis.   NATURAL ORDER: *Liliaceæ — Lily Family.*

PEOPLE in towns and cities are familiar with the vegetable Asparagus as they find it in their markets, tied in bundles of straight stalks without the least appearance of foliage. There the stalks are almost white, as gardeners cut the stems deep in the soil. Those having their own gardens cut them after they are four or five inches above the ground, when they are green, sweet, and quite brittle. The soil should be very rich for its growth. It is one of the oldest of table plants, having been a favorite from the time of the ancient Greeks; and grows about four feet high into a large herbaceous bush, with leaves like so many green bristles. A mass at a distance looks as if the fairies had disrobed and left their green illusion garments behind. The flowers are small; the berries, in autumn, are a brilliant scarlet.

Emulation.

IN poet's lore, and sentimental story,
  It seems as 't were this life's supremest aim
For heroes to achieve what men call glory,
  And die intoxicate with earth's acclaim.
Ah me! how little care the dead for breath
Of vain applause that saved them not from death.
—Mackellar.

YET, press on!
  For it shall make you mighty among men;
And, from the eyrie of your eagle thought,
Ye shall look down on monarchs. O, press on!
For the high ones and powerful shall come
To do you reverence; and the beautiful
Will know the purer language of your soul,
And read it like a talisman of love.
Press on! for it is godlike to unloose
The spirit and forget yourself in thought.
—Byron.

MAN was mark'd
  A friend, in his creation, to himself,
And may, with fit ambition, conceive
The greatest blessings, and the brightest honors
Appointed for him, if he can achieve them
The right and noble way. *—Massinger.*

WHO never felt the impatient throb,
  The longing of a heart that pants
And reaches after distant good!
—Cowper.

Aspen.

Populus tremuloides.   NATURAL ORDER: *Salicaceæ — Willow Family.*

CELEBRATED in ancient lore was Phaëton, one of the sons of Phœbus Apollo. Epaphus, a reputed son of Zeus and Io, denied that Phaëton was the son of Apollo, whereupon he, acting upon the advice of Clymene, his mother, went to the "palace of the sun to test his paternity." Phœbus acknowledged him as his son, taking oath that anything he should demand as proof should be granted. Phaëton, probably desiring to excite the envy of Epaphus and to pass in glory before his jealous gaze, asked to drive his father's chariot of the sun for one day. Apollo, dismayed, but mindful of his inviolable oath, granted the request. Phaëton ascended with joy, but his steeds ran away, and threatened to set fire to the earth, whereupon Jupiter killed him with a thunderbolt, and he fell into the river Po. His three sisters mourned him incessantly, and were at last changed into poplars by the pity of the gods, and their tears into amber. The Aspen is a species of poplar, whose leaves are attached to the branches by long, slender petioles or leaf-stems, which keep them tremulous with the slightest breeze.

Excessive Sensibility.

WHY tremblest thou, Aspen? no storm threatens nigh;
Not a cloud mars the peace of the love-beaming sky;
'Tis the spring of thy being — no autumn is near
Thy green boughs to wither, thy sweet leaves to sear!
The sun, like a crown, o'er thy young head shines free,
Then wherefore thus troubled? what fear'st thou, fair tree?
—*Charles Swain.*

A DELICATE, frail thing — but made
For spring sunshine, or summer shade —
A slender flower, unmeet to bear
One April shower — so slight, so fair.
—*Miss Landon.*

ROSES bloom, and then they wither;
Cheeks are bright, then fade and die;
Shapes of light are wafted hither,
Then, like visions, hurry by.
—*Percival.*

FEELING hearts — touch them but lightly — pour
A thousand melodies unheard before! —*Rogers.*

Asphodel.

Asphodelus luteus. NATURAL ORDER: *Liliaceæ — Lily Family*

VERY fine among the family of lilies is the Asphodel, a garden plant from the island of Sicily. It is very easily cultivated, and multiplies rapidly. The stem is nearly three feet high, and adorned with hollow, three-cornered leaves. The flowers, which are yellow, bloom closely along the stalk, almost covering its whole length. There is also a white variety, a native of Europe. The name is from the Greek, and means not to be equaled. They planted it beside the tombs, and fancied that beyond the Acheron the deceased roamed through fields of Asphodel, quaffing the waters of Lethe.

Remembered Beyond the Tomb.

THE dead! the much-loved dead!
    Who doth not yearn to know
The secret of their dwelling-place,
And to what land they go?
What heart but asks, with ceaseless tone,
For some sure knowledge of *its own?*
        —*Mary E. Lee.*

WHEN the summer moon is shining
    Soft and fair,
Friends she loved in tears are twining
    Chaplets there.
Rest in peace, thou gentle spirit,
    Throned above —
Souls like thine with God inherit
    Life and love! —*James T. Fields.*

IN my left hand I held a shell,
    All rosy-lipped and pearly red;
I laid it by his lowly bed,
    For he did love so passing well
The grand songs of the solemn sea.
Oh! shell, sing well! wild! with a will!
When storms blow loud and birds be still,
    The wildest sea-song known to thee!
        —*Joaquin Miller.*

FADE! flowers, fade! nature will have it so;
    'Tis what we must in our autumn do!
And as your leaves lie quiet on the ground,
The loss alone by those that lov'd them found,
So in the grave shall we as quiet lie,
Miss'd by some few that loved our company.
        —*Waller.*

Aster.

Aster corymbosus.   NATURAL ORDER: *Compositæ — Aster Family.*

OUR native Aster grows about two feet high, and is found frequently in dry, open woodlands in the Northern and Middle States. The name is derived from the Greek word *aster*, signifying a star, as the petals spread out like rays of light from the center. There are none of our native plants that are equal to the Chinese Asters, though the same assiduity in culture would undoubtedly improve them. On the western prairies there are some whose colors are really handsome in their exquisite tints, standing tall among the grass; in some places so abundant that it would seem that a rose or purple glory had settled down over the fields for the birds to sing in.

Cheerfulness in Old Age.

ALIKE all ages. Dames of ancient days
   Have led their children through the mirthful maze;
And the gay grandsire, skill'd in gestic lore,
Has frisk'd beneath the burden of threescore.
                             —*Goldsmith.*

OH, no! I never will grow old,
   Though years on years roll by,
And silver o'er my dark brown hair,
   And dim my laughing eye.
      —*Sara Jane Clarke.*

WHY grieve that time has brought so soon
   The sober age of manhood on?
As idly should I weep at noon
   To see the blush of morning gone.
      —*Bryant.*

HE look'd in years, yet in his years were seen
   A youthful vigor and autumnal green.
      —*Dryden.*

MY days pass pleasantly away,
   My nights are blest with sweetest sleep,
I feel no symptoms of decay,
   I have no cause to mourn or weep;
My foes are impotent and shy,
   My friends are neither false nor cold;
And yet, of late, I often sigh,
   I'm growing old!   —*John G. Saxe.*

THE spring, like youth, fresh blossoms doth produce,
   But autumn makes them ripe and fit for use. —*Sir J. Denham.*

Auricula.

Primula auricula.   NATURAL ORDER: *Primulaceæ — Primrose Family.*

EUROPE gave birth to this flower. It is a native of the Alps, where its fragrant and pure blossoms are one of Nature's first tributes to spring. It is greatly admired as an ornament to our gardens, and is said to bloom best when favored with a northern aspect. Its name is derived from two Latin words: Primula, from *primus*, first, because it blossoms so early in the spring, and Auricula, from its ear-shaped leaves. The species mostly cultivated are the Cowslip Primrose, a perennial from Great Britain, with yellow flowers; the purple, found on the mountains of Nepaul, Asia; the double-cupped, native of Austria; and the common Primrose of Europe.

Painting.

ALL that imagination's power could trace,
  Breath'd in the pencil's imitative grace;
O'er all the canvas, form, and soul, and feeling,
  That wondrous art infus'd with power of life;
Portray'd each pulse, each passion's might revealing;
  Sorrow and joy, life, hatred, fear and strife.
    —*From the Spanish.*

THEN first from love, in Nature's bowers,
  Did Painting learn her fairy skill,
And cull the hues of loveliest flowers,
  To picture woman lovelier still. —*Moore.*

ERE yet thy pencil tries her nicer toils,
  Or on thy palette lie the blended oils,
Thy careless chalk has half achieved thy art,
And her just image makes Cleora start.
    —*Tickell.*

COME! the colors and the ground prepare:
  Dip in the rainbow, trick her off in air;
Choose a firm cloud before it fall, and in it
Catch, ere she change, the Cynthia of this minute.
    —*Pope.*

IS she not more than painting can express,
  Or youthful poets fancy when they love?
    —*Rowe.*

'TIS in life as 'tis in painting:
  Much may be right, yet much be wanting.
    —*Prior.*

COME, thou best of painters,
  Prince of the Rhodian art;
Paint, thou best of painters,
  The mistress of my heart.
    —*Wm. Hay's Trans. Anacreon (Greek).*

Azalea.

Azalea Indica. NATURAL ORDER: *Ericaceæ — Heath Family.*

MOST of the few native shrubs of this family are inhabitants of the Southern States, but the plants chiefly in cultivation are of Asiatic origin, and are almost innumerable in their varieties. In color of blossom they run through every shade, from pure white into all the delightful tints of pink, scarlet, crimson, purple and salmon. Care should be taken to prevent a straggling growth, which can be done with proper pruning. They can be grown from seeds or from slips; the latter, however, produce flowers much sooner than seedlings. Blooming early in spring, they are a great acquisition for Easter decorations, a fine plant frequently being covered from base to apex with its elegant flowers.

Temperance.

TEMPERATE in every place — abroad, at home,
  Thence will applause, and hence will profit come;
And health from either he in time prepares
For sickness, age, and their attendant cares.
  —*Crabbe.*

HE who the rules of temperance neglects,
From a good cause may produce vile effects.
  —*Tuke.*

BEWARE the bowl! though rich and bright
  Its rubies flash upon the sight,
An adder coils its depths beneath,
Whose lure is woe, whose sting is death.
  —*Street.*

PUT down the cup! It is brimmed with blood,
  Crushed, throbbing, from hearts like mine!
For hope, for peace, and for love's dear sake,
Oh! pledge me not with wine!
  —*Josie E. Hun.*

'TIS to thy rules, O temperance! that we owe
  All pleasures which from health and strength can flow;
Vigor of body, purity of mind,
Unclouded reason, sentiments refined,
Unmixed, untainted joys, without remorse—
The intemperate sinner's never-failing curse.
  —*Mary Chandler.*

31

Baccharis.

Baccharis halimifolia. NATURAL ORDER: *Compositæ — Aster Family.*

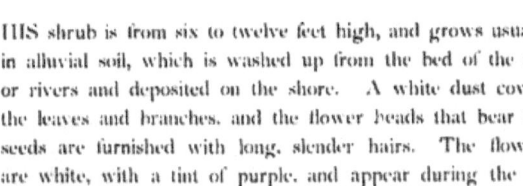

THIS shrub is from six to twelve feet high, and grows usually in alluvial soil, which is washed up from the bed of the sea or rivers and deposited on the shore. A white dust covers the leaves and branches, and the flower heads that bear the seeds are furnished with long, slender hairs. The flowers are white, with a tint of purple, and appear during the fall months. It has sufficient beauty to recommend it for cultivation. The name of this shrub is derived from Bacchus, the deity of wine and reveling, because its fragrance savors of wine. It is sometimes called Groundsel Tree, from its resemblance to the weedy plant of that name.

Intoxication.

IN what thou eat'st and drinkest seek from thence
Due nourishment, not gluttonous delight;
So thou may'st live, till, like ripe fruit thou drop
Into thy mother's lap, or be with ease
Gather'd, not harshly pluck'd, for death mature.
— *Milton.*

WINE is like anger; for it makes us strong,
Blind and impatient, and it leads us wrong;
The strength is quickly lost, we feel the error long.
— *Crabbe.*

OH thou invisible spirit of wine,
If thou hast no name to be known by, let
Us call thee devil. — *Shakespeare.*

SHALL I, to please another wine-sprung mind,
Lose all mine own? — *George Herbert.*

THE joy which wine can give, like smoky fires,
Obscures their sight, whose fancy it inspires.
— *Hill.*

COULD every drunkard, ere he sits to dine,
Feel in his head the dizzy fumes of wine,
No more would Bacchus chain the willing soul,
But loathing horror shun the poison'd bowl.
— *Merivale.*

THOU sparkling bowl! thou sparkling bowl!
Though lips of bards thy brim may press,
And eyes of beauty o'er thee roll,
And song and dance thy power confess,
I will not touch thee! for there clings
A scorpion to thy side, that stings. — *John Pierpont.*

Bachelor's Button.

Centauria cyanus.   NATURAL ORDER: *Compositæ—Aster Family.*

ENTAUREA is said to derive its name from the centaur Chiron, the fabled son of Saturn, who was cured by an application of it after having been wounded in the knee by a poisoned arrow from the bow of Hercules. Another mythological narrative says that Chiron's wound was incurable; but that, having been born of immortal parents, he could not die, and was consequently placed by the gods in the firmament as a constellation, being called Sagittarius. The plant is a hardy annual, and grows about two feet high. The blossoms vary much in color, appearing singly on the ends of the branches.

Single Blessedness.

HE meets the smile of young and old, he wins the praise of all.
He is toasted at the banquet, and distinguished at the ball;
When town grows dull and sultry, he may fly to green retreats,
A welcome visitor in turn at twenty country seats;
He need not seek society, for, do whate'er he can,
Invitations and attentions will pursue the single man.

A BACHELOR
   May thrive, by observation, on a little;
A single life's no burthen; but to draw
In yokes is chargeable, and will require
A double maintenance.   —*John Ford.*

IF I am fair, 'tis for myself alone;
   I do not wish to have a sweetheart near me,
Nor would I call another's heart my own,
   Nor have a gallant lover to revere me.

THE ills of love, not those of fate, I fear;
   These I can brave, but those I cannot bear.
      —*Dryden.*

A WIFE! Oh, fetters
   To man's bless'd liberty! All this world's prison,
Heav'n the high wall about it, sin the gaoler;
But th' iron shackles weighing down our heels
Are only women.   —*Decker.*

For surely I would plight my faith to none,   [me;
   Though many an amorous cit might jump to hear
For I have heard that lovers prove deceivers,
When once they find that maidens are believers.
      —*From Michael Angelo.*

LOVE is not in our power—
   Nay, what seems strange, is not in our choice.
      —*French.*

Balm—Molucca.

Moluccella lævis. NATURAL ORDER: *Labiatæ — Mint Family.*

OLUCCA BALM, or Shell Flower, is a native of the Molucca or Spice Islands, where it mingles with the odoriferous flowers of the clove, the citron and the lime. The stem is from one to two feet high, smooth, and of a sea-green color. It is an annual, often grown in the flower-garden as a curiosity, for its singular manner of inflorescence. The calyx or floral sheath is large and bell-shaped, which suggests the appearance of a hollow shell, while down in the bottom sits the flower itself, out of sight, the color being a yellowish-green. The blooming time is from May to August.

You Excite my Curiosity.

OH strange it is, and wide the new-world lore,
  For next it treateth of our native dust!
Must dig out buried monsters, and explore
  The green earth's fruitful crust;

Must write the story of her seething youth —
  How lizards paddled in her lukewarm seas:
Must show the cones she ripened, and forsooth
  Count seasons on her trees;

Must know her weight, and pry into her age,
  Count her old beach-lines by their tidal swell.
Her sunken mountains name, her craters gauge,
  Her cold volcanoes tell. —*Jean Ingelow.*

BETSY! art thou Eve's true daughter?
  Betsy! hast a peering eye?
Wouldst thou read as clear as water
All the honeyed terms that lie
Within that letter's fragile folds?
Spell every word that letter holds,
And know when thy young master Harry
Or Lady Jane intends to marry?

What! not yet in the secret, Betsy?
That's very puzzling — very! Let's see —
The letter's not from Lady Jane,
No, no! you need not peep again.
A lady's hand — the envelope
Perfumed — the seal expresses "Hope."
The waiter waits — no longer tarry!
Go, give the letter to Lord Harry!
    —*Anonymous.*

Eve,
With all the fruits of Eden blest,
Save only one, rather than leave
That one unknown, lost all the rest.
    —*Moore.*

Balm--Sweet.

Melissa officinalis.   NATURAL ORDER: *Labiatæ — Mint Family.*

WE here find naturalized a very common and well-known garden plant, introduced from Europe, and cultivated for its virtues. The stem is erect and branching, growing about two feet high, the whole plant being covered with a soft down, and emitting, when touched with the hand, the delightful fragrance of the lemon. The flowers are a sallow white, appearing during midsummer. Melissa is from the Greek word *melissa*, a bee, because it attracts innumerable bees that come to suck at the nectaries of the blossoms. Old apiarists like to rub the inside of the hives with its aromatic leaves, as an inducement for the young swarms to remain, especially if the hives have been previously used.

Charms.

SWEET-POUTING lips whose color mocks the rose,
   Rich, ripe, and teeming with the dew of bliss —
The flower of love's forbidden fruit which grows
   Insiduously, to tempt us with a kiss.
R. H. Wilde's Tasso Sonnets.

HER eyes outshine the radiant beams
   That gild the passing shower,
And glitter o'er the crystal streams,
   And cheer each fresh'ning hour.

Her lips are more than cherries bright,
   A richer dye has grac'd them;
They charm the admiring gazer's sight,
   And sweetly tempt to kiss them.
Burns.

THOUGH gay as mirth, as curious thought sedate;
As elegance polite, as power elate;
Profound as reason, and as justice clear;
Soft as compassion, yet as truth severe.
Savage.

HER tresses loose behind,
   Play on her neck, and wanton in the wind;
The rising blushes which her cheeks o'er-spread,
Are opening roses in a lily's bed. —*Gay.*

THERE was a soft and pensive grace,
   A cast of thought upon her face,
That suited well her forehead high,

The eyelash dark, and downcast eye;
The mild expression spoke a mind
In duty firm, composed, resigned.
Scott.

Balm--Wild.

Monarda didyma. NATURAL ORDER: *Labiatæ—Mint Family.*

UCH coarser, and less delicate in odor, than the garden varieties, is the Wild Balm, commonly called Mountain Mint, and scientifically named, as above, in honor of Monardes, a Spanish botanist of the sixteenth century, who wrote a work on the medicinal virtues of the botanical productions of the new world. It is a tall, herbaceous plant, found in the fields and woods, having fragrant leaves and crimson flowers that improve under cultivation. In medicine it possesses stimulating and carminitive properties. An infusion of the leaves is known as Oswego tea; and the flowers yield the coloring principle of cochineal.

I Value Your Sympathy.

THOU'RT like a star; for when my way was cheerless and forlorn,
And all was blackness like the sky before a coming storm,
Thy beaming smile and words of love, thy heart of kindness free,
Illumed my path, then cheered my soul, and bade its sorrows flee.

HAST thou no human friend
To whom in hours like these to turn,
When thine o'erburdened soul will yearn
Its bitterness to end? —*Miss M. H. Rand.*

WE pine for kindred natures
To mingle with our own;
For communings more full and high
Than aught by mortals known.
—*Mrs. Hemans.*

AND when the world looked cold on him,
And blight hung on his name,
She soothed his cares with woman's love,
And bade him rise again. ——.

OUR hearts, my love, were form'd to be
The genuine twins of sympathy,
They live with one sensation;
In joy or grief, but most in love,
Like chords in unison they move,
And thrill with like vibration. —*Moore.*

LOVE'S soft sympathy imparts
That tender transport of delight
That beats in undivided hearts.
—*Cartwright.*

KINDNESS by secret sympathy is tied,
For noble souls in nature are allied.
—*Dryden.*

Balm of Gilead.

Populus candicans.   NATURAL ORDER: *Salicaceæ—Willow Family.*

UTILITY and agreeableness are combined in this handsome tree, and it is often used, interspersed with others, to break the monotony in foliage groups, and yield a grateful shade, for which it is well adapted. The height averages from forty to fifty feet, the thickness being in good proportion, with an ample crown of dark green leaves. The buds are resinous, and possess strong tonic and other medicinal properties, whence they are frequently used as a domestic medicine. *Populus balsamifera* is a similar variety, found wild in swamps and other moist places, and is called Tacamahac or Balsam Poplar, as it yields a resinous gum from the buds in the same manner as the Balm of Gilead.

Sympathetic Feeling.

NO radiant pearl which crested fortune wears,
  No gem that twinkling hangs from beauty's ears,
Not the bright stars which night's blue arch adorn,
Nor rising sun that gilds the vernal morn,
Shines with such luster as the tear that flows
Down virtue's manly cheek for others' woes.
—*Dr. E. Darwin.*

AND when he read, they forward lean'd,
  Drinking with thirsty hearts and ears
His brook-like songs, whose glory never wean'd
  From humble smiles and tears.
Slowly there grew a tenderer awe,
  Sun-like, o'er faces brown and hard,
As if in him who read they felt and saw
  Some presence of the bard. —*James R. Lowell.*

YET a single cup of water,
  Or a crust to feed the starving,
E'en one word in kindness spoken,
Or a hand stretched to the falling
Shall receive as great reward as
Ever hero gained in battle,
Saint or martyr at the scaffold.
—*Lena I. Gifford.*

IT is the secret sympathy,
  The silver link, the silken tie,
Which heart to heart, and mind to mind,
In body and in soul can bind. —*Scott.*

Balsamine.

Impatiens balsamina.   NATURAL ORDER; *Balsaminaceæ — Jewel-Weed Family.*

LADY SLIPPER, or the ordinary Balsam, is familiar to all as a product of our gardens. It is a native of the East Indies, and is worthy of notice. Within the last few years the double varieties have been grown as pot-plants, in which state they require very rich soil, and to have the tip of the main branch pinched off, when it will throw out side branches and form larger plants. They appear in every variety of color, and the fancy ones are streaked or mottled, many of them being nearly as double as the blossoms of that beautiful shrub the camelia japonica. The seed-pods burst when slightly pressed, from which circumstance they receive their Latin name, *Impatiens, noli me tangere* (impatient, touch me not).

Impatience.

WHAT! canst thou not forbear me half an hour?
　Then get thee gone, and dig my grave thyself,
And bid the merry bells ring to thine ear
That thou art crown'd — not that I am dead.
　　　　　　　　　　　　　　— *Shakespeare.*

A WRETCHED soul, bruised with adversity,
　We bid be quiet, when we hear it cry;
But were we burdened with like weight of pain,
As much, or more, we should ourselves complain.
　　　　　　　— *Shakespeare.*

PREACH patience to the sea, when jarring winds
　Throw up her swelling billows to the sky!
And if your reasons mitigate her fury,
My soul will be as calm.　　— *Smith.*

GO, then, my song, speed swiftly to her;
　Sing to her, plead with her late and long;
Hover around her, and gently woo her;
　Perhaps she will hear thee some day, O Song!

Out of the depths of the soul comes sorrow;
　But, out of the depths of these days that cease,
May come, like light 'round the feet of the morrow,
　Love's soft glory, our love's calm peace.
　　　　　　　　　　　　Barton Grey.

OH! how impatience gains upon the soul,
　When the long-promised hour of joy draws near!
How slow the tardy moments seem to roll!　— *Mrs. Tighe.*

Bartonia—Golden.

Mentzelia Lindleyi.   NATURAL ORDER: *Loasaceæ — Loasa Family.*

IN the Golden Bartonia we have a beautiful annual from California, with an oval, lance-shaped leaf, indented similar to the thistle; the stems are procumbent and often a yard in length. The flowers, which much resemble a poppy, are of a most brilliant yellow, deepening toward the center into the true orange shade, and measuring from two to three inches in diameter. Within the center the numerous thread-like stamens spread themselves out over the petals, like a delicate fringe. The seeds should be sown where the plants are to grow, as they are transplanted with difficulty.

Does He Possess Riches?

HAD I but pearls of price—did golden pills
Of hoarded wealth swell in my treasury,
Easy I'd win the fawning flatterer's smile
And bend the sturdiest stoic's iron knee.
— *J. A. Locke.*

THINK'ST thou the man whose mansions hold
The worldling's pride, the miser's gold,
Obtains a richer prize
Than he who in his cot, at rest,
Finds heavenly peace a willing guest,
And bears the earnest in his breast
Of treasure in the skies?
— *Mrs. Sigourney.*

A MIGHTY pain to love it is,
And 'tis a pain that pain to miss;
But, of all pains, the greatest pain
It is to love but love in vain.
Virtue now, nor noble blood,
Nor wit, by love is understood;
Gold alone does passion move;
Gold monopolizes love.
— *Cowley.*

O KNEW I the spell of gold,
I would never poison a fresh young heart
With the taint of customs old;
I would bind no wreath to my forehead free,
In whose shadows a thought might die,
Nor drink, from the cup of revelry,
The ruin my gold would buy.
— *Willis.*

MADAM, I own 'tis not your person
My stomach's set so sharp and fierce on;
But 'tis your better part, your riches,
That my enamor'd heart bewitches!
— *Butler.*

A MASK of gold hides all deformities;
Gold is heaven's physic, life's restorative.
— *Decker.*

Basil—Sweet.

Ocimum basilicum. NATURAL ORDER: *Labiatæ — Mint Family.*

SWEET BASIL, or Royal Ocimum, is a very aromatic herb from Persia, where it is much planted in graveyards. It is also indigenous to the East Indies, where its seeds are considered an antidote to the poison of serpents. It is an annual, about a foot high, with a soft, oval leaf, various in color, which possesses a very agreeable fragrance. The flowers, which are nearly white, appear during the summer. French cooks are very partial to this herb in flavoring their various dishes, and for this purpose it is extensively grown in the vegetable gardens of Europe, as well as in America. Apparently from confounding the word with basiliscus, a basilisk, or possibly because of its use as an antidote, whence it may have come to represent a serpent hater, it has been taken as a symbol for hatred, but the following is the proper language.

Good Wishes.

SOFT be the sleep of their pleasant hours,
  And calm be the seas they roam!
May the way they travel be strewed with flowers,
  Till it bring them safely home!   *Oliver Twiss.*

TO wish thee fairer is no need,
  More prudent, or more sprightly,
Or more ingenious, or more freed
  From temper flaws unsightly.
What favor then not yet possess'd
  Can I for thee require,
In wedded love already blest
  To thy whole heart's desire?   —*Cowper.*

SO may'st thou live, dear! many years,
  In all the bliss that life endears,
Not without smiles, nor yet from tears,
  Too strictly kept.   —*Thomas Hood.*

IF, then, a fervent wish for thee
  The gracious heavens will heed from me,
What should, dear heart, its burden be?
    J. G. Whittier.

AND what am I to you? A steady hand
  To hold, a steadfast heart to trust withal;
Merely a man that loves you, and will stand
  By you, whate'er befall.   —*Jean Ingelow.*

Bayberry.

Myrica cerifera. NATURAL ORDER: *Myricaceæ — Sweet Gale Family.*

BAYBERRY, a useful shrub, varying in height from two to eight feet, and flowering in April or May, is found in dry forests from Nova Scotia to Florida. It has a grayish bark and branching top, and its fruit consists of a globular stone, covered with white wax, which is separated by heat, usually boiling water. This product constitutes the Bayberry tallow of commerce, sometimes called myrtle wax. A bushel of berries yields about four pounds of wax. The botanical name comes from the Greek *muro*, to flow, because the stamens contract on the slightest touch, and are thence conceived to be easily irritated, even to tears.

I Respect thy Tears.

BE temperate in grief? I would not hide
   The starting tear-drop with a stoic's pride,
I would not bid the o'erburthen'd heart be still,
And outrage nature with contempt of ill.
Weep! but not loudly! He whose stony eyes
Ne'er melt in tears, is hated in the skies.
Euphorion.

THE rose is fairest when 'tis budding new,
   And hope is brightest when it dawns from fears;
The rose is sweetest wash'd with morning dew,
And love is loveliest when embalmed in tears.
          — *Scott.*

LET me wipe off this honorable dew
   That silverly doth progress on my cheeks.
       Shakespeare.

WITH a shriek heart-wounding loud she cried,
   While down her cheeks the gushing torrents ran,
Fast falling on her hands.
          — *Rowe.*

TWO other precious drops that ready stood,
   Each in their crystal sluice, he, ere they fell,
Kiss'd, as the gracious signs of sweet remorse
And pious awe, that fear'd to have offended.
          — *Milton.*

COME, chase that starting tear away,
   Ere mine to meet it springs.   *Moore.*

HIDE not thy tears! weep boldly, and be proud
   To give the flowing virtue manly way:
'Tis nature's mark, to know an honest heart.
          Hill.

Beech.

Fagus sylvatica. NATURAL ORDER: *Cupuliferæ—Oak Family.*

AS nothing beautiful escapes the eye of the poet, numerous have been the tributes paid to this noble tree. It is lofty and abundant in the forests of the Eastern States, and not unfrequently found throughout all sections of the United States, as well as in Europe. It grows straight and tall, rising sometimes to the height of one hundred feet on the banks of the Ohio, with a trunk nine feet in circumference. It has a gray, unbroken bark and long, sweeping branches, but not so pendulous as those of the elm, and is scarcely equaled by any other tree in the shade it affords. Cattle are fond of its leaves in spring, when they are very tender, with a slight acid flavor. The nuts are partially triangular, and, though troublesome to eat, are sweet and nutritious. A valuable oil, but little inferior, it is said, to the olive, can be extracted from them.

Lovers' Tryst.

I KNOW a walk where beeches grow —
  Where feathered songsters fill the air
With music sweet, and flowers blow
  Blooming and fair.
And there I've oft with pleasure wooed
The muses nine in solitude. — *Fred. W. Webber.*

SIX: nay, at six in any case
  He could not come! 'tis evening chime,
And if I reach the trysting place
  Whole hours before the trysting time,
'Tis not with any hope to see
  Unseemly soon my love appear;
He is no idle maid like me;
  He has high things to do and bear.
And not for worlds would I that he
  For love should weakly eager be.
      — *Mrs. Eliza S. Randolph.*

SHE starts, for she doth hear
  My loving footstep near;
She turns to bid me stay,
With cheeks that burn for joy.
With looks half kind, half coy —
  This is her heart's sweet way!
So am I nothing loath,
But answer oath for oath,
  And linger lovingly
In silken chains — *ma mie!*
      — *Edward Renaud.*

Begonia.

Begonia discolor. NATURAL ORDER: *Begoniaceæ — Begonia Family.*

BEGONIAS were so named by the French Botanist, Plumier, in honor of Michael Begon, a governor of Santo Domingo, and a patron of science. They are natives of Jamaica, Brazil, the East and West Indies, and other tropical countries. The large-leaved varieties have been vulgarly called Elephant's Ears, which they may perhaps resemble in shape, but the exquisite beauty of their coloring eliminates from the mind every ugly and unpleasant synonym. Some of them are a dark green with a band of silver, or groupings of silver blotches; or again entirely bronze, according to the individual plant. This species is grown chiefly for its foliage; the flowers are mostly white or faintly tinted, blooming on short stems. There are several kinds, however, with small waxy leaves that make a splendid appearance when in bloom, being handsome in color and of fine texture. The stems of the large foliage variety are very much distorted.

Deformity.

SHE did corrupt frail nature with some bribe
To shrink mine arm up like a wither'd shrub,
To make an envious mountain on my back,
Where sits deformity to make my body;
To shape my legs of an unequal size;
To disproportion me in every part
Like to a chaos.   —*Shakespeare.*

AM I to blame if nature threw my body
In so perverse a mold? yet when she cast
Her envious hand upon my supple joints,
Unable to resist, and rumpled them
On heaps in their dark lodging; to revenge
Her bungled work, she stamped my mind more fair.

DEFORMITY is daring;
It is its essence to o'ertake mankind
By heart and soul, and make itself the equal —
Ay, the superior of the rest. There is
A spur in its halt movements, to become
All that others cannot, in such things
As are still free for both.   *Byron.*

And as from chaos, huddled and deform'd,
The gods struck fire, and lighted up the lamps
That beautify the sky; so she inform'd
This ill shap'd body with a daring soul,
And, making me less than man, she made me more.
            —*Lee.*

Bellflower.

Campanula rotundifolia.   NATURAL ORDER: *Campanulaceæ — Bellwort Family.*

DAMP, cool and rocky places are the favorite abodes of this simple little flower (known also as the Harebell), and it is accordingly found in great abundance in the New England States and the Dominion of Canada. The family of the Campanulas is quite extensive, numbering about five hundred species. The flowers, though simple, are various in colors, and are worthy of attention. In this species they are blue, which is the prevailing tint, though others run through different shades of purple, from violet to lilac, and white. The Campanula pyramidalis is the handsomest and most stately, growing from three to five feet, blooming the second year from the seed, and producing blossoms by the hundred

A Constant Heart.

THEN come the wild weather, come sleet or come snow,
   We will stand by each other however it blow.
Oppression and sickness, and sorrow, and pain,
Shall be to our true love as links to the chain.
                    — *Longfellow.*

TO keep one sacred flame
   Through life unchilled, unmoved,
To love in wintry age
   The same that first in youth we lov'd,
To feel that we adore

With such refined excess,
   That tho' the heart would break with more,
It could not live with less;
   This is love — faithful love;
Such as saints might feel above.

WHEN all things have their trial, you shall find
   Nothing is constant but a virtuous mind. — *Shirley.*

LOVE, constant love!
   Age cannot quench it — like the primal ray
From the vast fountain that supplies the day.
   Far, far above
Our cloud-encircled region, it will flow
As pure and as eternal in its glow.
                Park Benjamin.

COULD genius sink in dull decay,
   And wisdom cease to lend her ray;
Should all that I have worshiped change,
   Even this could not my heart estrange;
Thou still would'st be the first — the first
That taught the love sad tears have nursed.
                — *Mrs. Embury.*

Berberry.

Berberis vulgaris.   NATURAL ORDER: *Berberidaceæ — Berberry Family.*

GROWN in our gardens as an ornament, this graceful, bushy shrub is very generally known. The leaves are a dark green, with serrated edges, each notch being bristly. The flowers are yellow, hanging in small clusters. The fruit is brilliant and attractive, of a bright scarlet in color, oblong in shape, and appearing more like pendulous groups of coral ear-drops, than anything else. The leaves, as well as fruit, have a sharp acid taste, the latter being frequently used for making jelly, while from the root can be prepared a yellow dye.

A Sour Disposition.

THOSE hearts that start at once into a blaze,
  And open all their rage, like summer storms
At once discharged, grow cool again and calm.
— *C. Johnson.*

FIE! wrangling queen!
  Whom everything becomes — to chide, to laugh,
To weep. Whose every passion fully strives
To make itself in thee, fair and admired.
— *Shakespeare.*

THE ocean lash'd to fury loud,
  Its high wave mingling with the cloud,
Is peaceful, sweet serenity,
To anger's dark and stormy sea.
— *J. W. Eastburn.*

WHEN anger rushes, unrestrain'd, to action,
  Like a hot steed, it stumbles in its way:
The man of thought strikes deepest, and strikes safest.
— *Savage.*

MY rage is not malicious; like a spark
  Of fire by steel enforc'd out of flint,
It is no sooner kindled, but extinct.
— *Goffe.*

ALL furious as a favor'd child
  Balk'd of its wish; or, fiercer still,
A woman piqued, who has her will.
— *Byron.*

SHE is peevish, sullen, froward,
  Proud, disobedient, stubborn, lacking duty;
Neither regarding that she is my child,
Nor fearing me as if I were her father.
— *Shakespeare.*

Birch.

Betula lenta.   NATURAL ORDER: *Betulaceæ — Birch Family.*

KNOWN as the black, cherry or sweet Birch, and sometimes called mountain mahogany from the hardness of its wood, this valuable tree abounds in the United States from New England to Ohio, and often reaches a height of seventy, and a diameter of three, feet. Children are very fond of the inner bark of this tree in springtime, when it has an aromatic fragrance and pleasant flavor. It is from the Paper Birch that the Indians obtain the bark for their light and buoyant canoes, in which they glide in safety through the most dangerous waters. The Yellow or Silver Birch is the artist's tree *par excellence*. Its beautiful outer bark, like satin in luster, peels from around the trunk and branches, and hangs in the most fantastic rolls and curls, resting on an undertone of warm and tender brown, making it one of the choicest and most illuminating trees in a woodland sketch, and one that always delights a painter's heart.

Elegance.

FOR faultless was her form as beauty's queen,
And every winning grace that love demands,
With mild attemper'd dignity was seen
Play o'er each lovely limb, and deck her angel mien.
— *Mrs. Tighe.*

HER face so fair, as flesh it seemèd not,
But heavenly portrait of bright angels' hue,
Clear as the sky, withouten blame or blot,
Through goodly mixture of complexion's dew.
— *Spenser.*

GRACEFUL to sight, and elegant to thought,
The great are vanquish'd, and the wise are taught.
— *Young.*

THE silk star-broidered coverlid
Unto her limbs itself doth mold,
Languidly ever; and, amid
Her full black ringlets, downward rolled,
Glows forth each softly shadowed arm,
With bracelets of the diamond bright
Her constant beauty doth inform
Stillness with love, and day with light.
— *Tennyson.*

Black Hoarhound.

Ballota nigra.   NATURAL ORDER: *Labiatæ — Mint Family.*

HERE is an unattractive foreign plant supposed to have been introduced into this country through the commerce of the nations, as many of our now obnoxious weeds have found their way, concealed in various grains imported for seed. It is now frequently found naturalized in the fields and by the waysides. The stem is from two to three feet high, having broad, opposite leaves covered with a soft down. It derives its name from the Greek word *ballo*, to throw, or reject, on account of its offensive odor. It blooms in July, the flowers being either purple or white, and of little beauty.

I Reject You.

TAKE my esteem, if you on that can live;
  But frankly, sir, 'tis all I have to give.
        —*Dryden.*

HE came too late! Her countless dreams
  Of hope had long since flown.
No charms dwelt in his chosen themes,
  Nor in his whisper'd tone;
And when with word and smile he tried
  Affection still to prove,
She nerved her heart with woman's pride,
  And spurn'd his fickle love. —*Elizabeth Bogart.*

WHERE is another sweet as my sweet,
  Fine of the fine, and shy of the shy?
Fine little hands, fine little feet—
  Dewy blue eye.
Shall I write to her? shall I go?
  Ask her to marry me by-and-by?
Somebody said that she'd say no.
        —*Tennyson.*

IF you oblige me suddenly to choose,
  My choice is made—and I must you refuse.
        —*Dryden.*

LIKE a lovely tree
  She grew to womanhood, and between whiles
Rejected several suitors.   —*Byron.*

I HAVE heard—
  But you shall promise ne'er again
To breathe your vows or speak your pain.
        —*Prior.*

DO I not in plainest truth
  Tell you,—I do not, nor I cannot love you?
        —*Shakespeare.*

Bladdernut.

Staphylea trifolia. NATURAL ORDER: *Sapindaceæ — Soapberry Family.*

PECULIAR to this handsome shrub, found in various sections of the United States, are the bladder-like capsules or pods, from which it derives its name, and in which are contained the seeds or nuts. These are hard, bony, smooth and polished. The flowers, which bloom in May, are white and hang in short, pendulous clusters, somewhat like bunches of grapes, whence the scientific Greek name, Staphylea. It grows to the height of six, eight, or even ten feet, chiefly in low lands, in moist woods, amongst the underbrush. The wood is firm and white, and well adapted for cabinet work.

A Trifling Character.

OH! there are some
   Can trifle, in cold vanity, with all
The warm soul's precious throbs; to whom it is
A triumph, that a fond, devoted heart
Is breaking for them; who can bear to call
Young flowers into beauty, and then crush them.
—Letitia E. Landon.

AROUND him some mysterious circle thrown
  Repell'd approach and show'd him still alone;
Upon his eye sat something of reproof,
That kept at least trivility aloof.   *Byron.*

HE was perfumed like a milliner;
  And twixt his finger and his thumb he held
A pouncet-box, which, ever and anon
He gave his nose —
And still he smiled and talked;
And as the soldiers bare dead bodies by,
He called them "untaught knaves unmannerly,
To bring a slovenly, unhandsome corse
Betwixt the wind and his nobility." — *Shakespeare.*

YOU oftentimes can mark upon the street
  The gilded toy whom fashion idolizes;
Heartless and fickle, swelled with self-conceit.
Avoiding alway what good sense advises.
—W. H. C.

THE joy that vain amusement gives,
  O, sad conclusions that it brings,
The honey of a crowded hive,
  Defended by a thousand stings.
'Tis thus the world rewards the fools
  That live upon her treacherous smiles,
She leads them blindfold by her rules,
  And ruins all whom she beguiles.
—Cowper.

Borage.

Borago officinalis.   NATURAL ORDER: *Boraginaceæ — Borage Family.*

ENGLAND and the rest of Europe as well as America now own this plant in a naturalized state, though it is generally believed to have been originally indigenous to the region of Aleppo, in Turkey. It is cultivated in the kitchen garden for its young leaves, which are considered excellent for salads, pickles and pot-herbs. It is an annual, about two feet high, with oval leaves growing alternately on each side of the stem, the whole plant being rough and covered with hairs. It is also grown as an ornamental plant in the flower garden. The flowers are a pale blue, appearing in spring on the ends of the branches. The plants of this whole family abound in mucilaginous juices containing much niter, and are said never to possess any poisonous or harmful quality.

Abruptness.

THE reed in storms may bow and quiver,
Then rise again; the tree must shiver.
— *Bryan.*

SUDDENLY all the sky is hid
As with the shutting of a lid.
— *James Russell Lowell.*

I do not love
Much ceremony; suits in love should not,
Like suits in law, be rock'd from term to term.
— *Shirley.*

Although
The air of Paradise did fan the house,
And angels offic'd all, I will begone.
— *Shakespeare.*

THIS is some fellow,
Who, having been prais'd for bluntness, doth affect
A saucy roughness, and constrains the garb;
Quite from his nature! he can't flatter, he.
An honest mind and plain — he must speak truth!
And they will take it so; if not, he's plain.
These kind of knaves I know, which in this plainness
Harbor more craft, and far corrupter ends,
Than twenty silly ducking observants,
That stretch their duty nicely.   — *Shakespeare.*

Bouncing Bess.

Saponaria officinalis.   NATURAL ORDER: *Caryophyllaceæ — Pink Family.*

IN dooryards of old-fashioned country houses, and by the roadsides throughout the country, this plant may be found in abundance. The place of its nativity is Europe, but it has long been naturalized in America. It is about two feet high, of a succulent, herbaceous growth, and nearly allied to the bunch pinks, though much coarser. The flowers bloom in clusters, and are the palest possible shade faltering between pink and white. The root is perennial, and inclined to spread and become obtrusive. As one means of curtailing its obtrusiveness, its seeds, which are very fertile and abundant, should be clipped and destroyed before they ripen. The bruised stalks make a lather in water, which quality gives it the name of Soapwort in our vernacular, as well as its scientific appellation Saponaria, from the Latin *sapo*, soap.

Intrusion.

A SUDDEN rush from the stairway,
  A sudden raid from the hall,
By three doors left unguarded,
  They enter my castle wall.

They climb up into my turret,
  O'er the arms and back of my chair;
If I try to escape, they surround me;
  They seem to be everywhere.
      — Longfellow.

I had much rather see
  A crested dragon, or a basilisk:
Both are less poison to my eyes and nature.
      — Dryden.

BUT the sound grew into word
  As the speakers drew more near —
Sweet, forgive me that I heard
  What you wished me not to hear.
      Elizabeth Barrett Browning.

LOVE knoweth every form of air,
  And every shape of earth,
And comes unbidden everywhere,
  Like thought's mysterious birth.
      — N. P. Willis.

A LADY! In the narrow space
  Between the husband and the wife,
But nearest him — she showed a face
  With dangers rife.   *— Jean Ingelow.*

Box.

Buxus sempervirens.   NATURAL ORDER: *Euphorbiaceæ — Spurge Family.*

ENGRAVERS on wood are much indebted to this tree for the blocks they use to work on, which, after having been sawed and made perfectly smooth, receive a slight coating of some white substance, usually white lead or Chinese white, to render the drawing more conspicuous. The artist's work is done in pencil or India ink. The engraver then follows with delicate touch the lines before him, and cuts the picture into the wood beneath. The botanical name of this shrub comes from the Latin. The word Buxus, box, is itself derived from the Greek *puxos*, pyx, or small box, and *sempervirens* is from the two Latin words *semper*, always, and *virens*, present participle of the verb *virere*, to be green. There are several varieties of this genus which are natives of Europe. The species known scientifically as the Buxus Nana, or Dwarf Box, is much used as a bordering for walks both here and abroad.

Stoicism.

On his dark face a scorching clime
 And toil, had done the work of time,
Roughen'd the brow, the temples bared,
And sable hairs with silver shared,
Yet left — what age alone could tame —
The lip of pride, the eye of flame;

The full-drawn lip that upward curl'd,
The eye that seem'd to scorn the world.
That lip had terror never blench'd;
Ne'er in that eye had tear-drop quench'd
The flash severe of swarthy glow,
That mock'd at pain and knew not woe.
— *Sir Walter Scott.*

Nor box, nor limes, without their use are made,
 Smooth-grain'd and proper for the turner's trade;
Which curious hands may carve, and seal
With ease invade.   — *Virgil.*

The rolling wheel, that runneth often 'round,
 The hardest steel in tract of time doth tear;
And drizzling drops, that often do redound,
Firmest flint doth in continuance wear:

Yet cannot I, with many a dropping tear,
And long entreaty, soften her hard heart,
That she will once vouchsafe my plaint to hear
Or look with pity on my painful smart.
— *Spenser.*

Broom.

Genista tinctoria. NATURAL ORDER: *Leguminosæ—Pulse Family.*

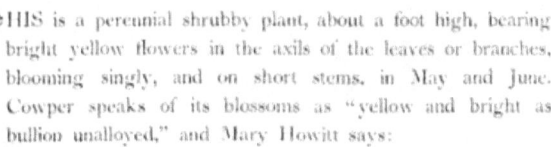

THIS is a perennial shrubby plant, about a foot high, bearing bright yellow flowers in the axils of the leaves or branches, blooming singly, and on short stems, in May and June. Cowper speaks of its blossoms as "yellow and bright as bullion unalloyed," and Mary Howitt says:

> "But ne'er was flower so fair as this,
> In modern days or olden;
> It groweth on its nodding stem
> Like to a garden golden."

It is a native of Europe, but is found naturalized in some parts of the United States, and is useful to the dyer in forming a yellow dye, or a green when combined with woad. The color is obtained from any part of the plant.

Humility.

HUMBLE we must be, if to Heaven we go;
High is the roof there, but the gate is low;
Whene'er thou speak'st, look with lowly eye—
Grace is increased by humility. — *Robert Herrick.*

THE cedar's shade like a cloud may lie
Athwart the lily's brightness—
Yet why complain? it leaves no stain
To mar the blossom's whiteness;
And darkly thus may pride and power
Appear to press the lowly,
Yet never may the shadow stay
Where Faith, like blossom holy,
Keeps white the heart; to such there will be given
A blest assurance of the love of Heaven.
— *Mrs. Hale.*

HUMILITY is the eldest-born of virtue,
And claims the birthright at the throne of
heav'n. — *Murphy.*

HEAVEN'S gates are not so highly arched
As princes' palaces; they that enter there
Must go upon their knees. — *John Webster.*

I AM content to touch the brink
Of the other goblet, and I think
My bitter drink a wholesome drink,
Because my portion was assigned
Wholesome and bitter. Thou art kind,
And I am blessèd to my mind.
— *Elizabeth Barrett Browning.*

Broom Corn.

Sorghum vulgare. NATURAL ORDER: *Gramineæ—Grass Family.*

VARIOUS parts of the United States are favorable to the cultivation of this corn, which is manufactured into brooms, constituting a special industry of most of the Shaker communities, besides many private persons. It looks very much like the Indian corn as regards its leaves and height. When the panicle is sufficiently mature, the stalk is bent down at the top until ripe enough to cut. It is a native of the East Indies, and has been chosen as an emblem of labor. The Sorghum saccharatum, or Chinese sugar cane, is supposed to be another variety, which yields a saccharine juice, whence its name; but even this, it is said, does not give a product equal to the crystallized syrup of the East India species of the same character.

Labor.

LABOR is health. Lo! the husbandman reaping,
How through his veins goes the life current leaping!
How his strong arm in its stalwart pride sweeping.
True as a sunbeam the swift sickle guides. —*Mrs. Osgood.*

GIVE me the fair one, in country or city,
Whose home and its duties are dear to the heart,
Who cheerfully warbles some rustical ditty,
While plying the needle with exquisite art.
—*Wordsworth.*

MAN hath his daily work of body or mind
Appointed, which declare his dignity;
While other animals inactive range,
And of their doings God takes no account.
—*Milton.*

COME, my fair love, our morning task we lose.
Some labor e'en the easiest life would choose;
Ours is not great, the dangling boughs to crop,
Whose too luxuriant growth our alleys stop.
Dryden.

"GO till the ground," said God to man,—
"Subdue the earth, it shall be thine;"
How grand, how glorious was the plan!
How wise the law divine. *Mrs. Hale.*

THIS my mean task
Would be as heavy to me as odious; but
The mistress, which I serve, quickens what's dead,
And makes my labors pleasures. *Shakespeare.*

Browallia.

Browallia cœrulea.   NATURAL ORDER: *Scrophulariaceæ — Figwort Family.*

FROM Peru and Brazil comes this delicate little annual, one among many recent additions to our gardens. It received its name from Linnæus in honor of his intimate friend (who was afterward his enemy), Johan Browall, bishop of Abo, in Sweden. It is about a foot high, and is delicate and graceful in appearance, being covered continually with innumerable flowers, which are very peculiar in shape, bearing a fanciful resemblance to a salver with two deep indentations in the sides. The plant is well calculated for pot culture. The varieties are white, rose, and a purplish blue.

Can You Bear Poverty?

MY crown is in my heart, not on my head;
  Not deck'd with diamonds and Indian stones,
Nor to be seen: my crown is call'd content;
A crown it is that seldom kings enjoy.
                                                  —*Shakespeare.*

O GRANT me, heav'n, a middle state —
  Neither too humble nor too great,
More than enough for nature's ends,
With something left to treat my friends.
                                  —*Mallet.*

UNFIT for greatness, I her snares defy,
  And look on riches with untainted eye.
To others let the glitt'ring baubles fall;
Content shall place me far above them all.
                                  —*Churchill.*

HAPPY the life that in a peaceful stream,
  Obscure, unnoticed, through the vale has flow'd;
The heart that ne'er was charm'd by fortune's gleam
Is ever sweet contentment's blest abode.   —*Percival.*

MERE store of money is not wealth, but rather
  The proof of poverty and need of bread.
Like men themselves is the bright gold they gather;
  It may be living, or it may be dead.

It may be filled with love and life and vigor,
  To guide the wearer, and to cheer the way;
It may be corpse-like in its weight and rigor,
  Bending the bearer to his native clay.
                                  —*John Boyle O'Reilly.*

BE honest poverty thy boasted wealth;
  So shall thy friendships be sincere, tho' few,
So shall thy sleep be sound, thy waking cheerful.   —*Harvard.*

Bugloss.

Anchusa officinalis.   NATURAL ORDER: *Boraginaceæ — Borage Family.*

OUR gardens, fields and roadsides everywhere furnish this rough perennial plant, which produces an abundance of sweet-scented purple flowers during the entire summer. The leaves are long and rough, from which it has received in England the name of Ox-tongue, and the stem is covered with bristly hairs. The root is used in medicine, producing a gentle moisture through the system. The root of one of the species yields the red dye that was so much used by the Athenian ladies as a rouge when that classic city was in its prime.

Hypocrisy.

THERETO when needed, she could weep and pray,
   And when she listed she could fawn and flatter,
Now smiling smoothly, like to summer's day,
Now glooming sadly, so to cloak the matter:
Yet were her words but wind, and all her tears but water.
          —*Spenser.*

EVERY man in this age has not a soul
  Of crystal, for all men to read their actions
Through; men's hearts and faces are so far asunder
That they hold no intelligence.
     —*Beaumont and Fletcher.*

A glittering volume may cover
  A story of sorrow and woe;
And night's gayest meteors may hover
  Where danger lies lurking below.

SO smooth he daubed his life with show of virtue,
  He lived from all attainder of suspect.
     —*Shakespeare.*

YET there came a time
  To my proud love's prime.
When that proved base I had deemed sublime.
  By the cool stream's bed
  My flowers hung dead,
And the serpent, hissing, upreared its head!
    —*Mary E. Bradley.*

SO, friend, be warned! He is not one
  Thy youth should trust, for all his smiles;
Frank foreheads, genial as the sun,
  May hide a thousand treacherous wiles,
And tones like music's honeyed flow
May work—God knows!—the bitterest woe.
    —*Paul H. Hayne.*

Bulrush.

Scirpus lacustris. NATURAL ORDER: *Cyperaceæ — Sedge Family.*

MOST uncommon and peculiar is the appearance of the Bulrush or Clubrush, as it is occasionally called, which makes it quite noticeable wherever it appears among other grasses; the leaves being tubular, with various fine grooves or channels running up and down their length. The Lake Bulrush is the largest of the species; growing in low lands, muddy marshes, and on the margins of streams and ponds. In early times it was much used in scouring tin, copper and pewter ware, but modern arts having supplied us with much better substitutes, it now remains unmolested. It was in some species of Bulrush or reed found along the borders of the Nile, that the infant Moses was discovered and rescued by the maids of the Egyptian princess.

Indecision.

SHE will, and she will not — she grants, denies,
Consents, retracts, advances, and then flies.
—*Granville*

THREE things a wise man will not trust:
The wind, the sunshine of an April day,
And woman's plighted faith. I have beheld
The weathercock upon the steeple point
Steady from morn till eve, and I have seen
The bees go forth upon an April morn,
Secure the sunshine will not end in showers;
But when was woman true?
—*Southey*

THE shepherd told me all his pain;
I ran and told it all again;
But Phillis gave herself such airs
It fills poor Colin's breast with cares;
And I can hardly tell, I'm sure,
If she will grant at last a cure.—
I've told you all, and what think you?
I won't repeat, so tell me — do! —*Mrs. Norton*

MOST fair is e'er most fickle. A fair girl
Is like a thousand beauteous things of earth,
But most like them in love of change.
—*Freebald*

CLOUDS turn with every wind about;
They keep us in suspense and doubt;
Yet oft perverse, like woman-kind,
Are seen to scud against the wind;
Is not this lady just the same?
For who can tell what is her aim? —*Swift*

Burdock.

Lappa major. NATURAL ORDER: *Compositæ — Aster Family.*

JUDGED by the popular verdict, the Burdock is an unattractive weed, one of the coarsest and most obnoxious of the plants that infest the roadsides, barnyards and fields, yet the roots are used in medicine as a tonic and alterative and to produce a gentle perspiration. The leaves are large, often nearly two feet long, with coarse cords or veins running through them, and the entire plant is pervaded by a bitter, disagreeable odor and taste. It grows about three or four feet in height, and is pyramidal in shape. The burrs are the most disagreeable part, as each little scale that forms the floral sheath is armed with a hook, by which it fastens to anything it may touch, and if ripe and dry it adheres most tenaciously. It is a naturalized plant from Europe, and blooms in July and August. The flowers are a delicate pink.

Proximity Undesirable.

THERE is some soul of goodness in things evil,
    Would men observingly distil it out;
For our bad neighbors make us early stirrers;
    Which is both healthful and good husbandry.
                              —*Shakespeare.*

I TO my chimney's shrine
    Brought him, as Love professes,
And chafed his hands with mine,
    And dried his dripping tresses.

But when that he felt warmed;
    Let's try this bow of ours,
And string, if they be harmed,
    Said he, with these late showers.

Forthwith his bow he bent,
    And wedded string and arrow,
And struck me, that it went
    Quite through my heart and marrow.

Then laughing loud, he flew
    Away, and thus said, flying:
Adieu, mine host, adieu!
    I'll leave thy heart a-dying
                    —*Anacreon.*

AH! charming isle in the warm, green sea!
    O sirens' tempting me to wrong,
What value have your meads to me?
                  —*James Maurice Thompson.*

Buttercup.

Ranunculus acris.   NATURAL ORDER: *Ranunculaceæ — Crowfoot Family.*

QUAINT is the fancy that attaches in the minds of the young to this common plant, so beautifully characterized by the poet Robert Browning as "the little children's dower." The very name calls up the picture of children crouching in the grass, and holding the golden blossoms under each other's chin to see if by the reflection they love butter, feeling assured that the least yellow gleam is indicative that their bread should be thickly spread with that golden and necessary product of the dairy. The leaves drop from the plant easily, and frequently the least touch will cause the petals of the flowers to fall in a golden shower.

Distrust.

THOU hast no truth to prove, fair Eloise,
   And I say thou art false, who loved thee most;
Then spare us both these feints and artful words.
I could forgive thee if thou didst not play
The actress with me now. And now I go;
But ere I go, I'll say I *do* forgive thee. — *Frances A. Fuller.*

WHO should be trusted now, when one's right hand
Is perjur'd to the bosom? Proteus,
I am sorry, I must never trust thee more,
But count the world a stranger for thy sake;
The private wound is deepest. — *Shakespeare.*

THIS, this has thrown a serpent to my heart,
   While it o'erflowed with tenderness, with joy,
With all the sweetness of exulting love;
Now naught but gall is there, and burning poison. — *Thompson.*

O DOUBT! O doubt! I know my destiny;
   I feel thee fluttering bird-like in my breast;
I cannot loose, but I will sing to thee,
   And flatter thee to rest.

Our doubts are traitors,
And make us lose the good we oft might win,
By fearing to attempt. — *Shakespeare.*

LIFE'S sunniest hours are not without
   The shadow of some lingering doubt.
                     — *Whittier.*

There is no certainty, "my bosom's guest."
No proving for the things whereof ye wot,
For, like the dead to sight unmanifest,
They are, and they are not. — *Jean Ingelow.*

Butterfly Orchis.

Oncidium Papilio majus.   NATURAL ORDER: *Orchidaceæ — Orchis Family.*

FLORISTS have had their interest much aroused by a very expensive class of plants called Orchids, partly on account of their curious and beautiful flowers, and partly because of their strange manner of growth and individual appearance. They are divided into two classes, terrestrial and aerial. The aerial ones are confined chiefly to tropical climates, some growing in damp woods, resting on trees, while others are found on dripping rocks among mountains and near water courses. The large Butterfly Orchis is one among the finest of that family known as Oncidium, and is a native of Trinidad. The blossom has the form of a butterfly, from which it takes its specific name papilio, a Latin word having the same significance. In color the flower is of a dark brown striped or barred with yellow. The large projection, called the lip, is yellow at the center with a brown edge or margin. The flowers come successively from the old flower-stems for years, one coming continuously to supply the place of the faded one.

Gaiety.

> WHAT nothing earthly gives, or can destroy,
> The soul's calm sunshine, and the heartfelt joy.
> —*Pope.*

THE valley rings with mirth and joy.
  Among the hills the echoes play
A never, never ending song,
  To welcome in the May.
The magpie chatters with delight.
  The mountain raven's youngling brood

Have left the mother and the nest;
  And they go rambling east and west
In search of their own food;
Or through the glittering vapors dart,
  In very wantonness of heart.
  — *Wordsworth.*

THE weak have remedies, the wise have joys;
  Superior wisdom is superior bliss.   *Young.*

A LITTLE of thy merriment,
  Of thy sparkling light content,
Give me, my cheerful brook,—
  That I may still be full of glee

And gladsomeness where'er I be,
  Though fickle fate hath prison'd me
In some neglected nook.
  — *Lowell.*

Cacalia.

Cacalia coccinea. NATURAL ORDER: *Composite—Aster Family.*

SCARLET Cacalia is a native of the East Indies, where nature revels in the most brilliant hues conceivable to the human mind, and where flowers assume shapes more innumerable than in this our cool and more temperate climate. Yet we must admit the most of them behave admirably in their adopted homes, sometimes diminishing their stature, but always remaining objects worthy of attention. The Cacalia blossom is shaped like a beautiful little brush or tassel, and is sometimes called Venus's Paint Brush, or Tassel Flower. There are two varieties grown in our gardens, one an orange scarlet, the other a golden yellow. They appear to better advantage in masses when not too thickly sown, and if the withered flowers are removed, will bloom profusely until frost.

Adulation.

IF we from wealth to poverty descend,
Want gives to know the flat'rer from the friend.
— *Dryden.*

THOU delightest the cold world's gaze,
When crowned with the flower and the gem,
But thy lover's smile should be dearer praise
Than the incense thou prizest from them.

And gay is the playful tone,
As to the flattering voice thou respondest;
But what is the praise of the cold and unknown
To the tender blame of the fondest?
— *John Everett.*

NO adulation; 'tis the death of virtue!
Who flatters is of all mankind the lowest,
Save he who courts the flatterer. — *Hannah More.*

I AM not form'd, by flattery and praise,
By sighs and tears, and all the whining trade
Of love, to feed a fair one's vanity;
To charm at once and spoil her.
— *Thompson.*

A SPIRIT, pure and fine and true
As ever dwelt in human form;
A love as deep, as fond, as warm,
As ever loving woman knew.
— *Kate J. Hi(?)*

Cactus--Night Blooming.

Cereus grandiflorus. NATURAL ORDER: *Cactaceæ*—Cactus Family.

HERE is one of a class of plants which we should more frequently find in our dwellings than we do, as there are none that demand so little attention, requiring only a rough soil, containing a free admixture of coarse sand and small fragments of rocks or potsherds, and a little water once or twice a week. They endure any amount of heat, but will not withstand a positive frost. The Cereus grandiflorus is a native of Mexico and the West Indies, where it grows to a large size, as do the other varieties. The blossom is magnificent, appearing at night, and wasting before day approaches. The flower is sometimes cut when in its prime, and preserved in a large glass jar with alcohol, as a curiosity.

Transient Beauty.

FLOWER of the night! mysteriously awake
    When earth's green tribes repose, why stealthful thus
Com'st thou to meet the stars—unfolding soft,
Beneath their tranquil ray, thy peerless form?
Flower of the night! chaster than Alpine snows—
Unvisited by aught save Heaven's sweet breath—
Why hide thy loveliness from mortal eye,
Why pour thy fragrance to the unconscious night?
                    —*H. I. Johns.*

'TIS not the fairness of the brow,
    Nor brightness of the eye;
Nor yet the cheek whose radiant glow
    Can with carnation vie,
That has a power to chain my gaze,
    Or hold it in control;
The beauty that I most admire
    Shines spotless from the soul.
                    —*Mrs. R. T. Eldredge.*

WHO hung such beauty on such rugged stalk,
    Thou glorious flower?
        Who pour'd the richest hues
In varying radiance o'er thy ample brow?
                    —*Mrs. Sigourney.*

Cactus--Snake.

Cereus flagelliformis. NATURAL ORDER: *Cactaceæ—Cactus Family.*

WHIP or Snake Cactus, as it is familiarly called, is from the arid plains of South America. The stem is about half an inch in diameter, having ten angles, and attaining the length of five or six feet. It is much too frail to stand alone, and should be supported on a trellis or tied to an upright stick. The flowers are extremely handsome, coming out from the clusters of spines that adorn the stem. The tube is long and slender, and the petals a brilliant pink, remaining in perfection a number of days, when they are succeeded continuously by others for several weeks.

You Terrify Me.

I FEEL my sinews slacken'd with the fright,
    And a cold sweat thrills down all o'er my limbs,
    As if I were dissolving into water.
        —*Dryden.*

WHEN the sun sets, shadows that show'd at noon
    But small appear most long and terrible;
So when we think fate hovers o'er our heads,
Our apprehensions shoot beyond all bounds. —*Lee.*

HIS hand did quake
    And tremble like a leaf of aspen green,
And troubled blood through his pale face was seen
As it a running messenger had been. —*Spenser.*

NEXT him was fear, all arm'd from top to toe,
    Yet thought himself not safe enough thereby,
But fear'd each shadow moving to or fro,
And his own arms when glittering he did spy,
Or clashing heard, he fast away did fly;
As ashes pale of hue, and wingéd heel'd,
And evermore on danger fix'd his eye,
'Gainst whom he always bent a brazen shield,
Which his right hand unarmed fearfully did wield.
    —*Spenser.*

IMAGINATION frames events unknown
    In wild fantastic shapes of hideous ruin,
And what it fears creates! —*Hannah More.*

I AM fearful: wherefore frowns he thus?
    'Tis an aspect of terror. All's not well.
    —*Shakespeare.*

Calceolaria.

Calceolaria hybrida.   NATURAL ORDER: *Scrophulariaceæ — Figwort Family.*

CALCEOLARIAS came originally from South America and New Zealand. There are two species of this plant, differing entirely from each other, in regard to the foliage. One is herbaceous, with large, oval, downy leaves, and grows about a foot and a half high; the other is a shrub with small, oval leaves resembling those of the sage, except that they are a purer green. The flowers are alike in shape, the herbaceous having rather the largest. They are like a pouch or bag of velvet, sometimes of a plain color, and again covered with dots; indeed they often remind one of the plump body of a beautiful spider, only they have not spinarets and legs. The blossoms, which are superb in color, are often large enough to hold a teaspoonful of water.

Novelty.

OF all the passions that possess mankind,
   The love of novelty rules most the mind;
In search of this, from realm to realm we roam;
Our fleets come fraught with ev'ry folly home.
                    —*Foote.*

STILL sighs the world for something new,
   For something new;
Imploring me, imploring you
   Some will-o'-wisp to help pursue.
Ah, hapless world! What will it do,
   Imploring me, imploring you,
      For something new?   *Ralph Hoyt.*

CHANGE is written on the tide,
   On the forest's leafy pride;
On the streamlet, glancing bright,
On the jewel'd crown of night;
All where'er the eye can rest
Show it legibly imprest.
               Clack.

I HAVE lived in cities all my birth,
   Where all was noise, and life, and varying scene;
Recurrent news which set all men agape,
New faces, and new friends, and shows and revels,
Mingling in constant action and quick change.
                    Beles.

Calla Lily.

Richardia Aethiopica. NATURAL ORDER: *Araceæ — Arum Family.*

BEAUTIFUL in name (from the Greek *kallos*) and justly meriting the distinction, is this lily-like plant. Its scientific name does joint honor to the French botanist, L. C. Richard, and its supposed original seat, Ethiopia, though its true habitat is farther south, in the region of the Cape of Good Hope, this charming, familiar plant is only adapted to house culture in cold climates. It has large, arrow-shaped leaves on long leafstalks. The flower is of a beautiful creamy white, and similar to a cornucopia in shape, or to our own wild-wood plant, Jack-in-the-pulpit, and blooms during winter and spring. The plants of this order are pervaded by a volatile substance which in some becomes poisonous. The corms and root-stalks abound in starch, which in a few cases are rendered edible when the volatile substance is expelled by cooking.

Feminine Beauty.

I AM come, I am come! from the purple-browed sky,
   The spirit of beauty to thee;
I ride on the wings of the rose-scented air,
I sit on the lips of the violet fair,
And weave me a wreath of the sun's golden hair,
   As his tresses go glancingly by,
     And glimmer the foam of the sea.   —*Carlos D. Stuart.*

A NATIVE grace
  Sat fair proportion'd on her polish'd limbs,
Veil'd in a simple robe, their best attire,
Beyond the pomp of dress; for loveliness
Needs not the foreign aid of ornament,
But is, when unadorn'd, adorn'd the most;
Thoughtless of beauty, she was Beauty's self,
Recluse amid the close embowering woods.
     —*Thompson.*

I NEVER saw aught like to what thou art,
  A spirit so peculiar in its mold,
With so much wildness and with yet a part
Of all the softer beauties we behold.
     —*Frances I. Fuller.*

Calycanthus.

Calycanthus floridus.   NATURAL ORDER: *Calycanthaceæ — Calycanth Family.*

OUR Southern States, more especially the Carolinas, are the native seats of this fragrant shrub, whence it is sometimes called Carolina Allspice. It is generally found in fertile soils along water courses, is of a straggling growth, and does not attain a very great height — usually from three to four feet only. It is also frequently cultivated in gardens and shrubberies, where it has received the praise of many for the odor of its blossoms, which have a strawberry or fruit-like fragrance. The bark when broken also exhales a spicy perfume. The flowers are of a dull, lurid purple, and bloom on very short stems.

Benevolence.

O BLESSED bounty, giving all content!
   The only fautress of all noble arts,
That lend'st success to every good intent,
A grace that rests in the most godlike hearts,
By heav'n to none but happy souls infused,
Pity it is that e'er thou wast abused.
— Drayton.

HOW few, like thee, inquire the wretched out,
   And court the offices of soft humanity!
Like thee, reserve their raiment for the naked,
Reach out their bread to feed the crying orphan,
Or mix the pitying tears with those that weep!
— Rowe.

HALF his earn'd pittance to poor neighbors went;
   They had his alms, and he had his content.
— Walter Hart.

FROM thy new hope, and from thy growing store,
Now lend assistance, and relieve the poor.
— Dryden.

GODLIKE his unwearied bounty flows;
   First loves to do, then loves the good he does.
— Sir J. Denham.

He that's liberal
To all alike may do good by chance,
But never out of judgment.
— Beaumont and Fletcher.

For his bounty,
There was no winter in 't; an autumn 'twas,
That grew the more by reaping.
— Shakespeare.

Camellia.

Camellia Japonica. NATURAL ORDER: *Camelliaceæ — Tea Family.*

JAPAN is the original habitat of this shrub, whence its name in part — Japonica, Japanese; while the first part is derived from the German botanist, Kamel, Latinized into Camellus. It is a native of China, as well as of Japan, where it grows to a large tree. It is graceful and handsome as one could desire for any place or occasion. Its blossoms are among the loveliest that nature yields, but lack the fragrance of those of its rival, the rose, which they much resemble; they are, however, more stately, the petals being much thicker, more waxy and symmetrical. There are, it is said, now nearly a thousand varieties, chiefly derived from seed. In order to perpetuate the same variety in color, they are propagated from slips.

Perfect Loveliness.

NE'ER shall thy dangerous gifts these brows adorn,
 To me more dear than all their rich perfume,
The chaste Camellia's pure and spotless bloom,
That boasts no fragrance and conceals no thorn.
— *Wm. Roscoe.*

SHE, the gayest, sweetest blossom,
 Smiling 'neath the summer skies,
Glorious lips and swelling bosom,
 Golden hair and sparkling eyes,

Softly breathing amorous sighs,
While the doves around are cooing,
And the simple lovers wooing,
Holds the moonbeams in surprise.
— *Carlos D. Stuart.*

EACH ornament about her seemly lies,
 By curious chance, or careless art, composed.
 — *Tasso.*

THE fairness of her face no tongue can tell,
 For she the daughters of all women's race,
And angels eke, in beautie doth excel,
Sparkled on her from God's own glorious face,

And more increast by her own goodly grace,
That it doth far exceed all human thought,
Ne can on earth compared be to aught.
— *Spenser.*

Canary Grass.

Phalaris Canariensis.   NATURAL ORDER: *Gramineæ — Grass Family.*

DERIVING its name from the Greek word *phalaris*, meaning white or brilliant, as the seeds are shining and smooth, the Canary Grass is a native of the Canary Islands, and its seeds form the chief food of the delightful little Canary bird, as well as some other small wild birds. It is sometimes found sparingly naturalized in the fields in America. There is a native plant belonging to the same genus found in low, wet grounds and ditches, known technically as the Phalaris arundinacea, or Reed Canary Grass, and familiarly as Ribbon Grass.

Perseverance.

ATTEMPT the end, and never stand to doubt,
Nothing 's so hard, but search will find it out.
— *Herrick.*

NEW things are possible to listless indolence;
But unto him whose soul is in his task,
Who scorns 'mid ease or sloth to bask
Till it 's accomplished, there is no chance,
No prison which long in durance
Can keep success; the unconquerable will
Bends all before it; pierces through each maze
Impenetrable to superficial gaze.
Encounters every obstacle and still
Bears off from each the palm; then, human soul,
If for some noble object thou dost strive
And wouldst triumphant reach the final goal,
Swerve not aside ere yet thou dost arrive;
Be patient, faithful, firm, and even fate shall not control.
— *James Walker.*

REVOLT is recreant when pursuit is brave,
Never to faint doth purchase what we crave.
Machen.

HOW noble is a good resolve,
There 's heavenly hope attending it,
And fair and pleasant thoughts involve
A latent bliss befriending it; —
If strong the strife and great the pain,
Greater 's the triumph — try again.
— *John Swain.*

PERSEVERANCE is a Roman virtue,
That wins each godlike act, and plucks success
E'en from the spear-proof crest of rugged danger.
— *Harvard.*

Candytuft.

Iberis umbellata. NATURAL ORDER: *Cruciferæ—Mustard Family.*

IBERIS, or Candytuft, is so well adapted for bouquets that an ample bed of it should be found in every garden, for it will bear any amount of clipping and still yield an abundance of flowers until destroyed by frost. The plants bear removal so poorly that it is best to sow them where they are to bloom, and to pull up all the superfluous ones. It is a native of Spain, and takes its name from the ancient appellative of that country, which was Iberia. It is most excellent for winter use, grown in pots or in vases; and is also planted as a border in flower gardens. The flowers are white, purple or crimson, and some of them are very fragrant.

Architecture.

IN the well-framed models,
 With emblematic skill and mystic order,
Thou show'dst where tow'rs on battlements should rise;
Where gates should open, or where walls should compass.
— Prior.

OUR fathers next, in architecture skill'd,
 Cities for use, and forts for safety, build.
Then palaces and lofty domes arose;
These for devotion, and for pleasure those.
— Sir R. Blackmore.

WESTWARD a pompous frontispiece appear'd,
 On Doric pillars of white marble rear'd,
Crown'd with an architrave of antique mold,
And sculpture rising on the roughen'd gold.
— Pope.

HIS son builds on, and never is content
 Till the last farthing is in structure spent. — *Dryden.*

HERE stair on stair, with heavy balustrade,
 And columned hybrids cut in rigid stone,
And vase, and sphinx, and obelisk, arrayed,
 And arched wide bridges over wheelways thrown.
Valleys of heaven the gardens seemed to be,
Or Isles of cloudland in a sunset sea. ———.

LET my due feet never fail
 To walk the studious cloister's pale,
And love the high embowed roof,
With antique pillars massy proof;
And storied windows richly dight,
Casting a dim, religious light.
— Milton.

71

Canterbury Bells.

Campanula medium.   NATURAL ORDER: *Campanulaceæ—Bellwort Family.*

UNPRETENDING but handsome is this species of the Campanula, introduced into this country from Germany. The stem is from two and a half to three feet high, and produces flowers that are large and attractive, continuing in bloom from early summer until fall. The blossoms are bell-shaped, as in the other varieties, the distinctive differences consisting in diversity of foliage, and dissimilarity of style. Some are tall and stately, while others are mere cushions of verdure and flowers. The color of their blossoms is usually blue, though sometimes lavender or white.

Gratitude.

FOUNTAIN of mercy! whose pervading eye
   Can look within and read what passes there,
Accept my thoughts for thanks, I have no words;
My soul, o'erfraught with gratitude, rejects
The aid of language.   —*Hannah More.*

THE benefits he sow'd in me met not
   Unthankful ground, but yielded him his own
With fair increase; and I still glory in it.
      —*Massinger.*

TO a generous mind
   The heaviest debt is that of gratitude,
When 'tis not in our power to repay it.
      —*Franklin.*

WHEN gratitude o'erflows the swelling heart,
   And breathes in free and uncorrupted praise
For benefits received; propitious heaven
Takes such acknowledgments as fragrant incense,
And doubles all its blessings.   *Lillo.*

I FIND a pious gratitude disperse
   Within my soul; and at every thought of him
Engenders a warm sigh within me, which,
Like curls of holy incense, overtake
Each other in my bosom, and enlarge
With their embrace his sweet remembrance.
      Shirley.

I GROW impatient, till I find some way
   Great offices with greater to repay.   —*Dryden.*

Cardamine.

Cardamine hirsuta.   NATURAL ORDER: *Cruciferæ — Mustard Family.*

GROWING wild, this plant is found in various parts of the United States, in some instances adding the name of the State in which the variety is produced to its own. It is also called Cuckoo Flower, and Bitter Cress. It flourishes in wet places, near streams or springs. The flowers are white and small. The blossoms of some of the other species are larger than the above, and are frequently rose or purple in color. Its name is derived from *kardia*, heart, and *damao*, to overcome, alluding to some supposed medicinal properties.

Infatuation.

OH! blest is the fate of the one who hath found
   Some loadstar to guide through the wilderness round;
And such I have found, my beloved one, in thee.
   For thou art the star of the desert to me.
       — *Samuel Lover.*

'TIS his one hope — all else that round his life
   So fairly circles, scarce he values now;
The pride of name, a lot with blessings rife,
Determined friends, great gifts that him endow —
Are shrunk to nothing in a woman's smile;
Counsel, reproof, entreaty, all are lost
Like windy waters, which their strength exhaust
And leave no impress; worldly lips revile
With sneer and stinging jibe, but idly by,
Unfelt, unheard, the impatient arrows fly;
Careless he joins a parasitic train,
Fops, fools and flatterers, whom her arts enchain,
Nor counts aught base that may to her pertain.
Immersed in love — or what he deems is such.
       — *F. G. Tuckerman.*

DO but look on her eyes! they do light
   All that Love's world compriseth!
Do but look on her hair! it is bright
   As Love's star when it riseth!
Do but mark — her forehead 's smoother
   Than words that sooth her!
And from her arched brows such a grace
   Sheds itself through the face,
As alone there triumphs to the life,
All the gain, all the good of the elements' strife.
       — *Jonson.*

OH! then speak, thou fairest fair!
   Kill not him that vows to serve thee;
But perfume this neighboring air
   Else dull silence sure will starve me;
   'Tis a word that 's quickly spoken,
   Which, being restrained, a heart is broken.
       — *Beaumont and Fletcher.*

ALL nature fades extinct; and she alone
Heard, felt and seen, possesses every thought,
Fills every sense, and pants in every vein.
       — *Thompson.*

Cardinal Flower.

Lobelia Cardinalis.   NATURAL ORDER: *Lobeliaceæ—Lobelia Family.*

MATHIEU LOBEL, a French botanist resident in England and physician to James the First, was honored by having this class of flowers named for him, while this variety obtained its distinctive title from its rich scarlet or cardinal color. It is a tall plant of exceeding beauty, found in meadows, especially near streams of running water, where its bright face is mirrored on the gleaming surface. It was introduced into England from America, of which it is a native, during colonial times, and has ever since enjoyed the admiration of florists and amateur cultivators. The flowers are of a deep scarlet, and each blossom about two inches in length, arranged on a fine, nodding stem. These appear during the whole summer.

Preferment.

WHEN knaves come to preferment, they rise as
   Gallows are raised in the low countries, one
Upon another's shoulders.
Webster.

'TIS sweet, beloved, to have thee nigh,
   In pleasant converse thus with me,
For while these social moments fly,
   I feel my heart still clings to thee.
Yes, clings to thee with stronger ties
   Than e'er I felt or knew before,
As day by day some charm supplies
   That makes me bless thee more and more.
Thomas G. Spear.

IF to feel the deep devotion
   Of a pilgrim at a shrine,
If to weep with fond emotion
   Be to love thee, I am thine.
If to treasure every token,
   Every look and every sign,
Every light word thou hast spoken,
   Be to love thee, I am thine.
Mrs. V. E. Howard.

HE who cannot merit
   Preferment by employments, let him bare
His throat unto the Turkish cruelty,
Or die or live a slave, without redemption.
—John Ford.

Carnation.

Dianthus caryophyllus.   NATURAL ORDER: *Caryophyllaceæ — Pink Family.*

AMONG the most delightful of all our flowers are the Carnations, in all their diverse colors, being called the flower of Jove or Jupiter, the chief god among the Romans, whence its name — *Dios*, of Zeus, or Jupiter, and *anthos*, a flower; the distinctive epithet is also from two other Greek words, *karuon*, a nut, and *phyllon*, a leaf. They are variously called bizarres, flakes, or picotees, according to their colors and markings, being spotted, striped or plain. The varieties number, it is said, over four hundred, and many of them yield the exquisite odor of the clove, or other sweet perfume.

Contempt.

AND where his frown of hatred darkly fell,
  Hope withering fled — and mercy sigh'd farewell!
                               — *Byron.*

HARSH scorn hath hail'd thy blighted name,
  Thou frail but lovely thing;
And the precious flower of fame
  Is slowly withering!   — *Mrs. Norton.*

SHALL it not be scorn to me
  To harp on such a molder'd string?
I am sham'd through all my nature
  To have lov'd so slight a thing. — *Tennyson.*

THINK not there is no smile
  I can bestow upon thee. There is a smile,
A smile of nature too, which I can spare,
  And yet perhaps thou wilt not thank me for it.
                            — *Joanna Baillie.*

TAKE back, take back thy promises;
  Take back, take back thy love,
They say 'tis all ideal bliss
  Fleeting as sunbeams move;
And that 'twill quickly pass away,
  And not a chord remain

To vibrate at affection's touch,
  With such sweet joy again.
Then give me back the light, warm heart
  I held in youth's bright morn;
It can't endure indifference,
  'Twould break beneath thy scorn.
                     — *Mrs. Locke.*

HENCE! Leave my door!
  I know thee not, dark woman! Hence away! — *Mrs. Sigourney.*

Catchfly.

Silene Armeria.   NATURAL ORDER: *Caryophyllaceæ — Pink Family.*

VARIETIES of this plant to the number of about one hundred, of which perhaps a dozen are indigenous to the United States, have been noted by botanists. It is cultivated as a garden annual, many varieties having been introduced from Europe — the rose-colored from Sicily, and the red from Portugal, while Russia has furnished a perennial species. They all bloom plentifully, and are appropriate for planting in the borders, or for rockwork. The stem is about a foot and a half high, and the flowers mostly a purplish pink, white, and red. Beneath each joint there is a glutinous substance that retains any light insect that touches it. It derives its name from Silenus, the reputed foster-father and drunken companion of Bacchus, who, when caught asleep and encircled with a cordon of flowers by mortals, could be compelled to prophesy; so the ancient Greeks imagined.

I am Thy Prisoner.

HIGH walls and strong the body may confine,
   And iron gates obstruct the prisoner's gaze,
And massive bolts may baffle his design,
   And vigilant keepers watch his devious ways;
Yet scorns the immortal mind this base control!
   No chains can bind it and no cells enclose;
Swifter than light it flies from pole to pole,
   And in a flash from earth to heaven it goes.
                  — *Anonymous.*

O LIBERTY! the prisoner's pleasing dream,
   The poet's muse, his passion and his theme;
Genius is thine, and thou art Fancy's nurse;
Lost without thee the ennobling powers of verse;
Heroic song from thy free touch acquires
Its clearest tone, the rapture it inspires. — *Cowper.*

HE gives the signal of command,
   He waves — he drops — the lifted hand!
It was a sound of clashing steel —
Why starts he thus? what doth he feel?
The clanking of his iron chain
Hath made him prisoner again! — *Mrs. Norton.*

Cedar--Red.

Juniperus Virginiana.   NATURAL ORDER: *Coniferæ — Pine Family.*

NEARLY all the Pine family are pleasing to the eye for the diversity as well as the continuity of their foliage. There are somewhat over a hundred species in the order, and all of them of infinite importance to man, growing as some of them do in immense forests, they yield an unbounded supply of timber for various architectural purposes, being light, easily wrought and durable. This includes all the pines, hemlocks, spruces and cedars. The large, straight trunks of the White Pine are in great demand for the masts of vessels, while other varieties yield the resinous sap from which resin, tar, pitch and turpentine are manufactured. The Red Cedar is a middle-sized tree, found in the United States, but principally in rocky situations near the sea-coast. Its wood is of a reddish cast, compact, fine grained, and almost imperishable, so well does it resist all the processes of decay.

I Live for Thee.

FOR thee I will arouse my thoughts to try
   All heavenward flights, all high and holy strains;
For thy dear sake I will walk patiently
   Through these long hours, nor call their minutes pain.
                              Frances Anne Kemble.

NOW, the plaintive tones inspiring
   Still more sweet and yearning swell,
Till my spirit bursts its bondage,
   That had chained it with its spell;

And I'm hastening with affection
   To my hidden darling there,
Where the cedar boughs are waving
   In the rustling evening air.
                              — L. Sylvestre.

WE will walk this world,
   Yok'd in all exercise of noble aim,
And so through those dark gates across the wild
That no man knows.
                              Tennyson.

Celandine.

Chelidonium majus.   NATURAL ORDER: *Papaveraceæ — Poppy Family.*

QUITE familiar, from growing wild by the roadsides and in the fields, especially in moist places, as well as from being cultivated in gardens, is this plant of the poppy family. It is a fleshy herb, with leaves formed of leaflets arranged in pairs on a central stem, and one odd one to finish the tip; they are of a sea or bluish green in color, and are quite smooth. The flowers are yellow, and are not lasting. Its name is derived from the word *chelidon*, the Greek name for the swallow, as it was supposed to blossom with the arrival of that bird. It has become a naturalized plant in the United States, its native place being Europe.

Future Happiness.

THERE is a gentle element, and man
  May breathe it with a calm, unruffled soul,
And drink its living waters till his heart
Is pure; and this is human happiness. —*Willis.*

IF solid happiness we prize,
  Within our breast the jewel lies,
And they are fools who roam;
The world has nothing to bestow,
From own selves our joys must flow,
And that dear hut — our home. —*Cotton.*

HAPPINESS depends, as nature shows,
  Less on exterior things than most suppose;
Vigilant over all that He has made,
Kind Providence attends with gracious aid,
Bids equity throughout His works prevail,
And weighs the nations in an even scale.
  —*Cowper.*

HE is the happy man whose life e'en now
  Shows somewhat of that happier life to come;
Who, doomed to an obscure but tranquil state,
Is pleased with it, and, were he free to choose,
Would make his fate his choice; whom peace, the fruit
Of virtue, and whom virtue, fruit of faith,
Prepare for happiness; bespeak him one
Content indeed to sojourn while he must
Below the skies, but having there his home.
  —*Cowper.*

Chamomile.

Anthemis nobilis. NATURAL ORDER: *Compositæ — Aster Family.*

THERE are two species of this humble plant; the first inodorous, naturalized in fields, byways and lanes, and is called Corn Chamomile; and the second a perennial from Great Britain and other parts of Europe. It is frequently cultivated in gardens, and is well known for its strong, agreeable odor. The flowers are much used in medicine for their tonic and anodyne properties. It was called Anthemis, from *anthos*, Greek for flower, by reason of its profusion of flowers.

Mercy.

IS love so very plenty in this weary world of pain,
That you cannot let all else go by and trust me once again?
Christian Reid.

THE end will soon come, and tho' outcast I be,
Perhaps there is One will have pity on me;
Who will to the injured His mercy extend,
And be to the outcast protector and friend. — *J. H. S.*

THEN gently scan thy brother man,
Still gentler sister woman;
Though both may gang a kennie wrang.
To step aside is human. — *Burns.*

'TIS mercy! mercy!
The mark of heav'n impress'd on human kind,
Mercy that glads the world, deals joy around;
Mercy that smooths the dreadful brow of power,
And makes dominion light; mercy that saves,
Binds up the broken heart, and heals despair
Rowe.

COME unto me, when weary of life's burdens,
When, oh! so tired of all its hopes and fears —
When, 'midst the fury of the storms and tempests,
Thou shalt be waiting as the heaven nears.

NAY, the divine in it lingers there still,
God's care in all;
Rose leaves but drop at the beck of His will,
Fetters which thrall.
— *Mary B. Dodge.*

IN mercy and justice both,
Through heaven and earth, so shall my glory excel.
But mercy first and last shall brightest shine. *Milton.*

Chestnut.

Castanea vesca. NATURAL ORDER: *Cupuliferæ—Oak Family.*

FRANCE and Italy, or parts of them, use the nut of this tree to some extent as an article of diet, a substitute for flour and potatoes, principally among the poorer classes, who prepare it by some process of cooking; the nut there, however, being nearly double the size of the ones we are familiar with. The Italian nut venders are also found on street corners of our large cities. In some portions of the United States the tree grows plentifully, though seldom forming masses in the woods. In July the blossoms hang like tassels all over the tree, completely covering it as if with a yellowish mantle. The nut is of a beautiful brown, and is inclosed in a formidable burr, beset on all sides with sharp, thorny spines. The timber is useful in some kinds of building, being strong, elastic and durable, without much weight. The Chestnut was a favorite tree of Salvator Rosa, and flourished in the mountains of Calabria. It is said to have derived its name from Casthanæa, a city of ancient Greece.

Deceptive Appearances.

HOW little do they see what is, who frame
Their hasty judgments upon that which seems.
—*Southey.*

WITHIN the oyster's shell uncouth
The purest pearl may hide;—
Trust me, you'll find a heart of truth
Within that rough outside.
—*Mrs. Osgood.*

THE deepest ice that ever froze
Can only o'er the surface close;
The living stream lies quick below,
And flows, and cannot cease to flow.
—*Byron.*

'TIS not the fairest form that holds
The mildest, purest soul within;
'Tis not the richest plant that folds
The sweetest breath of perfume in.
—*Percy.*

THY plain and open nature sees mankind
But in appearances, not what they are.
—*French.*

APPEARANCES to save, his only care;
So things seem right, no matter what they are.
—*Churchill.*

Chickweed.

Stellaria media. NATURAL ORDER: *Caryophyllaceæ — Pink Family.*

NEARLY everywhere north of Mexico the Chickweed may be found generally in moist, shady places. It is a small, delicate, grain-like herb. The leaves are oval, the stem round and jointed, and rather procumbent. The flowers are small, white and star-like, whence its botanical name. At night the leaves, in pairs, close around the young stems. Birds are very fond of picking at the seeds, as well as the green leaves, especially canaries, giving rise to its popular name, Chickweed. The leaves possess certain cooling and nutritive properties that render them desirable for consumptives. They are also useful to allay external inflammation, by being moistened and applied warm.

Star of my Existence.

I HAVE sought the intensest ways to best adore you,
   I have lain my soul's last treasure at your feet;
Yet I tremble as in thought I bend before you,
   With abasement and abashment and defeat,
Knowing well that all the love I ever bore you
   Is requital weak of worth and incomplete!
                    —*Edgar Fawcett.*

I'VE seen grand ladies plumed and silked,
   But not a sweeter maiden —
But not a sweeter, fresher maid
   Than this in homely cotton,
Whose pleasant face and silky braid
   I have not yet forgotten.
      —*Christina Georgina Rossetti.*

THERE ever is a form, a face,
   Of maiden beauty in my dreams,
Speeding before me like the race
To ocean of the mountain streams —
With dancing hair, and laughing eyes,
That seem to mock me as it flies.
                —*Halleck.*

MY spirit bows before a nameless shrine,
   Seeking to offer there
The heart's devotion to some nymph divine
   As pure and true as fair.
                —*W. F. Langer.*

Chicory.

Cichorium intybus. NATURAL ORDER: *Composite — Aster Family.*

HERE is an oriental herb in height from two to three feet, found naturalized in fields and byways. The flowers are large and conspicuous, blooming in pairs in the axils of the leaves, and are a pale blue in color. The root is used in France, and indeed in America, for the adulteration of coffee, for which purpose it is roasted, ground, and flavored with burnt sugar. Its name is of Egyptian origin, being in Egypt called *chikouryeh*. It is known in England as Succory. The Endivia variety, so called, is a native of the East Indies, and is sometimes used for salads.

Prudent Economy.

FOR him light labor spread her wholesome store,
   Just gave what life requir'd, but gave no more;
His best companions, innocence and health;
And his best riches, ignorance of wealth.   —*Goldsmith.*

PRUDENCE, thou virtue of the mind, by which
   We do consult of all that's good or evil,
Conducting to felicity; direct
My thoughts and actions by the rules of reason;
Teach me contempt of all inferior vanities;
Pride in a marble portal gilded o'er,
Assyrian carpets, chairs of ivory,
The luxuries of a stupendous house,
Garments perfum'd, gems valued not for use,
But needless ornament; a sumptuous table,
And all the baits of sense.   *Noble.*

LOOK forward what's to come, and back what's past;
   Thy life will be with praise and prudence graced;
What loss or gain may follow, thou mayst guess;
Thou then wilt be secure of the success.   —*Sir J. Denham.*

THE wise with prudent thought provide
   Against misfortune's coming tide.   —*Pittacus.*

WHEN any great designs thou dost intend,
   Think on the means, the manner and the end.
        —*Sir J. Denham.*

China Aster--Double.

Callistephus Chinensis.   NATURAL ORDER: *Composite — Aster Family.*

THE Chinese are exceedingly fond of flowers, and often take exquisite pains in their cultivation, the Aster being one of their especial favorites. With infinite patience they place the various colors so as to form, according to their taste, an artistic mass in gardens and pleasure grounds. The varieties now supplied by seedsmen are numerous, the colors the most perfect that one could wish, and filled with petals to the center. They bloom from midsummer until late in the autumn, or until frost sets its sharp teeth in their prodigal blossoms. On the approach of winter, those that have unexpanded buds can be lifted and transferred to the house, and if wasted flowers are clipped will remain in bloom some time. The scientific name is derived from the Greek, and signifies beautiful crown.

Bounty.

WHAT you desire of him, he partly begs
   To be desir'd to give. It much would please him,
That of his fortunes you would make a staff
To lean upon.
— *Shakespeare.*

LARGE was his bounty, and his soul sincere;
   Heaven did a recompense as largely send;
He gave to misery all he had — a tear;
He gain'd from heav'n — 'twas all he wished, a friend.
— *Gray.*

IN all places, then, and in all seasons,
   Flowers expand their light and soul-like wings,
Teaching us, by most persuasive reasons,
   How akin they are to human things.
— *Longfellow.*

SUCH moderation with thy bounty join
   That thou may'st nothing give that is not thine to give.
— *Denham.*

AND, more than all, ye speak
   Of might and power, of mercy, of the One
Eternal, who hath strew'd you fair and meek.
   To glisten in the sun;

To gladden all the earth
With bright and beauteous emblems of His grace,
That showers its gifts of uncomputed worth
   In every clime and place.
— *Mary Anne Browne.*

China Aster—Single.

Callistephus Chinensis.   NATURAL ORDER: *Compositæ—Aster Family.*

DESCRIPTION of this flower would be unnecessary, were it not the progenitor of all our handsome double, quilled, bouquet, pyramid and the many other varieties of asters that have originated under careful and discriminating cultivation. The blossom originally presented a yellow disk or center, surrounded by a single row of petals, of a purple color; now we have nearly all colors and shades, except yellow. Such is the wonderful power of human thought, skill, patience and perseverance, when applied to flowers; who can doubt its equal power when enlisted in the elevation of mankind or in the improvement of the individual.

I will Think of It.

LOVE'S heralds should be thoughts,
Which ten times faster glide than sunbeams,
Driving back the shadows over lowering hills.
—*Shakespeare.*

ROSE leaves, when the rose is dead,
Are heaped for the beloved's bed;
And so thy thoughts, when thou art gone,
Love itself shall slumber on.   —*Shelly.*

THOUGHTS of my soul, how swift ye go!
Swift as the eagle's glance of fire,
Or arrows from the archer's bow,
To the far aim of your desire!   —*Whittier.*

THE car without horses, the car without wings,
Roars onward and flies
On its pale iron edge,
'Neath the heat of a thought sitting still in our eyes.
—*Miss Barrett.*

THOUGHTS flit and flutter through the mind,
As o'er the waves the shifting wind;
Trackless and traceless is their flight,
As falling stars of yesternight,
Or the old tidemarks on the shore,
Which other tides have rippled o'er.   —*Bowring.*

MANY are the thoughts that come to me
In my lonely musing;
And they drift so strange and swift,
There's no time for choosing
Which to follow, for to leave
Any, seems a losing.   —*C. P. Cranch.*

Chrysanthemum.

Chrysanthemum carinatum.   NATURAL ORDER: *Composite — Aster Family.*

KEELSHAPED goldflower is the significance of the scientific name of this plant — carinatum, from the Latin *carina*, a keel; and Chrysanthemum, from two Greek words, *chrysos*, golden, and *anthemon*, a flower. It is not naturalized in this country, though it has now been cultivated here for a number of years. It is nearly a century since they were introduced into Great Britain (in 1789). They are indigenous to Northern Africa, China, Japan, and other Oriental countries. The primitive color was yellow, hence the Greeks called it Chrysanthemum; but now the colors are various, being white, crimson, maroon, and yellow of several shades. They blossom very late in the fall, and, if transferred to the house, will bloom until Christmas, requiring only to be kept from positive freezing.

Slighted Affections.

SOUL, wilt thou love, where to love is losing?
   Long wilt thou wander in ways that err.
Dally with hopes, that thy barren choosing
   Finds fleeting as steps of a wayfarer.
Wilt thou not turn and say to her spirit,
   Lo! I that love thee will love no more?
This is a hard thing that we inherit:
   To love and to weep, lo! this is sore.   —*Barton Grey.*

WAN brightener of the fading year,
   Chrysanthemum;
Rough teller of the winter near,
   Chrysanthemum;
Gray, low-hung skies and woodlands sere,
Wet, leaf-strewn ways with thee appear;
Yet well I love to see thee here,
   Chrysanthemum!
Yes, well I love to see thee here,
   Chrysanthemum!

Thou comest when the rose is dead,
   Chrysanthemum —
When pink and lily both have fled,
   Chrysanthemum;
When hollyhocks droop low the head,
And dahlias litter path and bed,
Thou bloomest bright in all their stead,
   Chrysanthemum,
And back recall'st their beauty fled.
   —*W. C. Bennett.*

Cineraria.

Cineraria amelloides.   NATURAL ORDER: *Compositæ — Aster Family.*

BRIGHT and beautiful, the flower-stalks of this plant raise their aster-like clusters of blossoms well above their broad and handsome leaves, in our greenhouses in spring, when flowers are scarce, sometimes as many as fifty flowers in a crowning mass. The plant has been called Cape Aster, one of the first varieties having come from the South of Africa; but as we have species now from the colder latitudes of Siberia, as well as from the tropical climes of Jamaica and the Canary Isles, that name has been almost universally abandoned for the Latin one embracing them all. The colors are the various shades of purple or blue, usually with a white or lighter ring at the base of the petals.

Always Delightful.

HOW brilliant and mirthful the light of her eye,
   Like a star glancing out from the blue of the sky.
                               —*Whittier.*

BRIGHTLY shines the sun today,
   Perhaps it brings but little sorrow;
We'll be happy while we may;
   'Twould be folly now to borrow
Griefs and cares, which may not stray,
   May not darken our tomorrow.

Sweet content, with winning smiles,
   Brightens every simple pleasure;
Happiness, with merry smiles,
   Adds its gold to all our treasure;
Thus our path for many miles
   May be crowned from joy's full measure.
                     —*Tamar Anne Kermode.*

HE is so full of pleasant anecdote,
   So rich, so gay, so poignant in his wit,
Time vanishes before him as he speaks,
And ruddy morning through the lattice peeps.

HIS sports were fair, his joyance innocent,
   Sweet without sour, and honey without gall;
And he himself seem'd made for merriment,
Merrily masking both in bower and hall.
                     —*Spenser.*

WHEN thou art near,
   The sweetest joys still sweeter seem,
The brightest hopes more bright appear,
   And life is all one happy dream,
When thou art near.   —*Robert Sweney.*

Citron.

Citrus medica. NATURAL ORDER: *Aurantieæ — Orange Family.*

EIGHT or nine feet high in its native seats in tropical climates, the Citron differs but slightly in appearance from the lemon and orange trees, with which we are familiar, though only as house shrubs. The foliage is evergreen, the flowers resembling the orange blossom; the fruit is fragrant, the pulp being acid like the lemon, and grateful and cooling to the taste. The trees of this class are all easily grown in the conservatory, and in Louisiana and Florida in the open air, yielding a delightful perfume when in bloom. It gets its distinctive title, *medica*, from the two essential oils (citron and cedrat) which it yields.

Marriage.

NO power in death shall tear our names apart,
As none in life could rend thee from my heart.
— *Byron.*

COME from the woods with the citron flowers,
 Come with your lyres for festal hours,
Maids of bright Scio! They came, and the breeze
Bore their sweet songs o'er the Grecian seas;
They came, and Endora stood robed and crowned
The bride of the morn, with her train around.
— *Mrs. Hemans.*

WHEN on thy bosom I recline,
 Enraptured still to call thee mine,
 To call thee mine for life,
I glory in the sacred ties,
Which modern wits and fools despise,
 Of husband and of wife.
— *Lindley Murray.*

THE citron groves their fruit and flowers were strewing
 Around a Moorish palace, while the sigh
Of low, sweet summer winds the branches wooing
 With music through their shadowy bowers went by;
Music and voices from the marble halls
Through the leaves gleaming, and the fountain falls.
— *Mrs. Hemans.*

ACROSS the threshold led,
 And every tear kissed off as soon as shed,
His house she enters, there to be a light
Shining within, when all without is night;
A guardian angel o'er his life presiding,
Doubling his pleasure, and his cares dividing.
— *Rogers.*

Clianthus.

Clianthus Dampieri.   NATURAL ORDER: *Leguminosæ—Pulse Family.*

IT is but a few years since this beautiful flower was first introduced into Europe and the United States from New Zealand, and, as it was at first considered a delicate plant to cultivate, it commanded a very high price, and was with difficulty persuaded to bloom. The trouble was too much care. It is now grown from seeds, requiring a well-drained soil, and only a reasonable supply of water, as too liberal drenching causes it to decay at the root. The leaves grow in pairs opposite each other, similar to the pea family, to which class it belongs. The flowers appear in clusters of about half a dozen, each being from two to three inches long, and of a rich scarlet, with an intensely black blotch in the center.

Glorious Beauty.

HER eyes, her lips, her cheeks, her shape, her features,
  Seem to be drawn by love's own hands, by love
Himself in love.
          —*Dryden.*

THE beautiful are never desolate,
  But some one always loves them.
          —*Bailey.*

HEART on her lips, and soul within her eyes,
  Soft as her clime, and sunny as her skies.
          —*Byron.*

HER grace of motion and of look, the smooth
  And swimming majesty of step and tread,
The symmetry of form and feature, set
The soul afloat, even like delicious airs
Of flute or harp.
          —*Milman.*

SHE has such wondrous eyes,
  The saints in paradise
Must veil their own from her.
Around her snow-white neck
Great pearls, like foam-bells fleck,

The lustrous depths that stir
  With rhythmic rise and fall,
To hide her heart from all—
  I hold a hidden key
To ope the gates, *ma mie!*
          —*Edward Renaud.*

Clotbur.

Xanthium strumarium.   NATURAL ORDER; *Composite — Aster Family.*

LIKE some of the human family, certain plants have but very little biography, and what they have is not very favorable. They necessarily have had progenitors or ancestors, but not the illustrious, the noted, the famous; neither have they beauty or attractions sufficient to redeem them from obscurity. The Clotbur resembles the burdock, the Spanish needles, and some others of those provoking plants that scatter their seeds by adhering to whatever comes in contact, which they do readily by the hooked spines with which they are provided. They are mostly coarse plants, found in byways, fields, woods and barnyards.

Detraction.

DETRACTION is a bold monster, and fears not
　　To wound the fame of princes, if it find
But any blemish in their lives to work on.　—*Massinger.*

'TIS not the wholesome, sharp morality,
　Or modest anger of a satiric spirit,
That hurts or wounds the body of a State;
But the sinister application
　　　　Of the malicious, ignorant and base
　　　　Interpreter; who will distort, and strain
　　　　The gen'ral scope and purpose of an author
　　　　To his particular and private spleen.　—*Jonson.*

VIRTUE itself 'scapes not calumnious strokes;
　The canker galls the infants of the spring,
For oft before their blossoms be disclos'd,
And in the morn and liquid dew of youth,
Contagious blastments are most imminent.
　　　　　　　—*Shakespeare.*

NO skill in swordsmanship, however just,
　Can be secure against a madman's thrust.
And even virtue so unfairly match'd,
Although immortal, may be prick'd or scratch'd.
　　　—*Cowper.*
　　　　　　I'M one whose whip of steel can with a lash
　　　　　　　Imprint the characters of shame so deep,
　　　　　　Ev'n in the brazen forehead of proud sin,
　　　　　　That not eternity shall wear it out.
　　　　　　　　　—*Randolph.*

HAPPY are they that hear their detractions,
　And can put them to mending.　—*Shakespeare.*

Clover.

Trifolium pratense.   NATURAL ORDER: *Leguminosæ — Pulse Family.*

KNOWN more commonly, from one variety, as the Red Clover, this three-leaved product of the meadow (whence its scientific name) is, next to common grass, the most useful plant to the husbandman for the feeding of his cattle; and of it they are exceedingly fond. It is usually grown as a mixture in with other grasses, but sometimes whole fields are devoted to it. All such crops should really be grown and stored separately, so as to be used at discretion, for cattle, as well as people, have a discerning taste, and know as well as we that "variety is the spice of life." The blossoms are fragrant, and are very enticing to bees and butterflies as well as other honey-loving insects.

Industry.

LIKE clocks, one wheel another on must drive —
Affairs by diligent labor only thrive.   —*Chapman.*

AND cheerfully she plodded through
   Her many household cares;
And led the flock her father left,
   To feed upon the hill;
And guided them at sunset
   To the bubbling silver rill;
And put them safe in fold at night,
   And left the watch-dog nigh,
That at his honest, angry bark

The coward wolf might fly;
And train'd the woodbines higher yet
   Upon the cottage wall,
And pruned the roses, where they grew,
   So sweet and fresh and tall;
And planted flowers and strawberries,
   In her small plot of ground,
And painted all the railing green,
   That fenced her garden 'round.
     —*Mrs. Norton.*

OFT did the harvest to the sickle yield,
   Their harrow oft the stubborn glebe hath broke;
How jocund did they drive their teams afield,
How bow'd the woods beneath their sturdy stroke.
     —*Gray.*

SHORTLY his fortune shall be lifted higher:
   True industry doth kindle honor's fire.
     Shakspeare.

ABSENCE of occupation is not rest,
   A mind quite vacant is a mind distressed.
     —*Cowper.*

Cobæa.

Cobæa scandens.   NATURAL ORDER: *Polemoniaceæ — Polemonium Family.*

CLIMBING COBÆA, so called from Barnabas Cobo, a Spanish missionary in Mexico (whence the common species has been introduced), is a very luxuriant and beautiful plant, often growing a hundred and fifty feet or more in a single season. The most common kind produces large, bell-shaped flowers, nearly the size of a teacup, which when they first appear are a pale green, changing gradually to a beautiful dark purple under the influence of the sun and air. There is also a variegated kind, and very recently a white variety has been introduced. The seeds are large and flat, and should be planted edgewise, as, if placed flat, they are apt to rot before sprouting. It can be cultivated as an annual, or as a permanent house-plant; in either case care should be taken in pruning if entirely cut back, to see that there are young shoots sprouting from the root near the earth, to absorb the superfluity of sap, or the plant will perish.

Gossip.

TALKERS are no good doers; be assured
We go to use our hands, and not our tongues.
—*Shakspeare.*

SWEET were the tales she used to tell
When summer's eve was dear to us,
And fading from the darkening dell,
The glory of the sunset fell.
—*Whittier.*

NEVER with important air
In conversation overbear;
My tongue within my lips I rein:
For who talks much must talk in vain.
—*Gay.*

MY lord shall never rest;
I'll watch him tame, and talk him out.
—*Shakespeare.*

A MIRTH-MOVING jest,
Which his fair tongue, conceit's expositor,
Delivers in such apt and gracious words
That aged ears play truant at his tales.
—*Shakespeare.*

HOW hard soe'er it be to bridle wit,
Yet memory oft no less requires the bit.
How many, hurried by its force away,
Forever in the land of gossips stray!
—*Stillingfleet.*

Cockscomb.

Celosia cristata.   NATURAL ORDER: *Amarantaceæ — Amaranth Family.*

A FEW years ago the crimson Celosia was the only variety to be met with, and now we have the white, yellow, and rose. They bloom in a flattened, pyramidal spike, frequently a foot broad, and resemble a mass of plush gathered into a grotesque shape, the crest of the flower being usually deeper in tint and softer in texture. They are garden annuals, but are equally adapted for pot culture, looking well as greenhouse or conservatory ornaments when placed against a background of striking foliage. Their flowers are lasting, and are a fine addition to winter bouquets, in which case they should be plucked before frost, and before too much wasted by the ripening of the seeds.

Foppery.

OH! save me, ye powers, from these pinks of the nation,
These tea-table heroes! these lords of creation.   —*Salmagundi.*

SOME positive, persisting fops we know,
Who, if once wrong, will needs be always so;
But you with pleasure own your errors past,
And make each day a critique on the last.   —*Pope.*

COXCOMBS are of all ranks and kind,
They're not to sex or age confined;
Of rich, or poor, or great, or small,
'Tis vanity besets them all.   —*Gay.*

SHINE out, fair sun, till I have bought a glass,
That I may see my shadow as I pass.   —*Shakespeare.*

EV'RY morning does
This fellow put himself upon the rack,
With putting on 's apparel, and manfully
Endures his tailor, when he screws and wrests
His body into the fashion of his doublet.   —*Shirley.*

FOPS take a world of pains
To prove that bodies may exist *sans* brains;
The former so fantastically dress'd,
The latter's absence may be safely guess'd.   —*Park Benjamin.*

NATURE made ev'ry fop to plague his brother,
Just as one beauty mortifies another.   —*Pope.*

Columbine.

Aquilegia Canadensis.   NATURAL ORDER: *Ranunculaceæ — Crowfoot Family.*

PERHAPS ten varieties of this plant are in cultivation, some of them being our own wild ones naturalized, while others have been imported from Siberia, Mexico and elsewhere. They are various in color of blossom, usually combining two shades or complementary tints in one flower, as red and yellow, blue and white, some even having three. The petals are curiously spurred, from which they have been compared to the talons of the eagle, whence their Latin name, from *aquila*, an eagle. The resemblance of its flowers to a fool's cap has given rise to its symbolism.

Folly.

LEAVE such to trifle with more grace and ease,
  Whom folly pleases, or whose follies please.
           —*Pope.*

FAME'S but a hollow echo; gold, pure clay;
  Honor, the darling of but one short day;
Beauty, the eye's idol, but a damask'd skin;
State, but a golden prison to live in.
           Sir Henry Wotton.

WHAT is social company
  But a babbling summer stream?
What our wise philosophy
  But the glancing of a dream?
           —*Christopher Pearse Cranch.*

OTHERS the siren sisters compass 'round,
  And empty heads console — with empty sound.
           —*Pope.*

HIS passion for absurdity 's so strong,
  He cannot bear a rival in the wrong.
Tho' wrong the mode comply: more sense is shown
In wearing others' follies than our own.
           —*Young.*

THE morning's blush, she made it thine,
  The morn's sweet breath, she gave it thee;
And in thy look, my Columbine!
  Each fond-remember'd spot she bade me see.
           —*Jones Very.*

TOO many giddy, foolish hours are gone,
  And in fantastic measures danced away.
           —*Rowe.*

THEIR passions move in lower spheres,
  Where'er caprice or folly steers.   —*Swift.*

THUS in a sea of follies toss'd,
  My choicest hours of life are lost.
           —*Swift.*

Corcopsis.

Corcopsis tinctoria.   NATURAL ORDER: *Composita — Aster Family.*

MANY are the varieties of this truly handsome annual, which derives its name from two Greek words, *koris*, a bug, and *opsis*, appearance. The flowers are about an inch or an inch and a half in diameter, and in shape like a diminutive sunflower, the rays or petals being yellow, crimson, maroon and red; or yellow with one of the darker colors forming a circle at the base. They bloom profusely during the whole summer. The plants are delicate in growth and are about two feet high. They are natives of all the Southern States.

Happy at all Times.

COULD you chain the blithe waves dancing wild in their glee?
  Could you check the glad mockbird his carol repeating.
Hold the laughing leaves still that are fluttering free,
  Or the sungleams that o'er the green meadows are fleeting?

And why is my voice attuned like a lute
  To the music that all things around me are feeling,
If its voice in that concert alone must be mute,
  If I shut out the doctrine of nature's revealing?
—Elizabeth F. Ellet.

ROWS of liquid eyes in laughter,
  How they glimmer, how they quiver!
Sparkling one another after,
  Like bright ripples on a river.
Tipsy band of rubious faces,
  Flushed with Joy's ethereal spirit,
Make your mocks and sly grimaces
  At Love's self, and do not fear it.
—George Darley.

OH! why delight to wrap the soul
  In pall of fancied sadness?
'Twere best be merry while we live,
  And paint our cheeks with gladness;
What if hope tells a "flattering tale,"
  And mocks us by deceiving,
'Tis better far to be content,—
  There's nothing made by grieving.
—L. Labree.

AND her against sweet cheerfulness was placed,
  Whose eyes like twinkling stars in evening clear
Were deck't with smyles, that all sad humors chased,
  And darted forth delights, the which her goodly graced.
—Spenser.

Coriander.

Coriandrum sativum.   NATURAL ORDER: *Umbelliferæ—Parsley Family.*

PORTIONS of Southern Europe along the coast of the Mediterranean, and the East generally, are the native seats of the Coriander in a wild state; but the cultivated varieties are to be found in all countries. The seeds, for which it is grown, are very aromatic, and are used by confectioners in manufacturing many of their sweets, they being passed through some process by which their exterior is covered with a coating of sugar, each seed still retaining its individuality. The leaves of the plant are much divided; the flowers are white, grouped in umbels, and bloom in the month of July.

Merit.

THE sweet eye-glances that like arrows glide,
   The charming smiles that rob sense from the heart,
The lovely pleasaunce, and the lofty pride,
   Cannot expressed be by any art.   —*Spenser.*

OH! how much more doth beauty beauteous seem
  By that sweet ornament which truth doth give!
The rose looks fair, but fairer we it deem
  For that sweet odor which doth in it live.
               —*Shakspeare.*

HAPPEN what there can, I will be just;
  My fortune may forsake me, not my virtue;
That shall go with me and before me still,
And glad me doing well, though I hear ill.
               —*Jonson.*

HERE only merit constant pay receives;
  Is blest in what it takes, and what it gives.
               —*Pope.*

THE noble mind, unconscious of a fault,
  No fortune's frown can bend, or smiles exalt.

THE fame that a man wins himself, is best;
  That he may call his own.   —*Middleton.*

BE thou the first, true merit to befriend;
  His praise is lost who waits till all commend.
               —*Pope.*

WITHOUT the stamp of merit, let none presume
  To wear undeserved dignity.   —*Shakspeare.*

MERIT like his, the fortune of the mind,
  Beggars all wealth.   —*Thompson.*

Corn Cockle.

Agrostemma githago.   NATURAL ORDER: *Caryophyllaceæ—Pink Family.*

GROWING uncultivated in fields of grain, this plant is nearly allied to the species of Lychnis that are grown in the flower garden. The stem is from two to three feet high, with foliage of a pale green, and the leaves three or four inches in length. The flowers are rather pretty, though not brilliant, being in color somewhat of a dull purple. Its name, Agrostemma, signifies crown of the field, derived from the Greek; and the epithet githago is allied to gith, the Welsh name for Corn Cockle.

Worth above Beauty.

O FATAL beauty! why art thou bestow'd
  On hapless woman still to make her wretched?
Betrayed by thee, how many are undone.   —*Patterson.*

BEAUTY, like ice, our footing does betray;
  Who can tread sure on the smooth, slip'ry way?
Pleased with the passage, we glide swiftly on,
And see the dangers which we cannot shun.
    —*Dryden.*

'TIS not a set of features or complexion
  The tincture of a skin I admire,
Beauty soon grows familiar to the lover,
Fades in his eye, and palls upon the sense.
    —*Addison.*

WHY did the gods give thee a heavenly form,
  And earthly thoughts to make thee proud of it?
Why do I ask? 'Tis now the known disease
That beauty hath, to bear too deep a sense
Of her own self-conceived excellence.   —*Jonson.*

BEAUTY, my lord, 'tis the worst part of woman,
  A weak, poor thing, assaulted ev'ry hour
By creeping minutes of defacing time;
A superficies, which each breath of care
Blasts off; and ev'ry hum'rous stream of grief,
Which flows from forth these fountains of our eyes
Washeth away, as rain doth winter's snow.
    —*Goffe.*

THINK not, 'cause men flat'ring say,
  Y' are fresh as April, sweet as May,
Bright as the morning star,
That you are.   —*Carew.*

BEAUTY is excell'd by manly grace,
  And wisdom, which alone is truly fair.
    —*Milton.*

BEAUTY, fair flower, upon the surface lies,
  But worth with beauty soon in aspect vies.   —*Sappho.*

Coronilla.

Coronilla glauca.   NATURAL ORDER: *Leguminosæ — Pulse Family.*

CORONILLA is a shrubby plant growing to some three or four feet in height, and blossoms freely and early in the greenhouse or window. There are but few varieties, none of which are natives, being all of European origin. Three produce yellow flowers; the Coronilla varia has purple ones; and the Coronilla Emerus, frequently called Scorpion senna, a native of France, has blossoms of a rose color. They should have partial shade in summer, and be grown in a light, open soil well drained. The significance of the name is a little crown, from the shape of the flower.

Success Crown Your Wishes.

GOOD actions crown themselves with lasting bays,
  Who deserves well needs not another's praise
    — *Heath.*

CROWN'D with my constellated stars I stand
  Beside the foaming sea,
And from the Future with a victor's hand,
  Claim empire for the Free. — *Bayard Taylor.*

O SUCH a day,
  So fought, so follow'd, and so fairly won,
Came not till now, to dignify the times,
Since Cæsar's fortunes. — *Shakespeare.*

THUS far our fortune keeps an onward course,
  And we are graced with wreaths of victory.
    — *Shakespeare.*

APPLAUSE waits on success; the fickle multitude,
  Like the light straw that floats along the stream,
Glide with the current still, and follow fortune.
    — *Franklin.*

TO do is to succeed — our fight
  Is wag'd in Heaven's approving sight —
The smile of God is victory.
    — *Whittier.*

OUR toils, my friends, are crown'd with sure success;
  The greater part perform'd, achieve the less.
    — *Dryden.*

WISDOM he has, and to his wisdom courage;
  Temper to that, and unto all success.
    — *Sir J. Denham.*

SUCCESS, the mark no mortal wit,
  Or surest hand, can always hit.
    — *Butler.*

Cotton Plant.

Gossypium herbaceum. NATURAL ORDER: *Malvaceæ—Mallow Family.*

THIS plant is a native of the East Indies, or is, perhaps, indigenous to all tropical regions. It is now at least extensively grown in various tropical and semi-tropical countries for the product which it yields. It is an annual, growing, if left unpruned, some five feet high. Sown in spring, and tended with care during the summer months, it is harvested in autumn. The seeds are ensconced in the most delightful of beds, soft and white. When they are ripe the pods burst, and if left to nature, would eventually float out on the wide, wide world, till they had found a resting place in the soil, to become plants themselves; but man seizes their downy covering and applies it to his own use. The flowers are a pale yellow, and are from two to three inches broad. The Nankin Cotton is similar to the common, except in the color of the fiber, which is yellow or tawny. The Gossypium Barbadense, Barbadoes or Sea-Island cotton, grown in a narrow belt of our Southern States and adjacent islands, is unrivaled for length, softness and strength.

Greatness.

As some tall cliff, that lifts its awful form,
   Swells from the vale, and midway leaves the storm;
Tho' round its breast the rolling clouds are spread,
Eternal sunshine settles on its head.   *Goldsmith.*

LIVES of great men all remind us
   We can make our lives sublime,
And, departing, leave behind us
   Footprints on the sands of time:—

Footprints, that perhaps another,
   Sailing o'er life's solemn main,
A forlorn and shipwreck'd brother,
   Seeing, shall take heart again.
         Longfellow.

OUR greatness, thou art but a flattering dream,
   A wat'ry bubble, lighter than the air.   *Tracy.*

GREAT souls by instinct to each other turn,
   Demand alliance and in friendship burn.
         Addison.

HIGH stations tumult, but not bliss create;
   None think the great unhappy, but the great.
         Young.

Cranberry.

Oxycoccus palustris. NATURAL ORDER: *Ericaceæ—Heath Family.*

NEARLY every one is familiar with the handsome, bright and glossy fruit of the Cranberry, which is so frequently exposed for sale in our markets, and from which such luscious jellies and appetizing tarts are concocted. The literal translation from the Greek would be sour-berry, from *oxus*, acid, and *kokkos*, berry, than which nothing could be more appropriate. It is also called moss-berry, or moor-berry, as it thrives best in low, boggy grounds, such as will-o'-the-wisp delights to dance over, and where the soil sucks up water like a sponge. The shrub being procumbent, or trailing, creeps along the ground, and under cultivation forms dense masses, yielding an abundant product. The flowers are of a light pink, and are clustered near the tips of the branches. There is also a variety called the Upland Cranberry.

Hardihood.

THE mind I sway by, and the heart I bear,
  Shall never sagg with doubt, nor shake with fear.
                    — *Shakespeare.*

A MIGHTY man is he,
  With large and sinewy hands;
And the muscles of his brawny arms
Are strong as iron bands.
         — *Longfellow.*

UPON his ample shoulders
  Clangs loud the four-fold shield,
And in his hand he shakes the brand
Which none but he can wield.
         — *Lord Macaulay.*

LET fortune empty all her quiver on me,
  I have a soul that, like an ample shield,
Can take it all, and verge enough for more.
         — *Dryden.*

LIKE a mountain lone and bleak,
  With its sky-encompass'd peak,
    Thunder riven,
Lifting its forehead bare,
Through the cold and blighting air,
    Up to heaven,
Is the soul that feels its woe,
And is nerved to bear the blow.
         — *Mrs. Hale.*

Crape Myrtle.

Lagerstræmia Judica.   NATURAL ORDER: *Lythraceæ — Loosestrife Family.*

SWEDEN was the birthplace of Magnus Lagerstrœm, the noted traveler and botanist for whom this beautiful exotic shrub was named, and as it was supposed to have come originally from the East Indies, the qualifying adjective, Indica, was added. The petals of the flowers are very delicate, and are attached to the calyx by long, slender claws, which give it a light and airy appearance. The shrub is frequently found in the Southern States, where it is quite hardy, but in the northern section of the United States it is found only in conservatories. Very recently a white-blooming plant was found in Arkansas, growing wild; it being the first discovered of that color, it was of course very choice, and was at once removed by an enthusiastic amateur for propagation.

Eloquence.

METHOUGHT I heard a voice
 Sweet as the shepherd's pipe upon the mountains
When all his little flock's at feed before him.   —*Otway.*

OH! I know
 Thou hast a tongue to charm the wildest temper;
Herds would forget to graze, and savage beasts
Stand still and lose their fierceness, but to hear thee,
As if they had reflection; and by reason
Forsook a less enjoyment for a greater.   —*Rowe.*

HIS eloquence is classic in its style,
 Not brilliant with explosive coruscations
Of heterogeneous thoughts, at random caught,
And scattered like a shower of shooting stars,
That end in darkness; no — his noble mind
Is clear, and full, and stately, and serene.
—*Mrs. Hale.*

THAT voice was wont to come in gentle whispers,
 And fill my ears with the soft breath of love.
—*Otway.*

THE charm of eloquence — the skill
 To wake each secret string.
And from the bosom's chords at will
 Life's mournful music bring;

The o'ermastering strength of mind, which sways
 The haughty and the free,
Whose might earth's mightiest ones obey;
 This charm was given to thee.
—*Mrs. Embury.*

Crocus—Spring.

Crocus vernus. NATURAL ORDER: *Iridaceæ — Iris Family.*

ONE of the first flowers that greet the eye in early spring is this inhabitant of the snowy Alps, brightening the earth with its gay blossoms often before any verdure is visible. The root is bulbous, and cheap enough to have in abundance. They are exceedingly attractive for house cultivation, planted in some of the pretty devices that are made for hyacinths and similar plants. The colors vary through the different shades of purple, yellow and white. The ancient legend relates that Crocus was an unfortunate lover, whose unrequited passion awakened the sympathy of the gods, and procured his metamorphose into this flower.

Cheerfulness.

SO my storm-beaten heart likewise is cheer'd
With that sunshine, when cloudy looks are clear'd.
— *Spenser.*

WHEN cheerfulness, a nymph of healthiest hue,
Her bow across her shoulders flung,
Her buskins gemm'd with morning dew,
Blew an inspiring air, that dale and thicket rung.
— *Collins.*

JOY, like the zypher that flies o'er the flower,
Rippling into it fresh fairness each hour,—
Joy has wav'd o'er thee his sun-woven wing,
And dimpled thy cheek like the roses of spring.
— *Mrs. Osgood.*

AT sight of thee my gloomy soul cheers up,
My hopes revive, and gladness dawns within me.
— *Ambrose Philips.*

WELCOME, wild harbinger of spring!
To this small nook of earth;
Feeling and fancy fondly cling
Round thoughts which owe their birth
To thee, and to the humble spot
Where chance has fix'd thy lowly lot.

To thee — for thy rich, golden bloom,
Like heaven's fair bow on high,
Portends, amid surrounding gloom,
That brighter hours draw nigh,
When blossoms of more varied dyes
Shall ope their tints to warmer skies.
— *Bernard Barton.*

LET cheerfulness on happy fortune wait,
And give not thus the counter-time to fate.
— *Dryden.*

Crown Imperial.

Fritillaria imperialis. NATURAL ORDER: *Liliaceæ — Lily Family.*

IMPERIAL chessboard is the significance of the name of this plant. Persia, a land of roses, of beautiful women, and of kingly power in one of its most arbitrary forms, gave it birth; and, in selecting a floral emblem of imperial sovereignty, there is an appropriateness in choosing a native of that country, which gave birth to one of the earliest of the world's great emperors, Cyrus, and where also a despotism worse than his still prevails. The root of the Crown Imperial is bulbous, and when placed in the ground should remain undisturbed for years if possible. The lower leaves are long and narrow, like most lilies. The flower stalk rises to the height of from three to four feet without leafage, and on the summit appear numerous large, bell-shaped flowers, surrounding the stem in a circle, the mouth of the flower turned downward. Surmounting these is a tuft of narrow leaves, which appear in fine contrast to the brilliant color of the blossom, which is red or yellow.

Imperial Power.

OH! not a minute, king, thy power can give;
  Shorten my days thou canst with sullen sorrow,
And pluck nights from me, but not lend a morrow;
Thou canst help Time to furrow me with age,
But stop no wrinkle in his pilgrimage;
Thy word is current with him, for my death;
But dead, thy kingdom cannot buy my breath.
                      —Shakespeare.

THIS was a truth to us extremely trite,
  Not so to her who ne'er had heard such things;
She deemed her least command must yield delight,
Earth being only made for queens and kings.
                —Byron.

OH! covet not the throne and crown,
  Sigh not for rule and state;
The wise would fling the scepter down,
  And shun the palace gate.
                —Eliza Cook.

HE is a king,
  A true, right king, that dares do aught, save wrong.
                —Marston.

Cuphea.

Cuphea viscosissima.   NATURAL ORDER: *Lythraceæ — Loosestrife Family.*

WET grounds in some parts of the United States produce this annual, the stems and calyx of which are covered with a viscid or gummy substance, whence the epithet viscosissima, while the Greek word *kuphea* denotes gibbous or curved, from the shape of the calyx. The flowers appear singly at the axils of the leaves, the seed capsule bursting before ripe. The Cuphea platycentra (broad-centered) is a foreign variety grown as a house plant, which blooms profusely at all seasons, and accomodates itself to nearly all locations. Its flowers are small, scarlet, and tubular, with a black and white tip.

Impatience.

DOST thou so hunger for my empty chair,
That thou wilt needs invest thee with my honors
Before thy hour be ripe?
  —*Shakespeare.*

O NOTHING rash, my sire! By all that's good
Let me invoke thee — no precipitation.
  —*Coleridge.*

"NAY, let me in," said she,
 "Before the rest are free,
In my loneness, in my loneness,
All the fairer for that oneness.
For I would lonely stand,
Uplifting my white hand,
On a mission, on a mission,
To declare the coming vision.
See mine, a holy heart,
To high ends set apart,—
All unmated, all unmated,
Because so consecrated."
  —*Elizabeth Barrett Browning.*

SPREAD the sails! behold!
The sinking moon is like a watchtower blazing
Over the mountain yet; — the City of Gold
Yon cape alone does from the sight withhold.
The stream is fleet — the north breathes steadily
Beneath the stars, they tremble with the cold!
Ye cannot rest upon the dreary sea!—
Haste, haste to the warm home of happy destiny.
  —*Shelly.*

Currant.

Ribes rubrum.   NATURAL ORDER: *Grossulariaceæ—Currant Family.*

BOTANICALLY named from a misapplied Arabic word, and vernacularly from Corinth in Greece, with which it has no special connection, while even the qualifying Latin epithet, *rubrum* (red) is a misnomer, as not only red but white currants are included, it must be confessed this excellent shrub has been unfortunate in its godfathers. It is, however, quite familiar to everyone, or if not they have missed one of the blisses of childhood in lying under its branches to pluck the bright, gleaming fruit, hanging like strung rubies in such clusters and bountiful abundance, filled with a healthful and agreeable wine-like juice. The flowers are a delicate green, and would be pretty if of some brilliant tint. The yellow Currant, that grows wild in Missouri and Oregon, is grown as a garden shrub, for the bright and cheering flowers that appear so early in springtime, and like the robin, are among nature's earliest harbingers of her awakening, and of earth's returning joy.

You Please All.

HER every tone is music's own, like those of morning birds,
And something more than melody dwells ever in her words;
The coinage of her heart are they, and from her lips each flows,
As one may see the burden'd bee forth issue from the rose.
— *Edward C. Pinkney.*

THY words had such a melting flow,
  And spoke the truth so sweetly well,
They drop'd like heaven's serenest snow,
  And all was brightness where they fell.
— *Moore.*

AH! simple is the spell, I ween,
  That doth that grace impart;
It dwells its own sweet self within—
  It is—a loving heart.
— *Mrs. Osgood.*

ALL are lovely, all blossom of heart and of mind;
  All true to their natures, as Nature designed,
To cheer and to solace, to strengthen, caress,
And with love that can die not to buoy and to bless.
— *William Howitt.*

Cyclamen.

Cyclamen Persicum. NATURAL ORDER: *Primulaceæ—Primrose Family.*

PERSIA gave birth to this variety of the Cyclamen, which, like the others of the same genus, is a bulbous (or, as some botanists call it, tuberous) plant, because the root or bulb is solid, like a turnip, while the true bulb is composed of layers, like the onion, or scales, like most lilies. In cultivation they should not be too much watered; and when not in bloom, should have less. There are but few varieties, and it is difficult to make choice of one possessing advantages above another, except in time of flowering—a few blooming in winter, others in summer. The foliage of some is rich and varied; others send up their flowers from the bare bulb before the leaves appear. The Cyclamen Persicum blooms from January to April, the C. hederæfolium from September to December, and the C. Neapolitanum from July to September; so with one of each, one could have blossoms almost the whole year. The word Cyclamen comes from the Greek word *kuklos*, a circle, because after the flower has withered and the seed pods appear, the stalk or stem begins to curl like the tendril of a vine, until the seed vessel is drawn down to and under the ground where it ripens.

Diffidence.

STILL from the sweet confusion some new grace
Blushed out by stealth and languished in her face.
—*Ensden.*

BUT cyclamen I choose to give,
Whose pale-white blossoms at the tips
(All else as driven snow) are pink,
And mind me of her perfect lips;
Still, till this flower is kept and old,
Its worth to love is yet untold.

MY lady comes at last,
Timid and stepping fast,
And hastening hither.
With modest eyes downcast
She comes! she's here! she's past!
May heaven go with her!
—*William Makepeace Thackery.*

UNTO the ground she cast her modest eye,
And, ever and anon, with rosy red,
The bashful blush her snowy cheeks did dye. —*Spenser.*

Cypress.

Carodinm distychum. NATURAL ORDER: *Conifera—Pine Family.*

THE scepter of Jupiter is said to have been made from the wood of this tree, being symbolical of the eternity of his empire, as the wood is almost imperishable. It is one of the largest trees of the forest, having light green, open foliage, resembling the yew. There are large swamps of it in the Southern States. The timber is light and durable. It is said that the Athenian heroes and mummies of Egypt were deposited in coffins made of it, and the Romans and all succeeding nations have associated it with mourning and graveyards. Shakespeare and innumerable other poets have immortalized its emblematic meaning.

Sorrow.

BE of comfort, and your heavy sorrow
 Part equally among us; storms divided,
Abate their force, and with less rage, are guided.
    —*Heywood.*

WHY dost thou come to me, sorrow?
 Why dost thou darken my soul?
Why dost thou point to a morrow
 Engraven on destiny's scroll?
    —*O. G. Hughan.*

OH! weary years, ye have crushed my hopes,
 The altar fire burns dim and low;
In sorrow's night my spirit gropes,
 Her smiting shadow on my brow.
    —*Edith Malcolm.*

AFTER singing, silence; after roses, thorns;
 All the blackest midnights built o'er golden morns;
After flowering, fading; bitter after sweet;
Yellow, withered stubble, after waving wheat.
    Howard Glyndon.

IN my bosom sorrow reigneth,
 Soul and sense are sick with care;
Bitterly my heart complaineth,
 At the load it needs to bear.

O there are, amid earth's pleasures,
 Hours of bitter gloom and grief,
When her dearest worldly treasures
 Bring us, sorrowing, no relief.
    —*P. W. Russell.*

GNARLING sorrow hath less power to bite
 The man that mocks at it, and sets it light.
    Shakespeare.

Daffodil.

Narcissus pseudo-narcissus. NATURAL ORDER: *Amaryllidaceæ—Amaryllis Family.*

DURING the early spring, as soon as the frost begins to leave the ground, among the first green things to appear are the tips of the tapering leaves of this plant, in company with the tulips, hyacinths and other early flowering bulbs. Nearly all the species of the Narcissus produce yellow flowers. The botanical name is derived from the Greek word *narke*, stupor, as it is supposed the odor of some of them possess sodorific influence when inhaled. They require a more than ordinarily rich soil, and the bulbs should be renewed when they begin to deteriorate through age.

Chivalry.

THE champions all of high degree,
  Who knighthood loved, and deeds of chivalry,
Throng'd to the lists, and envied to behold
The names of others, not their own, enroll'd.
            —*Dryden.*

ME ye call great: mine is the firmer seat,
  The truer lance; but there is many a youth
Now present, who will come to all I am
And overcome it; and in me there dwells
No greatness, save it be some far-off touch
Of greatness to know well I am not great.
      —*Tennyson.*

HE is a man setting his fate aside,
  Of comely virtues;
Nor did he soil the fact with cowardice
(An honor in him, which buys out his fault),
But, with a noble fury, and fair spirit,
Seeing his reputation touch'd to death,
He did oppose his foe.   —*Shakespeare.*

THEY reel, they roll in clanging lists,
  And when the tide of combat stands,
Perfume and flowers fall in showers,
  That lightly rain from ladies' hands.
      Tennyson.

THE daffodil most dainty is,
  To match with these in meetness;
The columbine compared to this,
  All much alike for sweetness.
      Nicholas Drayton.

'TIS much he dares;
  And to that dauntless temper of his mind,
He hath a wisdom that doth guide his valor.
      —*Shakespeare.*

Dahlia.

Dahlia variabiles.   NATURAL ORDER: *Composite — Aster Family.*

ANDREW DAHL, a native of Sweden, the friend and pupil of Linnæus, was honored by having this magnificent flower named for him. It was introduced into Spain by the Spaniards about the year 1789, from the sandy plains of South America, and Humboldt, one of the world's most-observing, enthusiastic and scientific discoverers, found it growing on the elevated plateaux of Mexico. Under cultivation it sports into a variety of hues, blooming freely from midsummer until late in fall. The blossom is very symmetrical in shape, and each petal is arranged in the most exquisite order, one layer above another, forming a most beautiful rosette. The roots are removed from the ground as soon as the foliage is destroyed by frost, and kept in a dry, warm cellar until spring.

Dignity.

WHERE ambition of place goes before fitness
Of birth, contempt and disgrace follow.
— *Chapman.*

HERE the supercilious dahlia
In imperial splendor shone,
While, beneath, the white-crowned daisy,
Unobtrusive, bloomed alone;

I, stooping, kissed the blossom
The proud dahlia seemed to scorn,
Feeling that within my bosom
A new impulse had been born.
—*Lucy M. Sanford.*

I KNOW myself now, and I feel within me
A peace above all earthly dignities;
A still and quiet conscience. The king has cur'd me,
I humbly thank his grace; and from these shoulders,
These ruin'd pillars, out of pity taken
A load would sink a navy; too much honor:
O 'tis a burden, Cromwell, 'tis a burden,
Too heavy for a man that hopes for heaven.
—*Shakespeare.*

Daisy.

Bellis perennis. NATURAL ORDER: *Compositæ — Aster Family.*

BELLIS, the botanical name, is from the Latin *bellus*, pretty, and the French name *marguerite*, from the Latin *margarita*, a pearl; while the English name is from the Saxon *dæges-eye*, day's eye, as it opens early in the morning. It is a delightful little plant, blooming freely throughout the spring and summer months, and used in mediæval times to be worn by ladies and knights when they frequented the tournament. Alcestis, wife of Admetus, king of Pheræ, in Thessaly, was called the daisy queen, as she was supposed to have been transformed into this flower.

Innocence and Beauty.

INNOCENT maid, and snow-white flower;
  Well are ye pair'd in your opening hour;
Thus should the pure and lovely meet,
Stainless with stainless, and sweet with sweet.
                              — *Whittier.*

CHILD of the year! that 'round dost run
  Thy pleasant course, — when day 's begun,
As ready to salute the sun
  As lark or leveret —
Thy long-lost praise thou shalt regain,
Nor be less dear to future men
Than in old time; — thou not in vain
  Art nature's favorite.   — *Wordsworth.*

THE daisy scatter'd on each mead and down,
  A golden tuft within a silver crown;
Fair fall that dainty flower! and may there be
No shepherd graced that doth not honor thee!
                              — *Browne.*

STAR of the mead! sweet daughter of the day,
  Whose opening flower invites the morning ray,
From the moist cheek and bosom's chilly fold
To kiss the tears of eve, the dew drops cold!
Sweet daisy, flower of love, when birds are paired,
'Tis sweet to see thee, with thy bosom bared,
Smiling in virgin innocence serene,
Thy pearly crown above thy vest of green.
                              — *Dr. Leyden.*

BY dimpled brook and fountain brim,
  The wood-nymphs, deck'd with daisies trim,
Their merry wakes and pastimes keep. — *Milton.*

Dandelion.

Taraxacum dens-leonis.   NATURAL ORDER: *Compositæ — Aster Family.*

CURIOUS — extremely so sometimes — is the formation of our English words; thus, Dandelion is from the French *dent de lion*, this being itself from the Latin *dens leonis* — each signifying lion's tooth, because of the indentation of the leaves; but the *e* in the original first word is changed to *a*, because that approaches nearer to the sound than does our *e*. There are two species of this plant: the one above named, and one called the Dwarf Dandelion, the Latin name of which is Kriegia Virginica, named after Dr. Daniel Krieg, an eminent German botanist, who visited this country to pursue his favorite study. The Taraxacum (from the Greek *tarasso*, I change, on account of its medicinal properties) is larger, and is familiar to everyone, as its golden blossoms gleam bright and frequent through the grass. The stalks are round and hollow, bearing each a single flower; and the seeds, when ripe, possess a globular fringe of feathery down, which buoys them up, and they float off like the thistle seed on the surrounding air. In spring, when the leaves are tender, they are boiled and dressed for the table.

Youthful Recollections.

DANDELION, with globe of down,
   The schoolboy's clock in every town,
Which the truant puffs amain,
   To conjure lost hours back again.   —*Howitt.*

THINE full many a pleasing bloom
   Of blossoms lost to all perfume;
Thine the dandelion flowers,
Gilt with dew like sun with showers.
                Clare.

THE sunny days of childhood
   In simple joys are passed;
And, like the early summer flower,
Too frail and fair to last.

THE singing of the happy birds
   Again I like to hear;
They carry back my memory
   To many a bygone year.
              S. A. Munson.

Yet memory, ever in delight,
   Turns to those happy hours,
When skies above were ever bright,
   The pathway strewn with flowers.
          —*William R. Lawrence.*

Daphne.

Daphne odorata. NATURAL ORDER: *Thymelaeceæ — Mezereum Family.*

MOST of the Daphnes are from those distant climes so rich and luxuriant in all forms of vegetation, Southern Africa, China and Australia; but few of the species being disseminated in other countries. They are worthy a choice place in the greenhouse, window, or conservatory, as they bloom in the bleakest season of the year, beginning in December and lasting until spring. The foliage is beautiful and evergreen, the flowers white, abundant and fragrant. Some of the varieties have rosy purple, and the Daphne oleoides lilac, blossoms. All are highly odoriferous. The name is derived from the nymph Daphne, beloved of Apollo, who was changed into this plant to escape his pursuit.

Sweets to the Sweet.

WHILE writing verses for my love, I looked up from the paper,
   And there she stood! I rose in haste, and overturned the taper.
"How careless to put out the light!" she said. "Is it surprising,"
I answered, "that I quenched my lamp when I saw the sun arising?"
— Hone.

TO gild refined gold, to paint the lily,
   To throw a perfume on the violet,
To smooth the ice, or add another hue
Unto the rainbow, or with taper light,
To seek the beauteous eye of heaven to garnish,
Is wasteful and ridiculous excess. —*Shakspeare.*

WHEN first I saw my darling's face,
   I know I did not see the grace
That afterward, unbidden,
Seemed filling all her dainty form,
As day by day, love, gently born,
Disclosed some trait long hidden. —C. C. C.

A LOVELIER nymph the pencil never drew,
   For the fond Graces form'd her easy mien,
And heaven's soft azure in her eye was seen.
Howley.

SHE hath the art, *ma belle,*
   To praise most sweetly well.
Yet only in love's service doth she use it.

For me, between her voice
And all songs were there choice,
Always 'twould well rejoice my soul to choose it
Edgar Fawcett.

Darnel.

Lolium perenne.   NATURAL ORDER: *Gramineæ — Grass Family.*

THE Darnel is a grass of a shining green, found naturalized in cultivated fields and meadows, and is sometimes called Ray or Rye Darnel. It is of perennial growth, the stalk being from one to two feet in height. The Poisonous Darnel is a plant similar to the above in appearance, the seeds, which are poisonous, distinguishing it from all other grasses or grains, as it is the only one recognized with that pernicious quality. The seeds of the first species, in their arrangement on the stem, resemble the elaborate stitches in needlework called herringbone.

Vice.

WHEN vice prevails and impious men bear sway,
  The post of honor is a private station.   —*Addison.*

SIN, like a bee, unto thy hive may bring
  A little honey, but expect the sting. —*Watkyns.*

THERE dwelleth in the sinlessness of youth
  A sweet rebuke that vice may not endure.
        —*Mrs. Embury.*

NO penance can absolve our guilty fame,
  Nor tears, that wash out sin, can wash out shame.
        —*Prior.*

AH, me! from real happiness we stray,
  By vice bewilder'd; vice, which always leads,
However fair at first, to wilds of woe.   *Thompson.*

CROWS are fair with crows;
  Custom in sin gives sin a lovely dye;
Blackness in Moors is no deformity.   —*Dekker.*

FALSEHOOD and fraud grow up in every soil,
  The products of all climes.   —*Addison.*

I NE'ER heard yet,
  That any of these bolder vices wanted
Less impudence to gainsay what they did,
Than to perform at first.   *Shakespeare.*

VICE is a monster of so frightful mien,
  As to be hated needs but to be seen;
Yet seen too oft, familiar with her face,
We first endure, then pity, then embrace.
        —*Pope.*

COUNT all the advantage prosperous vice attains,
  'Tis but what virtue flies from, and disdains.
        —*Pope.*

Day Lily.

Hemerocallis fulva.   NATURAL ORDER: *Liliaceæ — Lily Family.*

EMEROCALLIS, meaning, in Greek, the beauty of a day, is a very handsome plant, and although the flowers perish soon, others continually replace them during their season. There are three species of the Day Lilies. The first is an inhabitant of the countries bordering on the Mediterranean, and has large, red flowers on a tall, naked stalk. Another not so tall is from Liberia, with bright yellow blossoms. The third was imported from Japan, and produces white flowers on long footstalks.

Coquetry.

BUT when I plead, she bids me play my part;
   And when I weep, she says tears are but water;
And when I sigh, she says I know the art;
   And when I wail, she turns herself to laughter;
So do I weep and wail, and plead in vain,
While she as steel and flint doth still remain.
—Spenser.

THEN in a kiss she breath'd her various arts
   Of trifling prettily with wounded hearts;
A mind for love, but still a changing mind,
The lisp affected, and the glance design'd,
The sweet confusing blush, the secret wink,
The gentle, swimming walk, the courteous sink,
The stare for strangeness, fit for scorn the frown,
For decent yielding, looks declining down;
The practic'd languish where well-feign'd desire
Would own its melting in a mutual fire;
Gay smiles for comfort, April showers to move
And all the nature all the art of love.
—Parnell.

THERE'S danger in the dazzling eye,
   That woos thee with its witching smile.
Another, when thou art not by,
   Those beaming looks would fain beguile.
— Mrs. Osgood.

FOR such are the airs
   Of these fanciful fairs,
They think all our homage a debt;
Yet a partial neglect
Soon takes an effect,
And humbles the proudest coquette.
—Byron.

Deadly Nightshade.

Atropa Belladonna. NATURAL ORDER: *Solanaceæ — Nightshade Family.*

FATE personified (not as one, but threefold) was described in ancient Greek mythology as three women with robes of ermine, as white as snow, bordered around with purple. The first is named Clotho, the second, Lachesis, and the third, Atropos (literally, not turning), because she is immutable and unalterable. "To them is intrusted the management of the thread of life: for Clotho draws the thread between her fingers; Lachesis turns the wheel; and Atropos cuts the thread. That is, Clotho gives life and brings into the world, Lachesis determines the fortunes that shall befal us here, and Atropos concludes our lives." The flower of this plant is of a pale purple, the berries of a glossy black, freely charged with a purple juice. The whole plant is poisonous, especially the berries. Fortunately it is not naturalized in the United States.

Death.

DEATH is the crown of life;
   Were death deny'd, poor men would live in vain.
Were death deny'd, to live would not be life;
Were death deny'd, ev'n fools would wish to die.
— *Young.*

DEATH'S but a path that must be trod,
  If man would ever pass to God.
— *Parnell.*

THE bad man's death is horror; but the just
  Keeps something of his glory in his dust.
— *Babington.*

THE world recedes; it disappears!
  Heav'n opens on my eyes! my ears
With sounds seraphic ring.
— *Pope.*

I BREATHE in the face of a maiden,
  I kiss the soft mouth of a rose;
Yet not that I hate them, but love them,
My black wings are spread forth above them.

And round them my pinions enclose,
  I love them so well that they die.
Yet my heart with their sorrow is laden,
  And sad with their cry
— *Ellis.*

Dodder.

Cuscuta epilinum. NATURAL ORDER: *Convolvulaceæ—Convolvulus Family.*

EUROPE is the native seat of the Dodders, which are of several kinds, yet so similar in nature that the description of one gives an idea of all. This plant is an inhabitant of the fields, being destitute of foliage, having a reddish orange stem of a parasitical nature — that is, having no power of providing nutriment for itself, as it depends upon some neighboring plant around which it twines. The root then decays, when it receives its nourishment from the plant that supports it, by means of small projecting filaments, with which it penetrates them, absorbing their juices. This particular species grows on flax, whence its name, from the Greek *epi*, on, and *linon*, flax: the origin of the name Cuscuta is unknown. The flowers are a yellowish white.

Baseness.

IF the tears I shed were tongues, yet all too few would be,
To tell of all the treachery that thou hast shown to me.
—*Bryant.*

FOR vicious natures, when they once begin
To take distaste, and purpose no requital,
The greater debt they owe, the more they hate.
—*Thomas May.*

THE proudest of you all
Have been beholden to him in his life:
Yet none of you would once plead for his life
—*Shakespeare.*

I COULD stand upright
Against the tyranny of age and fortune;
But the sad weight of such ingratitude
Will crush me into earth. —*Denham.*

I HAVE been base;
Base ev'n to him from whom I did receive
All that a son could to a father give:
Behold me punish'd in the self-same kind;
Th' ungrateful does a more ungrateful find.
—*Dryden.*

DISHONOR waits on perfidy. The villain
Should blush to think a falsehood; 'tis the crime
Of cowards. —*C. Johnson.*

SEE how he sets his countenance for deceit,
And promises a lie before he speaks. —*Dryden.*

Dogwood.

Cornus florida. NATURAL ORDER: *Cornaceæ—Dogwood Family.*

GROWING in our Northern States, and generally throughout the temperate zone, this tree is well known. Anyone living near woodlands must be familiar with its white blossoms that lie like a pall of snow over the tree. It is about twenty or twenty-five feet in height, the body being small and covered with a rough bark, which possesses excellent tonic properties, similar to the celebrated barks of the cinchona trees of Peru, and known as Peruvian or Jesuit's bark, as it was first introduced into medical practice by the missionaries of that society. The name is from the Latin *cornu*, horn, because of the hardness of its wood: and *florida*, flowery.

Honesty true Nobility.

EACH thought was visible that roll'd within,
  As through a crystal case the figured hours are seen:
And heaven did this transparent veil provide
Because she had no guilty thought to hide.
— *Dryden.*

THERE still exists a rank which far transcends
  The stars and coronets that shine in courts;
It takes no sounding name to make men stare;
No blazoning heraldry proclaims its pomp,
Its modest title is, plain honesty.

Though homely be its garb, though coarse its fare.
And though it live unnoticed by the crowd,
Still, spite of fashion's fools, the honest man
Is yet the highest noble of the land!
— *Alex Bell.*

HONOR and glory were given to cherish:
  Cherish them, then, though all else should decay;
Landmarks be these, that are never to perish,
  Stars that will shine on the duskiest day.
— *From the German.*

THE gentle mind by gentle deeds is known,
  For man by nothing is so well bewrayed
As by his manners, in which plain is shown
Of what degree and what race he is grown.
— *Spenser.*

BUT let not all the gold which Tagus hides,
  And pays the sea in tributary tides,
Be bribe sufficient to corrupt thy breast,
Or violate with dreams thy peaceful rest.
— *Dryden.*

Dragon's Claw.

Corallorhiza odontorhiza. NATURAL ORDER: *Orchidaceæ — Orchis Family.*

IN old woods, from Canada to Carolina and Kentucky, this singular plant may be found. It consists in a collection of small, fleshy tubers, connecting and branching like coral, whence it is called Coral root, which is a literal translation of its Greek botanical name; while odontorhiza in the same language signifies tooth root. It has no leaves or verdant foliage, the flower stalk being fleshy, about a foot high, with a number of flowers in a long spike. The color of the blossom is brownish green, with a white lip spotted with purple. It usually grows in old woodlands throughout the northern and middle States.

Danger.

GOOD I would now repay with greater good,
Remain within — trust to thy household gods
And to my word for safety, if thou dost
As I now counsel — but if not, thou art lost!
— *Byron.*

SPEAK, speak, let terror strike slaves mute,
Much danger makes great hearts most resolute.
Marston.

HE that stands upon a slippery place
Makes nice of no vile hold to stay him up.
— *Shakespeare.*

THUS have I shun'd the fire for fear of burning;
And drench'd me in the sea, where I am drown'd.
— *Shakespeare.*

OUR dangers and delights are near allies;
From the same stem the rose and prickle rise.
Aleyn.

THE absent danger greater still appears,
Less fears he who is near the thing he fears.
Daniel.

THOU little know'st
What he can brave, who, born and nurst
In danger's paths, has dared her worst!
Moore.

NOW I will unclasp a secret book,
And to your quick-conceiving discontents
I'll read you matter deep and dangerous;

As full of peril and advent'rous spirit,
As to o'erwalk a current, roaring loud,
On the unsteadfast footing of a spear!
— *Shakespeare.*

Dwarf Pink.

Houstonia cœrulea.   NATURAL ORDER: *Rubiaceæ — Madder Family.*

WILLIAM HOUSTON, M. D., the friend and correspondent of the botanist Miller, has received the distinction of having the name of this elegant little plant changed in his honor. It was formerly called Hedyotis from the Greek *hedus*, sweet, and *oti*, to the ear, from its supposed value in curing deafness. Its flowers are a pale blue with a yellowish center, and when found in large patches, as it sometimes is, it gives the ground quite a cœrulean tinge. The Dwarf Pinks are found usually in low, moist grounds by the roadsides and in the fields, blooming during most of the summer. Some of the other varieties have pink or white flowers.

Innocence.

THE bloom of opening flowers' unsullied beauty,
 Softness and sweetest innocence she wears,
And looks like nature in the world's first spring.
— *Rowe.*

THE angels watch the good and innocent,
 And where they gaze it must be glorious.
— *Mrs. Hale.*

HOPE may sustain, and innocence impart
 Her sweet specific to the fearless heart.
— *Sprague.*

MISFORTUNE may benight the wicked; she
 Who knows no guilt, can sink beneath no fear.
— *Habbington.*

FAIR sunbright scene! —
 (Not sunny all — ah! no) — I love to dwell,
Seeking repose and rest, on that green track,
Your farthest verge, along whose primrose path

Danced happy childhood, hand in hand with Joy,
And dove-eyed Innocence, (unwaken'd yet
Their younger sister Hope), while flowers sprang up
Printing the fairy footsteps as they passed.
— *Mrs. Southey.*

HAPPY the innocent whose equal thoughts
 Are free from anguish as they are from faults.
— *Waller.*

I AM arm'd with innocence,
 Less penetrable than the steel-ribb'd coats
That harness round thy warriors.   — *Madden.*

INNOCENCE shall make
 False accusation blush, and tyranny
Tremble at patience.   — *Shakespeare.*

Dyer's Weed.

Reseda luteola. NATURAL ORDER: *Resedaceæ — Mignonette Family.*

KNOWN familiarly as the Dyer's Weed, but botanically by the Latin words *reseda*, from its medicinal value in assuaging pain, and *luteola*, yellow, from the dye which it furnishes, sometimes called Dutch pink, this plant is of the same species as our well-known garden favorite, the mignonette. Both are mostly native on the coast of the Mediterranean; this one, however, has become partially naturalized in the United States. It is said that its flowers follow the course of the sun, inclining east, south and west by day, and north by night.

Design.

WHEN men's intents are wicked, their guilt haunts them,
But when they are just, they're armed, and nothing daunts them.
— *Middleton.*

PURPOSE is but the slave to memory,
Of violent birth, but poor validity;
Which now like fruits unripe, stick on the tree,
But fall unshaken when they mellow be.
— *Shakespeare.*

ACTIONS rare and sudden do commonly
Proceed from fierce necessity; or else
From some oblique design, which is asham'd
To show itself in the public road.
— *Sir Wm. Davenant.*

YOU have sent so many posts
Of undertakings, they outride performance;
And make me think your fair pretences aim
At some intended ill, which my prevention
Must strive to avert. — *Nabb.*

HONEST designs justly resemble our devotions,
Which we must pay, and wait for the reward.
— *Sir Robert Howard.*

WHEN any great design thou dost intend,
Think on the means, the manner and the end.
— *Denham.*

BRING, therefore, all the forces that you may,
And lay incessant battery to her heart;
Plaints, prayers, vows, ruth, and sorrow, and dismay,
These engines can the proudest love convert. — *Spenser.*

Ebenaster.

Diospyros ebenus.   NATURAL ORDER: *Ebenaceæ — Ebony Family.*

ONE hundred and sixty species, most of which are found within the tropics, are included in this order. The Ebony is the wood of the above named, and some others which are found in Madagascar and Ceylon. Its usual colors are green, black and red, the black being the most valuable when free from rind or veins, and is of a very astringent taste. It is often used in the manufacture of chess-men and toys, and is also suitable for inlaid or mosaic work. In its green or unseasoned state it readily ignites, owing to the abundance of grease it contains, and, if placed on burning coals, yields an agreeable perfume. Sir Samuel W. Baker, in his "Eight Years in Ceylon," says: "The Ebony grows in great perfection and large quantity. The tree is at once distinguished from the surrounding stems by its smaller diameter and its sooty trunk. The bark is crisp, jet-black, and has the appearance of being charred. Beneath the bark the wood is perfectly white until the heart is reached, which is the fine black ebony of commerce."

Night.

SLEEP chains the earth, the bright stars glide on high,
  Filling with one effulgent smile the sky;
And all is hush'd so still, so silent there,
That one might hear an angel wing the air.
                                    —*Mrs. Lewis.*

OH, Night! most beautiful, most rare!
  Thou giv'st the heavens their holiest hue!
And through the azure fields of air
  Bring'st down the golden dew!
For thou, with breathless lips apart,
  Didst stand in that dim age afar,
And hold upon thy trembling heart
  Messiah's herald star!
                        —*T. B. Read.*

NIGHT is the time when nature seems
  God's silent worshiper,
And ever with a chastened heart
  In unison with her.
I lay me on my peaceful couch,
  The day's dull cares resigned,
And let my heart fold up like flowers
  In the twilight of the mind.
                        —*Sarah J. Clark.*

Eglantine.

Rosa rubiginosa.   NATURAL ORDER: *Rosaceæ — Rose Family.*

RUSTY ROSE is the literal meaning of the Latin botanical name of this shrubby plant, the epithet rusty being applied because of the parasitic fungus that attaches to it. Familiarly known as the Sweetbrier, or Eglantine, it is one of our sweetest native roses, so simple and unpretending that it has a home in the hearts of all lovers of plants. A golden Eglantine, a violet and marigold constituted the three prizes at the Floral Games of Toulouse, the most ancient in Europe, which still survive, with the addition of four other prizes, after the lapse of more than four hundred years. Planted beneath our windows and around our doors, it freights the atmosphere with its odor, and gratifies the eye with its delicate blossoms. There are many varieties cultivated, some of which are double. Its stem is armed with stout thorns, and the color of the berry when ripe is orange red.

Home.

HOME is the sphere of harmony and peace,
  The spot where angels find a resting place,
When, bearing blessings, they descend to earth.
— *Mrs. Hale.*

'TIS sweet to hear the watchdog's honest bark
  Bay deep-mouth'd welcome as we draw near home;
'Tis sweet to know there is an eye will mark
  Our coming, and look brighter when we come.
— *Byron.*

HOME is the resort
  Of love, of joy, of peace and plenty, where,
Supporting and supported, polish'd friends
And dear relations mingle into bliss.
— *Thompson.*

I LOVE that dear old home! my mother lived there
  Her first sweet married years, and last sad widow'd ones.
The sunlight there seems to me brighter far
Than wheresoever else. I know the forms
Of every tree and mountain, hill and dell;
Its waters gurgle like a tongue I know;—
It is my home.
— *Mrs. Frances K. Butler.*

Elder.

Sambucus Canadensis. NATURAL ORDER: *Caprifoliaceæ — Honeysuckle Family.*

NAMED botanically Sambucus, this shrub is known in Denmark as the *Hylde*, and in England and America as the Elder. Its scientific name is closely related to *sambuca*, a musical instrument of the Romans made from the wood of the Elder, triangular in shape, and crossed with strings, the music of which was held in little esteem, as its tones were sharp and shrill in quality. It is found in thickets in the United States and Canada, growing about old stumps and fence corners. The flowers are small and of a creamy white, bloom in large clusters as broad as a plate, and have a heavy, sweetish odor, though not disagreeable. The berries are round and of a dark purple color, and full of juice; they are used for pies, preserves, and also canned for winter use.

Zeal.

IN duty prompt at ev'ry call,
   He watch'd and wept, he prayed and felt, for all;
And as a bird each fond endearment tries
To tempt its new-fledged offspring to the skies,
He tried each art, reproved each dull delay,
Allured to brighter worlds, and led the way.
—*Goldsmith.*

PRESS bravely onward! not in vain
   Your generous trust in human kind;
The good which bloodshed could not gain
Your peaceful zeal shall find.
—*Whittier.*

WHERE zeal holds on its even course,
   Blind rage and bigotry retire;
Knowledge assists, not checks, its force,
And prudence guides, not damps, its fire.
—*J. Wesley.*

SPREAD out earth's holiest records here,
   Of days and deeds to reverence dear;
A zeal like this what pious legends tell?
—*Sprague.*

ON such a theme 'twere impious to be calm,
Passion is reason, transport, temper, here.
—*Young.*

ZEAL and duty are not slow,
   But on occasion's forelock watchful wait.
—*Milton.*

Enchanter's Nightshade.

Circæa Lutetiana.   NATURAL ORDER: *Onagraceæ — Evening Primrose Family.*

LUTETIA of the Parisians is the name by which the city of Paris was known to Julius Cæsar, and Lutetiana is therefore equivalent to Parisian. Circe was, according to heathen mythology, the wife of the king of the Sarmatians, whom she poisoned, and for which she was banished by her subjects. She fled to Italy, and fell in love with Glaucus, a sea-god, who was in love with Scylla. Circe poisoned the water in which Scylla bathed, and thus turned her into a sea-monster. The two words constitute the botanical name of this plant, which is found in our own country from Carolina to Illinois. It grows in damp, shady places. Its flowers are rose color, and small; its fruit is inversely heart-shaped, having conspicuous hooks.

Sorcery.

IF you can look into the seeds of time,
 And say which grain will grow and which will not,
Speak then to me, who neither beg nor fear
Your favors, nor your hates.
— *Shakespear.*

'TIS thine to sing, how, framing hideous spells
 In Sky's lone isle, the gifted wizard seer,
Lodg'd in the wintry cave with fate's fell spear,
Or in the depths of Uist's dark forest dwells;
How they, whose sight such dreary dreams engross,
With their own vision oft astonish'd droop;
When, o'er the watery strath or quaggy moss,
They see the gliding ghosts unbodied troop.
Or, if in sports, or on the festive green,
Their destin'd glance some fated youth descry,
Who now, perhaps, in lusty vigor seen,
And rosy health, shall soon lamented die —
For them the viewless forms of air obey;
Their bidding heed, and at their beck repair,
They know what spirit brews the stormful day,
And heartless, oft like moody madness, stare
To see the phantom train their secret works
 repair.
—*Collins.*

PITY me! I am she whom man
 Hath hated since ever the world began;
I soothe his brain in the night of pain,
But at morning he waketh — and all is vain.
—*Barry Cornwall.*

Endive.

Cichorium endiva.   NATURAL ORDER: *Compositæ — Aster Family.*

SCATTERED widely throughout Europe and America, though a native of the East Indies, the Endive is of the same genus as the Chicory, already described on page 82. Its name in the vernacular is a formation from the Latin name *intybus*. It is an annual of a hardy nature, and is often cultivated for and forms an excellent salad, but is more used abroad than in America. It is of value in medicine, possessing cooling and anti-scorbutic properties, and French physicians use it as a remedy for jaundice. The leaves are a dark green and much curled.

Medicine.

BETTER to hunt in fields for health unbought,
   Than fee the doctor for a nauseous draught,
The wise for cure on exercise depend,
God never made His work for man to mend.
                                — *Dryden.*

WE own that numbers join with care and skill,
   A temperate judgment, a devoted will;
Men who suppress their feelings, but who feel
The painful symptoms they delight to heal;
Patient in all their trials, they sustain

The starts of passion, the reproach of pain;
   With hearts affected, but with looks serene,
Intent they wait through all the solemn scene,
Glad if a hope should rise from nature's strife
To aid their skill and save a lingering life.
                                — *Crabbe.*

WHEN nature cannot work, the effect of art is void,
   For physic can but mend our crazy state,
Patch an old building, not a new create.
                                — *Dryden.*

HE intent on somewhat that may ease
   Unhealthy mortals, and with curious search
Examines all the properties of herbs.
                                — *John Philips.*

THE ingredients of health and long life are
   Great temperance, open air,
Easy labor, little care.
                                — *Sir Philip Sidney.*

O MICKLE is the powerful grace that lies
   In plants, herbs, stones, and their true qualities.
                                — *Shakespeare.*

English Moss.

Sedum acre. NATURAL ORDER: *Crassulaceæ—Orpine Family.*

PLANTS of this genus grow in very thin soil, sometimes in the crevices of bare rocks, and, as the Latin name indicates, would seem to be sitting there. The English Moss, which is so often called Wall Pepper, is frequently cultivated as a border for flower beds, and as an ornament to old walls, the surface of which it soon covers, as it spreads rapidly and requires so little for sustenance. The whole plant contains an acrid juice. The flowers are yellow.

Fortitude.

WHEN the whole host of hatred stood hard by,
    To watch and mock thee shrinking, thou hast smiled
With a sedate and all-enduring eye;
    When fortune fled her spoiled and favorite child,
He stood unbowed beneath the ills upon him piled.
                      — *Byron.*

THE star of the unconquered will,
    He rises in my breast,
Serene, and resolute, and still,
    And calm, and self-possessed.

O fear not in a world like this,
    And thou shalt know ere long—
Know how sublime a thing it is
    To suffer and be strong.
            — *Longfellow.*

TRUE fortitude is seen in great exploits
    That justice warrants, and that wisdom guides;
All else is towering phrensy and distraction.
            — *Addison.*

GIRD your hearts with silent fortitude,
    Suffering yet hoping all things.
            — *Mrs. Hemans.*

IN war was never lion's rage so fierce;
    In peace, was never gentle lamb more mild.
            — *Shakespeare.*

FORGETFUL of ourselves,
    Giving but little heed
To the confusing strife,
    The winding ways of life,
Yet careful of its anxious cry of need

Thus we may meet the storm,
    Still brave, and true, and strong;
And, like a golden chain,
    Some lives may take the gain,
Some hearts be gladdened by our simple song.
            — *Tamar Anne Kesmode.*

Escallonia.

Escallonia rubra. NATURAL ORDER: *Saxifragaceæ—Saxifrage Family.*

QUITE an acquisition to the flora of our Southern States will be made whenever these plants shall become naturalized there. They are native of South America, and are confined exclusively to mountainous regions. In cold climates all the Escallonias (of which there are about seven genera and sixty species) are confined entirely to the greenhouse or conservatory, but where the temperature is warm or comparatively mild they survive the winter in open air. They are shrubby in growth; the leaves are evergreen, appearing alternately on each side of the branches; the blossoms are scarlet, white or pink, and are delicate and waxy in texture. The plants require a light and friable soil, and are said to bloom and thrive best when planted in the ground in the conservatory.

Opinion.

OPINION is that high and mighty dame
  Which rules the world; and in the mind doth frame
Distaste or liking; for, in human race,
She makes the fancy various as the face.
—*Havel.*

OH, breath of public praise,
  Short-lived and vain! oft gain'd without desert,
As often lost unmerited. —*Harvard.*

HE lov'd his kind, but sought the love of few;
  And valued old opinions more than new.
—*Park Benjamin.*

YET in opinions look not always back;
  Your wake is nothing, mind the coming track.
—*O. W. Holmes.*

OPINION, the blind goddess of fools, for
  To the virtuous, and only friend to
Undeserving persons. —*Chapman.*

LET not opinion make thy judgment err.
  The evening conquest crowns the conqueror
—*Lady Altmony.*

OPINION governs all mankind,
  Like the blind's leading of the blind.
—*Butler.*

OH, he sits on high in all the people's hearts;
  And that which would appear offense in us,
His countenance, like richest alchemy,
Will change to virtue and to worthiness.
—*Shakespeare.*

Eternal Flower.

Xeranthemum annuum.　　Natural Order: *Composite—Aster Family.*

UNUSUAL favor marks the progress of this class of plants, which is steadily advancing in the estimation of flower fanciers; for where a few years ago we had only the Gomphrena, we now have a dozen different kinds, all interesting, and most excellent for winter bouquets on account of their imperishable flowers. They are noticeable, when the flower is expanded, for the lack of moisture in their petals, being crisp under the fingers, whence their botanical name, signifying, in Greek, a dry flower. They usually bloom solitary, or one on a stem. The colors of the various kinds are rose, white, purple, yellow, and red, each kind of plant having a variety of colors. Most any seedsman would gladly furnish their names, and the cultivator would experience a new sensation in seeing them bloom. For winter use they should be cut when most perfect, and dried in the shade.

Eternity.

'TIS the Divinity that stirs within us,
　'Tis Heav'n itself that points out an hereafter,
And intimates eternity to man.　　—*Addison.*

THE dream, which tells me life is short,
　Foretells its endless day;
The mind, which wakes one thought of heaven,
　May never know decay.
I love those dreams which link to heaven
　The soul with friendly ties;

Though sin makes dark the vale of tears,
　These brighten distant skies.
Oh! when the spirit, freed from clay,
　Its wings impatient furls,
How will it soar in haste away,
　To live in mystic worlds!
　　　　—*W. R. Montgomery.*

THE eternal life beyond the sky,
　Wealth cannot purchase, nor the high
　And proud estate;
The soul in dalliance laid—the spirit
Corrupt with sin—shall not inherit
　A joy so great　　—*From the Spanish.*

Eupatorium.

Eupatorium elegans.   NATURAL ORDER: *Compositæ — Aster Family.*

VERY few of these plants are under cultivation, and though the species is quite numerous, they are with few exceptions entirely unattractive. The Eupatorium elegans is admitted to the greenhouse for its fragrant flowers, which are white; the Eupatorium aromaticum, also admired for its odor, has flowers of the same color, which bloom in the fall. The boneset and hoarhound belong to this same family, and, though useful, are homely herbs. They are said to have been named for Mithridates the Great (also called Eupator, that is, of a noble father, or well born), king of Pontus, who brought about a war with the Romans, and when conquered by Pompey, and conspired against by his own son, Pharnaces, rather than be taken prisoner by the Romans, committed suicide by taking poison, B. C. 63.

Delay.

OH, my good lord, that comfort comes too late;
'Tis like a pardon after execution.   —*Shakespeare.*

THINK not tomorrow still shall be your care;
Alas! tomorrow like today will fare.
Reflect that yesterday's tomorrow's o'er,—
Thus one "tomorrow," one "tomorrow" more,
Have seen long years before them fade away,
And still appear no nearer than today.
—*Gifford.*

HOIST up sail while gale doth last,
Tide and wind stay no man's pleasure;
Seek not time when time is past,
Sober speed is wisdom's leisure.
After-wits are dearly bought,
Let thy fore-wit guide thy thought.
—*Robert Southwell.*

YOUR gift is princely, but it comes too late,
And falls, like sunbeams, on a blasted blossom.
—*Suckling.*

OMISSION to do what is necessary
Seals a commission to a blank of danger;
And danger, like an ague, subtly taints
Even then when we sit idly in the sun.
—*Shakespeare.*

HE came too late! Neglect had tried
Her constancy too long;
Her love had yielded to her pride,
And the deep sense of wrong.
—*Elizabeth Bogart.*

Euphorbia.

Euphorbia splendens.   NATURAL ORDER: *Euphorbiaceæ — Spurge Family.*

THIS is a class of plants that are widely dispersed. Many of them are entirely wanting in beauty or any other quality to recommend them to notice, particularly those found in the temperate regions of North America. The few admitted within the precincts of the conservatory, greenhouse or dwelling are from the tropics, chiefly from South America. The above variety much resembles some of the Cacti; the stem is thick, fleshy and branching, and fortified with strong, sharp thorns. The leaves are few and oval; the flowers small, but of a brilliant scarlet. It is a native of Madagascar, and is only grown as a greenhouse or parlor plant, where it can have heat in winter. According to Pliny, it was named by Juba II., the king of Mauretania, in honor of his physician, Euphorbus.

Reproof.

SOME did all folly with just sharpness blame,
  While others laughed, and scorned them into shame;
But, of these two, the last succeeded best,
As men aim rightest when they shoot in jest.
  —*Dryden.*

DEAR heart, for whom I wait from year to year,
  Counting as beads each slowly-lagging day,
What joy detains thee? In what distant sphere
Art thou content to keep so long away?
  —*Joel Benton.*

REPROVE not in his wrath incensed man,
  Good counsel comes clean out of season then;
But when his fury is appeas'd and pass'd,
He will conceive his fault and mend at last.
  —*Randolph.*

FORBEAR sharp speeches to her. She's a lady
  So tender of rebukes that words are strokes,
And strokes death to her.   —*Shakespeare.*

Prithee forgive me;
I did but chide in jest; the best loves use it
Sometimes; it sets an edge upon affection.
  —*Middleton.*

How dare you let your voice
Talk out of tune so with the voice of God
In earth and sky?   —*Mrs. Osgood.*

Eutoca.

Eutoca viscida.   NATURAL ORDER: *Hydrophyllaceæ—Waterleaf Family*

CALIFORNIA is the native seat of this charming little annual, which has proved quite attractive and desirable for the various shades of the blue flowers, which retain their freshness well when severed from the plant for bouquets. There is some diversity in their habit, some being erect or almost so, and others are represented in botanical works as nearly procumbent. The flowers are tubular bell-shaped, about an inch long, blooming in racemes. There are a few novelties in this genus with different colored flowers, some of which are biennials. They bloom freely, but require a light soil.

A Gift.

AND his gift, though poor and lowly it may seem to other eyes,
  Yet may prove an angel holy, in a pilgrim's guise.   —*Whittier.*

ACCEPT of this; and could I add beside
  What wealth the rich Peruvian mountains hide;
If all the gems in eastern rocks were mine,
On thee alone their glittering pride should shine.
                                                —*Lyttleton.*

I FORM'D for thee a small bouquet,
  A keepsake near thy heart to lay,
Because 'tis there, I know full well
That charity and kindness dwell.
                                                —*Miss Gould.*

SHE prizes not such trifles as these are;
  The gifts she looks from me are pack'd and lock'd
Up in my heart, which I have given already,
But not delivered.   —*Shakespeare.*

I GAVE the jewel from my breast,
  She played with it a little while
As I sailed down into the west,
  Fed by her smile;

Then weary of it—far from land,
  With sigh as deep as destiny,
She let it drop from her fair hand
  Into the sea.   —*Jean Ingelow.*

WIN her with gifts, if she respects not words;
  Dumb jewels often, in their silent kind,
More quick than words do move a woman's mind.
                                                —*Shakespeare.*

Eyebright.

Euphorbia hypericifolia. NATURAL ORDER: *Euphorbiaceæ — Spurge Family.*

EYEBRIGHT is a simple little plant found in dry soils in the United States. It is an annual, about a foot and a half high, with smooth, purple stem, and leaves marked with oblong blotches. The blossoms are white, appearing in clusters during the summer. A medicine prepared from it was formerly used for diseases of the eye. There is also another plant called Eyebright, a native of the White Mountains, with bluish-white flowers appearing in spikes. Its classic name is Euphrasia, meaning cheerfulness, in Greek, from the same root as Euphrosyne, one of the three graces.

Your Eyes are Bewitching.

AND then her look — O, where's the heart so wise,
    Could, unbewilder'd, meet those matchless eyes?
Quick, restless, strange, but exquisite withal,
    Like those of angels.
—*Moore.*

SOME praise the eyes they love to see,
    As rivaling the western star;
But eyes I know well worth to me
    A thousand firmaments afar.
—*John Stirling.*

THOSE laughing orbs that borrow
    From azure skies the light they wear,
Are like heaven — no sorrow
    Can float o'er hues so fair.
—*Mrs. Osgood.*

NINE things to sight required are:
    The power to see, the light, the visible thing,
Being not too small, too thin, too nigh, too far,
Clear space and time, the form distinct to bring.
—*Sir J. Davies.*

I NEVER saw an eye so bright,
    And yet so soft as hers;
It sometimes swam in liquid light,
And sometimes swam in tears;
    It seem'd a beauty set apart
For softness and for sighs.
—*Mrs. Welby.*

HER eyes, in heaven,
    Would through the airy region stream so bright
That birds would sing, and think it were not night
—*Shakespeare.*

Fennel.

Anethum graveolens. NATURAL ORDER: *Umbelliferæ — Parsley Family.*

FENNEL, also called Dill, is found in country gardens along with coriander, anise and caraway, all of which produce seeds valuable for their pungent and aromatic flavor. The Fennel grows abundantly along the chalk cliffs of England in a wild and uncultivated state. Another species is cultivated to a great extent in Italy. It is also found wild in the United States, and once introduced it propagates itself for years. The leaves are much divided, and spread out like a fine, thready plume. The flowers are small and yellow, blooming in umbels like the parsnip. Its botanical name is from the Greek *anethon*, through the Latin *anethum*, both signifying Dill or anise; and *graveolens* (Latin), heavy-smelling. Fennel is from *fœniculum*, Latin diminutive of *fœnum*, hay; the etymology of Dill seems lost; the Anglo-Saxon, German and Danish have the word substantially in the same form, but of what significance is not known.

Worthy all Praise.

TO sing thy praise, would heav'n my breath prolong,
Infusing spirits worthy such a song.
Not Thracian Orpheus should transcend my lays. —*Dryden.*

HE gave you all the duties of a man;
Trimm'd up your praises with a princely tongue,
Spoke your deservings like a chronicle;
Making you even better than his praise.
—*Shakespeare.*

FOR praise too dearly loved, or warmly sought,
Enfeebles all internal strength of thought,
And the weak soul, within itself unblest,
Leans for all pleasure on another's breast.
—*Goldsmith.*

IN praise so just let ev'ry voice be join'd,
And fill the general chorus of mankind!
—*Pope.*

NATURE did her so much right
As she scorns the help of art;
In as many virtues dight

As e'er yet embraced a heart.
So much good so truly tried,
Some for less were deified.
—*William Browne.*

Fennel Flower.

Nigella Damascena. NATURAL ORDER: *Ranunculaceæ—Crowfoot Family.*

A NATIVE of the south of Europe and the Levant, deriving its distinctive epithet from the world-renowned and ancient Damascus, this curious annual is grown as an ornamental flower in gardens and borders of walks. It is called Nigella from its black seeds, and has a variety of popular names— Love-in-a-mist, Devil-in-a-bush, and Ragged Lady. The blossoms of the different kinds are purple, blue, and white. They bloom single or solitary, and are encircled with fine, feather-cleft leaves, like the foliage on other parts of the plant, which much resembles the aromatic garden fennel.

Artifice.

WHAT's the bent brow, or neck in thought reclin'd?
　The body's wisdom to conceal the mind.
A man of sense can artifice disdain,
As men of wealth may venture to go plain.　　—*Young.*

YOU talk to me in parables;
　You may have known that I'm no wordy man;
Fine speeches are the instruments of knaves,
Or fools, that use them when they want good sense.
　　　　—*Otway.*

OTHERS by guilty artifice and arts
　Of promised kindness practice on our hearts;
With expectation blow the passion up;
She fans the fire without one gale of hope.
　　　　—*Granville.*

O SERPENT heart, hid with a flowering face!
　Did ever dragon keep so fair a cave?　—*Shakespeare.*

PATIENCE! I yet may pierce the rind
　Wherewith are shrewdly girded round
The subtle secrets of his mind.

A dark, unwholesome core is bound,
Perchance, within it. Sir, you see,
Men are not what they seem to be.
　　　　—*Paul H. Hayne.*

THEN quit her, my friend!
　Your bosom defend,
Ere quite with her snares you're beset.
　　　　—*Byron.*

Fern--Walking.

Antigramma rhizophylla.   NATURAL ORDER: *Filices — Fern Family.*

WHAT is more beautiful than the gracefully sweeping Fern, that clothes the ragged, rocky cliffs, hanging like so many plumes from every crevice, to catch the moisture of the timid spring that slips out to trickle over the green moss and hide in its bosom? Oh, marvelous is nature in her simplest simplicity! The Walking Fern is one of the rare ones, to be found in rocky woods. The frond or leaf is about six or seven inches in length, and its peculiarity consists in bending the long, slender tip backward until it reaches the ground, when it takes root, from which a plant arises the following year. The botanical names were probably given it because of its peculiarities, and denote, in Greek, root-leaved counterpart or transcript.

Curiosity.

THE enquiring spirit will not be controll'd;
  We would make certain all, and all behold.
      — *Sprague.*

THE skies in the darkness stoop nearer and nearer,
  A cluster of stars hangs like fruit in the tree.
The fall of the water comes sweeter comes clearer;
  To what art thou list'ning, and what dost thou see?
    Let the star-clusters glow,
    Let the sweet waters flow,
    And cross quickly to me.
      — *Jean Ingelow.*

SEARCHING those edges of the universe,
  We leave the central fields a fallow part;
To feed the eye more precious things amerce,
  And starve the darkened heart.
      — *Jean Ingelow.*

THRO' the buzzing crowd he threads his way,
  To catch the flying rumors of the day.
      — *Sprague.*

CURIOSITY! who hath not felt
  Its spirit, and before its altar knelt?
      — *Sprague.*

CONCEAL yersel' as weel's ye can
  Fra' critical dissection;
But keek thro' every other man
  With lengthen'd, sly inspection.
      — *Burns.*

BUT love is such a mystery,
  I cannot find it out;
For when I think I'm best resolved,
  Then I am most in doubt.
      — *Sir John Suckling.*

Feverfew.

Matricaria parthenium. NATURAL ORDER: *Composite—Aster Family.*

PYRETHRUM (hot, or spicy, from the Greek *pur*, fire) was formerly the botanical name of this plant, but the classification of Tournefort has recently been given precedence, and it is now called Matricaria, from its supposed value in certain forms of disease. The English name, identical in meaning with febrifuge, or fever-dispelling, from its medicinal properties, is familiar to all. It is a very desirable plant for the garden, continuing in bloom the entire season. The double variety is as full of petals as a daisy, and is most excellent where many cut flowers are desired. It is in great favor among florists, as the white blossoms retain their freshness for a considerable time, even though out of water. There are varieties with red flowers mentioned, but they are not as frequent in cultivation.

Beneficence.

WOULD'ST thou from sorrow find a sweet relief,
Or is thy heart oppressed with woe untold;
Balm would'st thou gather for corroding grief,
Pour blessings round thee like a shower of gold.
—*Carlos Wilcox.*

WITH a look of sad content
Her mite within the treasure-heap she cast;
Then, timidly as bashful twilight, stole
From out the temple. But her lowly gift
Was witnessed by an eye whose mercy views
In motive all that consecrates a deed
To goodness; so He blessed the widow's mite
More than the gifts abounding wealth bestowed.
—*Montgomery.*

THE charities that soothe, and heal, and bless,
Are scattered at the feet of man like flowers.
—*Wordsworth.*

THINE not the good,
The gentle deeds of mercy thou hast done,
Shall die forgotten all; the poor, the pris'ner,
The fatherless, the friendless and the widow,
Who daily own the bounty of thy hand,
Shall cry to heaven, and pull a blessing on thee.
—*Rowe.*

Fir Balsam.

Abies balsamea. NATURAL ORDER: *Coniferæ — Pine Family.*

BALSAMIC FIR (or Fir Balsam for the sake of euphony) sends out its branches in an almost horizontal line from the trunk, the fine shape being formed by the gradual diminution of the length of the branches until it reaches the apex, thus giving a pyramidal outline to its form. The leaves are white on the lower surface, and green above. The sap or resinous juice is obtained from the bark, from which it exudes, being about the consistency of thick honey, of a light amber tint. It is useful medicinally, both internally and externally.

Health.

REASON'S whole pleasure, all the joys of sense,
  Lie in three words, health, peace, and competence.
                                    — *Pope.*

AH! what avail the largest gifts of heaven,
  When drooping health and spirits go amiss?
How tasteless, then, whatever can be given!
  Health is the vital principle of bliss,
  And exercise of health. In proof of this,
Behold the wretch who slugs his life away,
  Soon swallow'd in disease's sad abyss;
While he whom toil has brac'd, or manly play,
  Has light as air each limb, each thought as clear as day.
                                    — *Thomson.*

WHAT health promotes, and gives unenvied peace,
  Is all expenseless, and procured with ease.
                              — *Sir R. Blackmore.*

THE surest road to health, say what they will,
  Is never to suppose we shall be ill.
Most of those evils we poor mortals know,
From doctors and imagination flow. — *Churchill.*

KNOW, then, whatever cheerful and serene
  Supports the mind supports the body too.
Hence the most vital movement mortals feel
Is hope: the balm and life-blood of the soul.
                             — *Dr. John Armstrong.*

NATURE does require
  Her time of preservation, which, perforce,
I, her frail son amongst my brethren mortal,
Must give attendance. — *Shakespeare.*

I REMEMBER, I remember
  The fir trees dark and high;
I used to think their slender tops
  Were close against the sky. — *Leigh Hunt.*

Flax.

Linum usitatissimum. NATURAL ORDER: *Linaceæ—Flax Family.*

COMPARED with plants not grown directly for food, the Flax is probably the most useful as well as the most ancient known to man. In various parts of the world it is grown in large quantities, forming the industry of a large population, furnishing employment both summer and winter in raising, gathering and caring for the crop, considerable attention being required in preparing the fiber for the manufacturing arts. The fields have a fine appearance when the Flax is in bloom, presenting an uninterrupted blue surface to the eye that is truly pleasing. There are some handsome varieties of tropical Flax for both garden and greenhouse, with flowers of scarlet, yellow, white, and rose color, some of them being perennial.

Domestic Industry.

WHAT happiness the rural maid attends,
In cheerful labor while each day she spends
She gratefully receives what heaven has sent,
And, rich in poverty, enjoys content. —*Gay.*

NEAT little housewife, so demure,
Plying the needle swift and sure,
In quiet places,
What charm is in those darksome eyes,
What magic in your beauty lies,
And lovely graces!

SWEETER and sweeter,
Soft and low,
Neat little nymph,
Thy numbers flow,
Urging thy thimble,
Thrift's tidy symbol,
Busy and nimble,
To and fro;

No sound to break your gentle dream;
Those lily hands from seam to seam
Are ever stirring;
All hushed—as summer's noonday hour,
When sleep the bee, and leaf, and flower—
Save pussy's purring.

Prettily plying
Thread and song,
Keeping them flying
Late and long,
Though the stitch linger,
Kissing thy finger,
Quick—as it skips along.

—*T. W. Palmer.*

Flower-of-an-Hour.

Hibiscus Trionum. NATURAL ORDER: *Malvaceæ — Mallow Family.*

EVANESCENT, as its familiar name indicates, this handsome annual was imported some years since from Italy; its botanical name is made up of the generic hibiscus, or mallow, and Trionum, of the constellation known by that name to the Romans, and to us as Charles's Wain. The flowers are similar in shape to the single hollyhock blossom, and are about two inches across the top, the petals being a sulphur or greenish yellow, and the base of each a rich maroon brown. There are various other plants and shrubs under the general name Hibiscus, some of which in the South Sea Islands grow sufficiently large to be used with the bamboo in the erection of houses, such as the people of that latitude require. They thrive best in moist, sandy soil.

Trifling Beauty.

TRUST not too much to that enchanting face;
 Beauty's a charm, but soon the charm will pass.
 — *Dryden.*

THAT transitory flower, even while it lasts,
 Palls on the roving sense when held too near,
Or dwelling there too long; by fits it pleases,
And smells at distance best; its sweets, familiar
By frequent converse, soon grow dull and cloy you.
 — *Jeffery.*

BEAUTY, like the fair Hesperian tree, [guard
 Laden with blooming gold, had need the
Of dragon-watch with unenchanted eye,
To save her blossoms and defend her fruit
From the rash hand of bold incontinence.
 — *Milton.*

DO not idolatrize, beauty's a flower,
 Which springs and withers almost in an hour.
 — *William Smith.*

LOVE raised on beauty will like that decay;
 Our hearts may bear its slender chain a day,
As flow'ry bands in wantonness are worn —
A morning's pleasure, and at evening torn.
 — *Pope.*

BEAUTY, sweet love, is like the morning dew,
 Whose short refresh upon the tender green
Cheers for a time, but till the sun doth show,
And straight is gone, as it had never been.
 — *Daniel.*

LOVE built on beauty, soon as beauty dies;
 Choose this face, changed by no deformities.
 — *Donne.*

Four-o'clock.

Mirabilis Jalapa. NATURAL ORDER: *Nyctaginaceæ — Four-o'clock Family.*

IT is from the roots of this plant, which is a native of the West Indies, that the Jalap of commerce is obtained. The stem is about two feet high, having numerous branches, with smooth, oval, pointed leaves, and tuberous root. Its flowers are large, blooming in clusters, very sweet and fragrant, and various in colors. This, with the few species from Mexico, all open about the time of day their name indicates, and continue a perfect succession of bloom during the whole summer. The plants bloom better the second year, if the roots are removed to a dry cellar during the winter, kept from frost, and replanted in the spring.

Time.

DESIRE not to live long, but to live well;
How long we live, not years, but actions tell.
— *Watkyns.*

TIME is a feathered thing,
And whilst I praise
The sparkling of thy locks, and call them rays,
Takes wing.   — *Mayne.*

ART is long and time is fleeting,
And our hearts, though stout and brave,
Still, like muffled drums, are beating
Funeral marches to the grave.
— *Longfellow.*

TIME, as he passes, has a dove's wing,
Unsoiled and swift, and of a silken sound.
— *Cowper.*

TOUCH us gently, Time!
Let us glide down thy stream
Gently — as we sometimes glide
  Through a quiet dream.
— *Bryan W. Procter.*

THE hours are viewless angels,
That still go gliding by,
And bear each minute's record up
  To Him who sits on high
— *C. P. Cranch.*

EVEN such is Time, that takes on trust
Our youth, our joys, our all we have,
And pays us with but age and dust;
  Who in the dark and silent grave,
When we have wandered all our ways,
Shuts up the story of our days!   — *Sir W. Raleigh.*

Foxglove.

Digitalis purpurea. NATURAL ORDER: *Scrophulariaceæ — Figwort Family.*

LITERALLY, the purple finger-flower, this plant is of easy culture, and well adapted for the borders of walks and beds. The blossoms, which grow in a long spike, are many, and thimble-shaped, with dots of a color differing from the flower in the interior. The whole plant is a violent and dangerous poison when taken internally in any considerable quantity, producing delirium, convulsions and death. It becomes a valuable medicine in the hands of a skillful physician. It thrives best in partially shaded locations. There are a number of varieties, the flowers being white, purple, carmine, brown, and yellow.

Delirium.

O THIS poor brain! ten thousand shapes of fury
  Are whirling there, and reason is no more.
                                            — *Fielding.*

HE raves, his words are loose
  As heaps of sand, and scattering wide from sense;
So high he 's mounted on his airy throne,
That now the wind has got into his head,
And turns his brains to phrenzy.   — *Dryden.*

HIS brain is wrecked —
  For ever in the pauses of his speech
His lip doth work with inward mutterings,
And his fixed eye is riveted fearfully
On something that no other sight can spy.
                                            — *Maturin.*

I AM not mad; too well, too well I feel
  The different plague of each calamity.
                                            — *Shakespeare.*

I AM not mad; I would to heaven I were!
  For then 'tis like I should forget myself;
O, if I could, what grief should I forget!
                                            — *Shakespeare.*

THIS wretched brain gave way,
  And I became a wreck, at random driven,
Without one glimpse of reason or of heaven.
                                            — *Moore.*

IF a phrenzy do possess the brain,
  It so disturbs and blots the form of things,
As fantasy proves altogether vain,
  And to the wit no true relation brings.
                                            — *Sir John Davis.*

Fritillaria.

Fritillaria maleagris. NATURAL ORDER: *Liliaceæ — Lily Family.*

NOT inappropriately named, from the Latin *fritillus*, a dice-box, as the flower is more nearly of that shape than in the other lilies, this plant is a sister to the crown imperial, already described, both blooming in the month of May. The flower is large, nodding, and beautifully checked with pale-red, purple or yellow spots, from which circumstance the name has sometimes been interpreted "chessboard." It is indigenous throughout Europe. It is usually solitary in bloom. In Spain it is called Checkered Lily, and in other places Guinea-Hen-Flower.

Persecution.

I HAVE learn'd to endure, I have hugg'd my despair;
I scourge back the madness that else would invade;
On my brain falls the drop after drop, yet I bear,
Lest thou should'st discover the wreck thou hast made.
—*Mrs. E. Oakes Smith.*

THIS you have practiced,
Practiced on us with rigor, this hath forced us
To shake our heavy yokes off; and, if redress
Of these just grievances be not granted us,
We'll right ourselves, and by strong hand defend
What we are now possessed of.
—*Massinger.*

THEY lived unknown
Till persecution dragged them into fame,
And chased them up to heaven. Their ashes flew,
No marble tells us whither. With their names
No bard embalms and sanctifies his song;

BUT what avail her unexhausted stores,
Her bloomy mountains and her sunny shores,
With all the gifts that heaven and earth impart,
The smiles of nature, and the charms of art,
While proud oppression in her valleys reigns,
And tyranny usurps her happy plains?
—*Addison.*

And history, so warm on meaner themes,
Is cold on this. She execrates, indeed,
The tyranny that doomed them to the fire,
But gives the glorious suff'rers little praise.
—*Cowper.*

NEITHER bended knees, pure hands held up,
Sad sighs, deep groans, nor silver-shedding tears,
Could penetrate her uncompassionate sire.
—*Shakespeare.*

Fuchsia.

Fuchsia coccinea.   NATURAL ORDER: *Onagraceæ — Evening Primrose Family.*

DELICATE and beautiful for a house plant is the Scarlet Fuchsia, a native of South America; and the story of its general introduction into England is somewhat singular and not without a touch of romance. A gentleman, while traveling, passed through some town not far from the great metropolis, and there saw a plant with hanging bells, like ear-drops, which attracted his attention. Upon his arrival in London, he informed an eminent gardener of what he had seen, eulogizing the beautiful and graceful arrangement of its flowers. The gardener went immediately to the place designated, but the poor cottager declared that she could not part with it, as her "good man, who was at sea, had brought it as a present the last time he was at home, and she did not know if she should ever see him again." He however finally possessed himself of it by offering her a large sum, and promising her the first slip. He brought it home, divided and subdivided it, soon having a large number of plants, for which he obtained a rapid sale.

Grace.

HER laugh, full of life, without any control,
   But the sweet one of gracefulness, rung from her soul;
And where it most sparkled no glance could discover,
In lip, cheek, or eyes, for she brightened all over.   —*Moore.*

THE light of love, the purity of grace,
   The mind, the music, breathing from her face.
              —*Byron.*

GRACE was in all her steps, heav'n in her eye,
   In ev'ry gesture dignity and love!
              —*Milton.*

A LOVELIER nymph the pencil never drew.
   For the fond Graces form'd her easy mien,
And heaven's soft azure in her eye was seen.   —*Hayley.*

HER ivory-polish'd front with seemly cheer,
   Graced at the bottom with a double bow,
Where all the Graces in their throne appear,
Where love and awful majesty do grow,
   Expends itself, and shows a field more clear
     Than candid lilies or the virgin snow;
   Her eyes, like suns, shoot rays more sharp than darts,
   Which wound all flinty, love-despising hearts.
              —*Pordage.*

Gentian.

Gentiana acaulis. NATURAL ORDER: *Gentianaceæ — Gentian Family.*

GENTIAN is a plant of excellent tonic and febrifuge properties, which are said to have been first discovered by Gentius, king of ancient Illyria, in whose honor it was named. It is found abundantly in the Western States, where the land lies low and is more or less moist, which soil seems most congenial to its growth. It is not unusual to find acres of land dotted freely with its blue blossoms, particularly in openings in the woods. Besides our native plants, we have other specimens from Wales, Australia, and the Alps. The two from the first-named countries have blue flowers, the latter yellow ones. The more dwarf varieties are the best adapted for rock culture.

Intrinsic Worth.

FIRM and resolved by sterling worth to gain
   Love and respect, thou shalt not strive in vain.
                                 —*Sir S. E. Brydges.*

O HOW thy worth with manners may I sing,
   When thou art all the better part of me?
What can mine own praise to mine own self bring?
And what is 't but mine own, when I praise thee?
              —*Shakespeare.*

ALL that is best of beauty is its dower,
   All that is pure in piety its bequest.
The subtle spring of truth, the soul of power.
It gives our dreams their scope, our life its zest.
             —*Isidore G. Ascher.*

I KNOW transplanted human worth
   Will bloom to profit otherwhere.
                 —*Tennyson.*

THERE is a joy in worth,
   A high, mysterious, soul-pervading charm,
Which, never daunted, ever bright and warm,
Mocks at the idle, shadowy ills of earth,
Amid the gloom is bright, and tranquil in the storm.
            —*Robert T. Conrad.*

'TIS what the heart adores, where'er the eye
   Doth rest, on ocean, earth, or in the sky;
For love ne'er worships willingly a blot,
But looks for what is pure, for what is fair.
For what is good, as heaven and angels are.
            —*Sallie A. Brock.*

BEAUTIES that from worth arise,
   Are like the grace of deities,
Still present with us, though unsighted.
            —*Sir J. Suckling.*

Geranium.

Geranium sanguineum. NATURAL ORDER: *Geraniaceæ — Geranium Family.*

ANY are the varieties of this beautiful plant, most of which are nurtured in the window or greenhouse, either for their beauty of blossom or the delightful fragrance of their leaves. Some of them are from the Cape of Good Hope, but this beautiful species, with its blood-red flowers, is a native of Europe. It is well adapted to make a brilliant show in the garden in summer, being again removed to the house in the fall. The name is derived from *geranos*, a Greek word meaning crane, the seeds having a long spur (supposed to resemble a crane's bill), which in planting should be cut off with the scissors, as it tends to push the seeds out of the ground before sprouting.

Confidence.

TRUST in thee? Aye, dearest, there 's no one but must.
  Unless truth be a fable in such as they trust;
For who can see heaven's own hue in those eyes,
And doubt that truth with it came down from the skies?
While each thought of thy bosom, like morning's young light,
Almost ere 'tis born, flashes there on his sight.
— C. F. Hoffman.

OUT of the depths of the starlit distance   [up,
  A pale gleam shows where the moon comes
And here in the dregs of this strange existence
  May lurk the sweetness that crowns the cup,

And faith and hope and the spirit's patience
  Strengthen the heart and lighten the eyes.
Ah, soul! my soul! there is hope for the nations,
  And God is holy and just and wise.
— Barton Grey.

I TRUST in thee, and know in whom I trust;
  Or life or death is equal; neither weighs;
All weight is this: O let me live to thee! — *Young.*

HAVE I not brought thee roses fresh with youth,
  And snow-white lilies, pale with pure desire?
Beheld in thee my inmost dream of Truth,
  And felt no beauty thou didst not inspire?
— Joel Benton.

OH! emblem of that steadfast mind
  Which, through the varying scenes of life,
By genuine piety refined,
  Holds on its way 'midst noise and strife!

Gladiolus.

Gladiolus communis.   NATURAL ORDER: *Iridaceæ—Iris Family.*

OF recent introduction into general cultivation in the United States, the Gladiolus has more than answered all anticipations, and too much praise cannot be elicited in its behalf. It has a bulbous root, round and flattened like an onion, though less perfect in shape; the leaves are long and pointed, and shaped like a small sword (*gladiolus*), from which it takes its name. The flower stalk rises about two feet. The flowers are large and handsome, arranged around the stem for nearly half its length, the lower ones blooming first. The colors are brilliant in the highest degree, and the variety of hues and shades is almost numberless. The new colors are derived from seedlings.

Ready Armed.

'TIS ours by craft and by surprise to gain;
   'Tis yours to meet in arms, and battle in the plain.
          —*Prior.*

I'LL ride in golden armor like the sun,
  And in my helm a triple plume shall spring,
Spangled with diamonds dancing in the air,
To note me emperor of the threefold world.
          —*Marlo.*

SWORD, on my left side gleaming,
  What means thy bright eye's beaming?
It makes my spirit dance
To see thy friendly glance.
          —*From the German of Körner.*

A GENERAL sets his army in array
  In vain, unless he fight and win the day.
          —*Sir J. Denham.*

IMPETUOUS, active, fierce, and young,
  Upon the advancing foes he sprung.
Woe to the wretch at whom is bent
His brandish'd falchion's sheer descent.
          —*Scott.*

I'LL do the best that do I may,
  While I have power to stand;
While I have power to wield my sword,
I'll fight with heart and hand.
          —*Anonymous.*

In that day's feats
He proved the best man i' th' field; and for his mead
Was brow-bound with oak.
          —*Shakespeare.*

Globe Flower.

Trollius Europæus.   NATURAL ORDER: *Ranunculaceæ—Crowfoot Family.*

HERE and there in swamps throughout the north and west, the Trollius laxus, or wild Globe Flower, may be found, but the varieties in cultivation are from abroad, Europe and Asia each furnishing its quota. They can be grown from seeds, as well as by division of the roots. They are ornamental plants, handsome in growth, with flowers varying through the different shades of yellow. The Japan Globe Flower belongs to another class of plants, and is of shrubby growth, usually six or seven feet high. The flowers appear in small clusters near the ends of the branches, being also yellow in color.

Fancy.

NOT nobler are the hearts that work than hearts that only dream;
For real, as the things that are, are all the things that seem.
The waters gleam among the hills, the mirage on the sands,
And yet alike both image forth the selfsame Maker's hands.
— *L. Bruce Moore.*

FANCY high commissioned; send her!
    She has vassals to attend her;
She will bring in spite of frost,
Beauties that the earth hath lost;
She will bring thee, all together,
All delights of summer weather.
— *John Keats.*

TELL me where is fancy bred;
    Or in the heart or in the head?
How begot, how nourished?
It is engendered in the eyes,
With gazing fed; and fancy dies
In the cradle where it lies.
— *Shakespeare.*

FANCY is a fairy, that can hear,
    Ever, the melody of nature's voice,
And see all lovely visions that she will.
— *Mrs. Osgood.*

A SILVERY haze hangs o'er the earth,
    And through its gauzy sheen
We look in vain for summer's garb,
    Or spring-tide's dewy green;
Bright, gorgeous tints, like Tyrian dies,
    Gleam on the ravished sight;
I fancy an enchanted realm
    Revealed in mystic light. — *Sallie A. Brock.*

Gourd.

Lagenaria vulgaris.   NATURAL ORDER: *Cucurbitaceæ*—*Gourd Family.*

KNOWN scientifically as Lagenaria, from the Latin *lagena*, a bottle, the common Bottle Gourd, or Calabash, is familiar to all. It grows like a round ball, gradually extended into a handle. When ripened, a slice is cut from one side, and the seeds are removed, thus forming a very convenient vessel for dipping water, for which purpose it was used in early times. There are upward of fifty different kinds of this interesting plant, all of them being natives of tropical countries. Some are large and grotesque, others small, fanciful, delicate, beautiful in shape and color, and worthy of enthusiastic admiration. Hawthorne said they were "worthy of being wrought in enduring marble."

Extent.

HE who, from zone to zone,
Guides through the boundless sky thy certain flight,
In the long way that I must tread alone
Will lead my steps aright.   —*William Cullen Bryant.*

AND yet I know past all doubting, truly—
A knowledge greater than grief can dim—
I know, as he loved, he will love duly,
Yea, better—e'en better than I love him;

And as I walk by the vast, calm river
The awful river so dread to see,
I say, "Thy breadth and thy depth forever
Are bridged by his thoughts that cross to me."
—*Jean Ingelow.*

MY wingéd boat,
A bird afloat,
Swims round the purple peaks remote:—
Round purple peaks
It sails, and seeks
Blue inlets and their crystal creeks,
Where high rocks throw,
Through deeps below,

A duplicated golden glow.
Far, vague, and dim,
The mountains swim;
While on Vesuvius' misty brim,
With outstretched hands
The gray smoke stands,
O'erlooking the volcanic lands.
—*Thomas Buchanan Read.*

FROM the low earth round you,
Reach the heights above you;
From the stripes that wound you,
Seek the loves that love you.

God's divinest burneth plain
Through the crystal diaphane
Of our loves that love you.
—*Elizabeth Barrett Browning.*

Grass.

Anthoxanthum odoratum. NATURAL ORDER: *Gramineæ—Grass Family.*

WHAT is more delightful to the senses of one pent up amid the brick and dust of a crowded city than to behold a spot of refreshing verdure? It rejoices the eye, and fills the soul with gladness. Who can look abroad at the waving meadows and close-cropped pastures and not acknowledge the beneficence of the all-wise Creator? No other color would be so grateful to the vision, and no other color would always appear so fresh and new. The grass, along with all grains, belongs to the extensive order Gramineæ, which contributes more to the sustenance of man and beast than all others combined. It has an element of poetry in its botanical name, which signifies sweetly-scented yellow flower; and has for ages been considered an emblem of utility.

Utility.

HERE may I always on this downy grass,
   Unknown, unseen, my easy minutes pass!
        —*Roscommon.*

THUS is nature's vesture wrought,
  To instruct our wandering thought;
Thus she dresses green and gay,
To dispense our cares away. —*Dyer.*

NOT enjoyment and not sorrow
  Is our destin'd end or way,
But to act that each tomorrow
Finds us farther than today. —*Longfellow.*

THE chiefest action for a man of spirit,
  Is never to be out of action; we should think
The soul was never put into the body,
Which has so many rare and curious pieces
Of mathematical motion, to stand still.
Virtue is ever sowing her seeds. —*Webster.*

THE even grass beneath our feet
  Was something greener and more sweet
Than that which grew below.

We breathed a purer, better air;
Our lives seemed wider and more fair,
And earth with love aglow.
        —*Henry Abbey.*

Ground Ivy.

Nepeta Glechoma.   NATURAL ORDER: *Labiatæ — Mint Family.*

GROUND IVY, or Gill-over-the-ground, is a very pretty plant of rapid growth, to be found about hedges, old walls, and among the rocks along the margins of creeks and small streams. The stem, which is naturally prostrate, if suffered to lie on the ground, takes root at every joint, sending out in turn new creepers, which grow from a few inches to two feet in length. In a hanging basket it trails from the sides, completely enveloping it, delighting in shade and plenty of moisture. The flowers are of a bluish purple, blooming in May. The leaves are aromatic, and were formerly used in brewing ale. It is sometimes called Alehoof, and Tunhoof. It derives its scientific name from Nepete, now Nepi, in Italy; and Glechoma was the name given it by Linnæus.

Enjoyment.

JOY is no earthly flower, nor framed to bear
  In its exotic bloom life's cold, ungenial air.
— *Mrs. Hemans.*

WE are all children in our strife to seize
  Each pretty pleasure, as it lures the sight;
And like the tall tree, swaying in the breeze,
Our lofty wishes stoop their tow'ring flight,
Till, when the prize is won, it seems no more
Than gather'd shell from ocean's countless store,
And ever those who would enjoyment gain,
Must find it in the purpose they pursue.
— *Mrs. Hale.*

WITH much we surfeit, plenty makes us poor,
  The wretched Indian scorns the golden ore.
— *Drayton.*

AH! here how sweet, my love, my own,
  To dream, aloof from any sorrows,
Of one fair, changeless monotone —
  Serene tomorrows and tomorrows!
Ah! sweet, in sooth, when God had furled
  All colors at the calm sky-verges,
And night came silencing the world,
  And loudening the long sea-surges!
— *Edgar Fawcett.*

WISE heaven doth see it as fit
  In all our joys to give us some alloys,
As in our sorrows, comforts.   — *Fountain.*

Ground Pine.

Lycopodium complanatum. NATURAL ORDER: *Lycopodiacea — Club Moss Family.*

LYCOPODIUM is one of the humbler types of vegetation that in the earlier stages of our globe occupied a place of higher rank, and attained a size more worthy of consideration, as some of the specimens now existing in a fossil state amply show. When other and more important vegetation made its appearance, the less useful descended to a minor and more obscure position, till now it scarcely more than lends variety to the scene. This mossy plant has a round stem, and is frequently found creeping along the ground in woods that are moist and shady, being some five or six feet in length. There are several greenhouse varieties useful for ferneries and hanging-baskets, but they require considerable moisture to grow well. The name signifies leveled or horizontal wolf's-foot.

Complaint.

THERE are fancies strangely bitter in the surge of this restless sea,
   And hopes, and dreams, and memories, all rising mournfully;
The waves that are softly breaking, with starry luster kissed,
   Summon a host of phantoms out of the ocean-mist.
—Christian Reid.

GRIEV'ST thou that hearts should change?
  Lo! where life reigneth
Or the free sight doth range,
  What long remaineth?

Spring with her flowers doth die;
  Fast fades the gilded sky;
And the full moon on high
  Ceaselessly waneth. —*Anonymous.*

COME, now again thy woes impart,
  Tell all thy sorrows, all thy sin;
We cannot heal the throbbing heart,
  Till we discern the wounds within.
—Crabbe.

A WIND HARP swelled into perfect song
  'Neath Zephyr's soft touch;
But Boreas did it a grievous wrong,
  For he smote it too much—

He smote it so rudely, its delicate chords
  Wailed in musical pain,
Saying, in plaintive and mystical words,
  "We accord not again!"
—Howard Glyndon.

Gum Tree.

Nyssa Multiflora.   NATURAL ORDER: *Cornaceæ — Dogwood Family.*

THIS is a tall tree found throughout the United States, either in woodlands or along the roadside, growing both in dry and wet locations. The bark is of a light gray, and rough or broken on the surface, and at the height of fifty feet or more is a fine head of large, glossy, dark-green leaves. Its flowers are small and of a greenish color, blooming in clusters. The wood is much twisted and soft, but fine grained, and is used in the manufacture of naves of wheels and hatters' blocks. One of the species bears a small, blue fruit, which is the favorite food of the opossum.

Enthusiasm.

NO wild enthusiast ever yet could rest,
Till half mankind were like himself possessed.
—*Cowper.*

THE restless spirit charm'd thy sweet existence,
Making all beauteous in youth's pleasant maze,
While gladsome hope illumed the onward distance,
And lit with sunbeams thy expectant days.
—*Willis G. Clark.*

SHE caught th' illusion — blest his name,
And wildly magnified his worth and fame;
Rejoicing life's reality contained
One, heretofore, her fancy had but feigned.
—*Campbell.*

YOUTH with swift feet walks onward in the way,
The land of joy lies all before his eyes.
—*Mrs. Butler.*

I GAZE upon the thousand stars
That fill the midnight sky;
And wish, so passionately wish,
A light like theirs on high.

I have such eagerness of hope
To benefit my kind;
I feel as if immortal power
Were given to my mind.
—*Miss Landon.*

Oh! the joy
Of young ideas painted on the mind,
In the warm, glowing colors fancy spreads
On objects not yet known, when all is new,
And all is lovely.   —*Hannah Moore.*

Hawkweed.

Hieracium Gronovii.   NATURAL ORDER: *Composite—Aster Family.*

A FEW varieties of the Hawkweed from France and Italy are to be found in our gardens. The blossoms of the cultivated plants are yellow, silvery, or red in color. The flowers of the above native plant are yellow, and throughout Canada and the United States it is found in the woods in dry situations. The stalk is about two feet high, and the blossom appears during the months of August and September. The ancients supposed this, as well as the other species, to strengthen the sight of birds of prey. The classic name is derived from *ierax*, a hawk, on account of the properties ascribed to it.

Quick-Sightedness.

LONG while I sought to what I might compare
  Those powerful eyes, which lighten my dark spirit,
Yet found I nought on earth to which I dare
Resemble the image of their goodly light. —*Spenser.*

CREATURES there be of sight so keen and high
  That even to the sun they bend their gaze;
Others, who, dazzled by too fierce a blaze,
Issue not forth till evening vails the sky.
  —*Petrarch.*

HER lively looks a sprightly mind disclose,
  Quick as her eyes, and as unfixed as those;
Favors to none, to all she smiles extends,
Oft she rejects, but never once offends.
  —*Pope.*

HIS blazing eyes, like two bright shining fields,
  Did burn with wrath, and sparkled living fire;
As two broad beacons set in open fields
Send forth their flames. —*Spenser.*

YOUR hawkeyes are keen and bright,
  Keen with triumph, watching still
To pierce me through with pointed light;
But oftentimes they flash and glitter
Like sunshine on a dancing rill.
  —*Tennyson.*

IN her two eyes two living lamps did flame,
  Kindled above, at the heavenly light,
And darting fiery beams out of the same.
So passing pearceant, and so wondrous bright,
That quite bereaved the rash beholders of their sight.
  —*Spenser.*

Heath.

Erica odorata.   NATURAL ORDER: *Ericaceæ—Heath Family.*

WE find but few Heaths among the plants of a mixed greenhouse, as the idea prevails that they require a particular atmosphere and condition of temperature to grow them well. In Europe, houses are devoted exclusively to their culture. The British Heaths grow in bleak and barren places, and are utilized by the poorer class to thatch their cabins, who, like the poor of every nation, are driven by necessity to make use of all the gifts of nature, when they can so ill afford the gifts of art. The most cherished Heaths come from Southern Africa, of which there are several hundred in cultivation. Anyone who has torn a fern from its place in a wild retreat, has noticed its hair-like roots. This is the case with the Heath; and a desideratum of its culture is that its roots must never become dry, neither must it rest in sodden soil; for once dry, the foliage becomes sere and brown beyond recovery, and too much water decays the roots.

Solitude.

SWEET, solitary life! lovely, dumb joy,
  That need'st no warnings how to grow more wise
By other men's mishaps, nor the annoy
  Which from sore wrongs done to one's self doth rise;
The morning's second mansion, truth's first friend,
  Never acquainted with the world's vain broils,
When the whole day to our own use we spend,
  And our dear time no fierce ambition spoils.
              —*Earl of Ancrum.*

OH! to lie down in wilds apart,
  Where man is seldom seen or heard,
In still and ancient forests, where
Mows not his scythe, plows not his share,
  With the shy deer and cooing bird!

To go, in dreariness of mood,
  O'er a lone heath, that spreads around
A solitude like a silent sea,
Where rises not a hut or tree,
  The wide-embracing sky its bound!
              —*Howitt.*

Helenium.

Helenium autumnale. NATURAL ORDER: *Compositæ — Aster Family.*

THIS plant is named for the celebrated Helen, a daughter of Jupiter, who was so renowned for her beauty that she was seized by Paris, son of Priam, and carried to Troy, thereby causing the Trojan war. She is said to have "availed herself of its cosmetic properties." In medicine it is a tonic, produces an insensible perspiration; and it is also made into a snuff for medical use, which gives it the common name of Sneezewort. It grows in low ground or moist places in fields and by-ways, wholly uncultivated, having an herbaceous growth of from two to three feet in height. The plant blooms in August; the flowers are yellow.

Tears.

WHAT gem hath dropp'd, and sparkles o'er his chain?
   The tear most sacred shed for others' pain,
That starts at once — bright, pure — from pity's mine,
Already polish'd by the hand divine.   *Byron.*

RAISE it to heaven, when thine eye fills with tears,
   For only in a watery sky appears
The bow of light; and from the invisible skies
Hope's glory shines not, save through weeping eyes.
   —*Mrs. F. A. Butler.*

BLEST tears of soul-felt penitence!
   In whose benign, redeeming flow
Is felt the first, the only sense
   Of guiltless joy that guilt may know!
   Moore.

BUT these are tears of joy! to see you thus, has fill'd
   My eyes with more delight than they can hold.
   —*Congreve.*

THANK God, bless God, all ye who suffer not
   More grief than ye can weep for. That is well—
That is light grieving! lighter, none befell,
Since Adam forfeited the primal lot.
Tears! what are tears? The babe weeps in its cot,
The mother singing,— at her marriage-bell
The bride weeps,— and before the oracle
Of high-faned hills, the poet has forgot
Such moisture on his cheeks.
   —*Elizabeth Barrett Browning.*

THOU weep'st: O stop that shower of falling sorrows,
   Which melts me to the softness of a woman,
And shakes my best resolves.   —*Trap.*

Heliotrope.

Heliotropium Peruvianum.   NATURAL ORDER: *Boraginaceæ—Borage Family.*

ELIOTROPE is a small and elegant shrub about two feet high, a native of Peru. The flowers bloom in clusters, and are of a delicate lavender or purple tint, with the fragrance of vanilla, and are especially desirable for bouquets. It is said that Clytie, who had been loved and deserted by Apollo, seeing his attachment for her sister Leucothea, pined away, with her eyes gazing continually upon the sun, and was at last turned into a flower called Sunflower, or Heliotrope. The name is derived from the Greek *Helios*, sun, and *trepo*, to turn. It is also called Turnsole, from its turning to *Sol*, the Latin for sun. It was introduced into France by Jessieu, about 1740. There are several other flowers that follow the course of the sun, the best known being probably the common yellow Sunflower.

Devotion.

DEVOTION'S self shall steal a thought from heaven;
One human tear shall drop, and be forgiven.
— *Pope.*

I GIVE thee prayers, like jewels strung
On golden threads of hope and fear;
And tenderer thoughts than ever hung
In a sad angel's pitying tear.

As earth pours freely to the sea
Her thousand streams of wealth untold,
So flows my silent life to thee,
Glad that its very sands are gold.
— *Rose Terry.*

IN vain doth man the name of just expect,
If his devotions he to God neglect.
— *Sir J. Denham.*

I LOVE her for that loving trust
That makes the one she loves all just,
And faith that's blind in loving;

A love that smiles away all tears,
And looks not way beyond these years,
To see what love is proving.
— *C. C.*

ONE grain of incense with devotion offered
'S beyond all perfumes or Sabæan spices
By one that proudly thinks he merits it.
— *Massinger.*

155

Hellebore.

Helleborus viridis.   NATURAL ORDER: *Ranunculaceæ—Crowfoot Family.*

SEVERAL plants are known under the name of Hellebore, and though belonging to different and distinct families, they all possess highly poisonous qualities, as the literal translation of their botanical name would signify, "food of death," from the combination of two Greek words, *elein,* to cause death (literally to take away), and *bora,* food. Though fatal in inexperienced hands, they are exceedingly useful in the hands of educated medical men. The ancients were also well acquainted with their merits, as they used them for all "mental diseases, such as madness and idiocy, the best growing on the island of Anticyra in the Ægean sea." This variety is from Europe, is about three feet high, with large, nodding flowers, and is grown as an ornamental plant.

Calumny.

NOR might nor greatness in mortality
Can censure 'scape; back-wounding calumny
The whitest virtue strikes; what king so strong
Can tie the gall up in the slanderous tongue?
— *Shakespeare.*

THE world with calumny abounds;
  The whitest virtue slander wounds;
There are whose joy is, night and day,
To talk a character away.   —*Pope.*

WHEN sland'rous tongue thy honor stings,
  This solace give thee rest:—
Whatever fruit the autumn brings,
  The wasp will choose the best.
— *G. A. Burger.*

THE ignoble mind
  Loves ever to assail with secret blow
The loftier purer beings of their kind.
— *W. G. Simms.*

NO wound which warlike band of enemy
  Inflicts with dint of sword, so sore doth light
As doth the poisonous sting which infamy
Infixeth in the name of noble wight;
For by no art, nor any leeches' might
It ever can receivéd be again.   —*Spenser.*

Hemp.

Cannabis sativa. NATURAL ORDER: *Urticaceæ — Nettle Family.*

CANNABIS (Greek and Latin for Hemp) is a common and well-known plant, naturalized in waste places in the United States. It came originally from Persia and the East Indies, where the natives make an intoxicating beverage from it. In some States it is largely cultivated for the fiber of the stalks, and when properly prepared is manufactured into the coarser grades of toweling and ropes. It grows quite tall and erect, branching at intervals, having foliage that is sharply cleft and palmate, giving the whole plant a light, airy appearance. The flowers are green, and the seeds are crowded up and down the summits of the branches. It is very appropriate for sowing along fences, and is admirable for forming screens to shut off unsightly objects in a rear yard. In the fall, the seeds attract the dear little birds, which sometimes visit them in large flocks, after the frost and late season have exhausted other sustenance.

Fate.

HEAV'N from all creatures hides the book of fate,
All but the page prescribed their present state.
— *Pope.*

THE Fates but only spin the coarser clue:
The finest of the wool is left for you.
— *Dryden.*

WHAT fate imposes, men must need abide;
It boots not to resist both wind and tide.
— *Shakespeare.*

THY downcast looks, and thy disorder'd thoughts
Tell me my fate: I ask not the success
My cause has found. — *Addison.*

SUPREME, all-wise, eternal Potentate!
Sole Author, sole Disposer of our fate,
Enthroned in light and immortality,
Whom no man fully sees, and none can see!
Original of beings! Power divine!
Since that I live, and that I think, is thine!
Benign Creator! let thy plastic hand
Dispose its own effect. — *Matthew Prior.*

FATE, show thy force: ourselves we do not owe;
What is decreed must be: and be this so.
— *Shakespeare.*

Hollyhock.

Althæa rosea.   NATURAL ORDER: *Malvaceæ—Mallow Family.*

BETWEEN the Hollyhocks of this generation and the unpretending flower of our ancestors there is a marked difference. Formerly its single blossoms used to cluster around the stalk as it grew beside the cabin of the early settler or mingled with the humble flowers in the dooryard of the villager. The Hollyhock of today—how superb! Ruffle after ruffle has it added to its rosette, so silky and soft, until it is full to repletion, and close has it crowded them along its tall stem; step by step has it advanced to the lawn, gaining admiration as it approached the acme of its perfection. The colors of the blossoms are various. The plants look well grouped, or planted in rows, or arranged as a background to lower-growing plants. It blooms the second year from the seed, or can be propagated by dividing the root.

Ambition.

AMBITION is an idol on whose wings
Great minds are carried only to extreme:
To be sublimely great, or to be nothing.
— *Southern.*

AMBITION is at a distance
A goodly prospect, tempting to the view;
The height delights us, and the mountain top
Looks beautiful because 'tis nigh to heaven.
— *Otway.*

BE not with honor's gilded baits beguiled,
Nor think ambition wise, because 'tis brave;
For though we like it, as a forward child,
'Tis so unsound, her cradle is her grave.
— *Sir W. Davenant.*

WHO soars too near the sun, with golden wings,
Melts them;—to ruin his own fortune brings.
— *Shakespear.*

WHERE ambition of place goes before fitness
Of birth, contempt and disgrace follow.
— *George Chapman.*

YOU have deeply ventured,
But all must do so who would greatly win.
— *Byron.*

AMBITION is a spirit in the world,
That causes all the ebbs and flows of nations.
— *Crown.*

Holly.

Ilex aquifolium. NATURAL ORDER: *Aquifoliaceæ — Holly Family.*

ILEX, signifying originally in Latin a species of oak, came finally to be appropriated as the botanical name of the Holly; and aquifolium, from the Latin words *acus*, a needle, and *folium*, a leaf, has been added to designate its marked characteristic of sharp-pointed leaves. We have in the United States several species, some of which are shrubs from six to twelve feet in height, others attaining the size of trees. The leaves are glossy and evergreen, the lower ones being armed with thorns. In autumn, bright red berries deck their branches. There are over a hundred varieties now cultivated in Europe, where they are all hardy, and most of them of fine appearance. In this country in northern latitudes they nearly all require protection from the severity of the frost, by a covering of some kind. The wood of the Ilex opaca is fine grained and compact, and is useful in wood turning: some of the others possess properties useful in medical science.

Foresight.

I LOVE to view these things with curious eyes,
    And moralize;
And in this wisdom of the holly tree
    Can emblems see
Wherewith, perchance, to make a pleasant rhyme,
One which may profit in the after-time.

Thus though abroad, perchance, I might appear
    Harsh and austere
To those who on my leisure would intrude,
    Reserved and rude;
Gentle at home amid my friends I'd be,
Like the high leaves upon the holly tree.

And should my youth, as youth is apt, I know,
    Some harshness show,
All vain asperities I, day by day,
    Would wear away,
Till the smooth temper of my age should be
Like the high leaves upon the holly tree.
    — *Robert Southey.*

WALK boldly and wisely in that light thou hast;
There is a hand above will help thee on.
    — *Bailey.*

Honesty.

Lunaria biennis.　Natural Order: *Cruciferæ — Mustard Family.*

LUNARIA, from the Latin *luna*, the moon, has two varieties: the rediviva, a handsome perennial, with light-purple flowers, and rather rare in the United States; and the biennis, a large biennial with lilac-colored flowers. Both are natives of Germany, and received the name from the distinguished Swiss botanist, DeCandolle, on account of their transparent moon-shaped silicles or pods, which are the most attractive feature of the plant. The name has a special appropriateness not altogether arising from the shape of the pods, which is more nearly oval, but from the additional peculiarity of the *silvery* separating tissues or dissepiments. As the silicles remain unchanged, they are quite an acquisition to a winter bouquet if plucked and carefully dried in autumn.

Honesty.

TAKE heed what you say, sir!
　An hundred honest men! why, if there were
So many i' th' city, 'twere enough to forfeit
Their charter.　　　　　　　　　　—*Shirley.*

AN honest man is still an unmov'd rock,
　Wash'd whiter, but not shaken with the shock;
Whose heart conceives no sinister device;
Fearless he plays with flames, and treads on ice.
　　　　　　　　　　　　—*Davenport.*

HIS words are bonds, his oaths are oracles;
　His love sincere, his thoughts immaculate;
His tears, pure messengers sent from his heart,
His heart as far from fraud as heaven from earth.
　　　　　　　　　　　　—*Shakspeare.*

TO be honest, as this world goes,
　Is to be one pick'd out of ten thousand.
　　　　　　　　　　　　—*Shakspeare.*

AN honest soul is like a ship at sea
　That sleeps at anchor when the ocean's calm;
But when she rages, and the wind blows high,
He cuts his way with skill and majesty.
　　　　　　　—*Beaumont and Fletcher.*

THE man who consecrates his hours
　By vig'rous effort, and an honest aim,
At once he draws the sting of life and death,
He walks with nature, and her paths are peace.
　　　　　　　　　　　　—*Young.*

Honeysuckle.

Lonicera periclymenum. NATURAL ORDER: *Caprifoliaceæ—Honeysuckle Family.*

OF the numerous varieties of this beautiful climbing shrub, the one called periclymenum, or Woodbine, is perhaps the most common. The name is derived from the German naturalist Adam Lonicer, or Lonitzer. Its delicate flowers are so laden with sweets that they attract that little opalescent jewel of a humming-bird more frequently from his hiding-place than any other blossom, over which it floats like the spirit of another and more gorgeous flower. For a number of years there have been several very desirable imported plants of this species in cultivation. The Tartarian is from Russia, having either delicate purple or white flowers; the Lonicera Japonica, a tribute from China, has yellow blossoms; and able to vie with either is our own Coral Honeysuckle—bright, brilliant and fragrant.

Bonds of Love.

WHOSE heart is at rest, he alone is a lover:
　The winters shall change not, the storms leave unshaken,
Whose love shall endure, though all blossoms be taken,
Whose love shall endure when earth's durance is over,
Whose love shall enfold, though the world have forsaken.
　　　　　　　　　　— *Edward Ellis.*

SEE the honeysuckle twine
　Round this casement;—'tis a shrine
Where the heart doth incense give,
And the pure affections live
In the mother's gentle breast
By her smiling infant press'd.
　　— *Countess of Blessington.*

BECAUSE of this, *ma belle,*
　Thou knowest how richly well
My worship till death's ending serves and sues thee.
　Thou knowest, because of this,
　To have thee means all bliss,
All anguish were to miss, to mourn, to lose thee!
　　　　　　　　　　— *Edgar Fawcett.*

STILL I'm thy captive, yet my thoughts are free:
　To be love's bondsman is true liberty.
　　　　　　　— *Marston.*

THE humming-bird, with busy wing,
　In rainbow beauty moves,
Above the trumpet-blossom floats,
　And sips the tube he loves.
　　　　　— *Caroline Gilman.*

Hop.

Humulus lupulus. NATURAL ORDER: *Urticaceæ — Nettle Family.*

UTILIZED mainly in brewing, the Hop is a coarse, though not unsightly, vine, which has been named Humulus from the Latin *humus*, the ground, because of its tendency to creeping, unless properly supported. It is cultivated for its fertile catkins, which are of great importance in the manufacture of beer and ale, as they tend to preserve and give body to those liquids. The stem is an annual, decaying every fall, and springing again from the ground in the spring. It grows to a great length, and twines around its supports with the sun, from east to west. It is cultivated in large fields in various parts of the country, and in the fall calls together large concourses of laborers who are paid a certain sum per pole to gather the hops, which is done usually amid great hilarity.

Injustice.

HE 'S poor, and that 's suspicious — he 's unknown,
   And that 's defenceless: true, we have no proof
Of guilt — but what hath he of innocence?
                                — *Byron.*

A FINE and slender net the spider weaves,
   Which little and slight animals receives;
And if she catch a summer bee or fly,
They with a piteous groan and murmur die;
But if a wasp or hornet she entrap,
They tear her cords, like Samson, and escape;
So, like a fly, the poor offender dies;
But like the wasp the rich escapes, and flies.
                                — *Denham.*

IN the corrupted currents of this world,
   Offense's gilded hand may shove by justice;
And oft 't is seen, the wicked prize itself
Buys out the law.
                                — *Shakespeare.*

JUSTICE is lame, as well as blind, amongst us;
   The laws, corrupted to their ends that make them,
Serve but for instruments of some new tyranny,
That every day starts up t' enslave us deeper.
                                — *Otway.*

UNHEARD, the injured orphans now complain;
   The widow's cries address the throne in vain.
Causes unjudged disgrace the loaded file,
And sleeping laws the king's neglect revile.
                                — *Prior.*

Horse Chestnut.

Æsculus Hippocastanum. NATURAL ORDER: *Sapindaceæ—Soapberry Family.*

UCH admired for its beautiful foliage, the Horse Chestnut is mainly cultivated for the shade it affords. Its name in our vernacular is an exact translation from the Greek of the latter half of the scientific name; and Æsculus, from the Latin *esca*, food, was originally applied to a species of oak, and probably to other like trees with edible acorns or nuts. The flowers are white, marked with pink and yellow. It is of very rapid growth, and reaches the height of thirty or forty feet in a few years. The tree is a native of the northern part of the Asiatic continent. There is a similar tree, called the Æsculus glabra (smooth), found in Ohio and other western States, generally known by the name of Buckeye. The nuts are an irregular, rounded shape, and a rich brown in tint. They are more or less injurious to all animals except deer.

Luxury.

THESE thoughts he strove to bury in expense.
   Rich meats, rich wines, and vain magnificence.
                 —*Harte.*

O LUXURY! thou curs'd by heaven's decree,
How ill-exchang'd are things like these for thee!
How do thy potions, with insidious joy,
Diffuse thy pleasures only to destroy!
     —*Goldsmith.*

IT is a shame that man, that has the seeds
   Of virtue in him, springing unto glory,
Should make his soul degenerous with sin,
And slave to luxury.
     —*Marmyon.*

FELL luxury! more perilous to youth
   Than storms or quicksands, poverty or chains.
     Hannah More.

WAR destroys men, but luxury mankind
   At once corrupts; the body and the mind.
     —*Crown.*

BUT just disease to luxury succeeds,
   And ev'ry death its own avenger breeds.
     —*Pope.*

'TIS use alone that sanctifies expense,
   And splendor borrows all her rays from sense.
     —*Pope.*

Houseleek.

Sempervivum tectorum.   NATURAL ORDER: *Crassulaceæ—Orpine Family.*

VARIOUS peculiar shapes are assumed by this and other plants of the same class. Some grow erect like the common Orpine or Live-forever, while the Houseleek assumes the shape of a rosette, each thick, pointed leaf arranged in the most symmetrical order, all being so hardy that they survive the most adverse treatment; growing in poor soil, or even on walls or housetops. Its name literally denotes, in Latin, the always alive of roofs. The Echeveria, a native of California and Mexico, is the handsomest of the family, as the leaves are covered with a fine bloom, such as one sees on the cheek of a plum or a cluster of freshly-plucked grapes. The blossoms of some are scarlet, others are yellow. Many of them are most excellent for the dry air of the sitting-room, and do not require as much attention as most other house or conservatory plants.

Vivacity.

HER merry fit she freshly 'gan to rear,
And did of joy and jollity devise,
Herself to cherish and her guest to cheer.
— *Spenser.*

THE long carousal shakes th' illumined hall,
Well speeds alike the banquet and the ball;
And the gay dance of bounding beauty's train
Links grace and harmony in happiest chain.
— *Byron.*

THE seasons all had charms for her,
She welcomed each with joy;
The charm that in her spirit liv'd
No changes could destroy.
— *Mrs. Hale.*

TEACH me half the gladness
That thy brain must know
Such harmonious madness
From my lips would flow,
The world should listen then, as I am listening now.
—*Percy Bysshe Shelly.*

164

Hoya.

Hoya carnosa. NATURAL ORDER: *Asclepiadaceæ — Milkweed Family.*

GREENHOUSES, conservatories and parlors in our latitudes gladly give shelter to these beautiful vines, which are indigenous to the warmer regions of India. It has been called Hoya in honor of T. Hoy, an English florist, and carnosa from the Latin *caro*, flesh, because of its thick, fleshy leaves. The branches are twining, and need a support to keep them in an upright position. The leaves are of an oval shape, terminating in a sharp point, and are beautiful and attractive in themselves, having the appearance of green wax; and the flowers, which bloom in dense umbels, are supremely beautiful, being waxy in texture, and in color a most delicate rose-flushed white. The old flower-stems should not be removed, as they bloom year after year. There is a variety that has a pale-yellow or whitish margin to the leaf. It does not require a rich soil. It has the habit, when well growing, of starting out its vine sometimes a yard or more before the leaves make their appearance, and care should be taken not to break these naked stems, as they are rather tardy in growing again.

Sculpture.

SO stands the statue that enchants the world,
So bending tries to veil the matchless boast,
The mingled beauties of exulting Greece.
—*Thompson.*

TO famed Apelles, when young Amnon brought
The darling idol of his captive heart,
And the pleased nymph with kind attention sat,
To have her charms recorded by his art.
—*Waller.*

AN hard and unrelenting she
As the new-crusted Niobe,
Or, what doth more of statue carry,
A nun of the Platonic quarry.
—*Cleveland.*

FANCIES and notions he pursues,
Which ne'er had being but in thought;
Each, like the Grecian artist, wooes
The image he himself has wrought.
—*Prior.*

MY share in pale Pyrene I resign,
And claim no part in all the mighty nine;
Statues with winding ivy crown'd belong
To nobler poets, for a nobler song.
—*Dryden.*

Hyacinth.

Hyacinthus orientalis.   NATURAL ORDER: *Liliaceæ—Lily Family.*

EVERY one is familiar with the Hyacinth, which is a great favorite and is very generally cultivated, both in the house and garden. The bulb is large and purple, having several lanceolate leaves which stand erect. The flower-stalk is about twice the height of the leaves, and beautified with many bell-like blossoms, varying in color in the different varieties. It is said to have received its name from Hyacinthus, a boy beloved by Apollo, and with whom he was playing quoits, when Zephyrus, who also loved the youth, becoming jealous and enraged, "blew the quoit which Apollo had cast against the head of Hyacinthus, thereby causing his death." Apollo then changed his blood into the above flower. It is a native of the Levant, but has long been cultivated in Europe and America.

Jealousy.

BEHOLD the blood which late the grass had dy'd,
Was now no blood; from which a flower full blown,
Far brighter than the Tyrian scarlet shone,
Which seem'd the same, or did resemble right
A lily, changing but the red to white.   —*Ovid.*

BUT there are storms whose lightnings never glare—
Tempests, whose thunders never cease to roll:
The storms of love when madden'd to despair—
The furious tempests of the jealous soul.
—*Isaac Clason.*

FOUL jealousy! that turnest love divine
To joyless dread, and mak'st the loving heart
With hateful thoughts to languish and to pine,
And feed itself with self-consuming smart;
Of all the passions in the mind thou vilest art.
—*Spenser.*

O JEALOUSY! thou merciless destroyer,
More cruel than the grave! what ravages
Does thy wild war make in noblest bosoms!   —*Mallet.*

AS envy pines at good possessed,
So jealousy looks forth distressed
On good that seems approaching;
And if success his steps attend,
Discerns a rival in a friend,
And hates him for encroaching.
—*Cowper.*

Hydrangea.

Hydrangea Hortensia. NATURAL ORDER: *Saxifragaceæ — Saxifrage Family.*

FROM the circumstance that much water is demanded for its sustenance, this plant has been called Hydrangea, from the Greek *udor*, water, and *aggos*, a pail. It was called Hortensia by the French botanist, Commerson, in honor of his friend, Madame Hortense Lapeaute. This species is supposed to be a native of China. Its stem is from one to three feet high, having large, oval leaves. The flowers, which continue in bloom for several months, are at first green, passing through the various hues of straw-color, sulphur, yellow, white, purple, and pink. They are said to bloom best in a rather shady location, as they become blasted or scorched by the extreme heat of the sun.

Boasting.

TAKE up no more than you by worth can claim;
   Lest soon you prove a bankrupt in your fame.
                      — *Young.*

SO spake the apostate angel, though in pain
   Vaunting aloud, but rack'd with deep despair.
                      — *Milton.*

WE rise in glory, as we sink in pride;
   Where boasting ends, there dignity begins.
                      — *Young.*

CONCEIT, more rich in matter than in words,
   Brags of his substance, not of ornament;
   They are but beggars that can count their worth.
                      — *Shakespeare.*

THIS self-conceit is a most dangerous shelf,
   Where many have made shipwreck unawares;
He who doth trust too much unto himself,
Can never fail to fall in many snares.
                      — *Earl of Sterline.*

DRAWN by conceit from reason's plan,
   How vain is that poor creature, man!
How pleas'd in ev'ry paltry elf
To prate about that thing, himself.
                      — *Churchill.*

WHAT art thou? Have not I
   An arm as big as thine? a heart as big?
Thy words, I grant, are bigger; for I wear not
My dagger in my mouth.   — *Shakespeare.*

Hyssop.

Hyssopus officinalis.   NATURAL ORDER: *Labiatæ—Mint Family.*

DURING the Jewish dispensation the Israelites used this plant in their purifications (Exodus xii, 22). It is found in abundance on the hills of Palestine near Jerusalem. It is about two feet high, with a bushy stalk, an aromatic smell, and a pungent taste. The common species is a native of Europe. It is a handsome plant, having bright blue flowers and delicate leaves. It is usually cultivated for its medicinal properties. The name of this plant is derived from the Hebrew *ezob*, through the Greek *ussopos*.

Purification.

BLEST are the pure! Would'st thou be blest?
  He'll cleanse thy spotted soul. Would'st thou find rest?
Around thy toils and cares He'll breathe a calm,
And to thy wounded spirit lay a balm:
From fear draw love, and teach thee where to seek
Lost strength and grandeur with the bowed and meek.
—*Dana.*

CAST my heart's gold into the furnace flame,
  And if it comes not thence refined and pure,
I'll be a bankrupt to thy hope, and heaven
Shall shut its gates on me.
—*Mrs. Sigourney.*

SHE grew a sweet and sinless child.
  In sun and shadow, calm and strife—
A rainbow on the dark of life,
From love's own radiant heaven down smiled.
—*Massey.*

FROM purity of thought all pleasure springs,
  And from an humble spirit all our peace.
—*Young.*

LIKE bright metal on a sullen ground,
  My reformation, glittering o'er my fault,
Shall show more goodly, and attract more eyes,
Than that which hath no foil to set it off.
—*Shakespeare.*

WASH me with thy tears! draw nigh me,
  That their salt may purify me!
Thou remit my sins, who knowest
All the sinning, to the lowest.
—*From the Greek strans, by E. B. Browning.*

YET time serves, wherein you may redeem
  Your banished honors, and restore yourselves
Into the good thoughts of the world again. —*Shakespeare.*

Ice-Plant.

Mesembryanthemum crystallinum. NATURAL ORDER: *Mesembryaceæ—Ice-Plant Family.*

NOT a little curious and attractive, this plant has its foliage entirely covered with protuberances about the size of grains of barley, that appear like the most transparent ice, whence it is called crystallinum; the other part of its scientific name, from the Greek, denotes Midday Flower. The branches are trailing, from ten to twelve inches in length, and produce white flowers during the whole summer. It is from Greece. There have been some new varieties introduced from the Cape of Good Hope, that are adapted for conservatory culture, the flowers of which are yellow, purple, purple and pink, and purple and white combined. They require very little moisture in winter, once or twice a month being sufficient, but the quantity should be increased to a generous allowance when the blossoms begin to appear. The different varieties, of which there are several hundred, have quite a diversity of foliage.

Formality.

OH, she is colder than the mountain's snow;
To such a subtle purity she's wrought,
She's pray'd and fasted to a walking thought.
—*Crown.*

NO dews of love can warm the iceberg heart,
Or melt the Alpine snows upon her breast;
E'en flowers cease to spread their leaves apart,
If by her chilling foot they're prest.

The sculptur'd beauty of her marble face
Is chill and cold as e'er was marble stone;
Those veinlets blue, that o'er her temples trace,
Are like a springlet from a glacier thrown.
—*C. H. T.*

THOSE glances work on me like the weak shine
The frosty sun throws on the Appenine,
When the hills' active coldness doth go near
To freeze the glimmering taper to his sphere.
—*Beaumont.*

CANST thou no kindly ray impart,
Thou strangely beauteous one?
Fairer than fairest work of art,
Yet cold as sculptured stone!
—*Ordway.*

Indian Mallow.

Abutilon Avicennæ.   NATURAL ORDER: *Malvaceæ — Mallow Family.*

RESIDENTS by natural selection of the warmer latitudes, the Mallows bear the colder climates with an easy adaptability to circumstances, and favor us with their flowers without stint. The plant, as the name indicates, is a native of the East and West Indies, growing about the height of the hollyhock, having broad, velvety leaves, and producing flowers about an inch across, the color of which is yellow. Another species of Abutilon, adapted only to house or conservatory growth, is a shrub from Brazil, growing several feet in height, with broad, palmate leaves, and handsome, bell-shaped flowers of yellow, curiously veined with a dark red. Planted in the ground in the greenhouse, the trunk becomes several inches in thickness, but can accommodate itself to limited quarters in pot culture. To bloom well it must have the sun. The origin of the name Abutilon is unknown; Avicenna was a celebrated Arabian physician and philosopher of the middle ages.

Estimation.

SHE attracts me daily with her gentle virtues,
So soft, and beautiful, and heavenly.
— *James A. Hillhouse.*

FRIENDSHIP is no plant of hasty growth,
Tho' planted in esteem's deep-fixed soil,
The gradual culture of kind intercourse
Must bring it to perfection. — *Joanna Baillie.*

HOW much to be priz'd and esteem'd is a friend,
On whom we can always with safety depend!
Our joys, when extended, will always increase,
And griefs, when divided, are hush'd into peace.
— *Mrs. Margaret Smith.*

THOU gav'st me that the poor do give the poor,
Kind words and holy wishes, and true tears;
The loved, the near of kin, could do no more,
Who changed not with the gloom of varying years,
But clung the closer when I stood forlorn,
And blunted slander's dart with their indignant scorn.
Mrs. Norton.

Ipomœa.

Quamoclit vulgaris.   NATURAL ORDER: *Convolvulaceæ — Convolvulus Family.*

QUAMOCLIT (an aboriginal Mexican name) is a vine of delicate and airy appearance, its leaves being small and feather-like, and the stem slender, growing to about eight or ten feet in length. The flowers are small but beautifully brilliant, and very abundant. One or two new varieties have appeared, introducing both white and pink, which, combined with the crimson or scarlet, produce a pretty effect when trained upon a trellis or other support. The seeds are somewhat difficult of germination, and should be soaked in warm water for a short time before planting, otherwise they are apt to decay before sprouting. This vine passes variously under the names Ipomœa (from the Greek, and signifying, like the ips, a vine worm), Quamoclit, and Cypress Vine, and is nearly related to the morning glories and others passing under the general name of Convolvulus.

Attachment.

PUT golden padlocks on truth's lips, be callous as ye will,
From soul to soul, o'er all the world leaps one electric thrill.
—*Lowell.*

OH! there is one affection which no stain
Of earth can ever darken; when two find,
The softer and the manlier, that a chain
Of kindred taste has fastened mind to mind:

'Tis an attraction from all sense refined;
The good can only know it; 'tis not blind,
As love is unto baseness; its desire
Is but with hands entwin'd to lift our being higher.
—*Percival.*

IN many ways does the full heart reveal
The presence of the love it would conceal.
—*Coleridge.*

YEA! but human love to me
Is so near divine,
That my heart clings yearningly
Even to life like mine.

Love is sweeter far than rest—
That alone I know—
And the soul that loves me best
Will not let me go.
—*Mary B. Dodge.*

Ipomopsis.

Gilia coronopifolia. NATURAL ORDER: *Polemoniaceæ — Polemonium Family.*

BECAUSE of its finely pinnatifid foliage, nearly resembling the cypress vine, this plant used to be, and perhaps is still, in some localities, called Standing Cypress; but it belongs to another class of plants. It is a handsome plant, though not blooming until the second year. Seeds should be sown every spring for the next year's blooming, as should be done with all biennials, in order to have them every summer. The first year, the Ipomopsis rests like a tuft of finely-cut leaves close to the ground, and should be removed and kept in sand free from moisture and hard frost, or, if left in the ground, the soil must be well drained, as they are liable to decay with much dampness. The second year, the stalk rises and branches, covering itself with thread-like foliage, while its tubular flowers of scarlet, yellow, or rose, surround its stems for a foot or more.

Suspense.

HE has jumped the brook, he has climbed the knowe,
   There 's never a faster foot, I know,
   But still he seems to tarry. —*Sidney Dobell.*

BE not long, for in the tedious minutes,
   Exquisite interval, I 'm on the rack;
For sure the greatest evil man can know,
Bears no proportion to this dread suspense.
       Frowde.

OH! how impatience gains upon my soul
   When the long-promis'd hour of joy draws near;
How slow the tardy moments seem to roll,
What specters rise of inconsistent fear.
      —*Mrs. Tighe.*

O THAT man might know
   The end of this day's business, ere it come!
But it sufficeth that the day will end,
And then the end is known. —*Shakespeare.*

SO tedious is this day,
   As is the night before some festival
To an impatient child that hath new robes,
And may not wear them. —*Shakespeare.*

AND there are hearts that watch and wait
   For those who toil upon the shore;
Their welcome footstep at the gate
Is heard — ah! nevermore! —*George Cooper.*

Iris.

Iris sambucina. NATURAL ORDER: *Iridaceæ—Iris Family.*

PLANTS of this order are chiefly natives of the Cape of Good Hope; but the above species, sambucina (elder-scented), and some others, are natives of the southern part of Europe, and are quite common in our own gardens. There are three other varieties of the Iris which are very pretty. The first is a tall plant from the Levant, with sulphur-yellow flowers; the second is from China, being a small plant with striped flowers; and the Dwarf Iris, which is often used for the borderings of garden walks, as it blooms early in spring. Orris root is manufactured from the root of the Iris florentina, and has a fragrance resembling violets. It is used in various dentrifices, and to perfume the breath.

A Messenger.

EACH mind is press'd, and open every ear,
 To hear new tidings, though they no way joy us.
   — *Fairfax.*

THE rabble gather round the man of news,
 And listen with their mouths wide open: some
Tell, some hear, some judge of news, some make it,
And he that lies most loud is most believed.
   — *Dryden.*

LET me hear from thee by letters
 Of thy success in love; and what news else
Betideth here, in absence of thy friend.
   — *Shakspeare.*

HE whistles as he goes, light-hearted wretch,
 Cold and yet cheerful; messenger of grief
Perhaps to thousands, and of joy to some;
To him indifferent whether grief or joy.
   — *Cowper.*

YET the first bringer of unwelcome news
 Hath but a losing office; and his tongue
Sounds ever after as a sullen bell,
Remember'd knolling a departing friend.
   — *Shakspeare.*

IRIS there, with humid bow,
 Waters the odorous banks that blow
Flowers of more mingled hue
Than her purpled scarf can show.
   — *Milton.*

GIVE to a gracious message
 An host of tongues; but let ill tidings tell
Themselves, when they be felt.   — *Shakspeare.*

173

Ivy.

Hedera helix. NATURAL ORDER: *Araliaceæ—Ginseng Family.*

IVY is an evergreen vine, native of Great Britain, and attains the height of forty or fifty feet, sustaining itself by tufts of fibers, which insert themselves into the crevices of the walls that support it. Hedera is its old Latin name, and helix in Greek and Latin signifies twisted. After having grown to its utmost height, its climbing character ceases, "the leaf changes from a palmate to a lengthened oval shape; it then forms a bush two or three feet high, surmounted by an abundance of branches of interesting greenish flowers" that bloom in October. They frequently attain a great age. One is mentioned by De Candolle as being four hundred and thirty-three years old, which measured six feet in circumference at the base, covering a surface of over seventy square yards with its handsome foliage. It was used among the Greeks to decorate their heroes and poets, and also as a crown to Bacchus, although he is represented at other times crowned with grape leaves as the god of wine.

Lasting Friendship.

SHE clung to him with woman's love,
  Like ivy to the oak.
While on his head, with crushing force,
  Earth's chilling tempest broke.

FAST he stealeth on, though he wears no wings,
  And a staunch old heart has he!
How closely he twineth, how tight he clings
  To his friend, the huge oak tree!
And slily he traileth along the ground,
And his leaves he gently waves,
And he joyously twines and hugs around
  The rich mould of dead men's graves,
Creeping where no life is seen,
A rare old plant is the ivy green.
—*Charles Dickens.*

I HAD a friend that lov'd me —
  I was his soul; he liv'd not but in me;
We were so close within each other's breast
The rivets were not found that join'd us first.
—*Dryden.*

Jasmine--White.

Jasminum officinale.   NATURAL ORDER: *Jasminaceæ—Jasmine Family.*

WHITE JASMINE is a splendid shrub, climbing on supports to a height of fifteen or twenty feet, and is much used in Europe for the covering of arbors and trellises. It is not sufficiently hardy to endure the winters of our Northern States without the protection of a wall or other building to defend it from the fierce breath of the ungenial north wind. Its flowers are beautiful and fragrant, and their praises have been beautifully sung by Lord Morpeth (afterward earl of Carlisle), who says:

> "I ask not, while I near thee dwell,
> Arabia's spice or Syria's rose;
> Thy bright festoons more freshly smell,
> Thy virgin white more freshly glows."

There is in the tropical parts of the United States a fine Jasmine with beautiful yellow blossoms, that is heavily laden with delightful perfume. It is now cultivated in all warm climes, but was unknown in Europe until 1560, when it was introduced by the Spaniards from the East.

Amiability.

> THE twining jessamine and blushing rose
> With lavish grace their morning scents disclose.
> —*Prior.*

AND oft when from that scorching shore,
  In after years those odors came,
He pictured his green cottage door,
  The shady porch and window frame,

Far, far away across the foam:
  The very jasmine-flower that crept
Round the thatched roof about his home
  Where she he loved then safely slept.
    —*Miller.*

HOW lovelily the jasmine flower
  Blooms far from man's observing eyes;
And having lived its little hour,
  There withers,—there sequester'd dies!

Though faded, yet 'tis not forgot;
  A rich perfume, time cannot sever,
Lingers in that unfriended spot,
  And decks the jasmine's grave forever.
    —*Ryan.*

Juniper.

Juniper communis. NATURAL ORDER: *Coniferæ — Pine Family.*

JUNIPER belongs to an order which is among the most useful to mankind, not only for the lumber which they yield, but also for the medicinal properties which lie in their resinous juices. The Juniper inhabits hills, dry woods and groves, and is about eight feet high. The berries do not ripen until the second year after the blossom; they are sometimes used in medicine. The Juniper was formerly dedicated to Megæra, Tisiphone and Alecto, the three daughters of Nox and Acheron, who ministered the vengeance of the gods. They were called by the Greeks, Erinnyes and Eumenides; and by the Romans, Ferriæ and Diræ.

Asylum.

THE night, at least, with me forget your care;
Chestnuts, and curds, and cream, shall be your fare.
— *Dryden.*

HE knocked, was welcomed in, none asked his name,
Nor whither he was bound, nor whence he came;
But he was beckoned to the stranger's seat,
Right side the chimney fire of blazing peat
— *Campbell.*

THEREIN he them full fair did entertain,
Not with such forged shows as fitter been
For courting fools, that courtesies would faine,
But with entire affection and appearance plain.
— *Spenser.*

HE thought them folks that lost their way,
And ask'd them civilly to stay. — *Prior.*

HIS house was known to all the vagrant train,
He chid their wanderings but reliev'd their pain;
The long-remembered beggar was his guest,
Whose beard descending swept his aged breast,
The ruined spendthrift, now no longer proud,

Claimed kindred there and had his claim allowed;
The broken soldier, kindly bade to stay,
Sate by his fire and talked the night away;
Wept o'er his wounds, or tales of sorrow done,
Shoulder'd his crutch and show'd how fields were won.
— *Goldsmith.*

THE man their hearty welcome first express'd,
A common settle drew for either guest,
Inviting each his weary limbs to rest.
— *Dryden.*

Justicia.

Justicia carnea.   NATURAL ORDER: *Acanthaceæ—Acanthus Family.*

ALL the Justicias are half-shrubby plants from the tropical portions of the world, some of which are kept in the hot-house, and others, though few, in the greenhouse. The Justicia carnea has flowers of a flesh-colored tint, with many in bloom at one time, which appear successively for a long season. Justicia coccinea has scarlet blossoms which make their appearance during mid-winter, continuing until spring. There are some four or five other varieties, and all are fine plants. To make them fine, healthy specimens, they require a strong light, or to be kept near the glass, in moderately large pots, well drained.

Female Loveliness.

HER form was fresher than the morning rose
  When the dew wets its leaves; unstained and pure
As is the lily, or the mountain snow.   —*Thompson.*

NO wonder that cheek, in its beauty transcendant,
  Excelleth the beauty of others by far;
No wonder that eye is so rich and resplendent,
  For your heart is a rose, and your soul is a star.
    —*Mrs. Osgood.*

THOU art beautiful, young lady,—
  But I need not tell you this,
For few have borne, unconsciously,
  The spell of loveliness.   —*Whittier.*

THE fairness of her face no tongue can tell,
  For she the daughters of all woman race,
And angels eke in beautie doth excel.   —*Spenser.*

WHAT'S female beauty, but an air divine,
  Through which the mind's all gentle graces
    shine?
They, like the sun, irradiate all between;
The body charms, because the soul is seen.
    —*Young.*

WHEN I approach
  Her loveliness, so absolute she seems
And in herself complete, so well to know
Her own, that what she wills to do or say
Seems wisest, virtuousest, discreetest, best.
    —*Milton.*

A LAVISH planet reign'd when she was born,
  And made her of such kindred mould to heav'n,
She seems more heav'n's than ours.   —*Lee.*

Kennedya.

Kennedya monophylla. NATURAL ORDER: *Leguminosæ — Pulse Family.*

KENNEDYA, a native of New South Wales, is found in the conservatory or greenhouse, occupying a prominent position among the beautiful climbers, some of the species, however, being as yet quite rare. The commonest variety has either blue or crimson flowers. There are others with scarlet, purple, and one with nearly black, flowers. They grow readily from seed, which should be soaked in warm water previous to planting, and can be grown in pots, or placed in the ground when the weather is warm and settled. The pots should be well drained.

Mental Beauty.

ALL higher knowledge in her presence falls
Degraded, wisdom in discourse with her
Loses discountnanced, and like folly shows.
— *Milton.*

MARK her majestic fabric! she's a temple
Sacred by birth, and built by hands divine;
Her soul 's the deity that lodges there;
Nor is the pile unworthy of the god. — *Dryden.*

WHAT'S the brow,
Or the eye's luster, or the step of air,
Or color, but the beautiful links that chain
The mind from its rare elements. — *Willis.*

THINK of her worth, and think that God did mean
This worthy mind should worthy things embrace;
Blot not her beauties with thy thoughts unclean,
Nor her dishonor with thy passion base. — *Sir J. Davies.*

MIND, mind alone, (bear witness earth and heaven!)
The living fountains in itself contains
Of beauteous and sublime; here, hand in hand,
Sit paramount the graces; here enthron'd,
Celestial Venus, with divinest airs,
Invites the soul to never-fading joy.
— *Akenside.*

A MIND of broad and vigorous scope,
A penetration quick and keen,
An insight into things unseen,
A liberal dower of faith and hope.
— *Kate J. Hill.*

Lady's Slipper.

Cypripedium pubescens.   NATURAL ORDER: *Orchidaceæ — Orchis Family.*

MOST of these plants delight in damp, marshy ground, reveling beside brooks, bending over springs, hiding in the borders of woods, and sporting on the boundless prairie; dancing to the music of the wind or the rippling water with as much grace and ease as Terpsichore herself. Some of the blossoms of the species found in the western woods are very large, especially the above variety, which will hold at least two tablespoonfuls of fluid, and is of a bright yellow in color, with dark spots within the aperture. The shape is similar to the blossoms of the Calceolarias of the greenhouse — that is, like a pouch or bag.

Fickleness.

THEY know how fickle common lovers are,
   Their oaths and vows are cautiously believed,
For few there are but have been once deceived.
                                        — *Dryden.*

LIKE conquering tyrants you our breasts invade,
   Where you are pleased to ravage for a while;
But soon you find new conquests out, and leave
The ravag'd province ruinate and bare.
                                        — *Otway.*

INCONSTANT as the passing wind,
   As winter's dreary frost unkind;
To fix her, 'twere a task as vain
To count the April drops of rain.
                                        — *Smollett.*

REPROVE me not that still I change
   With every changing hour,
For glorious nature gives me leave
   In wave, and cloud, and flower.

You soft, light cloud, at morning hour,
   Looked dark and full of tears;
At noon it seemed a rosy flower —
   Now gorgeous gold appears.

So yield I to the deepening light
   That dawns around my way;
Because you linger with the night
   Shall I my noon delay.
                                        — *Frances S. Osgood.*

WE vary from ourselves each day in mind,
   Nor know we in ourselves, ourselves to find.   — *Heath.*

Lake-flower.

Limnanthemum lacunosa. NATURAL ORDER: *Gentianaceæ — Gentian Family.*

THIS is a curious water plant, usually found in stagnant ponds or quiet lakes, or even in rivers where the water has set back in some hollow on its shore, and where the current fails to stir its sleepy stillness. The leaves float on the surface, the stems always accommodating their length to the depth of the water. The flowers are small and white, from a half to three-quarters of an inch broad, and arranged in the form of an umbel, appearing one at a time on the top of the water and expanding. It is sometimes called Floating Heart, and is found most frequently in the States bordering on the Atlantic. Its botanical name is from the Greek *limne*, a lake or pool, and *anthemon*, a flower; the Latin *lacunosa* added, merely reduplicates the idea of pond or marsh. There are at present but nine species enumerated.

Retirement.

HOW much they err, who, to their interest blind,
   Slight the calm peace which from retirement flows!
And while they think their fleeting joys to bind,
Banish the tranquil bliss which heav'n for man design'd.
— *Mrs. Tighe.*

DEAR solitary groves where peace does dwell!
   Sweet harbors of pure love and innocence!
How willingly could I forever stray
Beneath the shade of your embracing greens,
List'ning to the harmony of warbling birds,
Tun'd with the gentle murmur of the streams!
Upon whose banks, in various livery,
The fragrant offspring of the early year,
Their heads, like graceful swans, bent proudly down,
See their own beauties in the crystal flood.
— *Rochester.*

THE shadowy desert, unfrequented woods,
   I better brook than flourishing, peopled towns:
There I can sit alone, unseen of any,
And to the nightingale's complaining notes
Tune my distresses, and record my woes.
— *Shakspeare.*

OH! by thy side,
   Far from the tumult and the throng of men,
And the vain cares that vex poor human life,
'Twere happiness to dwell alone with thee,
And the wide, solemn grandeur of the scene.
— *Mrs. Ellet.*

Lantana.

Lantana Mexicana.   NATURAL ORDER: *Verbenaceæ — Vervain Family.*

It is to the tropics that we are indebted for this beautiful addition to our flora. The plants are shrubby, and can be cultivated in the hothouse or conservatory, or may be placed in the garden during summer. It grows very rapidly in the ground, and many adopt the plan of placing it in a medium-sized pot, and putting the pot along with the plant in the ground, as that plan curtails the roots and prevents the plant from growing too straggling, and thereby rewarding the cultivator with more flowers. The blossoms have the peculiarity of coming out one color, and passing through different shades to another color; a quality which always gives a pleasing aspect to the plant. They are very susceptible to frost.

Rigor.

FULL many a stoic eye and aspect stern
Mask hearts where grief hath little left to learn.
— *Byron.*

WHY stand'st thou idle here? lend me thy sword!
Many a nobleman is stark and still
Under the hoofs of vaunting enemies,
Whose deaths are unrevenged.
— *Shakespeare.*

HIS awful presence did the crowd surprise,
Nor durst the rash spectator meet his eyes;
Eyes that confess'd him born for kingly sway,
So fierce they flashed intolerable day.
— *Dryden.*

MEN who their duties know,
But know their rights, and, knowing, dare maintain them.
— *Sir W. Jones.*

His eye
Had that compelling dignity,
His mien that bearing, haught and high,
Which common spirits fear.
— *Scott.*

MUST not earth be rent
Before her gems are found?
— *Mrs. Hemans.*

THIS too much lenity
And harmful pity must be laid aside.
To whom do lions cast their gentle looks?
Not to the beast that would usurp their den;
Whose hand is that the forest bear would lick?
Not his that spoils her young before her face.
— *Shakespeare.*

Larkspur.

Delphinium grandiflorum.   NATURAL ORDER: *Ranunculaceæ — Crowfoot Family.*

SIBERIA is the native country of two of the prettiest species of these plants, and they are consequently very hardy. All the varieties were much neglected a few years ago, but recently a great deal of care has been taken with the double ones, some of the shades of blue being very choice. Although the flowers bloom in spikes, which render them unsuitable to the modern style of bouquet, florists have overcome that difficulty by detaching each blossom, giving it an artificial stem of broom-straw, or something similar, secured by a bit of thread or wire, and arranging them as desirable. The perennial varieties are superior in every way to the annual ones. It is called Delphinium from a fancied resemblance of the flower in shape to the dolphin, and grandiflorum because of its large flowers.

Levity.

LAUGH not too much; the witty man laughs least:
  For wit is news only to ignorance.
Less at thine own things laugh; lest in the jest
  Thy person share, and the conceit advance.
                — *George Herbert.*

METHOUGHT it was the sound
  Of riot and ill-managed merriment,
Such as the jocund flute and gamesome pipe
Stirs up among the loose, unletter'd hinds.
          — *Milton.*

COME, sisters, cheer we up his sprights,
  And show the best of our delights:
We'll charm the air to give a sound,
While you perform your antic round.
          — *Shakespeare.*

CARE to our coffin adds a nail, no doubt;
  And every grin, so merry, draws one out.
          — *Dr. Walcot.*

FILL the bowl with rosy wine,
  Around our temples roses twine,
And let us cheerfully a while,
Like the wine and roses, smile.
Crowned with roses, we contemn
Gyges' wealthy diadem.

Today is ours; what do we fear?
Today is ours; we have it here;
Let's treat it kindly, that it may
Wish at least with us to stay.
Let's banish business, banish sorrow;
To the gods belongs tomorrow.
          — *Cowley.*

Laurel.

Laurens nobilis. NATURAL ORDER: *Lauraceæ — Laurel Family.*

LAUREL is a shrub which grows in height from four to six feet, having a liberal supply of beautiful evergreen foliage, which was much used by the ancients in decorating the brows of their heroes. Chaplets of Laurel were given as a reward to orators, philosophers and poets. Æsculapius, the god of physic, wears a crown of laurel, because of its power in the cure of diseases. Daphne is said to have been changed into a laurel when she fled from the embrace of Apollo, whence its botanical name; and laureola, laurus (laurel), seem allied to the Latin *laus*, praise. The Laurel tree is of a very hot, acrid nature. It is always flourishing, never old, and conduces, according to the ancients, to divination and poetic raptures. The leaves, when put under the pillow, are said to produce true dreams.

Glory.

GLORIES, like glow-worms, afar off shine bright;
But look'd too near, have neither heat or light.
—*Webster.*

AND should the aspiring man, that makes his gain
Of other's hurts, not hurt himself for gain?
Not, when he stabs another for a purse,
Prick his own bosom for a dearer price,
And wound his heart to laurel-crown his head.
—*Bird.*

ALAS for human greatness! and alas
For glory's splendor on a mortal brow!
The stateliest realms must down to ruin pass,
And mightiest monarchs to a mightier bow;
Alas! will death ne'er spare a gallant foe?
—*C. W. Everett.*

GLORY, like time, progression does require;
When it does cease t' advance, it does expire.
—*Lord Orrery.*

GLORY is like a circle in the water,
Which never ceaseth to enlarge itself,
Till, by broad spreading, it disperse to nought.
—*Shakespeare.*

WHAT is glory? What is fame?
The echo of a long-lost name;
A breath, an idle hour's brief talk.
—*Motherwell.*

FOR this world's glory
Is figur'd in the moon; they both wax dull,
And suffer their eclipses in the full. —*Alcyn.*

Laurestine.

Viburnum Tinus.   NATURAL ORDER: *Caprifoliaceæ—Honeysuckle Family.*

VIBURNUM or Laurestine is a fine, handsome, evergreen shrub, a native of Europe, and in our Northern States is considered as more adapted for the house than the lawn, where it can be placed, in the Southern States. The flowers bloom in small clusters, and are scarcely a pure white, having a slight tinge of red; they appear in early spring. There is a new, sweet-scented variety from China, but it is said to bloom less freely. Some few others are also desirable, and no doubt in a few years they will become thoroughly hardy, as they lack but little of the required amount of vigor.

I Die if Neglected.

MY heart seems breaking, Philip, as I linger all alone,
    And there comes no sound of comfort save the ocean's restless moan;
I stretch my arms to heaven, and pray for your return,
But the hope that dies, and the love that lives, can only pant and yearn.
—*Christian Reid.*

THERE, as she sought repose, her sorrowing heart
  Recall'd her absent love with bitter sighs;
Regret had deeply fix'd the poison'd dart,
Which ever rankling in her bosom lies:
In vain she seeks to close her weary eyes,
Those eyes still swim incessantly in tears;
Hope in her cheerless bosom fading dies,
Distracted by a thousand cruel fears,
While banish'd from his love forever she appears.
—*Mrs. Tighe.*

A BOAT at midnight sent alone
  To drift upon the moonless sea,
A lute whose leading chord is gone,
A wounded bird that hath but one
Imperfect wing to soar upon,
Are like what I am without thee.
Moore.

FAIR tree of winter! fresh and flowering,
  When all around is dead and dry;
Whose ruby buds, though storms are lowering,
  Spread their white blossoms to the sky.
Green are thy leaves, more purely green
  Through every changing period seen;
And when the gaudy months are past,
Thy loveliest season is the last.   —*Montgomery.*

Lavender.

Lavandula spica. NATURAL ORDER: *Labiatæ — Mint Family.*

EUROPE produces immense fields of Lavender, grown for the sake of the flowers, from which is obtained the perfume that is sold by all druggists and perfumers. It has a very pleasant, agreeable odor. The Latin word from which it is derived is *lavare*, to bathe, and brings to mind the marble baths of the early Greeks and Romans, when the most exquisite of sculpture, the most beautiful productions of art and nature, were gathered together for their adornment, and flowers and spices were rifled of their sweets to add to the sumptuousness and luxuriousness of their ablutions. It is a perennial of easy culture, about eighteen inches high, delightfully aromatic, and bears purple flowers. The oil possesses tonic and stimulative properties, and is used in medicine.

Confession.

AND lavender, whose spikes of azure bloom
Shall be erewhile in arid bundles bound,
To lurk amidst her labors of the loom,
And crown her kerchiefs clean with mickle rare perfume.
—*Shenstone.*

SWEET lavender! I love thy flower
  Of meek and modest blue,
Which meets the morn and evening hour,
  The storm, the sunshine, and the shower,
    And changeth not its hue.

Thou art not like the fickle train
  Our adverse fates estrange;
Who in the day of grief and pain
Are found deceitful, light and vain,
    For thou dost never change.

But thou art emblem of the friend,
  Who, whatsoe'er our lot,
The balm of faithful love will lend,
And, true and constant to the end,
  May die, but alter not. —*Strickland.*

I BLUSH to think what I have said —
But fate has wrested the confession from me;
Go on, and prosper in the paths of honor;
Thy virtue will excuse my passion for thee,
And make the gods propitious to our love.
—*Addison.*

Lemon Blossom.

Citrus limonum.   NATURAL ORDER: *Aurantieae—Orange Family.*

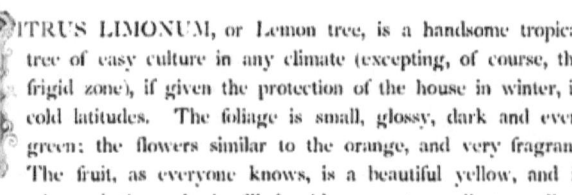

ITRUS LIMONUM, or Lemon tree, is a handsome tropical tree of easy culture in any climate (excepting, of course, the frigid zone), if given the protection of the house in winter, in cold latitudes. The foliage is small, glossy, dark and evergreen; the flowers similar to the orange, and very fragrant. The fruit, as everyone knows, is a beautiful yellow, and is very aromatic, and the pulp is filled with a most excellent, cooling, acid juice. When loaded with fruit, such as is to be seen in tropical climates, it presents a magnificent appearance. Mrs. Loudon says, "the golden apples of the heathen are supposed to belong to this family."

Discretion.

PRUDENCE protects and guides us; wit betrays;
  A splendid source of ill ten thousand ways.
     —*Dryden.*

BEAR me, Pomona, to thy citron groves,
  To where the lemon and the piercing lime,
With the deep orange glowing thro' the green,
Their lighter glories blend.   —*Thompson.*

CONSULT your means, avoid the tempter's wiles,
  Shun grinning hosts of unreceipted files,
Let heaven-ey'd prudence battle with desire,
And win the victory, though it be through fire.
     —*James T. Fields.*

BUT now, so wise and wary was the knight,
  By trial of his former harms and cares,
That he decry'd, and shunned still his sight.
The fish that once was caught, new bait will hardly bite.
     —*Spenser.*

THUS I shall be fairer to your untried thought,
  Than if all my living into yours were wrought.
Hearts' dreams are the sweetest in a lonely nest;
Leave me while you love me—this is surely best!
   —*Howard Glyndon.*

HE knows the compass, sail and oar,
  Or never launches from the shore;
Before he builds, computes the cost,
And in no proud pursuit is lost.
     Gay.

NONE pities him that's in the snare,
  And, warn'd before, would not beware.
     —*Herrick.*

Lettuce.

Lactuca sativa. NATURAL ORDER: *Compositæ — Aster Family.*

ONE of the most common of vegetables, Lettuce is also among the first to appear on the table in spring, when man as well as beast hungers for the green things of the field. Of the many kinds, each puts forward some especial claim to our attention, from the loose, curled leaves of the one, to the close, compact heads of the other; but crisp and tender they must be, to form the appetizing salads of which they are the chief ingredient. They are of very ancient cultivation, as they are mentioned by several Latin authors, and the selling of lettuce formed the occupation of people in those days as now in our own. Lettuce dealers were called Lactucarius, though they probably sold other vegetables. After the season is over, the plants are allowed to go to seed. The stalk is about two feet high, filled with a milky juice; and the flowers are a pale yellow, numerous, but rather small in size.

Cold Hearted.

I HAVE not from your eyes that gentleness
And show of love, as I was wont to have.
—*Shakespeare.*

YOUR coldness I heed not, your frown I defy;
Your affection I need not — the time has gone by,
When a blush or a smile on that cheek could beguile
My soul from its safety, with witchery's smile.
—*Mrs. Osgood.*

HIS heart was all on honor bent,
He could not stoop to love;
No lady in the land had power
His frozen heart to move.
—*Anonymous.*

NOT the basilisk
More deadly to the sight, than is to me
The cool, ingenious eye of frozen kindness.
—*Gay.*

YOUR breast is heaped like mountain snows,
Your cheek is like a blushing rose,
Your eyes are black as ripened sloes,
Like diamonds do they glitter.

I do not flatter like a fool —
The diamond is a cutting tool,
The rose is thorny, snow is cool,
And sloes are very bitter.

Lilac.

Syringa Persica.   NATURAL ORDER: *Oleaceæ—Olive Family.*

PERSIAN LILAC varies from the common varieties, both in size and foliage, which is sometimes entire, and again cleft. The flowers are white or purplish, and bloom in spikes. Our common Lilac is a native of Hungary, and is very popular as an early visitor in spring, when it gladdens the bower with its odor and blossoms. The Latin name Syringa, has its origin in the Greek tongue, where we find *suriggias* to be the name of any kind of reed or cane that can be hollowed out to form a pipe or rustic flute. The Greek and Latin shepherds were very fond of this humble instrument, upon which they used to improvise their simple tunes as they wandered with their flocks from one fragrant field to another, or played for each other's entertainment as they rested surrounded by their sleeping herds at night. The branches of the Lilac have a center filled with pith, which can be easily removed by running a stout wire or other substance through them.

Awakening Love.

LOVE never fails to master what he finds,
But works a different way in different minds:
The fool enlightens, and the wise he blinds.
— *Dryden.*

O MAID! with eyes whose azure
Holds a happy, joyous gleam,
What hath charmed thy listless leisure —
Made thy life a fairy dream?

Love hath found me sitting lonely,
Whispered soft a charmèd word;
Evermore my heart beats only
To the music of that word.
— *G. Hamlin.*

Love is a god,
Strong, free, unbounded; and, as some define,
Fears nothing, pitieth none: such love is mine.
— *Mason.*

I HAD so fixed my heart upon her,
That whatsoe'er I framed a scheme of life
For time to come, she was my only joy.

With which I used to sweeten future cares:
I fancied pleasures, none but one who loves
And doats as I did can imagine like them.
— *Otway.*

Lily.

Lilium candidum.   NATURAL ORDER: *Liliaceæ — Lily Family.*

GREEK *leirion*, interpreted to signify wanting in color, or pale, is the origin of the Latin *lilium*, as that is of the English lily. The Lilies are bulbous plants, having long, tapering leaves, and flowers of most exquisite beauty. They are cultivated without much labor. The above is pure white. The most beautiful of all lilies are those from China and Japan, being very rich in color, and larger in size than our native plants. The Lilium candidum is a native of the Levant. The Lily seems to vie with the daisy for its share of musical honors, for many is the lyre that has been tuned to its praises. Mrs. Tighe, in remarking that there is no beauty in the bulb, says:

> "Yet in that bulb, those sapless scales,
> The lily wraps her silver vest —
> Till vernal suns and vernal gales
> Shall kiss once more her fragrant breast."

Purity.

SPRING has no blossom fairer than thy form;
Winter no snow-wreath purer than thy mind;
The dewdrop trembling to the morning beam
Is like thy smile — pure, transient, heaven-refin'd.
— *Mrs. Lydia Jane Pierson.*

THERE is a pale and modest flower
In garb of green array'd,
That decks the rustic maiden's bower,
And blossoms in the glade;
Though other flowers around me bloom,
In gaudy splendor drest,
Filling the air with rich perfume,
I love the lily best.
— *Anonymous.*

I HAD found out a sweet, green spot
Where a lily was blooming fair;
The din of the city disturbed it not;
But the spirit that shades the quiet cot
With its wings of love was there.
— *James G. Percival.*

Lily of the Valley.

Convallaria majalis.   NATURAL ORDER: *Liliaceæ—Lily Family.*

WHEN wandering through the woods and sweetly-sleeping vales, in early May, we find this beautiful plant peering up its head, crowned with umbels of white, odoriferous, and modest flowers. It should be a frequent denizen of our gardens, for its own modest beauty, as well as for its classic association, having been the theme of poets of all ages. Clumps of the roots can be obtained of almost any seedsman, and once set will continue to increase, and give you bloom of which one can never have too many. In the vicinity of Matlock, England, there are many acres covered with this plant, which, when in bloom, attract many visitors, and the spot is known in that section of the country as the *Via Gellia*.

Return of Happiness.

MY sated senses seem afloat upon a waveless sea;
For all around me, all above, is beauteous harmony!
—*Sallie A. Brock.*

A BREEZY noise, which is not breeze,
   And white-clad children by degrees
Steal out in troops among the trees.

Fair little children, morning-bright,
With faces grave, yet soft to sight,
Expressive of restrained delight.

Some plucked the palm boughs within reach,
And others leaped up high to catch
The upper boughs, and shake from each

A rain of dew, till, wetted so,
The child who held the branch let go,
And it swang backward with a flow

Of faster drippings. Then I knew
The children laughed—but the laugh flew
From its own chirrup, as might do

A frightened song-bird; and a child
Who seemed the chief, said, very mild,
"Hush! keep this morning undefiled."
—*Mrs. Browning.*

FAIR flower, that, lapt in lowly glade,
   Do-t hide beneath the greenwood shade,
      Than whom the vernal gale
   None fairer wakes, on bank, or spray,
   Our England's lily of the May,
      Our lily of the vale! —*Mant.*

Lion's Heart.

Physostegia Virginiana. NATURAL ORDER: *Labiatæ—Mint Family.*

NATIVE to various portions of the Southern and Western States, this plant may occasionally be found beautifying our gardens, where it thrives well and increases rapidly. It is rather handsome in appearance, varying from one to four feet in height, with a square, thick, upright stem. The leaves appear opposite each other, and are large and glossy, and a dark green in color. The flowers are on the tops of the branches, in a four-rowed spike. They are a pale purple in tint, with spots on the inner side. The plant blooms freely during August and September. There are no special virtues ascribed to the Physostegia. The botanical name (from the Greek) signifies a bladder-like covering, from the puffed or inflated appearance of the corolla.

Bravery.

COMMANDING, aiding, animating all,
Where foe appear'd to press, or friend to fall.
—*Byron.*

THE brave man seeks not popular applause,
Nor, overpower'd with arms, deserts his cause;
Unshamed, though foiled, he does the best he can;
Force is of brutes, but honor is of man.
—*Dryden.*

THE brave man is not he who feels no fear,
For that were stupid and irrational;
But he whose noble soul its fear subdues,
And bravely dares the danger nature shrinks from.
—*Joanna Baillie.*

True valor
Lies in the mind, the never-yielding purpose,
Nor owns the blind award of giddy fortune.
—*Thompson.*

FIGHT valiantly today;
And yet I do thee wrong to mind thee of it,
For thou art framed of the firm truth of valor.
—*Shakespeare.*

NO fire nor foe, nor fate, nor night,
The Trojan hero did affright,
Who bravely, twice, renewed the fight.
—*Sir. J. Denham.*

I DARE do all that may become a man;
Who dares do more is none. —*Shakespeare.*

Loasa.

Loasa lateritia. NATURAL ORDER: *Loasaceæ — Loasa Family.*

FORMING a class of plants by themselves, the Loasas give their name to an order of which there have been discovered about seventy species; and those of peculiar beauty. Some of them recline their long, branching stems upon the ground, like the golden bartonia; others, like the Loasa, grow to a greater length, and have more aspiring natures, rendering them especially fine for the covering of trellises, arbors, or rock work. The flowers are curious; the outer petals, of which there are five, have each a hooded appearance, while within the center are five more of a different shape, the whole being filled with numerous stamens, like a delicate fringe. In training the plant, gloves should be used, as the hairs with which the plant is covered produce a stinging sensation. The blossoms are red or yellow. Pleasures, like this plant, require some precaution in handling, lest they sting in the enjoyment.

Pleasure.

PLEASURE with instruction should be joined;
So take the corn, and leave the chaff behind.
— *Dryden.*

BUT pleasures are like poppies spread —
You seize the flower, its bloom is shed;
Or like the snow-fall in the river, —
A moment white, then lost forever.
— *Burns.*

THERE rich varieties of joy
Continual feast the mind;
Pleasures which fill, but never cloy.
Immortal and refined.
— *Anne Steele.*

WE may roam through this world like a child at a feast,
Who but sips of a sweet and then flies to the rest;
And when pleasure begins to grow dull in the east,
We may order our wings and be off to the west.
— *Moore.*

AND while the face of outward things we find
Pleasant and fair, agreeable and sweet,
These things transport.
— *Sir J. Davies.*

'TIS time short pleasure now to take,
Of little life the best to make,
And manage wisely the last stake.
— *Cowley.*

Lobelia.

Lobelia fulgens.   NATURAL ORDER: *Lobeliaceæ — Lobelia Family.*

IT is difficult to select from this class of plants the one possessing the most claims to our attention, as they are all exceedingly pretty, though very diverse in habit. Some of them grow upright, others spread their slender branches in the most wanton manner. There are about eighty species of them, which, with the exception of about a dozen, are natives of the Cape of Good Hope. These have been improved by hybridizing. The flowers of most of them are an exquisite blue, a few are white, and others are of the different shades of crimson, purple, maroon and scarlet. The delicate varieties are fine for hanging-baskets, the upright ones for garden or window culture.

Malevolence.

HE hated men too much to feel remorse,
    And thought the voice of wrath a sacred call,
To pay the injuries of some to all.   —*Byron.*

I'LL keep my way alone, and burn away—
    Evil or good I care not, so I spread
Tremendous desolation on my road;
I'll be remember'd as huge meteors are;
From the dismay they scatter.   —*Proctor.*

I SEE thou art implacable, more deaf
    To prayers than winds and seas; yet winds and seas
Are reconciled at length, and sea and shore;
Thy anger, unappeasable, still rages,
Eternal tempest, never to be calm.   —*Milton.*

THERE are some things I cannot bear,
    Some looks which rouse my angry hate,
Some hearts whose love I would not share,
    Till earth and heaven were desolate.   —*Watts.*

BUT turn the heart's sweet current into gall,
    No earthly power can heal the deadly flow;
'T will poison the affections, till the blood
Grows venomous and fiery, and beneath
Its blasting influence are wither'd up
The springs of love and hope.   —*Mrs. Hale.*

THEY did not know how hate can burn
    In hearts once changed from soft to stern.
            —*Byron.*

Locust.

Robinia pseudacacia.   NATURAL ORDER: *Leguminosæ — Pulse Family.*

ROBINIA, the botanical name of the Locust, is derived from the Latinized surname of John Robin, an eminent botanist enjoying the patronage of Louis XIV., and was bestowed in honor of his memory; and pseudacacia denotes false acacia. There are no extensive forests of this tree on the American continent, but it is found mixed with other trees in various localities. It is much planted for groves and shade trees around rural residences. The foliage, though small, is beautiful, and during the spring an abundance of fragrant blossoms burden the air with their perfume. The wood is sometimes used in the mechanical arts, being hard, close grained and durable.

Vicissitude.

SUCH is life: all fair today, dark tomorrow, dull and gray;
Changing ever, like the moon, or the fleecy clouds of June.
—*L. H. Clinch.*

THUS doth the ever-changing course of things
Run a perpetual circle, ever turning;
And that same day that highest glory brings,
Brings us unto the point of back-returning
—*Daniel.*

ERE mirth can well her comedy begin,
The tragic demon oft comes thundering in,
Confounds the actors, damps the merry show,
And turns the loudest laugh to deepest woe.
—*Wilson.*

OH! life is a waste of wearisome hours,
Which seldom the rose of enjoyment adorns;
And the heart that is soonest awake to the flowers,
Is always the first to be touch'd by the thorn.
—*Moore.*

IS there no constancy in earthly things?
No happiness in us but what must alter?
No life, without the heavy load of fortune?

What miseries we are, and to ourselves!
Ev'n then when full content seems to sit us,
What daily sores and sorrows.
—*Beaumont and Fletcher.*

THE pang that wrings the heart today,
Time's touch will heal tomorrow.
—*Mrs. Filet.*

Lophospermum.

Lophospermum scandens. NATURAL ORDER: *Scrophulariaceæ—Figwort Family.*

THIS vine is more frequently found in our greenhouses, but it can be used in the garden if the seeds are started early in the house or hotbed. The flowers are extremely handsome, being from two to three inches in length, tubular in shape, expanding at the mouth, and in color pink or scarlet. There is a plant called Lophospermum rhodochiton (rose-clothed), that has brown flowers, and is sometimes called Rhodochiton volubile. Both are from Mexico and adjacent countries, and grow about ten feet in height. The name is composed of two Greek words, *lophos* and *sperma*, signifying crested seed; and *scandens*, Latin, is translated climbing. The plant has been selected as the emblem of ecstasy. Every heart should be filled with joy as abundantly and feelingly as a luxuriant vine that spreads and airs itself in sunny enjoyment.

Ecstasy.

SWELL, swell, my joys; and faint not to declare
Yourselves as ample as your causes are.
—*Jonson.*

I WAS born for rejoicing; a "summer child," truly!
And kindred I claim with each wild, joyous thing:
The light frolic breeze—or the streamlet unruly—
Or a cloud at its play—or a bird on its wing.
—*Mrs. Ellet.*

ALL in a mesh of dreams entangled;
Oh, breathe thy words of rapt delight,
Sweet lips—twin petals of the rose bespangled
With the diamond dews of night!
—*George Cooper.*

THERE is no state in which the bounteous gods
Have not placed joy, if men would seek it out
—*Crown.*

THE paths of bliss are joyous, and the breast
Of thoughtless youth is easy to be blest.
—*William Herbert.*

WELL, there is yet one day of life before me,
And, whatsoe'er betide me, I will enjoy it.
—*Joanna Baillie.*

JOY loves to cull the summer flower,
And wreathe it round his happy brow.
—*James G. Brooks.*

Lupine.

Lupinus polyphyllus. NATURAL ORDER: *Leguminosæ—Pulse Family.*

AMONG our handsomest native plants, the Lupines find a recognized place, more especially the above, which is a fine variety from Oregon. Its height is from three to four feet, the foliage soft and silky, and the flowers yellow, purple, or white. There are numerous other varieties from different parts of the United States, both annual and perennial. The Lupinus mutabilis (changeable) is from South America, and is said to be changeable in the color of its blossoms. The ancients used a species of Lupine for food, thinking it strengthened the intellect; and on the stage the seeds were used by the players instead of real money. The Latin name signifies wolfish, from *lupus*, a wolf, as it absorbs the fertility of the soil, to the detriment of other things; and polyphyllus, from the Greek, denotes many-leaved.

Voraciousness.

THE turnpike road to people's hearts, I find,
Lies through their mouths, or I mistake mankind.
—*Dr. Walcot.*

I'M quite ashamed—'tis mighty rude
To eat so much—but all's so good
I have a thousand thanks to give—
My lord alone knows how to live.
—*Pope.*

'TIS holyday; provide me better cheer.
'Tis holyday; and shall be round the year;
Shall I my household gods and genius cheat,
To make him rich who grudges me my meat?
—*Dryden.*

SOME men are born to feast, and not to fight;
Whose sluggish mind, e'en in fair honor's field,
Still on their dinner turn.
—*Joanna Baillie.*

BEYOND the sense
Of light refection, at the genial board
Indulge not often; nor protract the feast

To dull satiety; till soft and slow
A drowsy death creeps on th' expansive soul,
Oppress'd and smother'd the celestial fire.
—*Armstrong.*

NOT all on books their criticism waste,
The genius of a dish some justly taste,
And eat their way to fame.
—*Young.*

Magnolia.

Magnolia grandiflora.   NATURAL ORDER: *Magnoliaceæ—Magnolia Family.*

OF all the flowers bestowed upon the South, there is none to which a Southerner refers with more pride than to the blossoms of this elegant tree. The Magnolia grandiflora flourishes throughout most of the Gulf States and on the Atlantic coast as far north as North Carolina. It grows chiefly in swampy lands, yet attains its greatest height in a light, fertile soil, where, if planted by itself, it will assume the shape of a perfect pyramid. The leaves are evergreen, the old ones forming a striking contrast to the young and tender foliage, which is of a much lighter shade. The flowers are of the purest white, about eight or nine inches in diameter, and fill the air with their honeyed fragrance. As the slightest injury causes the blossom to soon turn brown, they have often been used as a medium of communication between lovers or friends. It was only necessary to write the message with some pointed instrument on one of the broad petals, and cause the flowers to be delivered in a bouquet to the person desired, and the wounded parts would soon betray the secret committed to the floral page.

Love of Nature.

NATURE is man's best teacher. She unfolds
   Her treasures to his search, unseals his eye,
Illumes his mind, and purifies his heart,
An influence breathes from all the sights and sounds
Of her existence; she is wisdom's self. —*Steel.*

I LOVE thee for the blossoms and the bees,
   The hills, the vales, the mountains and the seas;
The winds, the clouds, the skies of azure blue,
The moon, the stars, and planets circling through;

The earth, the sun, and everything that's fair,
   Above, below, all round and everywhere—
The soul, the mind, to their Creator call,
To him, the Father, First and Last of all.
                                     —*Lalor.*

O NATURE! how in every charm supreme!
   Whose votaries feast on raptures ever new!
O! for the voice and fire of seraphim,
To sing thy glories with devotion due! —*Beattie.*

THE green earth sends its incense up
   From every mountain shrine—
From every flower and dewy cup
   That greeteth the sunshine. —*Whittier.*

Mallow.

Malva sylvestris.   NATURAL ORDER: *Malvaceæ — Mallow Family.*

VALUED at all times for their emollient properties (whence the name from the Greek *malasso*, I make soft, through the Latin *malva*), the Mallows are a mucilaginous order of plants, allied to the hollyhock family. They are frequently found in rural gardens as ornaments. The above species is about three feet high, with purplish-red flowers, and is called High Mallow, to distinguish it from the Low Mallow, a prostrate species, the seeds of which children call cheeses. The Mallow crispa is a very tall annual from Syria, with very large, roundish leaves, the borders of which are adorned with a very full, crisped or curled ruffling, and would appear to advantage as a foliage plant in the borders in summer. The Musk Mallow is from Great Britain, having very pretty flowers of a rose color, blooming in midsummer; the whole plant being pervaded by the odor from which it takes name.

Goodness.

HOW far that little candle throws its beams!
  So shines a good deed in a naughty world.
                         — *Shakespeare.*

MORE sweet than odors caught by him who sails
  Near spicy shores of Araby the blest,
A thousand times more exquisitely sweet,
The freight of holy feeling which we meet
In thoughtful moments, wafted by the gales
From fields where good men walk, or bowers
Wherein they rest.
                         — *Wordsworth.*

GOOD, the more
  Communicated, more abundant grows;
The author not impair'd, but honor'd more.
                         — *Milton.*

TO be good is to be happy; angels
  Are happier than men because they're better.
                         — *Rowe.*

MAN should dare all things that he knows is right,
  And fear to do no act save what is wrong;
But guided safely by his inward light,
  And with a permanent belief, and strong,
In Him who is our Father and our Friend,
He should walk steadfastly unto the end.
                         — *Phœbe Carey.*

Maple--Rock.

Acer saccharinum. NATURAL ORDER: *Aceraceæ—Maple Family.*

CANADA and the New England States produce the Rock Maple in great abundance, forming in some districts a greater part of the forests. It grows to a great height, has a somewhat rough, gray bark, and in summer a fine crown of foliage, which in fall takes on itself the most brilliant hues that greet the eye in an autumn landscape, sporting through all the shades from yellow to crimson, as if it had caught and imprisoned the glorious colors of a sunset sky. The Black Maple is another tree of the same class, both yielding the sap from which the sugar bearing their name is manufactured.

Rescrue.

YOU know my wishes ever yours did meet;
   If I be silent, 'tis no more but fear
That I should say too little when I speak.
—*Lady Carew.*

THE maples in the forest glow;
  On the lawn the fall flowers blaze;
  The landscape has a purple haze;
My heart is filled with warmth and glow.

Like living coals the red leaves burn;
  They fall, then turns the red to rust;
  They crumble, like the coals, to dust;
Warm heart, must thou to ashes turn?
—*Sylvester Baxter.*

AH! what delight 't would be,
  Would'st thou sometimes by stealth converse with me!
How should I thy sweet commune prize,
  And other joys despise!
Come, then! I ne'er was yet denied by thee.
—*John Norris.*

I ABJURE your sight;
  Ev'n from my meditations and my thoughts
I banish your enticing vanities;
And, closely kept within my study walls,
As from a cave of rest, henceforth I'll see
And smile, but never taste your misery.
—*Goff.*

IF thou canst feel,
  Within thy inmost soul,
That thou hast kept a portion back,
  While I have staked the whole;
Let no false pity spare the blow,
  But in true mercy tell me so.
—*Adelaide Anne Procter.*

Marigold.

Tagetes erecta. NATURAL ORDER: *Composite — Aster Family.*

MARIGOLDS are mostly herbs of tropical America, and belong to the same order as the artemisia, chrysanthemum and China aster, which order is said to comprehend one-ninth of all flowering plants. The Tagetes is named in honor of Tages, an Etrurian deity, a grandson of Jupiter, who is said to have sprung from the plowed earth, in the form of a boy, and taught the Etrurians the art of foretelling events, or divination. A description of so familiar a plant is almost unnecessary, as everyone must know it has the yellowest of flowers and an abundance of them, interspersed with plumy foliage. The French Marigold has dark, velvety blossoms, which, varying through the different shades of maroon, are really pretty. All the varieties have a peculiar fragrance, rather balsamic than otherwise.

Cruelty.

OFT those whose cruelty makes many mourn,
   Do by the fires which they first kindle burn.
                                  — *Earl of Sterline.*

NO counsel from our cruel wills can win us,
  But ills once done, we bear our guilt within us.
             — *John Ford.*

YOU are more inhuman, more inexorable,
  O, ten times more, than tigers of Hyrcania.
             — *Shakespeare.*

WHY didst thou fling thyself across my path?
  My tiger spring must crush thee in its way,
  But cannot pause to pity thee.
             — *Maturin.*

LET me be cruel, not unnatural;
  I will speak daggers to her, but use none.
             — *Shakespeare.*

FANTASTIC tyrant of the amorous heart,
  How hard thy yoke! how cruel is thy dart!
             — *Prior.*

THOU art come to answer
  A stony adversary, an inhuman wretch,
Incapable of pity, void and empty
From ev'ry dracham of mercy.
             — *Shakespeare.*

Marjoram--Sweet.

Origanum majorana. NATURAL ORDER: *Labiatæ — Mint Family.*

WHEN our grandsires flourished, and almost every plant received some familiar, diminutive appellation that seemed to bring it into closer association with humanity than our now high-sounding names, this plant was called Sweet Marjory. It is very aromatic, and is grown more frequently as an herb for kitchen use than for ornament, and is useful in seasoning various articles of food. The flowers are pink, blooming in spikes. It is a native of Portugal. There is also a wild variety found in fields, and sometimes in the woods, that has nearly white flowers, and much the same properties as the other. The literal meaning of the name (from the Greek) is "joy of the mountain."

Blushes.

CONFUSION thrill'd me then, and secret joy,
   Fast throbbing, stole its treasures from my heart,
And mantling upward, turned my face to crimson.
          —*Brooks.*

ON Beauty's lids the gem-like tear
   Oft sheds its evanescent ray,
But scarce is seen to sparkle, ere
   'Tis chased by beaming smiles away;

Just so the blush is formed — and flies —
   Nor owns reflection's calm control;
It comes, it deepens — fades and dies,
   A gush of feeling from the soul.
      —*Anne Peyre Dinnies.*

FROM every blush that kindles in thy cheek,
   Ten thousand little loves and graces spring,
To revel in the roses.   —*Rowe.*

FOR I that old, old story had told —
   The story of anxious hopes and fears —
While over her ringlets' dark-brown gold
Was falling a shower of pearly tears —

Tears that hung on her eyelids' fringe
   Like dew on the fresh-born buds of May —
And her blushes deepened their roseate tinge,
   As I tenderly kissed those tears away.
      —*Sallie A. Brock.*

OH! little blush that comes and goes,
   Are you a blush, or yonder rose
I see reflected?   —*George Cooper.*

Matthiola.

Matthiola annua. NATURAL ORDER: *Cruciferæ—Mustard Family.*

DERIVING its name from the Italian physician and botanist P. A. Mattioli (1500-1577), this flower has always commanded more attention in Europe than it has in America. There it is really the flower of the people; and in cities nearly every window ledge must have its pot of Stock, to cheer by its presence, and serve as a reminder to its possessor, that there is a world of nature outside and beyond the turmoil and strife of city life. In the garden it is even more desirable, the plant assuming a pretty, upright habit, branching symmetrically, with the flowers arranged close around the upper parts of the stems or branches. The Tenweek Stock is an annual and requires no particular care. The perennial and biennial kinds should be protected during winter by some covering—a hotbed sash, or something equally good, as in cold climates they are apt to be winter-killed. They are all desirable plants; the colors are the various shades of red, crimson, yellow, purple, white, blue and rose.

Promptitude.

SEIZE, mortals, seize the transient hour;
  Improve each moment as it flies;
Life's a short summer—man a flower.
  —*Anonymous.*

WHILST timorous knowledge stands considering,
  Audacious ignorance hath done the deed,
For who knows most, the most he knows to doubt;
The least discourse is commonly most stout.
  —*Daniel.*

LET us take the instant by the forward top;
  For we are old, and on our quick'st decrees
The inaudible and noiseless foot of time
Steals, ere we can effect them.
  —*Shakespeare.*

TAKE the instant way;
  For honor travels in a strait so narrow,
Where one but goes abreast.
  —*Shakespeare.*

SHUN delays, they breed remorse;
  Take thy time, while time is lent thee;
Creeping snails have weakest force,

Fly their fault, lest thou repent thee.
Good is best when soonest wrought;
Lingering labors come to naught.
  —*Southwell.*

Maurandia.

Maurandia sempervirens. NATURAL ORDER: *Scrophulariaceæ — Figwort Family.*

HANDSOME and delicate, the Maurandia is a delightful vine for indoor culture, as its foliage is attractive and pretty, being small and neat in shape, similar to the point of a spear, and entirely unobtrusive. The flowers are about the size and shape of the foxglove, and, in color, purple, white, or rose-colored. They are most excellent for inserting in the sides of hanging-baskets or window-boxes, and are used by florists for that purpose. They are perennial, but as they bloom the first season after planting, are used for summer decoration out of doors, and of course perish on the approach of frost, except removed to the house. The name has been given in honor of Prof. Maurandy.

Courtesy.

SO gently blending courtesy and art,
That wisdom's lips seem'd borrowing friendship's heart
—*O. W. Holmes.*

SHEPHERD, I trust thy honest offered courtesy,
Which oft is sooner found in lowly sheds
With smoky rafters, than in tap'stry halls
And courts of princes. —*Milton.*

A SMILE for one of mean degree,
A courteous bow for one of high,
So modulated both that each
Saw friendship in his eye.
—*Henry B. Hirst.*

STUDY with care politeness, that must teach
The modish forms of gesture and of speech.
—*Stillingfleet.*

WOULD you both please and be instructed too,
Watch well the range of shining, to subdue;
Hear every man upon his favorite theme,
And ever be more knowing than you seem;
The lowest genius will afford some light,
Or give a hint that had escaped your sight.
—*Stillingfleet.*

ILL seemes (sayd he) if he so valient be,
That he should be so sterne to stranger wight;
For seldom yet did living creature see
That courtesie and manhood ever disagree.
—*Spenser.*

Mayweed.

Maruta cotula. NATURAL ORDER: *Composite — Aster Family.*

PERHAPS the commonest of all uncultivated plants is this roadside outcast, growing from the deep-rutted soil, utterly disregarding all the ordinary conditions required for herbal perfection, it sports its numerous blossoms, and during the whole summer its flowers make white the borders of the dusty way. It is an annual, though so abundant as to seem perennial, and only the greatest perseverance can eradicate it or reduce it to subjection. Of European origin, it was probably introduced with grain. The flower is really pretty, combining the purest of yellow, with the most opaque white, in an admirable and artistic manner, and could it only have been odorless and rare, would have been received with ecstatic admiration, instead of contumely and contempt. The origin of the botanic name Maruta is obscure, and its meaning is quite uncertain. Cotula was the half-pint measure of the Greeks and Romans.

Rumor.

RUMOR doth double like the voice and echo,
  The numbers of the fear'd.   —*Shakespeare.*

THE flying rumors gather'd as they roll'd;
  Scarce any tale was sooner heard than told,
And all who told it added something new,
And all who heard it made enlargement too;
In every ear it spread, on every tongue it grew.
  —*Pope.*

FROM the Orient to the drooping West,
  Making the wind my post-horse, still unfold
The acts commenced on this ball of earth:
Upon my tongues continual slanders ride,
The which in every language I pronounce,
Stuffing the ears of men with false reports.
  —*Shakespeare.*

A WHISPER woke the air—
  A soft, light tone, and low,
  Yet barb'd with shame and woe,—
Now, might it only perish there!
  No farther go!   —*Mrs. Osgood.*

RUMOR is a pipe
  Blown by surmises, jealousies, conjectures,
And of so easy and so plain a stop,
That the blunt monster with uncounted heads—
The still discordant, wavering multitude—
Can play upon it.   —*Shakespeare.*

Medick.

Medicago sativa.   NATURAL ORDER: *Leguminosæ — Pulse Family.*

EUROPE has long been the seat of the Medick, which has become thoroughly naturalized there, though it is supposed to have been originally derived from the ancient Media (now Northern Persia), whence its name. It is of the same order as the clover, and is somewhat naturalized and cultivated in America for the same purpose, but it has not proved as valuable, being probably not as well adapted to the climate. It is of perennial growth, with stems about a foot and a half high. The Medicago scutellata, is an annual of the same class, and is grown in the garden for its curious seed vessels, resembling snail shells, which gives the familiar name of Snails to the plant. The Medicago intertexta, called hedgehog, has prickly pods, and is cultivated for ornamental purposes, as are some others of the same species. The pods are used in winter bouquets along with dried grasses of various kinds.

Agriculture.

REAP well, scatter not, gather clean that is shorn,
Bind fast, shock apace, have an eye to thy corn.
— *Tusser.*

EARTH of man the bounteous mother,
Feeds him still with corn and wine;
He who best would aid a brother,
Shares with him these gifts divine.
— *John Stirling.*

WILT thou repine
To labor for thyself? and rather choose
To lie supinely, hoping heaven will bless
Thy slighted fruits, and give thee bread unearned?
— *John Philips.*

WHO abuseth his cattle and starves them for meat,
By carting or ploughing his gain is not great;
Where he that with labor can use them aright,
Hath gain to his comfort, and cattle in plight.
— *Tusser.*

GIVE me, ye gods, the product of one field,
That so I neither may be rich nor poor;
And having just enough, not covet more. — *Dryden.*

YOU sunburnt sickle men, of August weary,
Come hither from the furrow, and be merry.
— *Shakespeare.*

Melilot.

Melilotus alba.   NATURAL ORDER: *Leguminosæ — Pulse Family.*

A TALL herb, passing frequently under the cognomen of Sweet-scented Clover, the Melilot used to be cultivated in gardens for the fragrance of its foliage, as well as its flowers, which it retains for a long time in a dried state. By many it was considered as desirable to place among clothing, as the famed lavender and roseleaves was by the belles of the last century. It is usually about three feet high, and in an uncultivated state is found in meadows, particularly in soils left by running streams, in which it seems to delight. The flowers are small, arranged up and down the stem in the style of a loose raceme, and in color white, with a slight tinge of yellow intermixed. It derives its name from the Greek, and signifies honey lotus.

Philanthropy.

I WOULD bring balm, and pour it in your wound;
  Cure your distemper'd mind, and heal your fortunes.
—*Dryden.*

AND now philanthropy! thy rays divine
  Dart round the globe from Zembla's to the line;
O'er each dark prison plays the cheering light,
Like northern lustres o'er the vault of night.
—*Darwin.*

IN faith and hope the world will disagree,
  But all mankind's concern is charity:
All must be false that thwart this one great end,
And all of God that bless mankind or mend.
—*Pope.*

THE primal duties shine aloft, like stars;
  The charities that soothe, and heal, and bless,
Are scatter'd at the feet of man, like flowers.
—*Wordsworth.*

YET was she not profuse, but fear'd to waste,
  And wisely managed that the stock might last;
That all might be supplied, and she not grieve
When crowds appear'd she had not to relieve;
Which to prevent, she still increased her store;
Laid up, and spared, that she might the more.
—*Dryden.*

AND when the sickly taper shed
  Its light through vapors damp confined,
Hushed as a seraph's fell thy tread,
A new Electra by the bed
Of suffering human kind,
Pointing the spirit in its dark dismay
To that pure hope which fadeth not away.
—*Whittier.*

Mermaid Weed.

Proserpinaca palustris. NATURAL ORDER: *Onagraceæ — Evening Primrose Family.*

LIKE so many others, this plant, which inhabits moist places, such as ponds, swamps and ditches, has its mythological associations, being named, it is thought, from Proserpine, a Roman goddess stolen by Pluto and conveyed to his kingdom. Ceres, her mother, searched for her a long time in vain, but at last hearing that she had been taken to Pluto's kingdom, she expostulated with Jupiter, and finally obtained permission for her daughter to remain one half the year with her, the other half in the infernal regions. The name, however, may have been derived from the creeping habit of the plant (Latin *proserpo*, I creep), as the stems creep at the base in the mud or shallow water, the upper part only emerging.

Necessity.

FULL soon, I know it, while they shall strain to free not,
    From these idolatrous arms you shall be torn;
You are fated from my days to pass and be not,
    Like all of rare and fair they have ever worn!
I am doomed, although the stealthy doom I see not;
    I feast, albeit I die tomorrow morn!   —*Edgar Fawcett.*

THE ship which goes to sea inform'd with fire,—
    Obeying only its own iron force,
Reckless of adverse tides, breeze dead, or weak
As infant's sporting breath, too faint to stir
The feather held before it,—is as much
The appointed thrall of all the elements,
As the white bosom'd bark which wooes the wind,
And when it dies desists. And thus with man
However contrary he set his heart
To God, he is but working out His will,
And at an infinite angle, more or less
Obeying his own soul's necessity.   —*Bailey.*

THE grass withereth, the flower fadeth,
    Ay, and I know "'tis well."
For they shall live again when springtime's
    Sweet birdlings' songs shall tell.
Above their knell.   —*Charlotte Cordner.*

LATE - soon or late,
    The longest day hath end;
If the summer wait,
    The winter still must wend
With sad steps and slow unto the fields of Fate.
    —*L. Bruce Moore.*

Mignonette.

Reseda odorata. NATURAL ORDER: *Resedaceæ — Mignonette Family.*

IN France, Holland, and various other parts of Europe, the Mignonette, originally a native of Egypt and North Africa, is trained into a tree shape, by taking a straight, healthy plant, and bending a piece of willow or whalebone over it, in the shape of a hoop, and tying the shoot to it, and as it increases in height another hoop is added until the plant has become woody. A French writer remarks that she has seen them as old as fifteen years, and even double that age. The flowers, after they have withered, must be removed, in order that it may retain its vitality. It grows also in beds or masses, and perfumes the whole garden. Some of the varieties are dense and bushy. Though humble and insignificant, its fragrance makes it a general favorite. Its name in the vernacular is from the French and means little darling, its botanical name is from the Latin *resedo*, I assuage.

Your Qualities Surpass Your Charms.

IT is not mirth, for mirth she is too still;
It is not wit, which leaves the heart more chill,
But that continuous sweetness which with ease
Pleases all around it from the wish to please.
— *The New Timon.*

FOR you remember you had set,
That morning, on the casement edge,
A long, green box of mignonette,
And you were leaning from the ledge;
And when I raised my eyes, above
They met with two so full and bright —
Such eyes! I swear to you, my love,
That these have never lost their light.
— *Tennyson.*

BEAUTIES that from worth arise
Are, like the grace of deities,
Still present with us, though un-sighted.
— *Sir J. Suckling.*

I KNOW the gentleman
To be of worth and worthy estimation,
And not without desert so well reputed.
— *Shakespeare.*

THIS fragrant bloom of garden birth,
So modest, yet persuasive —
Because the sweet it saps from earth
By fullness is invasive — I've met
Is truest measure of my love, of all the flowers
Une "*herbe d'amour*" — *petite* in girth,
Delicious mignonette! — *Mary B. Dodge.*

Mint.

Mentha viridis. NATURAL ORDER: *Labiatæ — Mint Family.*

SEVERAL plants are known under the common name of mint, the Spearmint being probably the most agreeable to the taste. It is used in making sauces for some varieties of meat, especially lamb; medicinally it is said to allay fevers, and act against spasmodic affections. The Peppermint is well known through the essences sold by all pharmaceutists. Both plants are natives of Europe, and affect moist places, frequently growing beside shallow streams and in low, wet meadows, where they seem much more brittle and tender, from the amount of water they suck up into their stems. Either plant grows well in the garden, spreading rapidly by means of their creeping roots. The flowers are purple, and in slender racemes. According to mythology, Minthe, a nymph of the woods and streams, and beloved by Hades (Pluto), was turned by Proserpine into one of these plants.

Virtue.

VIRTUE stands like the sun, and all which rolls around
Drinks life, and light, and glory from her aspect.
—*Byron.*

COUNT life by virtues—these will last
When life's lame-footed race is o'er;
And these, when earthly joys are past,
Shall cheer us on a brighter shore.
—*Mrs. S. J. Hale.*

VIRTUE, dear friend, needs no defense;
The surest guard is innocence:
Quivers and bows and poison'd darts
Are only used by guilty hearts.
—*Roscommon.*

VIRTUE could see to do what virtue would
By her own radiant light, though sun and moon
Were in the flat sea sunk.
—*Milton.*

ONLY a sweet and virtuous soul,
Like season'd timber, never gives;
But, though the whole world turn to coal,
Then chiefly lives.
—*George Herbert.*

THE path to peace is virtue; what I show,
Thyself may freely on thyself bestow;
Fortune was never worship'd by the wise,
But set aloft by fools, usurps the skies.
—*Dryden.*

Mistletoe.

Phoradendron flavescens. NATURAL ORDER: *Loranthaceæ — Mistletoe Family.*

OUR hundred species or more of the Mistletoe are now known to botanists. The leaves are thick and fleshy, the flowers a whitish yellow, bearing a half transparent white berry, with a sticky pulp. It is more abundant on elm trees than on any other, and only when it was found on the oak was it considered a sacred thing by the Druids, or priests of the ancient Britons; when so found, they had a great triumphal procession to gather it, after which, with much solemnity, they laid it on a white cloth, and divided it among the people as a charm against disease. These plants are parasitic in nature, living on the juices of the trees on which they rest. This particular species, the American mistletoe, derives its name, which was given it by Nuttall, from two Greek words denoting thievish tree.

Obstacles to be Overcome.

OUR natures are like oil: compound us with anything.
Yet still we strive to swim upon the top.
- *Beaumont and Fletcher.*

COME, my soul, let us reason together;
  Come, for the shadows darken ahead;
Care and sorrow tighten the tether,
  Life's sun through the mists grows dim and red.

Come, ere the long, low light of the summer
  Fade to the brown of the autumn leaf;
Come, lest the foot of the careless comer
  Lag weary in paths made rough with grief.
- *Barton Grey.*

Great souls,
By nature half divine, soar to the stars,
And hold a near acquaintance with the gods.
- *Rows.*

NATURE, that framed us of four elements,
  Warring within our breasts for regimen,
Doth teach us all to have aspiring minds:
Our souls, whose faculties can comprehend
The wondrous architechture of the world,
And measure ev'ry wand'ring planet's course,
Still climbing after knowledge infinite,
And always moving as the restless spheres,
Wills us to wear ourselves, and never rest
Until we reach the ripest fruit of all.
- *Marlo.*

Monkshood.

Aconitum Napellus. NATURAL ORDER: *Ranunculaceæ—Crowfoot Family.*

THIS plant takes its name from the peculiar shape of its flowers, which resemble a monk's cowl or hood, and are of various colors — blue, white, and rose-color. It has a rather pleasant appearance, and when once established requires but little attention, as it grows well in any soil, and thrives from year to year. The extract of the plant is extremely poisonous, but, used medicinally, it is the strong bulwark of the homœopathic practice. It is used successfully in combating fevers, and the first stages of most diseases, as it acts against all inflammatory conditions of the body, but should never be used in the fluid state except as advised by a physician.

Knight Errantry.

SOLEMNLY he swore,
   That by the faith which knights to knighthood bore,
And whate'er else to chivalry belongs,
He would not cease till he revenged their wrongs.
—*Dryden.*

A TRUE knight,
   Not yet mature, yet matchless; firm in word,
Speaking in deeds, and deedless in his tongue;
Not soon provok'd, nor being provok'd, soon calm'd;
His heart and hand both open, and both free;
For what he has, he gives; what thinks, he shows;
Yet gives he not till judgment guide his bounty,
Nor dignifies an impure thought in breath.
—*Shakespeare.*

A FORM more active, light and strong,
   Ne'er shot the ranks of war along;
The modest, yet the manly mien,
Might grace the court of maiden queen.
—*Scott.*

NAUGHT is more honorable to a knight,
   Nor better doth beseem brave chivalry,
Than to defend the feeble in their right,
   And wrong redress in such as wend awry.
—*Spenser.*

MY good blade carves the casques of men,
   My tough lance thrusteth sure,
My strength is as the strength of ten,
   Because my heart is pure.
—*Tennyson.*

Morning Glory.

Ipomœa Nil. NATURAL ORDER: *Convolvulaceæ—Convolvulus Family.*

HERE is a well known climber and general favorite, though rejected by some for its commonness, or because it is found so frequently in the humble walks of life. It however forms a very grateful shade from the noonday sun, and is used more than any other annual vine for that purpose. The flowers are various in color; the bud is curiously twisted, which, when expanded is of a beautiful trumpet-shape, the tints being far more delicate than any brush could lay. In the Southern States it grows wild, adorning the hedges and byways with its blossoms, and supplying the humming-bird and bee with their morning repasts.

Repose.

MY heart is like the sleeping lake,
   Which takes the hue of cloud and sky,
And only feels its surface break
   When birds of passage wander by.
          — *Willis.*

WITHOUT, the happy birds are singing
   Their last song in the gathering gloom;
And languorous airs soft scents are bringing
   From musky buds and bloom.
          — *George Cooper.*

HERE let us couch in fern,
   And gaze adown the forest's dim arcade,
Where little patches of bright sunlight burn,
   Companioned of deep shade.

THE cricket on its bank is dumb;
   The very flies forget to hum;
And, save the wagon rocking round,
   The landscape sleeps without a sound.
          — *John Clare.*

HERE stretched, the pleasant turf I press,
   In luxury of idleness;
Sun-streaks, and glancing wings, and sky
Spotted with cloud-shapes, charm my eye;
While murmuring grass and waving trees,

Their leaf-harps sounding to the breeze,
And water-tones that tinkle near,
Blend their sweet music to my ear;
And by the changing shades alone
The passage of the hours is known.
          — *Alfred B. Street.*

Mourning Bride.

Scabiosa atropurpurea. NATURAL ORDER: *Dipsaceæ — Teasel Family.*

MOURNING BRIDE (Sweet Scabious) is a perennial plant, but as it is only half-hardy in the Northern climate, and blooms the first season, it is sown every summer and allowed to perish with the frost; although it would be worth the trial to see if some light protection would not save it, as most perennial plants bloom better when the roots are well established. For many years it has been a favorite garden flower, being neat in habit, with very pretty tapering foliage and desirable blossoms. The buds are bunched together like a semi-spherical cushion, the rounded side up, the lower row of florets of which open first, and, when all are expanded, fairly crowd each other for room. They are velvety in texture, and in some of the purples and maroons the colors are so intense that the eye can scarcely penetrate the depth of their tints, as they are only a shade or two from being black; hence the epithet, atropurpurea, or dark purple. There are some light varieties, also white. They have the odor of musk.

Unfortunate Attachment.

I HAVE thrust away in silence each loving thought of you;
I have laid to rest each memory, so tender and so true;
I have prayed upon my bended knees for power to forget,
And the answer to that prayer is this — I love you, love you yet!
—*Christian Reid.*

I NEED not say how, one by one,
Love's flowers have dropp'd from off love's chain,
Enough to say that they are gone,
And that they cannot bloom again.
—*Miss Landon.*

UNHAPPY he, who lets a tender heart,
Bound to him by the ties of earliest love,
Fall from him by his own neglect, and die,
Because it met no kindness. —*Percival.*

NOT one sigh shall tell my story,
Not one tear my cheek shall stain;
Silent grief shall be my glory,
Grief that stoops not to complain.
—*Mrs. Robinson.*

AH me! I thought you loved me well —
Our human eyes are blind;
He only reads life's parable,
Who never looks behind. —*Barton Grey.*

213

Mullein.

Verbascum thapsus.   NATURAL ORDER: *Scrophulariaceæ—Figwort Family.*

VERBASCUM, or Mullein, is a common wayside plant, that we will dignify with a place in this volume as a slight recompense for the abuse it has ever, and will ever, receive. Condemned as a weed, considered as evidence of an untidy landholder wherever it is seen occupying the fields, its stately stalk a target for every roadside rambler's stick, it has at least some virtues, and less vice than it generally obtains credit for, and shall receive a tribute for the memory of childhood, when we remember seeing its golden blossoms so far above our head. The whole plant presents a gray appearance, from the dense woolly texture that covers its leaves and stalk. It is said to have been used in ancient times as wicks for lamps, or was placed in small vessels of oil, and one end lighted, the oil continually creeping up its dense surface, supplying the flame with fuel; and many a country lassie has been indebted for her rosy cheeks to a pilfered leaf, whose rough surface she has furtively applied to her smooth skin. The plant has several medicinal properties, being demulcent, anti-spasmodic, and useful as an anodyne. The German name is *wollkraut*, signifying wool-plant.

Good Nature.

GOOD humor only teaches charms to last,
Still makes new conquests, and maintains the past.
— *Pope.*

HE keeps his temper'd mind serene and pure,
And ev'ry passion aptly harmonized,
Amid a jarring world.   — *Thompson.*

A SWEETER and a lovelier gentleman,
Framed in the prodigality of nature,
The spacious world cannot again afford.
— *Shakspeare.*

THOUGH time her bloom is stealing,
There's still beyond his art —
The wild-flower wreath of feeling,
The sunbeam of the heart.   *Halleck.*

Musk Plant.

Mimulus moschatus.   NATURAL ORDER: *Scrophulariaceæ — Figwort Family.*

BUT few things in nature have the odor of musk, particularly in the vegetable kingdom; and this little, unobtrusive plant, so delicate and fragile, is cultivated for this property, otherwise it would be passed by for its more showy sisters; yet its blossoms look like drops of yellow gold among its pale-green leaves. It is a native of Oregon. The other varieties of the Mimulus are grown for their curious and striking flowers, which are usually yellow, velvety, and spotted with crimson, maroon, or brown. They are well adapted for garden or house culture, but require moisture, and a little shelter from the scorching sun. Mimulus is derived from the Greek *mimo*, signifying an ape, from the grinning appearance of the corolla. Another variety is known as the Mimulus ringens, or Monkey-flower.

A Meeting.

A HUNDRED thousand welcomes! I could weep,
And I could laugh; I am light, and heavy; welcome.
—*Shakespeare.*

THERE'S not a fiber in my trembling frame
That does not vibrate when thy step draws near;
There's not a pulse that throbs not when I hear
Thy voice, thy breathing, nay, thy very name.
—*Frances Kemble Butler.*

WHEN lovers meet in adverse hour,
'Tis like a sun glimpse through a shower,
A watery ray an instant seen,
Then darkly-closing clouds between.
—*Scott.*

AND doth not a meeting like this make amends
For all the long years I've been wand'ring away—
To see thus around me my youth's early friends,
As smiling and kind as in that happy day?

IT gives me wonder, great as my content,
To see you here before me. —*Shakespeare.*

THE joy of meeting pays the pangs of absence,
Else who could bear it? —*Rowe.*

IN that same place thou hast appointed me
Tomorrow truly will I meet with thee.
—*Shakespeare.*

Mustard.

Sinapis alba. NATURAL ORDER: *Cruciferæ — Mustard Family.*

RECEIVED into this country probably from Germany or England, as it is a very ancient European herb, it has always been esteemed as a condiment for the table and for its excellent medical qualities. It is exceedingly prolific, and wherever once sown, will take care of its own reproduction. In England it is cultivated in quantities for its seed, and on a small scale in some parts of America. It is sometimes grown in hotbeds as a salad, and the young leaves of the garden Mustard are frequently boiled as greens. It sends up a strong, branching stalk, about four feet high, which is in summer covered with numerous small, sulphur-colored flowers. The seeds are formed in small, delicate pods, which, when ripe, burst, and let their contents scatter over the ground. The seeds are very pungent to the taste; but those of the Sinapis nigra, or Black Mustard, are still more so; the flour of mustard, the form in which it is used as a condiment, is a combination of both — two-fifths black, and three-fifths white. The pungency is developed only where the flour is brought under the influence of water.

Indifference.

ALAS! my lord, if talking would prevail,
I could suggest much better arguments
Than those regards you throw away on me.
— *Young.*

LET me this fondness from my bosom tear;
Let me forget that e'er I thought her fair;
Come, cool indifference, and heal my breast;
Wearied, at length, I seek thy downy rest —
Not all her arts my steady soul shall move,
And she shall find indifference conquers love.
— *Lyttleton.*

A GRACIOUS person; but yet I cannot love him:
He might have took his answer long ago.
— *Shakespeare.*

BUT in those lands where people are,
Few men at all take any heed;
While still he sings, and from afar,
So beautiful is the song, indeed
That twilight loiters hours to hear,
Eavesdropping with a roseate ear.
— *Edgar Fawcett.*

Myrtle.

Myrtus communis.   NATURAL ORDER: *Myrtaceæ — Myrtle Family.*

ATHENS adopted the Myrtle as an emblem of municipal authority, and the victors in the Olympic games were crowned with wreaths of it; it was also sacred to Venus, the goddess of love, and her temples were encompassed with groves of Myrtle. We find in Virgil, that in Baiae (a small town in Campania, on the coast between Cumae and Puteoli, a favorite resort of the Romans on account of its warm baths and pleasant location), "there was a large Myrtle grove, where a warm, sudorific vapor rose from the earth." King Faunus beat Bona Dea, his wife, to death with myrtle rods, because she lowered the dignity of a queen by becoming intoxicated with wine. He afterward repented his severity, deified, and paid her divine honors. It is a handsome, ornamental evergreen shrub, grown usually in the greenhouse, and was much admired by the ancients for its elegance and fragrance.

Love.

OH, love! thou sternly dost thy power maintain,
And wilt not bear a rival in thy reign;
Tyrants and thou all fellowship disdain.
— *Dryden.*

LOVE knoweth every form of air,
And every shape of earth;
And comes, unbidden, everywhere,
Like thought's mysterious birth.
— *Willis.*

LOVE is a pearl of purest hue,
But stormy waves are round it,
And dearly may a woman rue
The hour that first she found it.
— *Miss Landon.*

A SUBTLE, unbound power,
That slips the soul from its prison fair
And makes it buoyant and lighter than air.
— *C. H. T.*

TRUE, ah! true, and well I mark
All your words would teach —
And my soul beyond the dark
Stretches forth to reach

Faith yet fuller, more complete,
While my lips attest
It is love makes heaven sweet —
Love is more than rest!
— *Mary B. Dodge.*

Nasturtium.

Tropæolum majus.   NATURAL ORDER: *Tropæolaceæ — Nasturtium Family.*

OF this handsome class of plants, there exists quite a number of annual varieties, some of which are dwarf or low-growing, others climbing five or six feet high, adhering to their support by their long leaf-stalks. The flowers are brilliant, usually of some shade of orange or yellow, combined with red, crimson, maroon, or carmine, and in shape very aptly compared to a helmet, and the leaf to a shield. Hence the botanical name, from the Greek *tropæon* a trophy, which meant strictly the pile of captured helmets, shields etc., raised by the victorious party on the field of battle. The vernacular Nasturtium is from the Latin *nasus tortus*, twisted nose, because of the pungency of the plant. There are also two or three tuburous or bulbous varieties, that are as yet rather unfrequent in cultivation, and are more delicate in foliage and flower than the well known species mentioned above. The Canary Bird Flower, Tropeolum aduncum is said, when fully grown, to live on air alone if detached from the roots. They are all natives of Peru.

Heroism.

YET it may be more lofty courage dwells
  In one weak heart which braves an adverse fate,
Than his whose ardent soul indignant swells,
  Warm'd by the fight, or cheer'd through high debate.
— *Mrs. Norton.*

THE wise and active conquer difficulties
  By daring to attempt them; sloth and folly
Shiver and sink at sights of toil and hazard,
And make the impossibility they fear.
— *Rowe.*

THERE is a tear for all who die,
  A mourner o'er the humblest grave;
But nations swell the funeral cry,
  And triumph weeps above the brave.
— *Byron.*

THERE'S naught within the compass of humanity
  But I would dare and do.
— *Sir A. Hunt.*

AND though in peaceful garb arrayed,
  And weaponless except his blade,
His stately mien as well implied

A highborn heart and martial pride,
As if a baron's crest he wore,
And, sheathed in armor, tread the shore.
— *Scott.*

Nemophila.

Nemophila insignis. NATURAL ORDER: *Hydrophyllaceæ—Waterleaf Family.*

DEMOPHILA, meaning, in the Greek, lover of the grove, is a low-growing, delicate, herbaceous plant, about six inches high, and a native of California. The narrow leaves are notched deeply on the sides, and are slightly downy; the flowers are small, but pretty, some being white with a purple spot on each petal, as if fairy hands had given each a pinch with thumb and finger; another is blue, edged with white, and *vice versa* —blue with a white center; altogether a dozen or more different varieties. The plants delight in shady grounds, making themselves doubly desirable on that account, and present a nice appearance as a border for walks and margins of beds, or, if fancy dictate, they can be sown in a mass by themselves.

Prosperity.

DAME NATURE gave him comeliness and health,
And Fortune, for a passport, gave him wealth.
—*Walter Harte.*

WHEN fortune raiseth to the greatest height,
The happy man should most suppress his state,
Expecting still a change of things to find,
And fearing when the gods appear too kind.
—*Sir Robert Howard.*

OF both our fortunes, good and bad, we find
Prosperity more searching of the mind;
Felicity flies o'er the wall and fence,
While misery keeps in with patience.
—*Herrick.*

FORTUNE came smiling to my youth, and woo'd it,
And purple greatness met my ripen'd years.
—*Dryden.*

PROSPERITY puts out unnumbered thoughts
Of import high, and light divine, to man.
—*Young.*

NOW rising fortune elevates his mind,
He shines unclouded, and adorns mankind.
—*Savage.*

DAILY and hourly proof
Tell us, prosperity is at highest degree
The fount and handle of calamity.
—*Chapman.*

Nettle.

Urtica dioica. NATURAL ORDER: *Urticaceæ—Nettle Family.*

URTICA, from the Latin *uro*, I burn, is the very expressive and appropriate botanical name of this familiar nuisance, as one cannot come in contact with it without being stung. Through its innumerable tubular hairs there passes a viscous, venomous fluid into the pores of the skin, creating a sensation that is intensely disagreeable and indescribable. Hence the term nettled is a synonym for chagrin or any mortifying sensation. The Greek epithet *dioica* denotes belonging to the household, or familiar. The flowers of the nettle are small and green. The leaves of the young plants are sometimes used as a potherb, but of course have to be gathered with gloves. Some of the Asiatic varieties yield a fiber that is sometimes utilized as a substitute for hemp. There are in all about twenty-three genera and three hundred species of nettles.

Slander.

FROM door to door you might have seen him speed,
  Or plac'd amid a group of gaping fools,
And whispering in their ears with his foul lips.
          — *Pollock.*

SLANDEROUS reproaches and foul infamies,
  Leasings, backbitings and vainglorious crakes,
Bad counsels, praises, and false flatteries;
All these against that fort did bend their batteries.
        — *Spenser.*

OH! many a shaft, at random sent,
  Finds mark the archer little meant;
And many a word, at random spoken,
May soothe or wound a heart that's broken.
        —*Scott.*

IF I am traduc'd by tongues, which neither know
  My faculties nor person, yet will be
The chroniclers of my doing—let me say,
'Tis but the fate of place, and the rough brake
That virtue must go through.   —*Shakespeare.*

SKILL'D by a touch to deepen scandal's tints, While mingling truth with falsehood, sneers with smiles,
  With all the kind mendacity of hints, And thread of candor with a web of wiles.
        —*Byron.*

Oak.

Quercus alba. NATURAL ORDER: *Cupuliferæ — Oak Family.*

EVERY one is familiar with the appearance of this noble genus of trees, or has read more or less in its praise. The wood or timber of many of the varieties is exceedingly useful to man, in many of the mechanical arts, but more especially in ship-building, on account of its great strength and durability. It is also of historic interest to all Americans, as it was in the hollow of an oak at Hartford, that the Charter obtained by Gov. Winthrop, the younger, for the colonists of Connecticut, from Charles I. of England, was secreted from October 31, 1687, to May, 1689. Sir Edmund Andros made an unsuccessful attempt to rob them of it, but was thwarted by William Wadsworth, who spirited it off and hid it in the Oak, which from this circumstance was called the Charter Oak.

It is supposed to have been upward of three hundred years old when blown down by a storm, Aug. 20, 1856. The Oak has been considered by the heathen as honored above all other trees, because the sacred mistletoe grows upon its branches.

Honor.

THESE be the sheaves that honor's harvest bears;
The seed thy valiant acts; the world the field.
— *Fairfax.*

HONOR and shame from no condition rise;
Act well your part, there all the honor lies.
— *Pope.*

MINE honor is my life; both grow in one;
Take honor from me, and my life is done.
— *Shakespeare.*

HEAV'N, that made me honest, made me more
Than ever king did when he made a lord.
— *Rowe.*

SO much the thirst of honor fires the blood;
So many would be great, so few be good;
For who would virtue for herself regard,
Or wed without the portion of reward?
— *Dryden.*

THE tall oak, towering to the skies,
The fury of the wind defies;
From age to age, in virtue strong,
Inured to stand and suffer wrong.
— *Montgomery.*

Oats.

Avena sativa. NATURAL ORDER: *Gramineæ—Grass Family.*

FAMILIAR throughout our own and other lands is this tall, grasslike plant. It is grown in large fields for its useful and nutritious seeds, which grow in long, loose panicles. In Scotland much pains are taken to prepare a meal from it, and when boiled into a mush, as we use cornmeal, or baked into oat cake, forms an excellent article of diet, very wholesome and nutritious, so that the cannie Scot's time-honored predilection for oatmeal is found based upon sound physiological principles. The whole seed is used everywhere as food for horses and cattle. It is said to flourish in cold, but to degenerate in warm, climates.

Country Life.

I'LL cull the farthest mead for thy repast;
 The choicest I to thy board will bring,
And draw thy water from the freshest spring.
—*Prior.*

THERE health, so wild and gay, with bosom bare,
 And rosy cheek, keen eye, and flowing hair,
Trips with a smile the breezy scene along,
And pours the spirit of content in song.
—*Pindar.*

NATURE I'll court in her sequestered haunts,
 By mountain, meadow, streamlet, grove, or cell,
Where the pois'd lark his evening ditty chants,
 And health, and peace, and contemplation dwell.
—*Smollet.*

OUR fields are full with the time-ripened grain,
 Our vineyards with the purple clusters swell;
Her golden splendor glimmers on the main,
 And vales and mountains her bright glory tell.
—*Lord Thurlow.*

O HOW canst thou renounce the boundless store
 Of charms which nature to her votary yields;
The warbling woodland, the resounding shore,
 The pomp of groves, and garniture of fields.
—*Beattie.*

MINE be a cot beside the hill;
 A beehive's hum shall soothe my ear;
A willowy brook, that turns a mill,
 With many a fall shall linger near.
—*Rogers.*

O FIELDS, O woods, O when shall I be made
 The happy tenant of your shade?
—*Cowley.*

Oleander.

Nerium Oleander. NATURAL ORDER: *Apocynaceæ — Dogbane Family.*

GROWING erect and branching regularly, this tall evergreen shrub keeps a good shape with very little attention. The most common species have rose-colored, single or double flowers, while some of the others are red, striped, crimson and white, and one pure white, partly double. The flowers of the latter are apt to scorch if too much exposed to the burning rays of a midday sun when in bloom. All of these varieties are natives of the Levant and some parts of Palestine, growing near streams in those localities, but are quite common in house cultivation in America, being placed out of doors in summer. In Florida it is found in swampy lands, attaining the size of a tree. The Oleander belongs to a very poisonous family, and no part should be placed in the mouth, as instances of occasional fatality are on record.

Beware.

LET no man know thy business save some friend,
A man of mind.
— *Bailey.*

IF light wrongs touch me not.
No more shall great; it not a few, not many;
There's naught so sacred with us but may find
A sacrilegious person; yet the thing is
No less divine 'cause the profane can reach it.
— *Jonson.*

BEWARE of desperate steps; the darkest day,
Live till tomorrow, will have passed away.
— *Cowper.*

UNCERTAIN ways unsafest are,
And doubt a greater mischief than despair.
— *Sir J. Denham.*

THEN fly betimes, for only they
Conquer love, that run away.
— *Carew.*

THOSE edges soonest turn that are most keen,
A sober moderation stands sure,
No violent extremes endure.
— *Aleyn.*

A VALIANT man
Ought not to undergo or tempt a danger,
But worthily, and by selected ways.
— *Ben Jonson.*

HEAT not a furnace for your foe so hot
That it doth singe yourself.
— *Shakespeare.*

Oleaster.

Elæagnus argentea.   NATURAL ORDER: *Elæagnaceæ — Oleaster Family.*

SILVER-LEAVED Oleaster is a native of Missouri, and is considered a shrub worthy of introducing into ornamental shrubberies. The foliage is handsome, and covered with a silvery scurf; the branches are red. In Europe there is a variety cultivated which produces a fruit having, when dried, much the flavor of the date. It is of a reddish color, and about the shape and size of a plum. It is called Elæagnus angustiflora, or Narrow-leaved Oleaster. Several other of the species are worthy of attention, one being an evergreen variety from the East Indies. The botanical name seems to imply, in Greek, upright olive — a significance retained in the vernacular, which is derived from the Latin.

Providence.

PROVIDENCE, not niggardly, but wise,
  Here lavishly bestows, and there denies,
That by each other's virtues we may rise.
                — *Granville.*

GO mark the matchless working of the power
  That shuts within the seed the future flower;
Bids these in elegance of form excel,
In color these, and those delight the smell;
Sends Nature forth, the daughter of the skies,
To dance on earth, and charm all human eyes.
                — *Cowper.*

THERE, when the tangled web is all explained,
  Wrong suffered, pain inflicted, grief disdained,
Man's proud, mistaken judgments and false scorn
Shall melt like mists before the uprising morn,
And holy truth stand forth serenely bright,
In the rich flood of God's eternal light!
                — *Mrs. Norton.*

HE that doth the ravens feed,
  Yea, providently caters for the sparrow,
Be comfort to my age.
                — *Shakespeare.*

WHO is it that will doubt
  The care of heaven? or think th' immortal
Pow'rs are slow, 'cause they take the privilege
To choose their own time, when they will send
Their blessings down.
                — *Davenant.*

THUS wisdom speaks
  To man; thus calls him through this actual form
Of nature, through religion's fuller noon,
Through life's bewildering mazes, to observe
A Providence in all!
                — *Ogilvie.*

Olive.

Olea Europæa. NATURAL ORDER: *Oleaceæ—Olive Family.*

CHIEFLY cultivated for its fruit, the Olive abounds in Spain, Italy, and the southern parts of France. The fruit is first bruised to the consistency of paste, after which it is mixed with hot water, and strained through flannel sacks. The oil is then separated from the water, and bottled or barreled for transportation as the Olive oil of commerce. Minerva (in Greek, Athene), the goddess of war, wears a crown of Olive leaves as an emblem of peace; for, say ancient authors, "war is only made that peace may follow." It is said, also, that when she was disputing with Neptune about the name of a city, she caused an Olive tree to spring out of the ground, which being considered more useful to man than the horse her competitor brought, she had the privilege of calling the city Athenæ, after her own name. This is the Athens of our time.

Peace.

A PEACE is of the nature of a conquest;
  For then both parties nobly are subdued,
  And neither party loses.
      —*Shakespeare.*

ANGEL of Peace, thou hast wandered too long;
  Spread thy white wings to the sunshine of love,
Come while our voices are blended in song,
  Fly to our ark like the storm-beaten dove.
      —*O. W. Holmes.*

LOVELY concord, and most sacred peace,
  Doth nourish virtue, and fast friendship breeds;
Weak she makes strong, and strong things does increase,
  Till it the pitch of highest praise exceeds.
      —*Spenser.*

PEACE, thy olive wand extend,
  And bid wild war his ravage end.
      —*Burns.*

DOWN the dark future, through long generations,
  The echoing sounds grow fainter, and then cease;
And like a bell with solemn, sweet vibrations,
  I hear once more the voice of Christ say Peace.

Peace! and no longer from its brazen portals
  The blast of war's great organ shakes the skies!
But beautiful as songs of the immortals,
  The holy melodies of love arise. —*Longfellow.*

PEACE o'er the world her olive wand extend,
  And white-robed Innocence from heaven descend.
      —*Pope.*

Orange.

Citrus aurantium. NATURAL ORDER: *Auranticeæ—Orange Family.*

THIS tree is of the same family as the citron, the lime, and the lemon. It is an evergreen of middle size, and when covered with its bright, golden fruit, is one of the most attractive sights in nature. The pulp of the Orange is divided into sections of as great regularity as is that of the lemon, the outer covering of each being dry and of considerable strength, while within are little sacs of irregular length filled with a cooling, delightful and refreshing juice, that renders it popular with all. The flowers are of a creamy white. It is a native of tropical climates, yet can be grown in a good greenhouse with ease, requiring little attention. In the West Indies, where it is native, as well as in Florida, Louisiana and California, it is cultivated in orchards for exportation, and yields fruit plentifully. Seedling trees require budding or grafting to make them bear in the greenhouse.

Chastity.

BENEATH the cares of earth she does not bow,
 Though she hath ofttimes drained its bitter cup!
But ever wanders on with heavenward brow,
 And eyes whose lovely orbs are lifted up!
— Amelia B. Welby.

SO dear to heaven is saintly chastity,
 That when a soul is found sincerely so,
A thousand liveried angels lackey her,
Driving far off each thing of sin and guilt.
— Milton.

CHASTE as the icicle
 That's curded by the frost from purest snow,
And hangs on Dian's temple.
—Shakespeare.

THE summer's flower is to the summer sweet,
 Though to itself it only live and die;
But if that flower with base infection meet,
 The basest weed outbraves his dignity;
For sweetest things turn sourest by their deeds;
Lilies that fester, smell far worse than weeds.
—Shakespeare.

Orchis.

Orchis spectabilis. NATURAL ORDER: *Orchidaceæ—Orchis Family.*

WE have many varieties of this plant growing throughout the United States, on our prairies or in shady, rocky places. They usually produce very handsome and various colored flowers. The most beautiful, however, are the Tropical Orchids, found in the South Sea Islands, growing on branches of trees and other substances, and depending so much on the air for their sustenance, and so little on root nourishment, that they are called air plants. They are more gorgeous in bloom than any terrestrial plant. In England there are extensive houses for their culture alone, and we believe some few in this country. They are mostly grown in small cork boxes, or on pieces of wood, in a warm, moist atmosphere. Some few grow in rooms successfully, but no water must touch the foliage or flowers, only enough to moisten the substance containing the roots.

A Belle.

YET graceful ease, and sweetness void of pride,
  Might hide her faults, if belles had faults to hide;
If to her share some female errors fall,
Look on her face, and you'll forget 'em all.
              —*Pope.*

A ROSEBUD in its first green coat,
  You wrapped your shawl about your throat,
And crossed the lawn, when we went boating;
I touched the fragrance of your hand;
The fog came down and hid the land,
  As white as snow, and we were floating.
        —*Will Wallace Harney.*

IN her cheeks the vermil red did shew,
  Like roses in a bed of lilies shed;
The which ambrosial odors from them threw,
And gazer's sense with double pleasure fed.
            —*Spenser.*

BECAUSE thou wear'st, *ma belle*,
  A strong, pure, silent spell,
Safely from all dark ways my feet retrieving;
Because thou wert to me
As lulled air to wild sea,
Storm-furrowed, fiercely free, and strongly grieving.
         —*Edgar Fawcett.*

SHE was a form of life and light,
  That, seen, became a part of sight;
And rose, where'er I turned mine eye,
The morning star of memory.
         —*Byron.*

Osier--Basket.

Salix viminalis.   NATURAL ORDER: *Salicaceæ—Willow Family.*

VARIETIES of the Willow are very numerous, all of them delighting in soil in which there is an abundance of moisture, and are consequently oftener found along the margins of streams, or in low-lying, wet meadows, than in any other locality. This species does not develope into a tree, the stems rising singly to the height of ten or twelve feet; they are very pliable, and well adapted to the industry to which they are applied. Viminalis signifies twigs or branches adapted to plaiting. One of the seven Roman hills on which Jupiter was worshiped was called Viminalis Collis, from the Willow-copse which once stood there.

Frankness.

THE brave do never shun the light;
 Just are their thoughts, and open are their tempers;
Truly without disguise they love or hate;
Still are they found in the fair face of day,
And heav'n and men are judges of their actions.
    —*Rowe.*

THY words had such a melting flow,
 And spoke of truth so sweetly well,
They dropp'd like heav'n's serenest snow,
And all was brightness where they fell!
  —*Moore.*

WHATE'ER the emotions of her heart,
 Still shone conspicuous in her eyes—
Stranger to every female art,
 Alike to feign or to disguise.
  —*Shaw.*

HE 'LL suit his bearing to the hour,
 Laugh, listen, learn or teach,
With joyous freedom in his mirth,
 And candor in his speech.
  —*Eliza Cook.*

A STALWART form, a manly port,
 A fearless brow, an eye of truth,
A step as free as that of youth,
A presence fit for camp or court;

A knee a child would love to climb;
 A face a woman needs must trust,
Quite free from guile and clean from lust,
Nor marred, though nobly marked by time.
  —*Kate J. Hill.*

Osmunda.

Osmunda regalis. NATURAL ORDER: *Filices—Fern Family.*

IN England this fern is called Royal Osmunda, as its Latin name signifies, and is given a place in the ferneries of the most fastidious amateur. In America it is found in damp meadows and swampy lands, sending up its fronds sometimes three and four feet high, but in less damp and congenial places it diminishes its height nearly one half. There is scarcely anything more graceful than the Fern, of whatever species, from the common brake in the woods, or fence corners, to the most delicate tropical one cherished in hothouse or greenhouse. No glaring color to strike the eye, nothing but its own simple and elegant outline, and that ever-satisfying, restful and never-tiring tint of nature, the predominating green.

Dreams.

WHY, when the balm of sleep descends on man,
  Do gay delusions, wand'ring o'er the brain,
Soothe the delighted soul with empty bliss?
                       —*Dr. Johnson.*

WELL may dreams present us fictions,
  Since our waking moments teem
With such fanciful convictions
  As make life itself a dream.
              —*Campbell.*

WHEN sleep's calm wing is on my brow,
  And dreams of peace my spirit lull,
Before me like a misty star
  That form floats dim and beautiful.
             —*G. D. Prentice.*

INNOCENT dreams be thine! thy heart sends up
  Its thoughts of purity, like pearly bells,
Rising in crystal fountains. Would I were
A sound, that I might steal upon thy dreams,
And, like the breathing of my flute, distil
Sweetly upon thy senses.   —*Willis.*

DREAMS are the children of an idle brain,
  Begot of nothing but vain fantasy,
Which is as thin of substance as the air,
And more inconstant than the wind.
             —*Shakespeare.*

ALAS! that dreams are only dreams!
  That fancy cannot give
A lasting beauty to those forms,
  Which scarce a moment live!
             —*Rufus Dawes.*

Oxalis.

Oxalis floribunda. NATURAL ORDER: *Oxalidaceæ—Oxalis Family.*

ALMOST everyone is familiar with our native Oxalises, under the name of Wood Sorrel, that children are fond of plucking for its pleasant acid juice, which, when extracted and concentrated, is highly poisonous. The name denotes in Greek sour salt, which is sufficiently appropriate. The foreign species come from Chili, Cape of Good Hope, Europe, and Africa, and are cultivated for their bloom. The root is bulbous, and should be potted in the fall for winter bloom. Those that have merely fleshy roots bloom in summer, and should always remain in the soil. The bulbous variety should be kept in dry sand during the summer. The oxalic acid of commerce is prepared from saccharine and farinaceous substances through the action of nitric acid, and is used for removing spots of iron rust and ink stains from linen or other articles.

Parental Affection.

BUT does not nature for the child prepare
 The parent's love, the tender nurse's care,
Who, for their own forgetful, seek his good?
— *Blackmore.*

OH! mother's love is glorifying,
 On the cheek like sunset lying;
In the eyes a moistened light,
Softer than the moon at night!
— *Thomas Burbidge.*

FOR if there be a human tear
 From passion's dross refined and clear,
'Tis that which pious parents shed
Upon a duteous daughter's head.
— *Scott.*

SOMEHOW while lingering to watch you here,
 Thy tyrannous mother-love makes me forget
All else but that you are divinely dear!
— *Edgar Fawcett.*

SWEET is the image of the brooding dove!
 Holy as heaven a mother's tender love!
The love of many prayers, and many tears,
Which changes not with dim declining years,
The only love which, on this teeming earth,
Asks no return for passion's wayward birth.
— *Mrs. Norton.*

Pæony.

Pæonia officinalis. NATURAL ORDER: *Ranunculaceæ—Crowfoot Family.*

THE Pæony is supposed to have derived its name from Pæon, a disciple of Æsculapius, who used it for the healing of Pluto, thereby arousing the jealous feelings of his preceptor, so much so indeed that he compassed his death. Both the root and leaves are used in medicine as an antispasmodic and tonic. The flowers are very large and showy in all the species. The common variety is a native of Switzerland; the white, of Tartary; the Siberian, as its name indicates, of Siberia. The Chinese Pæony is a shrub from three to four feet high, with ample foliage, and very large, brilliant, fragrant flowers. They are mostly hardy, except in extreme northern latitudes, and produce various colored blossoms.

Shame.

SHAME sticks ever close to the ribs of honor,
    Great men are never found after it.
                —*Middleton.*

WHEN knaves and fools combined o'er all prevail,
    When justice halts and right begins to fail,
Even the boldest start from public sneers,
Afraid of shame, unknown to other fears.
                —*Byron.*

THAT holy shame, which ne'er forgets
    What clear renown it us'd to wear;
Whose blush remains when virtue sets,
    To show her sunshine has been there.
                —*Moore.*

CONFOUND me not with shame, nor call up all
    The blood that warms my trembling heart,
To fill my cheeks with blushes.   —*Trap.*

I CAN bear scorpion stings, tread fields of fire,
    In frozen gulfs of cold, eternal lie;
Be toss'd aloft through tracts of endless void,
But cannot live in shame.   —*Joanna Baillie.*

THE mind that broods o'er guilty woes
    Is like a scorpion girt by fire;
In circle narrowing as it glows,
    The flames around their captive close.
                —*Byron.*

SOME seek to salve their blotted name
    With others' blot, till all do taste of shame.
                —*Sir P. Sidney.*

Parsley.

Apium petroselinum. NATURAL ORDER: *Umbelliferæ—Parsley Family.*

PARSLEY, a well known herb from the kitchen garden, is used for flavoring food, chiefly soups, and the garnishment of meat and game dishes when brought to the table. It is very partial to rich soil, and agriculturists say that soot placed around the plant is very congenial to it. There are several varieties produced by cultivation, differing in size and also in the curliness of the leaf, which is of a dark green. The seeds should be soaked in warm water several hours before planting. All the varieties are natives of Greece and the island of Sardinia, and are nearly allied to that great table favorite, celery. The name Apium is by some thought to be derived from the Celtic *apon*, or *avon*, a river, because the plant delights in moist situations; according to others the Apium denotes its relationship to celery, (botanically, Apium, and this from *apis*, a bee, while Petroselinum is the equivalent to Parsley, denoting in Greek, rock-curly, or rock-marsh —*selinon*, parsley, from *elos*, a marsh, or *elisso*, I twist.

Festivity.

FRIENDSHIP shall still thy evening feasts adorn,
  And blooming peace shall ever bless thy morn.
                          —*Prior.*

BLEST be those feasts with simple plenty crown'd,
  Where all the ruddy family around
Laugh at the jests or pranks that never fail,
Or sigh with pity at some mournful tale.
                   —*Goldsmith.*

THE banquet waits our presence, festal joy
  Laughs in the mantling goblet, and the night,
Illumin'd by the taper's dazzling beam,
Rivals departed day.
                   —*Brown.*

'TIS pity wine should be so deleterious,
  For tea and coffee leave us much more serious.
                 —*Byron.*

WHEN the laugh is lightest,
  When wildest goes the jest,
When gleams the goblet brightest,
  And proudest heaves thy breast,
And thou art madly pledging
  Each gay and jovial guest,—
A ghost shall glide amid the flowers—
  The shade of Love's departed hours.
                 —*Mrs. Osgood.*

Passion Flower.

Passiflora cœrulea. NATURAL ORDER: *Passifloraceæ—Passion Flower Family.*

MOSTLY natives of the tropical portions of America, the Passion Flowers climb to a great height — frequently from thirty to forty feet, the stem attaining the thickness of three or four inches in diameter. The foliage is palmate, being divided into five lobes in the Brazilian variety, and into three parts in the North American plants. The flowers, though transient, are large and beautiful. The petals, which are blue without, are lined with purple and white within, and spread themselves out in a flattened manner, with a row of filaments arranged around an inner circle, while erect stands the supposed resemblance of the cross. Several varieties are native in the United States. Among them are found flowers of red, purple, crimson, and red and white. Some of the species are adapted to the hot-house, and others to the greenhouse or conservatory. All are beautiful and attractive. The flower was named *flos passionis* by the early missionaries, who in their religious zeal imagined they saw emblems of the crucifixion — the crown of thorns, nails, hammer, etc.— in the various parts of the curious blossom.

Holy Love.

WE see Thy hand — it leads us, it supports us;
We hear Thy voice — it counsels and it courts us;
And then we turn away, and still thy kindness
Forgives our blindness. —*John Bowring.*

THY wonders do singly stand,
Nor far removed where feet have seldom stray'd;
Around us ever lies the enchanted land,
In marvels rich to Thine own sons displayed.
—*Jones Very.*

A SINGLE passion flower pressed
Is what my wistful eye engages,
And all the sign of love once blest
Lies buried 'tween the written pages.

FOR this a hundred voices I desire, [tire,
To tell thee what a hundred tongues would
Yet never could be worthily exprest:
How deeply thou art seated in my breast.
—*Dryden.*

But oh! the flower to you and me
A deeper mystery unrolls,
For written on its leaves I see
The record of two burning souls!
—*H. H. Leech.*

Pea--Sweet.

Lathyrus odoratus. NATURAL ORDER: *Leguminosæ — Pulse Family.*

LATHYRUS ODORATUS, or Sweet Pea, is one of the favorites of olden times, that has been crowded out by more recent novelties; but as fashions rotate, old things return to us as new; so now we hope these really-beautiful flowers will again come to the front, and press their claims upon all flower-loving people. They are most excellent for screens or arbors (whence the botanical name, from the Greek *lathon*, lying hid), many of them growing to the height of six feet; and although not producing as much leafage as the morning glory, they fully make up for the remissness by the abundance and fragrance of their blossoms. They are mostly from tropical climates, being natives of Ceylon, Sicily, and Barbary. In color they are white, purple, blue, nearly black, and variegated; and are most easy of cultivation.

Departure.

"BUT why do you go?" said the lady, while both sate under the yew;
    And her eyes were alive in their depth, as the kraken beneath the sea-blue.
"Because I fear you," he answered; "because you are far too fair,
    And able to strangle my soul in a mesh of your gold-colored hair." — *Mrs. Browning.*

SO, closing his heart, the judge rode on,
    And Maud was left in the field alone.
         — *Whittier.*

SING on! we sing in the glorious weather
  Till one steps over the tiny strand,
So narrow, in sooth, that still together
  On either brink we go hand in hand.
The beck grows wider, the hands must sever,
  On either margin, our songs all done,
We move apart, while she singeth ever,
  Taking the course of the stooping sun.
He prays, "Come over" — I may not follow;
  I cry, "Return!" but he cannot come:
We speak, we laugh, but with voices hollow;
  Our hands are hanging, our hearts are numb.
     — *Jean Ingelow.*

HERE are sweet peas, on tiptoe for a flight —
  With wings of gentle flush o'er delicate white,
And taper fingers catching at all things,
To bind them all about with tiny rings.
     — *John Keats.*

Peach Blossom.

Persica vulgaris. NATURAL ORDER: *Rosaceæ—Rose Family.*

NATIVE to Persia, the Peach is one of the most delightful of fruit trees. The different named varieties, numbering nearly two hundred, have been mostly produced by a process called hybridizing, to which nurserymen pay assiduous attention. The flowers most frequently seen are a beautiful rose tint. There are those, however, that are pure white, and also a double variety. In size they are a little larger than the blossom of the cherry. The fruit is among the most delicious bestowed upon man, and its medicinal properties are considered healthful, nutritious, and cooling to the system. The bark of the tree, the blossoms, and the skins of the seeds, are poisonous, being highly impregnated with prussic acid, which is distinguishable even in the odor of the flowers. In Great Britain the Peach is usually cultivated and trained against a south wall, in order to have the fruit ripen rapidly, the seasons being too inclement for it to be grown in large orchards, as it is found in the United States, where its cultivation forms a considerable industry.

I am Your Captive.

BUT an imprison'd mind, though living, dies,
   And at one time feels two captivities:
A narrow dungeon which her body holds,
But narrower body, which herself enfolds.
—*Dr. King.*

THEY chain'd us each to a marble stone,
   And we were three—yet each alone;
We could not move a single pace,
We could not see each other's face,
But with that pale and livid light
That made us strangers in our sight.
—*Byron.*

MAKE haste and lock the fetters over him,
   Lest Zeus behold thee lagging.
—*Mrs. Browning.*

SHE meant to weave me a snare
   Of some coquettish deceit,
Cleopatra-like, as of old,
To entangle me when we met,
To have her lion in a silken net,
And fawn at a victor's feet.
—*Tennyson.*

Pentstemon.

Pentstemon campanulatus.   NATURAL ORDER: *Scrophulariaceæ — Figwort Family.*

RAPIDLY advancing in favor since its introduction from Mexico, the Pentstemon is a handsome plant, finding a place in every garden when its beauty is once beheld; but it should be wintered in a cool part of the greenhouse, or some place free from frost. It can be raised from seed, and is said to bloom the first year if sown early in the spring. The blossom is tubular in shape, hanging three or four in a group, with the mouth of the flower downward. The color differs in different individuals, being scarlet, blue, and yellow, all remarkably handsome in whatever hue they sport. The stalk is from eighteen to twenty inches or more in height. They make nice conservatory or window plants, and will please all amateurs.

High-Bred.

BOAST not these titles of your ancestors,
  Brave youths, they 're their possessions not your own;
When your own virtues equal'd have their names,
'Twill be fair to lean upon their fames,
  For they are strong supporters.
  — *Ben Jonson.*

ACROSS the garden path she went,
  Herself the sweetest flower there,
Though richest blooms of Orient
  Their fragrance mingled in the air.
Her swarthy bondmaids held aloft
  A canopy of colors gay,
Or brushed with tufts of plumage soft
  The humming insect tribe away.
For sun, nor wind, nor gauzy wing,
  Must venture on a touch too free;
She was the daughter of a king,
  And bore herself right royally.
  — *Mary E. Bradley.*

PUT off your giant titles, then I can
  Stand in your judgments' blank and equal man,
Though hills advanced are above the plain,
They are but higher earth, nor must disdain
Alliance with the vale; we see a spade
Can level them, and make a mount a glade;
Howe'er we differ in the herald's book,
He that mankind's extraction shall look
In nature's rolls, must grant we all agree
In our best parts, immortal pedigree.
  — *Dr. Henry King.*

Periwinkle.

Vinca major. NATURAL ORDER: *Apocynaceæ — Dogbane Family.*

THESE pretty little trailing plants are allied to the stately oleander, and are mostly found in the tropical or warm climates. One of the species has variegated foliage, and is an admirable plant for covering the ground beneath hedges and other high-growing shrubs, giving a succession of bloom during the whole summer. In cool latitudes it is grown in pots, being readily propagated by slips. The Vinca minor is an evergreen plant of straggling growth, the procumbent stems being several feet in length, and threadlike, fully illustrating its Latin name, which comes from *vincio*, I bind. The Vinca major is more erect in habit. It requires much heat in winter, but does well in summer in a sunny border. The Madagascar Periwinkle is a very handsome upright species, suitable for indoor culture, and has leaves of polished green, and pretty white or rose-colored flowers, with a dark eye in the center. All the species bloom freely, and are easily cultivated.

Early Friendship.

FRIENDSHIP our only wealth, our last retreat and strength,
Secure against ill fortune and the world. — *Rowe.*

FEW are the hearts that have proved the truth
Of their early affection's vow;
And let those few, the beloved of youth,
Be dear in absence now.

O, vividly in their faithful breast
Shall the gleam of remembrance play,
Like the lingering light of the crimson west,
When the sunbeam hath passed away!
— *Horace Twiss.*

LAY this into your breast:
Old friends, like old swords, still are trusted best.
— *Webster.*

THAT heart, methinks, [print
Were of strange mold, which kept no cherish'd
Of earlier, happier times, when life was fresh,
And love and innocence made holyday.
— *Hillhouse.*

YES, the summer of life passes quickly away,
Soon the winter of age sheds its snow on the heart,
But the warm sun of friendship that gilded youth's day,
Shall still thro' the dark clouds a soft ray impart.
— *A. Gibbs.*

Persimmon.

Diospyros Virginiana.   NATURAL ORDER: *Ebenaceæ — Ebony Family.*

PERSIMMON trees are found in the United States, attaining a larger growth in the south than in the north, where they seldom become more than a large shrub. The flowers are inconspicuous, and are succeeded by a plum-shaped, pulpy fruit, of a reddish-orange hue, containing several hard-shelled seeds. Persimmons are only ripened by the action of the frost, after which they become palatable and nutritious. In the Southern States they are used in various ways, but in the Middle States they are seldom found plentifully enough to be used in any way except to eat in their original state. They are allied to the date plum, a foreign variety. The bark is used to allay fevers, and it also possesses tonic and astringent properties. The species are numerous in the tropics.

Amid Nature's Beauties.

THE love of Nature's works
 Is an ingredient in the compound man,
Infused at the creation of the kind. — *Cowper.*

HOW blest the man who in these peaceful plains
 Plows his paternal field; far from the noise,
The care and bustle of a busy world!
All in the sacred, sweet, sequester'd vale
Of solitude, the secret primrose path
 Of rural life, he dwells; and with him dwell
Peace and content, twins of the sylvan shade,
And all the graces of the golden age.
— *Michael Bruce.*

THE green earth sends its incense up
 From every mountain shrine —
From every flower and dewy cup
 That greeteth the sunshine.
— *Whittier.*

IF thou art worn and hard beset
 With sorrows that thou wouldst forget,
If thou wouldst read a lesson that will keep
Thy heart from fainting, and thy soul from sleep,
Go to the woods and hills! — no tears
Dim the sweet look that Nature wears.
— *Longfellow.*

O nature! how in every charm serene.
Beattie.

Petunia.

Petunia argentea. NATURAL ORDER: *Solanaceæ — Nightshade Family.*

BELONGING to the same order of plants as the tobacco, the Petunia is a native of South America, and derives its name from *petun*, a name for tobacco among the aborigines of that quarter. Of late years foreign florists have taken infinite pains to improve it by hybridizing, and have succeeded in producing some that are most exquisite in color, being plain, blotched, or striped, and nearly as double as a rose. This has only been accomplished after numerous discouragements. As the double ones rarely produce seeds, and should they do so would seldom yield double flowers in return, the mode of procedure has been to take the pollen of the double flower and apply it to the stigma of the never-failing single flower, having previously removed the pollen of the latter. The plants must then be grown and allowed to ripen under cover, to be sure that no bee or truant insect, searching for hidden sweets, shall shake off from its tiny legs any of the pollen that may have adhered while wantoning over single blossoms.

Keep Your Promises.

MY deeds and speeches, sir,
  Are lines drawn from one centre; what I promise
To do, I'll do.
               — *Daniel.*

THE man that is not in the enemies' pow'r,
  Nor fetter'd by misfortune, and breaks promises,
Degrades himself; he never can pretend
To honor more.
               — *Sir Robert Stapleton.*

LET not thy tongue too often bind thy will,
  To render deeds unto thy foe or friend,
For words once utter'd thou must erst fulfill,
  Lest sweetest friendship have inglorious end

DIVINEST creature! bright Astrea's daughter!
  How shall I honor thee for this success?
Thy promises are like Adonis's gardens,
  That one day bloom'd, and fruitful were the next.
               — *Shakespeare.*

For hearts once lighten'd by a promise giv'n,
  May sink too low for rescue shouldst thou fail,
As ships reach not the port for which they've striv'n
  Except a favoring wind their sails prevail.
               C. H. T.

Phaseolus.

Phaseolus multiflorus.   NATURAL ORDER: *Leguminosæ — Pulse Family.*

ONE of the plants that have been utilized by man for food, the Phaseolus, is familiar to all under the name of Bean. Some few are indigenous to the soil, but most of those grown, either for food or ornament, are from foreign lands. The Phaseolus vulgaris, that is so much grown for its edible pods, is from the East Indies, as are also the short Bush and Lima Beans, all three of which produce white flowers. The Phaseolus multiflorus, or Scarlet Runner, is an annual from South America. The blossoms are a brilliant scarlet, in which there is a slight dash of orange. There is also a variety with white and lilac flowers. The Hyacinth Bean is another handsome bloomer, and, with the two previously mentioned, is cultivated as an ornamental climber for screens, trellises and arbors.

Opportunity.

THE means that heaven yields must be embraced,
  And not neglected; else, if heaven would,
And we will not, heaven's offer we refuse,
The proffer'd means of succor and redress.   —*Shakespeare.*

I FIND my zenith doth depend upon
  A most auspicious star; whose influence
If now I court not, but omit, my fortunes
Will ever after droop.   —*Shakespeare.*

MISS not occasion; by the forelock take
  That subtle power, the never-halting time,
Lest a mere moment's putting off should make
Mischance almost as heavy as a crime.
    —*Wordsworth.*

THE golden opportunity
  Is never offer'd twice; seize then the hour
When fortune smiles, and duty points the way.
    —*Old Play.*

THE old Scythians [wings,
  Painted blind Fortune's powerful hands with
To show her gifts come swift and suddenly,
Which, if her fav'rite be not swift to take,
He loses them forever.   —*Chapman.*

OCCASION, set on wing, flies fast away,
  Whose back once turned, no holdfast can we find;
Her feet are swift, bald is her head behind;
Whoso hath hold, and after lets her go,
Does lose the lot which fortune did bestow.
    —*Mirror for Magistrates.*

Phlox.

Phlox subulata. NATURAL ORDER: *Polemoniaceæ—Polemonium Family.*

IT is said that Drummond, an eminent botanist and collector of flowers, on seeing some of the above in blossom, smiling among the barren pine-lands in New Jersey, exclaimed, "the beauty of that alone is worth coming to America to see; it is so splendid!" and truly they are beautiful. The Phlox is found on rocky hills, from New Jersey west to Kentucky and south to Georgia, usually growing in clusters, and blooming in May. The flower is either pink or white, with a dark spot in the center. The most handsome garden Phloxes are those called Phlox Drummondii, named after the above botanist, and probably derived from our native variety. The blossoms, arraying themselves in almost every concievable tint of the various colors, are charming to the eye. The Greek word *phlox* denotes flame.

Equanimity.

THOU wast my nurse in sickness, and my comforter in health,
　So gentle and so constant, when our love was all our wealth.
　　　　　　　　　　—*Albert Pike.*

OH! we will walk this world,
　Yok'd in all exercise of noble aim,
And so through those dark gates across the wild
That no man knows.
　　　—*Tennyson.*

THERE are two hearts whose movements thrill
　In unison so closely sweet,
That pulse to pulse, responsive still,
They both must heave—or cease to beat.
　　　—*Barton.*

RAPTUROUS moment of full-fruited gleaning!
　Rapturous blending of spirit with kin!
　　One in the heavens but knoweth the meaning
　　　Of tenderest mystery hidden within
　　This meeting of waters, this harvested stieen.
　　　　　　　—*Mary B. Dodge.*

HOW gladly, then, the days would glide,
　How faultlessly the nights would follow,
With cadences of many a tide
　In many a cavern cool and hollow!

What peace our sheltered lives would hold,
　What rest our placid hearts discover,
While wind, and bird, and sea-wave told
　The joys of lover and of lover!
　　　　　　　—*Edgar Fawcett.*

Pimpernel.

Anagallis arvensis.   NATURAL ORDER: *Primulaceæ—Primrose Family.*

ANAGALLIS is found growing in an uncultivated state in many places in Europe, so plentiful as to be classed as a weed. The flowers of this variety, which are scarlet, with a purple circle at the eye, open at eight o'clock and close at noon, or at the approach of rain, thereby giving it the familiar cognomen of "poor man's weather glass." It possesses acrid properties useful in medicine—dropsy, epilepsy and mania being the ailments for which the remedy is used. Its Latin appellative is derived from the Greek word *anagelao*, to laugh aloud. It is supposed to be identical with the Samolus mentioned by Pliny, who says the ancient Druids gathered it fasting, and with the left hand, carefully refraining from casting their eyes upon it, and ascribing to it magical properties in the cure and prevention of diseases in their cattle. It is a pretty plant of a trailing habit, with beautiful flowers in the cultivated species, whose tints are blue, white, red, vermilion, and maroon. Its geographical distribution extends over various portions of the world.

Mirth.

THE broadest mirth unfeeling folly wears,
Less pleasing far than virtue's very tears.
—*Pope.*

WHERE is the man that has not tried
How mirth can into folly glide,
And folly into sin?   —*Sir W. Scott.*

WHERE is our usual manager of mirth?
What revels are in hand? Is there no play
To ease the anguish of a torturing hour?
—*Shakespeare.*

WHILE her laugh, full of life, without any control
But the sweet one of gracefulness, rung from her soul,
And where it most sparkled, no glance could discover,
In lip, cheek, or eyes, for she brightened all over,
Like any fair lake that the breeze is upon,
When it breaks into dimples, and laughs in the sun.
Moore.

Pine.

Pinus strobus.   NATURAL ORDER: *Coniferæ—Pine Family.*

ENTERING so largely into all of our building enterprises, as well as into cheap household furniture, the wood of this tree is easily recognized, especially from its softness and lightness. The trunk, which is usually very straight, often attains the height of two hundred feet, while about half the distance from the ground the branches stretch themselves like great self-sustaining arms, rendering the Pine one of the most noble trees of the forest. The needle-like foliage is clustered in small masses on the tips of the twigs. The tree is supposed to have received its name from its leaves, for the Saxon name *pinntreo* signifies pin-tree, as does also the Danish *pyn-boom*, and the Welsh *pin-bren*.

Philosophy.

DIVINE philosophy! by whose pure light
    We first distinguish, then pursue the right,
Thy power the breast from every error frees,
And weeds out all its vices by degrees.
— *Gifford.*

WHAT does philosophy impart to man
    But undiscovered wonders? Let her soar
Even to her proudest heights, to where she caught
The soul of Newton and of Socrates,
    She but extends the scope of wild amaze
    And admiration. All her lessons end
    In wider views of God's unfathomed depths.
— *Henry Kirk White.*

Blest are those
Whose blood and judgment are so well commingled,
That they are not a pipe for fortune's finger,
To sound what stop she please.   — *Shakespeare.*

AND when I stretched beneath the pines,
    Where the evening star so holy shines,
I laugh at the lore and the pride of man,
    At the sophist schools, and the learned clan;
    For what are they all in their high conceit,
    When man in the bush with God may meet?
— *Emerson.*

PHILOSOPHY and Reason! Oh! how vain
    Their lessons to the feelings! They but teach
To hide them deeper, and to show a calm,
Unruffled surface to the idle gaze.   — *Elizabeth Bogart.*

Pitcher Plant.

Sarracenia psittacina.   NATURAL ORDER: *Sarraceniaceæ — Pitcher Plant Family.*

SARRACENIA, so named in honor of Dr. Sarrasin, of Quebec, is found in low, wet situations in warm latitudes, and is remarkable for the peculiar construction of the leaves, which are not flat, as in most other foliage, but are like hollow tubes, tapering toward the bottom like a vase, with a sort of cap or lid for the top, the hollow being nearly always half filled or more with water. There is one species from the East Indies that is well adapted for the greenhouse. The leaves of this plant are narrow and tapering, and the middle vein appears to run on in a sportive mood, extending itself like a thread beyond the leaf some four or five inches, and then curls about and turns up at the extremity, forming a delightful little pitcher. When grown in a pot, it requires a great deal of moisture, and a layer of moss or cocoa fiber on the surface of the soil to check evaporation. Some varieties have leaves from one to three feet high. The flowers are yellow or purple.

Instinct.

LEARN from the birds what food the thickets yield;
 Learn from the beasts the physic of the field;
The art of building from the bee receive;
Learn of the mole to plough, the worm to weave.
— *Pope.*

SAY, where full instinct is the unerring guide,
 What hope or counsel can they need beside?
Reason, however able, cool at best,
Cares not for service, or but serves when prest;
Stays till we call, and then not often near;
But honest instinct comes a volunteer;
Sure never to o'ershoot, but just to hit;
While still too wide or short is human wit.
— *Pope.*

HOW can we justly different causes frame,
 When the effects entirely are the same?
Instinct and reason how can we divide?
'Tis the fool's ignorance, and the pedant's pride.
— *Prior.*

Plumbago.

Plumbago Capensis.   NATURAL ORDER: *Plumbaginaceæ — Leadwort Family.*

LEADWORT of the Cape, that is, of the Cape of Good Hope, is the meaning of the botanic name of this plant. In studying up the biography of a plant, one is frequently astonished to find it of such ancient origin. This one is recorded by Pliny as a plant reputed to cure a disease of the eyes, and we find it mentioned in other ancient authors. The varieties are numerous. Some of them can be grown out of doors until destroyed by frost, but most of them require some protection in the northern or colder latitudes. The Plumbago rosea is best adapted for hothouse culture, and produces a bountiful supply of red flowers; but for the greenhouse, the Plumbago Capensis is to be preferred, with its beautiful spikes of blue flowers, blooming from midsummer until midwinter. The other species are natives of the East Indies, Peru and Chili, and all have proved hardy in the Southern States. They flourish best in their native soil in the neighborhood of the sea, or marshes formed by salt water.

Meekness with Dignity.

A MEEK mountain daisy, with delicate crest,
   And the violet whose eye told the heaven of her breast.
                    — *Mrs. Sigourney.*

I LOVED thee for thy high-born grace,
  Thy deep and lustrous eye —
For the sweet meaning of thy brow,
  And for thy bearing high.

I loved thee for thy stainless truth,
  Thy thirst for higher things,
For all that to our common lot
  A better temper brings.   — *Willis.*

YET so much is my poverty of spirit,
  So mighty, and so many my defects,
That I would rather hide me from my greatness,
Being a bark to brook no mighty sea.
                    — *Shakespeare.*

HUMILITY, that low, sweet root,
  From which all heavenly virtues shoot.
                    — *Moore.*

HUMILITY is eldest-born of virtue,
  And claims the birthright at the throne of heav'n.
                    — *Murphy.*

Poinsettia.

Poinsettia pulcherrima. NATURAL ORDER: *Euphorbiaceæ — Spurge Family.*

JOEL ROBERTS POINSETT, United States minister to Mexico, discovered, in 1828, this magnificent plant, one that excites such universal admiration when in its holiday trim. It is commonly grown among hothouse plants, though it will thrive in other situations with care and attention. It is a half-shrubby plant, much inclined to a straggling growth, and requires pruning about the second spring month, when it should be cut back to within about two inches of the wood of the previous year. This causes the plant to send out side branches, which must be preserved with care lest the ends of the twigs be broken. In midwinter the scarlet bracts or leaves which surround the flowers begin to appear, crowning the tip of each shoot as it were with fire, when it is the most brilliant, most magnificent plant in our collections. For decorative purposes it is much sought, and as the demand nearly always exceeds the supply, high prices are paid without demur for these floral tips.

Brilliancy.

THE gay and glorious creatures! they neither "toil nor spin;"
   Yet lo! what goodly raiment they're all appareled in;
No tears are on their beauty, but dewy gems more bright
Than ever brow of eastern queen endiadem'd with light.
—*Mrs. Bowles.*

O ROSE! O pearl! O child! O things of light!
   O maiden's eye that melts with beams of love!
   O stars that sparkle in the vault above!
O peerless moon, thou radiant queen of night!
O golden sun, so glorious in my sight!

How doth my soul leap forth to soul in thee,
To that appealing mute divinity
Which gives thee glory as it gives thee might!
'Tis what we worship, though we know it not
—*Sallie A. Brock.*

HIS earnest and undazzled eye he keeps [words
   Fix'd on the sun of Truth, and breathes his
As easily as eagles cleave the air;
And never pauses till the height is won.
—*Mrs. Hale.*

DO what he will, he cannot realize
   Half he conceives — the glorious vision flies;
Go where he may, he cannot hope to find
The truth, the beauty pictur'd in his mind.
—*Rogers.*

Pomegranate.

Punica granatum. NATURAL ORDER: *Myrtaceæ—Myrtle Family.*

REQUIRING the protection of glass in the northern climate, the Pomegranate is generally cultivated in greenhouses, while in the south of Europe it is grown for hedges, being in its wild state a thorny bush. The flowers are large, handsome, and scarlet in color, both double and single. Its fruit has a hard rind, numerous seeds, a soft pulp of fine flavor, and is as large as an orange; while the root yields an extract valuable for its medical properties. Columella, a writer on husbandry in A. D. 42, makes mention of it. Josephus says, in his Antiquities of the Jews, "that the bells on the high priests' robes were the symbols of thunder, and the pomegranates, of lightning."

Lightning.

RED lightnings play'd along the firmament,
And their demolish'd works to pieces went.
— *Dryden.*

FROM cloud to cloud the rending lightnings rage;
Till, in the furious elemental war
Dissolv'd, the whole precipitated mass
Unbroken floods and solid torrents pour.
— *Thomson.*

THE low reeds bent by the streamlet's side,
And hills to the thunder peal replied;
The lightning burst on its fearful way,
While the heavens were lit in its red array.
— *Willis Gaylord Clark.*

LOOK! from the turbid south
What floods of flame in red diffusion burst!
Frequent and furious, darted thro' the dark,
And broken ridges of a thousand clouds,
Piled hill on hill; and hark! the thunder rous'd,
Groans in long roarings through the distant gloom!
— *Mallet.*

THROUGH the air
Mountains of clouds, with lurid summits roll'd,
The lightning kindling with its vivid glare
Their outlines as they rose, heap'd fold on fold.
— *Epes Sargent.*

THE winds grow high;
Impending tempests charge the sky;
The lightning flies, the thunder roars,
And big waves lash the frighted shores.
— *Prior.*

Poppy--Opium.

Papaver somniferum.   NATURAL ORDER: *Papaveraceæ — Poppy Family.*

FROM this plant is obtained that powerful narcotic, the opium of commerce. It has a milky juice that exudes from incisions made on the capsules of the plant. After it has been collected, it is worked in the sun until it is firm enough to be formed into cakes for exportation. Ceres is pictured carrying Poppies in her hand, because, when she lost her daughter, Jupiter gave her Poppies to eat, that she might get sleep and rest, which she could not before, for the intensity of her grief. The flowers are white, large and double. The Oriental Poppy from the Levant is a beautiful flower of a rich scarlet. The capsule is round, with a flat cap or covering, underneath which are small openings through which the seeds may be scattered as from a pepperbox.

Sleep.

SLEEP, sleep! be thine the sleep that throws
  Elysium o'er the soul's repose,
Without a dream, save such as wind,
Like midnight angels, through the mind.
— *Robert M. Bird.*

HOW beautiful is sleep!
  Yet if its purest beauties thou wouldst feel,
On the babe's slumber creep,
  And bid thy heart confess its mute appeal.

Yet sleep is awful, too —
So like to death's its features it can dress;
  Meek slumberer! while I view
Thine own, I deeply feel its awfulness.
— *Barton.*

O MAGIC sleep! O comfortable bird
  That broodest o'er the troubled sea of the mind
Till it is hush'd and smooth. O unconfined
Restraint! imprison'd liberty! great key
To golden palaces — ay, all the world
Of silvery enchantment!   *Keats.*

FROM a poppy I have taken
  Mortal's balm and mortal's bane;
Juice that, creeping through the heart,

Deadens every sense of smart;
Doomed to heal or doomed to kill,
Fraught with good, or fraught with ill.
— *Mrs. Robinson.*

Portulaca.

Portulaca grandiflora. NATURAL ORDER: *Portulacaceæ—Purslane Family.*

PLANTS cultivated under this name are mostly from South Africa, though the varieties are greatly improved, and florists have by a course of treatment produced a multiplicity of colors. In their native land they are found in very sandy soils, and there are no plants that stand drouth better than they, except, perhaps, the cacti. The flowers appear fresh every morning during flowering seasons, and the seeds when ripe are of a silvery appearance. The native weed known under the name of Purslane is an American sister-plant, entirely devoid of beauty. The latter has thick, fleshy stems and leaves, and is used as a pot-herb, also for pickles, salads, and garnishing, and for that reason is designated botanically Portulaca oleracea.

Variety.

THE earth was made so various, that the mind
   Of desultory man, studious of change,
And pleas'd with novelty, might be indulg'd.
— *Cowper.*

WHEREFORE did nature pour her bounties forth
   With such a full and unwithdrawing hand,
Covering the earth with colors, fruits and flocks,
Thronging the seas with spawn innumerable—
But all to please and sate a curious taste.
— *Milton.*

COUNTLESS the various species of mankind,
   Countless the shades which separate mind from mind;
No general object of desire is known;
Each has his will, and each pursues his own.
— *Gifford.*

YOUTH loves and lives on change.
   'Till the soul sighs for sameness; which at last
Becomes variety; and takes its place.   — *Bailey.*

VARIETY, the source of joy below,
   From which still fresh revolving pleasures flow;
In books and love the mind one end pursues,
And only change the expiring flame renews.
— *Gay.*

PLAY every string in love's sweet lyre,
   Set all its music flowing;
Be air, and dew, and light, and fire,
To keep the soul-flower growing.
— *Mrs. Osgood.*

THAT each from other differs, first confess;
   Next, that he varies from himself no less.
Pope.

Potentilla.

Potentilla formosa.   NATURAL ORDER: *Rosaceæ — Rose Family.*

THE habit of this plant, being similar to that of the strawberry, renders it superior for rock work, or the adornment of hanging-baskets; and some of the larger kinds, being free bloomers, make a very nice appearance when placed in the shrubbery borders. The flowers are various as well as handsome, being rose-colored, scarlet, yellow, and scarlet and buff combined, continuing in bloom from five to six months. One of the native species is sometimes called Cinquefoil, or Fivefinger; and the plant is used medicinally for its astringent and tonic properties, but scarcely merits its name (from the Latin *potens*, powerful), as it is rather a mild astringent. Although called hardy perennials, they are the better for some light protection in winter.

Beloved Daughter.

THOU art my daughter — never loved as now —
Thou mountain maid — thou child of liberty!
Urilda! well from Uri's height I named thee,
Free as its breezes — purer than its snows.
—*Maturin.*

SHE obeys with speedy will
Her grave parents' wise commands;
And so innocent, that ill
She nor acts, nor understands.
—*William Habington.*

REASON masters every sense,
And her virtues grace her birth;
Lovely as all excellence,
Modest in her most of mirth.
—*William Browne.*

SHE comforts all her mother's days,
And with her sweet, obedient ways
She makes her labor light;
So sweet to hear, so fair to see!
O, she is much too good for me.
—*Jean Ingelow.*

AND a stranger when he sees her
In the street, even, smileth stilly,
Just as you would at a lily;

And all voices that address her
Soften, sleeken every word,
As if speaking to a bird.
—*Mrs. Browning.*

Primrose.

Primula grandiflora. NATURAL ORDER: *Primulaceæ — Primrose Family.*

ONE of the first floral pages in the spring volume of nature may be said to be occupied by the Primroses, as they early peep from the ground, showing their blossoms in April; hence the name, from the Latin *primus*, first. They are natives of Europe, and by cultivation have been made double, and of a variety of colors, while in their wild state they are single and yellow. In greenhouses they are made to bloom in winter, and are gems for window culture, also. They bloom abundantly, and are so pure in their tints, and so delicate in their structure, as to make them perfectly charming to the amateur, as well as to the professional florist.

Youth.

YOUTH has sprightliness and fire to boast,
   That in the valley of decline are lost;
And virtue with peculiar charms appears,
   Crowned with the garland of life's blooming years.
          — *Cowper.*

AH! happy breasts! unknown to pain,
   I would not spoil your joys;
Nor vainly teach you to complain
   Of life's delusive toys.
Be jocund still, still sport and smile,

Nor dream of woe or future guile;
   For soon shall ye awaken'd find
The joys of life's sad, thorny way,
   But fading flowerets of a day,
Cut down by every wind. — *Enfield.*

LIVE, that thy young and glowing breast
   Can think of death without a sigh;
And be assured that life is best
Which finds us least afraid to die.
          — *Eliza Cook.*

WHAT is youth? A smiling sorrow,
   Blithe today, and sad tomorrow;
Never fixed, forever ranging,

Laughing, weeping, doating, changing,
Wild, capricious, giddy, vain,
Cloyed with pleasure, nursed with pain.
          — *Mary Robinson.*

YOUTH with swift feet walks onward in the way
   The land of joy lies all before his eyes.
          — *Mrs. Butler.*

Privet.

Ligustrum vulgare.   NATURAL ORDER: *Oleaceæ—Olive Family.*

GROUPS of the common Privet, or Prim, are frequently found adorning the fields and pastures in the New England States, and as far west as New York. It is a hardy shrub, from six to eight feet high, with small, delicate foliage, of a rather somber green, and strong, yellow, matted or tangled roots. The flowers are white, blooming in conical bunches, similar to the lilac, and are succeeded by a polished, black, bitter berry, that shows in strong contrast in winter's snow. It is well adapted for hedges, for which it is usually propagated by cuttings, although it is sometimes grown from seed. Noxious insects seldom disturb or destroy the foliage of this bush, as they do some others that are used for the same purpose. The wood is hard and compact, and when large enough can be used in the arts, and is sometimes burned for charcoal for gunpowder. From the berries is obtained a rose tint used for staining maps. The Privet is a very ancient shrub, as in Virgil we find the mention of *Alba Ligustra*, White Privets, and in Columella, *Ligustrum nigrum*, the Black Privet. There are several varieties with white, yellow and green berries, some being from China, Japan and the East Indies.

Defense.

THEN in the name of God, and all these rights,
Advance your standards, draw your willing swords.
—*Shakespeare.*

TIGER with tiger, bear with bear, you'll find
In leagues offensive and defensive joined;
But lawless man the anvil dares profane,
And forge that steel by which a man is slain,
Which earth at first for plowshares did afford,
Nor yet the smith had learned to form a sword.
—*Tate.*

HIS sword, edg'd with defense of right and honor,
Would pierce as deep as lightning, with that speed too;
And kill as deadly.   —*Beaumont and Fletcher.*

BEHOLD! I have a weapon;
A better never did itself sustain
Upon a soldier's thigh: I have seen the day,
That with this little arm and this good sword
I have made my way thro' more impediments
Than twenty times your stop.   —*Shakespeare.*

Queen of the Meadow.

Spiræa salicifolia.   NATURAL ORDER: *Rosaceæ — Rose Family.*

MEADOW lands in the United States and Canada are frequently the chosen seats of this small, slender shrub, which is on that account called Queen of the Meadow. It grows to a height of three or four feet, having a purplish stem, which is very brittle in texture. The flowers are commonly called white, but there is a flush of red over them, and they are remarkable for their fragrance. The stamens, which are those threadlike organs within the corolla, are very attractive. The roots are possessed of some medicinal value, having certain tonic properties. It is frequently called Meadow Sweet, and is sometimes cultivated as an ornamental shrub, as are also several other species of this beautiful genus.

Praise.

TELLING men what they are, we let them see,
And represent to them, what they should be.
—*Aleyn.*

THE love of Praise, howe'er conceal'd by art,
Reigns, more or less, and glows in every heart;
The proud, to gain it, toils on toils endure,
The modest shun it but to make it sure.
—*Young.*

OR who would ever care to do brave deed,
Or strive in virtue others to excel,
If none should yield him his deserved meed,
Due praise, that is the spur of doing well?
—*Spenser.*

PRAISE of the wise and good! it is a meed
For which I would long years of toil endure—
Which many a peril, many a grief, would cure.
—*Sir E. Brydges.*

CAST down thyself, and only strive to raise
The glory of thy Maker's sacred name;
Use all thy powers that bless'd power to praise,
Which gives the power to be and use the same.
—*Sir J. Davies.*

I HAVE no taste of the noisy praise
Of giddy crowds, as changeable as winds;
Servants to change, and blowing with the tide
Of swoln success, but veering with its ebb.
—*Dryden.*

THOU 'LT say anon he is some kin to thee.
Thou spend'st such heydey wit in praising him.
—*Shakespeare.*

Queen of the Prairie.

Spiræa lobata. NATURAL ORDER: *Rosaceæ — Rose Family.*

SPIRÆA, so called probably because of the spiral shape of the pod-cells, is a blossom from nature's wild bouquet, and is found waving its head amid the tall grass of the western prairies. It was formerly called the Siberian Red Spiræa, and is remarkable for its beauty, growing frequently from six to seven feet high. It blooms freely, the flowers being a deep rose-color. It is a sister plant of the Meadow Sweet, the Pride of the Meadow, the Goat's-beard, and several other of the Spiræas that are cultivated for their flowers, which, in the many varieties, appear during the whole summer.

Nobility.

FOND man! though all the honors of your line
  Bedeck your halls and round your galleries shine
In proud display, yet take this truth from me—
Virtue alone is true nobility.
                — *Gifford.*

THE noble ranks of fashion and birth
  Are fetter'd by courtly rule;
They dare not rend the shackles that tend
  To form the knave and fool.   — *Eliza Cook.*

HOW poor are all hereditary honors,
  Those poor possessions from another's deeds,
Unless our own just virtues form our title,
And give a sanction to our fond assumption!
                — *Shirley.*

VAINGLORIOUS man, when fluttering wind does blow
  In his light wings, is lifted up to sky;
The scorn of knighthood and true chivalry,
To think, without desert of gentle deed
And noble worth, to be advanced high,
Such praise is shame, but honor, virtue's meed,
Doth bear the fairest flower in honorable seed.
                — *Spenser.*

TRUE is that whilome that good poet said,
  That gentle mind by gentle deed is known,
For man by nothing is so well bewray'd
  As by his manners in which plain is shown
  Of what degree and what race he is grown.
                — *Spenser.*

WHOE'ER amid'st the sons
  Of reason, valor, liberty and virtue,
Displays distinguish'd merit, is a noble
Of nature's own creating. Such have risen,
Sprung from the dust; or where had been our honories?
                — *Thompson.*

Quince.

Cydonia vulgaris. NATURAL ORDER: *Rosaceæ—Rose Family.*

CYDONIA receives its name from a town in the island of Crete, called Cydonia, famous for this species of fruit; and its English name is supposed to be derived from the French *coin*, a corner, alluding to its irregular appearance. The Quince tree grows quite dwarfish and straggling, the flowers are larger than the apple blossoms, and the fruit is as large as an orange, irregular in shape, yellow when ripe, and of a delightful fragrance peculiar to itself. The Japan Quince, grown as an ornamental shrub, is much smaller in size, with flowers conspicuous for their beauty and brilliancy, ranging through the shades from white to scarlet. They are all hardy, and require little attention.

Allurement.

TEMPTATIONS and trials, without and within,
　From the pathway of virtue the spirit may lure;
But the soul shall grow strong in its triumphs o'er sin,
　And the heart shall preserve its integrity pure.
　　　　　　　　　　— *Burleigh.*

BEAUTIFUL apparition! go not hence!
　Surely thou art a goddess, for thy voice
Is a celestial melody, and thy form
Self-poised as if it floated on the air!
　　　　— *Longfellow.*

TEMPTATION hath a music for all ears,
　And mad ambition trumpeteth to all;
And the ungovernable thought within
Will be in every bosom eloquent.
　　　　— *Willis.*

THE wind is like a mellow tune
　That blows me round the siren's isle;
It is the fragrant lull of June
　Becalms me for a little while,
　Midmost their tuneful lure and wile.
　　　　—*James Maurice Thompson.*

COULD'ST thou boast, O child of weakness,
　O'er the sons of wrong and strife,
Were there strong temptations planted
　In thy path of life?　— *Whittier.*

IF you're idle, you're destroy'd;
　All his force on you he tries;
Be but watchful and employ'd,
　Soon the baffled tempter flies.　*Motten*

Ragged Robin.

Lychnis floscuculi. NATURAL ORDER: *Caryophyllaceæ — Pink Family.*

THIS species of Lychnis is a perennial herb from Europe, and is from one to two feet high, with smooth, narrow, tapering leaves. The flowers are a beautiful pink, with a brown calyx. It is sometimes called, in England, the Cuckoo flower (which is but a literal translation of the Latin *flos cuculi*), as it blooms about the time of the arrival of that bird in early summer. The Greek word *lychnis* primarily denotes a lamp, and is conjectured to have been given to the plant because the down of some varieties was used for wicks, or because of the bright scarlet or reddish-purple flower of some of the others. All the varieties of the Lychnis have been cultivated from time immemorial, the flowers being red, white, pink, and purple. Some of the species are as downy as the mullein.

Wit.

UNHAPPY wit, like most mistaken things,
  Atones not for that envy which it brings.
                — *Pope.*

WITH her mien she enamors the brave;
  With her wit she engages the free;
With her modesty pleases the grave;
  She is every way pleasing to me.
         — *Shenstone.*

FOR nature never gave to mortal yet
  A free and arbitrary power of wit;
But bound him to his good behavior for 't,
  That he should never use it to do hurt.
         — *Butler.*

WILL is the prince, and wit the counselor,
  Which doth for common good in council sit;
And when wit is resolved, will lends her power
  To execute what is advised by wit.
         — *Sir J. Davies.*

HIS eye begets occasion for his wit;
  For every object that the one doth catch,
The other turns to a mirth-loving jest.
         — *Shakespeare.*

SENSE is the diamond, weighty, solid, sound;
  When cut by wit it casts a brighter beam;
Yet, wit apart, it is a diamond still.
         — *Young.*

Ranunculus.

Ranunculus bulbosus. NATURAL ORDER: *Ranunculaceæ — Crowfoot Family.*

BULBOUS RANUNCULUS, or Crowfoot, is generally found in pasture lands. The root is fleshy, and the flowers are of a golden yellow. Some varieties are cultivated in our gardens, among which are the Asiatic and Persian, sporting through nearly every conceivable hue. "A good Ranunculus should have a stem eight or twelve inches high, flower not less than two inches in diameter, either of one color or variously diversified." Its name is the diminutive form of the Latin appellation *rana*, signifying a frog, from the aquatic habits of some of the species. It blooms in May and June.

Ingratitude.

THE wretch whom gratitude once fails to bind,
To truth or honor let him lay no claim.
— *Fenyde.*

ALL should unite to punish the ungrateful;
Ingratitude is treason to mankind.
— *Thompson.*

BY me thy greatness grew; thy years grew with it,
But thy ingratitude outgrew them both.
— *Dryden.*

HE that's ungrateful has no guilt but one;
All other crimes may pass for virtues in him.
— *Young.*

IF there be a crime
Of deeper dye than all the guilty train
Of human vices, 'tis ingratitude. — *Brooke.*

I AM rapt, and cannot
Cover the monstrous bulk of this ingratitude
With any size of word. — *Shakspeare.*

HE that doth public good for multitudes,
Finds few are truly grateful.
— *Marston.*

BLOW, blow, thou winter wind,
Thou art not so unkind
As man's ingratitude;

Thy tooth is not so keen,
Because thou art not seen,
Although thy breath be rude.
— *Shakspeare.*

INGRATITUDE is a monster
To be strangled in the birth; not to be cherish'd.
— *Massinger.*

Rhodora.

Rhodora Canadensis.   NATURAL ORDER: *Ericacea — Heath Family.*

IT is in Canada and the New England States that the Rhodora is to be most frequently met with, growing in moist places among the mountains, or in the bogs. It is very handsome when in bloom, as each branch bears on its tip a cluster of stemless flowers while there is yet no foliage visible. After the blossoming season is over, the leaves make their appearance. The shrub is from two to three feet high, is closely allied to the Rhododendron, and derives its name from its resemblance to the rose.

Beauty in Retirement.

THE bloom of opening flowers' unsullied beauty,
Softness and sweetest innocence she wears,
And looks like nature in the world's first spring.
— *Rowe.*

IN May, when sea winds pierced our solitudes,
I found the fresh Rhodora in the woods,
Spreading its leafless bloom in a damp nook,
To please the desert and the sluggish brook:
The purple petals, fallen in the pool,
Made the black waters with their beauty gay;
Here might the redbird come his plumes to cool,
And court the flower that cheapens his array.
Rhodora! if the sages ask thee why
This charm is wasted on the marsh and sky,
Dear, tell them, that if eyes were made for seeing,
Then beauty is its own excuse for being.
Why thou wert there, O rival of the rose!
I never thought to ask; I never knew,
But in my simple ignorance suppose
The selfsame Power brought me there, brought you.
— *Ralph Waldo Emerson.*

O MAIDEN! silent sitting,
Braiding still thy golden hair;
Round thy head the bees are flitting,
Deeming thee a lily fair.   — *G. Hamlin.*

IF thou wonder among women,
I am fretted to the heart,
Thinking how my words are few
To depict thee as thou wert:
What I will, I cannot do!
— *Howard Glyndon.*

THINE eyes' clear fervor dwell
Passionate on my own glad eyes so often,
Because I know thou art
My life's diviner part,
My other tenderer heart to soothe, to soften.
— *Edgar Fawcett.*

Rocket.

Hesperis matronalis. NATURAL ORDER: *Cruciferæ—Mustard Family.*

HESPERIS has three species: one a native of the United States and found growing near Lake Huron, another from the cold latitude of Siberia, and a third a maritime herb found on the sea coast. The flowers are the various shades of purple or white. The odor of the blossom is much the strongest toward evening; hence the name *Hesperis*, being Greek for evening. This spicy fragrance has been the cause of its being sometimes called gilliflower with which it is closely allied. The double varieties are produced by hybridizing, but yield no seeds themselves, fertile seeds being obtained from the single flower. The seeds should be sown in the early fall, and the plants kept in a place free from frost for spring blooming. Choice specimens may be kept from year to year by pruning and clipping the flowers as soon as they have perished. The maritime variety is a smooth, thick, juicy, trailing plant, called Sea-Rocket.

Rivalry.

WAS not one of the two at her side —
This new-made lord, whose splendor plucks
The slavish hat from the villager's head?
—*Tennyson.*

OF all the torments, all the cares,
With which our lives are curst;
Of all the plagues a lover bears,
Sure, rivals are the worst!
By partners in each other kind,
Afflictions easier grow;
In love alone we hate to find
Companions of our woe.

Sylvia, for all the pangs you see
Are lab'ring in my breast,
I beg you would not favor me
Would you but slight the rest!
How great soe'er your rigors are,
With them alone I'll cope;
I can endure my own despair
But not another's hope.
—*William Walsh.*

IF one must be rejected, one succeed,
Make him my lord within whose faithful breast
Is fix'd my image, and who loves me best. —*Dryden.*

Rose—Austrian.

Rosa eglanteria.   NATURAL ORDER: *Rosaceæ—Rose Family.*

ROSES, as well as flowers of all other kinds, are very much cultivated by the flower-loving people of Germany, of which land this Rose is a native. The flowers are of a brilliant yellow, and soon fall, but the green leaves of the bush are very fragrant. It is said that the essential oil, attar or otto of Roses, was first discovered by Nur Jehan, better known as Nur Mahal ("light of the harem"), wife of Jehanghir, Moghul emperor of Hindoostan, 1605-27. She observed an oily substance floating on a vessel of Rose-water that had been distilled by the heat of the sun. The attar is very fragrant, being so concentrated that one drop will perfume a whole dressing-case; and so expensive that an ounce will cost about one hundred dollars, requiring nearly half a million of average Roses for its production.

Loveliness.

THAT loveliness ever in motion, which plays,
Like the light upon autumn's soft, shadowy days,
Now here, and now there, giving warmth as it flies,
From the lips to the cheeks, from the cheek to the eyes.
— *Moore.*

O SWEET, pale face! O lovely eyes of azure,
Clear as the waters of a brook that ran
Limpid and laughing in the summer sun!
O golden hair, that, like a miser's treasure,
In its abundance overflows the measure!
O graceful form, that cloudlike floatest on,
With the soft, undulating gait of one
Who moveth as it motion were a pleasure.
— *Longfellow.*

AH! could you look into my heart,
And watch your image there,
You would own the sunny loveliness
Affection makes it wear.   — *Mrs. Osgood.*

HER face right wondrous fair did seem to be,
That her broad beauty's beam great brightness threw
Through the dim shade, that all men might it see.
— *Spenser.*

HER dress, her shape, her matchless grace,
Were all observed, as well as heavenly face;
With such peerless majesty she stands.
— *Dryden.*

Rosebay.

Rhododendron maximum.   NATURAL ORDER: *Ericaceæ — Heath Family.*

A NATIVE tree from ten to fifteen feet high, the Rosebay is found principally in the Middle States. The leaves are thick and leathery when mature, and are about five or six inches in length. The flowers, which appear in July and August, are rose-color, frequently dotted with purple or yellow, and appear in fine contrast to the evergreen foliage. The whole genus delights in shady woodlands and cool swamps; indeed, their geographical range is almost wholly confined to such localities or to the summits of the highest mountains of Europe, Asia and America. Some of the foreign varieties are found in greenhouses, and are admired for their brilliancy and diversity of color. The yellow variety is from Siberia and the Caucasus mountains, where it grows in low bushes.

Talking.

BE silent always when you doubt your sense,
  And speak, though sure, with seeming diffidence.
                —*Pope.*

UNLESS thou find occasion, hold thy tongue
  Thyself or others careless talk may wrong.
             —*Sir J. Denham.*

WHAT need there is to be reserved in speech,
  And temper all our thoughts with charity.
             —*Wordsworth.*

HIS air, his voice, his looks, and honest soul,
  Speak all so movingly in his behalf,
I dare not trust myself to hear him talk.
             —*Addison.*

SHE spake in language whose strange melody
  Might not belong to earth. I heard, alone,
What made its music more melodious be—
  The pity and the love of every tone.
             —*Shelly.*

MY tongue will tell the anger of my heart:
  Or else my heart, concealing it, will break:
And, rather than it shall, I will be free,
Even to the uttermost, as I please, in words.
             Shakespeare.

AS I listened to thee,
  The happy hours pass'd by us unperceived,
So was my soul fixed to the soft enchantment.
             Rowe.

Rose—Damask.

Rosa Damascena.   NATURAL ORDER: *Rosaceæ—Rose Family.*

DAMASCUS, a city one of the most ancient and renowned in Syria, gives its name to this particular variety of Rose, which blooms monthly, and, under favorable circumstances, at all seasons. The Rose is said to have been the favorite flower of Venus, and was formerly white, until she, being in haste to assist her dying lover, pierced her foot with a thorn, and some of the blood falling on it changed its color from white to red. It grows about four feet high, most of the monthly sorts being dwarfish in habit.

Blushing Beauty.

UNTO the ground she cast her modest eye,
   And ever and anon, with rosy red,
The bashful blush her snowy cheeks did dye.
            —*Spenser.*

IF Jove would give the leafy bowers
   A queen for all their world of flowers,
The rose would be the choice of Jove,
And reign the queen of every grove.
        —*Moore.*

GIVE me the eloquent cheek
   Where blushes burn and die;
Like time, its changes speak
   The spirit's purity.
      —*Frances Sargent Osgood.*

BEAUTY was lent to nature as the type
   Of heaven's unspeakable and holy joy.
        —*Mrs. Hale.*

WE are blushing roses,
   Bending with our fulness,
'Midst our close-capp'd sister buds,
   Warming the green coolness.

Whatsoe'er of beauty
   Yearns and yet reposes,
Blush, and bosom, and sweet breath,
   Took a shape in roses.
      —*Leigh Hunt.*

Of all flowers,
Methinks a rose is best.
It is the very emblem of a maid,
For when the west wind courts her gently,
How modestly she blows, and paints the sun
With her chaste blushes!
    —*Beaumont and Fletcher.*

THE lilies faintly to the roses yield,
   As on thy lovely cheek they struggling vie;
(Who would not strive upon so sweet a field
   To win the mastery?)
And thoughts are in thy speaking eyes reveal'd,
Pure as the fount the prophet's rod unseal'd.
      —*Hoffman.*

Rose-leaved Rubus.

Rubus rosæfolius. NATURAL ORDER: *Rosaceæ — Rose Family.*

ERECT and branching, the Rubus, sometimes called the Flowering Bramble, and sometimes the Brier Rose, is a bush well fortified with straight prickles, and with foliage resembling that of the raspberry bush, being smooth on the under, and velvety on the upper, surface. It is a very delicate plant, requiring the shelter of the greenhouse or conservatory in order to cultivate it successfully; but as it blooms at the season when nature has withdrawn her genial smiles, it has proved a very desirable acquisition to those who can give it such shelter, or a sunny window in the house. The blossoms are double, and a pure, snow white. The Island of Mauritius claims its nativity, as does China, also. It is an especial favorite in England, being familiarly called the Bridal or Christmas Rose. The root is bulbous, and should be repotted in a large pot as early as October, in order that it may bloom well the following season, which commences about Christmas, and continues till May. It is propagated by a division of the stems after the flowering season has ceased.

Threats.

OH! wert thou young again, I would put off
My majesty to be more terrible. — *L——*

I'LL note you in my book of memory,
To scourge you for this reprehension;
Look to it well, and say you are well warn'd.
— *Shakespeare*

I'LL make my heaven in a lady's lap,
And deck my body in gay ornaments,
And witch sweet ladies with my words and looks.
— *Shakspeare*

I HAVE learned thy arts, and now
Can disdain as much as thou.
— *Thomas Carew.*

BACK to thy punishment,
False fugitive, and to thy speed add wings,
Lest with a whip of scorpions I pursue
Thy lingering. — *Milton.*

THOUGH I'm young, I scorn to flit
On the wings of borrowed wit;
I'll make my own feathers rear me,
Whither others cannot bear me.
— *George Wither.*

Rosemary.

Rosmarinus officinalis. NATURAL ORDER: *Labiatæ — Mint Family.*

LITERALLY, Rosmarinus signifies, in Latin, sea-dew, and the name was no doubt given because of the fondness of this plant for the surf-beaten and spray-sprinkled sea shore, whence its aromatic odor, not unlike that of camphor, often greets the gladdened mariner as he sails along the coast. It is an evergreen shrub, with blue flowers, growing spontaneously in China, Asia Minor, Spain, Italy, and portions of France. It yields, by distillation, a great quantity of odoriferous oil, with which the whole plant is highly impregnated. Rosemary was used by our forefathers as an emblem of fidelity, constancy, remembrance, and affection, and was distributed at weddings and funerals.

Remembrance.

SHE plac'd it sad, with needless fear,
   Lest time should shake my wavering soul —
Unconscious that her image there
   Held every sense in fast control.   — *Byron.*

I THINK of thee when soft and wide
   The evening spreads her robes of light,
And like a young and timid bride,
   Sits blushing in the arms of night:
And when the moon's sweet crescent springs
   In light o'er heaven's wide, waveless sea,
And stars are forth like blessed things,
   I think of thee — I think of thee.
       — *George D. Prentice.*

THERE'S not a look, a word of thine
   My soul hath e'er forgot;
Thou ne'er hast bid a ringlet shine,
Nor given thy locks one graceful twine,
   Which I remember not.   — *Moore.*

ROSEMARIE is for remembrance
   Between us day and night,
Wishing that I might always have
   You present in my sight;
And when I cannot have,
   (As I have said before,)
Then Cupid, with his deadly dart,
   Doth wound my heart full sore.
       — *Poem, 1584.*

Rose--Musk.

Rosa moschata. NATURAL ORDER: *Rosaceæ -- Rose Family.*

OF a trailing habit, the Musk Rose is well adapted for trellises and arbors: it grows from eleven to twelve feet high, requiring always some support to keep it from the ground. The flowers, which are large and white, bloom in clusters and have that peculiar musky odor from whence it derives its name. It is said that Hymen, the god of matrimony, used to wear a crown of Roses, and that "his locks dropped perfume." The Rose, of whatever species, color, or name, holds the supremacy in the hearts of the people, and never will its glory wane until Roses cease to bloom.

Charms of Home.

HE was made all up of love and charms!
  Delight of every eye! when he appear'd,
A secret pleasure gladden'd all who saw him.
—*Addison.*

HER cheek had the pale, pearly tint
  Of sea shells, the world's sweetest tint, as though
She lived, one half might deem, on roses sopp'd
In silver dew. —*Bailey.*

THE passion you pretend,
  Was only to obtain;
But when the charm is ended,
  The charmer you disdain. —*Dryden.*

LIGHT as the angel shapes that bless
  An infant's dream, yet not the less
Rich in all woman's loveliness;
With eyes so pure, that from their ray
Dark vice would turn abash'd away.
—*Moore.*

TELL me where thy strength doth lie;
  Where the power that charms us so—
In thy soul, or in thine eye? —*Waller.*

THERE'S no miniature
  In her face, but is a copious theme,
Which would, discours'd at large of, make a volume
—*Massinger.*

SHE moved upon this earth a shape of brightness,
  A power that from its objects scarcely drew
One impulse of her being—in her lightness,
  Most like some radiant cloud of morning dew.
—*Shelly.*

Rose—White.

Rosa alba. NATURAL ORDER: *Rosaceæ—Rose Family.*

GERMANY produces, more extensively perhaps than any other country, the Rosa alba, or White Rose, a shrub growing from six to seven feet high. Its flowers are usually pure white, though sometimes delicately tinted with a blush. The White Rose has been selected as a symbol of secrecy, as the old Latin phrase *sub rosa* signifies under the rose, or secretly; and Booth says it was so considered by the ancients, who hung it up at their entertainments, as a token that anything there said was not to be divulged. The flowers are very fragrant, and bloom in clusters.

Secrecy.

SEARCH not to find what lies too deeply hid;
Nor to know things whose knowledge is forbid.
—*Denham.*

WELL, read my cheek, and watch my eye,—
Too strictly school'd are they,
One secret of my soul to show,
One hidden thought betray. —*Miss Landon.*

WHEN two know it, how can it be a secret?
And indeed with what justice can you
Expect secrecy in me, that cannot
Be private yourself? —*Marston.*

INDEED, true gladness doth not always speak;
Joy bred and born but in the tongue is weak.
—*Ben Jonson.*

MY list'ning powers
Were awed, and ev'ry thought in silence hung,
And wond'ring expectation. —*Akenside.*

I'LL keep this secret from the world,
As warily as those that deal in poison
Keep poison from their children. —*Webst.*

A SECRET in his mouth,
Is like a wild bird put in a cage;
Whose door no sooner opens, but 'tis out.
—*Jonson.*

INTO our calm today its ghost comes gliding—
Known all too late!
Take from my hand its emblem, and the emblem
Of our strange fate.

Silence! its pale lips say; the snow-white silence
Of yon sad stone.
Yet—lingering joy—the sharers, even of silence,
Are not alone! —*Howard Glyndon.*

Rudbeckia.

Rudbeckia laciniata. NATURAL ORDER: *Composite—Aster Family.*

VERY properly this plant has been dedicated to Olaus Rudbeck, a celebrated botanist of Upsal, Sweden, a man unequaled in the ardor and zeal with which he prosecuted his botanical researches. His son, of the same name, followed in his footsteps, and was scarcely less distinguished. The Swedes have a taste for the science, and Linnæus, one of the greatest of naturalists, was a countryman of the Rudbecks. His reputation has somewhat overshadowed the earlier workers. The Rudbeckia is a tall plant, resembling the sunflower, and is found growing freely around swamps and ditches throughout the United States and Canada, and blooms from August to September.

Justice.

WHAT stronger breastplate than a heart untainted?
   Thrice is he armed who hath his quarrel just,
And he but naked, though lock'd up in steel,
Whose conscience with injustice is corrupted.
— Shakespeare.

THOUGH with tardy step
   Celestial justice comes, that step is sure,
Unerring is her bolt, and where it falls,
Eternal will the ruin be.   —*Samuel Hays.*

JUSTICE, when equal scales she holds, is blind,
   Nor cruelty, nor mercy, change her mind:
When some escape for that which others die,
Mercy to those, to these is cruelty —*Denham.*

A HAPPY lot be thine, and larger light
   Await thee there; for thou hast bound thy will
In cheerful homage to the rule of right,
   And lovest all, and doest good for ill.
—Bryant.

THE sun of justice may withdraw his beams
   Awhile from earthly ken, and sit concealed
In dark recess, pavilioned round with clouds;
Yet let not guilt presumptuous rear her crest,
Nor virtue droop despondent; soon these clouds,
Seeming eclipse, will brighten into day,
And in majestic splendor he will rise,
With healing and with terror on his wings.
—Bailey.

Rue.

Ruta graveolens. NATURAL ORDER: *Rutaceæ — Rue Family.*

PLANTS of this order are usually found in the warmer parts of the Eastern Hemisphere and the tropical parts of South America. The name Ruté is of Peloponnesian origin, and is frequently mentioned by both ancient Greek and Latin authors; while peganon was apparently the synonym elsewhere in Greece. The whole plant is pervaded by an intensely bitter element and an ungrateful odor, though it has several qualities that render it useful in medicine, among which are its tonic and febrifugal properties. It is a very hardy shrub, frequently cultivated in gardens, growing about three feet high, and from June to September produces flowers of a dull yellow color, in loose clusters.

Repentance.

I have deeply felt
The mockery of the hollow shrine at which my spirit knelt;
Mine is the requiem of years in reckless folly pass'd,
The wail above departed hopes on a frail venture cast;
The vain regret that steals above the wreck of squander'd hours
Like the sighing of the autumn wind over the faded flowers.
—*Whittier.*

HE that lacks time to mourn lacks time to mend;
Eternity mourns that. 'Tis an ill cure
For life's worst ills, to have no time to feel them.
—*Henry Taylor.*

COME, fair Repentance! daughter of the skies!
Soft harbinger of soon returning virtue!
The weeping messenger of grace from heav'n!
—*Brown.*

WHO by repentance is not satisfied,
Is not of heav'n nor earth, for these are pleased;
By penitence the Eternal's wrath 's appeased. —*Shakespeare.*

SWEET tastes have sour closes;
And he repents on thorns that sleeps on beds
Of roses.
—*Quarles.*

SORROW for past ills doth restore frail man
To his first innocence.
—*Nabb.*

SO let us which this change of weather view,
Change eke our minds, and former lives amend;
The old year's sins forepast let us eschew,
And fly the faults with which we did offend. —*Spenser.*

Sage.

Salvia officinalis.   NATURAL ORDER: *Labiatæ—Mint Family.*

SAGE is an humble denizen of the kitchen-garden, never making its appearance on the lawn among the gay and brilliant companions that we find it associated with in the botany, but content to be surrounded by the less obtrusive though more useful plants — the crisp lettuces, the peas, the beans, and numerous others that garnish our tables during the summer months. In order to be well grown it requires a mellow soil, when it becomes a pleasing object to the eye, its peculiar green distinguishing it from other plants, even at a distance; and behold, what a pretty leaf! so rugous or wrinkly that if transparent it would be like the meshes of fine lace. The flowers are purple, blooming in spikes. Its Latin name, is derived from *salvo*, I save, as it possesses valuable medical properties, being classed in botanical works as a tonic and expectorant.

Domestic Virtue.

AND oh, the atmosphere of home! how bright
It floats around us when we sit together
Under a bower of vine in summer weather,
Or round the hearthstone on a winter night.
— *Park Benjamin.*

NO single virtue could we most commend,
Whether the wife, the mother or the friend;
For she was each in that supreme degree,
That as no one prevail'd, so all was she.
— *Dryden.*

THE sum of all that makes a just man happy,
Consists in the well choosing of his wife.   — *Massinger.*

ALL day, like some sweet bird, content to sing
In its small cage, she moveth to and fro —
And ever and anon will upward spring
To her sweet lips, fresh from the fount below,
The murmur'd melody of pleasant thought.
— *Mrs. E. Oakes Smith.*

SEEK to be good, but aim not to be great;
A woman's noblest station is retreat;
Her fairest virtues fly from public sight;
Domestic worth — that shuns too strong a light.
— *Lord Lyttleton.*

DOMESTIC happiness! thou only bliss
Of Paradise that has surviv'd the fall!
Though few now taste thee unimpair'd and free,
Or, tasting, long enjoy thee; too infirm,
Or too incautious, to preserve thy sweets
Unmix'd with drops of bitter.   — *Cowper.*

Salvia.

Salvia splendens. NATURAL ORDER: *Labiatæ—Mint Family.*

DELIGHTING in warm climes, these plants are found abundantly in South America and Mexico. The brilliancy of their blossoms has caused their introduction into our more northern latitudes, where they occasionally pass under the name of Scarlet Sage. They are perennials, and are usually grown in the greenhouse, though they do exceedingly well in the garden or the lawn. The flowers are of a vivid, bewildering scarlet tint, and abundant in their prodigality. There are varieties with pink and blue flowers, which, though desirable, are less conspicuous. They can be raised as annuals from seed, or from cuttings, which root easily and with less delay than many other plants.

Energy.

THEN we wring from our souls their applicative strength,
    And bend to the cord the strong bow of our ken;
And bringing our lives to the level of others,
Hold the cup we have filled, to their uses at length.
—*Mrs. Browning.*

THE keen spirit
  Seizes the prompt occasion — makes the thought
Start into instant action, and at once
Plans and performs, resolves and executes!
—*Hannah More.*

FROM this moment,
  The very firstlings of my heart shall be
The firstlings of my hand. And even now,
To crown my tho'ts with acts, be it tho't and done.
—*Shakespeare.*

AWAY, then work with boldness and with speed.
  On greatest actions greatest dangers feed.
—*Marloe.*

HOW slow the time
  To the warm soul, that, in the very instant
It forms, would execute a great design.
—*Thompson.*

NEVER change thy mind, [still,
  If aught obstructs thy course, yet stand not
But wind about till thou hast top'd the hill.
—*Denham.*

RUN, if you like, but try to keep your breath;
  Work like a man, but don't be worked to death.
—*O. W. Holmes.*

Sarsaparilla.

Smilax sarsaparilla. NATURAL ORDER: *Smilaceæ — Smilax Family.*

FOR cleansing impurities from the human system the root of the Sarsaparilla has long been held in high estimation, and, though it has been supplanted to some extent by other remedies, it is still imported in large quantities from South America, where the natives gather it in the woods on the banks of the Tigre, Ucayale and other rivers, and pack it in large bales ready for shipment. Another species of the same plant belonging to the order Araliaceæ, grows abundantly throughout the Northern States. It flourishes best in rich, rocky soil. The root differs materially from that of the first mentioned, which is long and slender, the North American variety being thick and fleshy. The latter is sometimes substituted for the former by druggists in their preparations, and is supposed to have similar properties.

Experience.

THIS sad experience cites me to reveal,
And what I dictate is from what I feel.
— *Prior.*

O FATE! all left behind,
I follow thee adown the bitter road,
With weary feet, and heavy eyes and blind,
That leadeth to thy far unknown abode.

No need, then, with thy stings my flesh to goad,
Keep them for those that strive with thee in vain,
And leave me to my constant, weary pain.
— *William Morris.*

WORLD'S use is cold — world's love is vain —
World's cruelty is bitter bane;
But pain is not the fruit of pain. — *Mrs. Browning.*

O TEACH him, while your lessons last,
To judge the present by the past;
Remind him of each wish pursued,

How rich it glow'd with promised good;
Remind him of each wish enjoy'd,
How soon his hopes possession cloy'd.
— *Scott.*

EXPERIENCE, join'd to common sense,
To mortals is a providence. — *Green.*

Sassafras.

Sassafras officinale. NATURAL ORDER: *Lauraceæ — Laurel Family.*

UNDER the order of laurels we find this tree classified, with many others, most of which possess aromatic properties, either in their bark, roots or leaves. Many of them are in common use, as the cinnamon, obtained from the bark of the Cinnamomum Zeylanicum, a native of Ceylon; and the camphor, an aromatic gum procured from several trees in India, China and Japan. The Sassafras is found abundantly throughout the United States and Canada. The bark of the root, along with the essential oil prepared from it, is the chief article of commerce, and possesses gentle stimulating, aromatic and alterative properties. The tree grows to the height of fifteen or twenty feet, and presents a rather pleasing appearance. The pith of the young wood is sometimes used in inflammation of the eyes. The flowers are a greenish yellow, appearing from April to June.

Favor.

FOR where my worthiness is poor,
   My will stands richly at the door,
To pay shortcomings evermore.
               — *Mrs. Browning.*

'TIS ever thus when favors are denied;
   All had been granted but the thing we beg,
And still some great unlikely substitute,
Your life, your souls, your all of earthly good,
Is proffer'd in the room of one small boon.
               — *Joanna Baillie.*

NO trifle is so small as what obtains,
   Save that which loses favor; 'tis a breath
Which hangs upon a smile! a look, a word,
A frown, the air-built tower of fortune shakes,
And down the unsubstantial fabric falls.
               — *Hannah More.*

WE give of what we take
   From life of outward things; our spirits leave,
Where they have been, a glory in their wake
More bright than they receive.
             — *Dora Greenwell.*

GIVE thy heart's best treasures —
   From fair Nature learn;
Give thy love — and ask not,
   Wait not a return!

And the more thou spendest
   From thy little store,
With a double bounty,
   God will give you more.
             — *Adelaide A. Procter.*

Sensitive Plant.

Mimosa pudica. NATURAL ORDER: *Leguminosæ — Pulse Family.*

A SENSITIVE soul shrinks when wounded or stung by the rudeness or sarcasm of a thoughtless tongue, and in this plant a curious analogy to this feeling is found. The Mimosa has the peculiar property of retraction, when touched by the hand or other substance. There are four plants which have the same peculiar power, the names of which are: Dwarf Cassia, called also Sensitive Pea, an elegant plant with yellow flowers; the Wild Sensitive plant, whose leaves close by night and when touched; the Sensitive Brier, and the above, which is about a foot high, with a shrubby stem. The flowers of the Mimosa pudica are small, and bloom in heads, and are of little beauty. It is a native of Brazil, and is often cultivated as a curiosity, as its leaves droop if touched, or if the stalk of the shrub is shaken all the stems sink down as if they felt a thrill of horror pass over them, and only recover after several hours.

Bashful Modesty.

WITHAL she laughed, and she blushed withal,
  That blushing to her laughter gave more grace,
And laughter to her blushing.
  — *Spenser.*

THE sensitive plant was the earliest
  Upgather'd into the bosom of rest;
A sweet child weary of its delight,
The feeblest and yet the favorite,
Cradled within the embrace of night.
  — *Shelly.*

THE sweet eyes that his eyes were set upon
  Were hid by shamefast lids as he did speak,
And redder color burned on her fresh cheek
And her lips smiled, as, with a half-sad sigh,
He 'gan to tell his lovesome history.
  — *William Morris.*

IF maids be shy, he cures who can;
  But if a man be shy — a man —
Why, then the worse for him!
  — *Jean Ingelow.*

SO bright the tear in beauty's eye,
  Love half regrets to kiss it dry;
So sweet the blush of bashfulness,
E'en pity scarce can wish it less.
  — *Byron.*

A CRIMSON blush her beauteous face o'erspread,
  Varying her cheeks, by turn, with white and red;
The driving colors, never at a stay,
Run here and there, and flush and fade away.
  — *Parnell.*

Shamrock.

Trifolium repens.   NATURAL ORDER: *Leguminosae — Pulse Family.*

WHITE CLOVER, as this plant is usually called, inhabits all soils, from the luxuriant meadow to the sterile mountains, hills or rocky places. It is highly useful for pasturage, and forms the chief food for cattle in some countries. The flowers are white and odoriferous. Bees are attracted from a considerable distance by it, as it freights the air very heavily where it grows in quantities. The Shamrock is an Irish plant, and St. Patrick having chosen it to illustrate to his simple hearers his idea of the Trinity, it became thenceforth the national emblem of Ireland. Brande and Benthant say the Shamrock is the Oxalis acetosella or common wood sorrel, and with some reason, as the White Clover is believed to be of only recent introduction into Ireland, but the above is more generally received. Pliny says no serpent will touch it, which is probably a classic superstition.

Light Heartedness.

EACH delighted and delighting, gives
The pleasing ecstacy which each receives.
Prior.

WHOM call we gay? that honor has been long
    The boast of mere pretenders to the name
The innocent are gay — the lark is gay,

That dries his feathers saturate with dew
Beneath the rosy cloud, while yet the beam
Of day spring overshoot his humble nest.
— *Cowper.*

AS poised on vibrant wings,
    Where its sweet treasure swings,
The honey lover clings,
    To the red flowers.

So, lost in vivid light,
So, rapt from day and night,
I linger in delight,
    Enraptured o'er the vision-freighted hours.
— *Rose Terry.*

O THOU sweet lark, that in the heaven so high,
    Twinkling thy wings, dost sing so joyfully,
I watch thy soaring with no mean delight;
And when at last I turn mine aching eye

That lags so far below that lofty flight,
Still silently receive thy melody.
O thou sweet lark, that I had wings like thee!
— *Southey.*

Snapdragon.

Antirrhinum majus.   NATURAL ORDER: *Scrophulariaceæ — Figwort Family.*

OF the many varieties of this plant, all are highly esteemed as ornaments in the flower-garden. The flowers are very brilliant, usually combining two or three colors in one blossom, and are most singular in shape. Each is tubular as it comes out of the calyx, and continues so for nearly an inch, when it terminates in two lips, a two-cleft one turning upward, and a three-cleft one turning downward, while between the two, and closing the orifice, is a puffed protuberance. The Greek words *anti rin*, whence the name, signify "opposite the nose," as it is supposed to resemble the snout of an animal. When the flower is pressed between the fingers it opens like a mouth, and when the pressure is slackened it snaps or closes quickly like a spring. The plants are perennials, growing about a foot or two in height, and bloom the first season if sown early.

Presumption.

DE LORGE'S love o'erheard the king, a beauteous, lively dame,
  With smiling lips and sharp, bright eyes, which always seemed the same;
She thought, The count, my lover, is brave as brave can be;
He surely would do wondrous things to show his love of me;
"King, ladies, lovers, all look on; the occasion is divine;
I'll drop my glove, to prove his love; great glory will be mine."
She dropped her glove, to prove his love, then looked at him and smiled,
He bowed, and in a moment leaped among the lions wild;
The leap was quick, return was quick, he has regained his place,
Then threw the glove, but not with love, right in the lady's face.
"By heaven!" said Francis, "rightly done!" and he rose from where he sat;
"No love," quoth he, "but vanity, sets love a task like that." —*Leigh Hunt.*

WHEN years began
  To reap the fruit of knowledge; ah! how then
Would she with graver looks, with sweet, stern brow,
Check my presumption and my forwardness;
Yet still would give me flow'rs; still would she show
What she would have me, yet not have me know. —*Daniel.*

Snowball.

Viburnum roseum. NATURAL ORDER: *Caprifoliaceæ — Honeysuckle Family.*

THIS shrub is a native of Europe, and attracts general attention in early spring, when it crowns itself with bloom. The flowers make their appearance at first in small, greenish masses, and are utterly devoid of beauty; but a few days of warm sunlight bleaches them to a creamy white, by which time the balls have expanded to their utmost, bringing full assurance that the loitering days of summer are at hand. The Viburnum assumes a rather straggling shape if left entirely to itself, but with a little attention and pruning can be trained into a well-shaped bush for a single specimen, or, where the luxury of space will allow, it may be planted in groups to adorn the lawn, where it harmonizes well with the delicate and simple tints of the lilac and other spring flowers. In England it is called the Guelder Rose. The significance of its botanical name is uncertain, but it is the old Latin appellative.

Thoughts of Heaven.

THE torch you turn to earth still upward lifts its flame;
And so the soul looks up, though turned to earth in shame.
Wm. W. Story.

HER thoughts were holy, saint-like,
  Ever pointing to her God;
And sweetest orisons were uttered
  By the lips beneath the sod.

So that queenly "Snowball" blooming,
  Was of her an emblem given;
For its flower language whispers —
  "My thoughts are all of heaven."
Lucy M. Sanford.

HEAVEN darkly works; yet where the seed hath been,
  There shall the fruitage, glowing, yet be seen.
— Hemans.

MY thoughts are not in this hour
  Unworthy what I see, though my dust is;
Spirit! let me expire, or see them nearer!
Byron.

EACH individual seeks a separate goal;
But heav'n's great view is one, and that the whole,
That counterworks each folly and caprice;
That disappoints th' effects of ev'ry vice.
Pope.

Snowdrop.

Galanthus nivalis. NATURAL ORDER: *Amaryllidaceæ—Amaryllis Family*

ZURICH, with the adjoining cantons of Switzerland and some other localities in Europe, may be considered the original habitats of this little plant, the botanical name of which signifies Snowy Milk-flower. It flourishes in the meadows and along the water courses that abound in the neighborhood of the Alps, where the pure and everlasting snow rests like a cloud between the blue sky above and the green and fertile valley beneath. It is very hardy, as it would indeed have to be to exist amid such surroundings. Having been many years cultivated, it has found its way from the parterres abroad into the gardens of America, where it may be seen peeping from its snowy coverlet long before other flowers burst from their wintry prisons, or nature awakes from her dreaming. The roots are bulbous, and in planting they show to better advantage where several (from six to eight) are set in a group, when, in a few years, the increase will warrant a division. The flower is of a fair size, and pendulous, with only a single blossom on a stem.

Consolation.

OH! sweetly beautiful it is to mark
　The virgin, vernal snowdrop! lifting up—
Meek as a nun—the whiteness of its cup,
From earth's dead bosom, desolate and dark.

SWEET flower, thou tell'st how hearts
　As pure and tender as thy leaf—as low
And humble as thy stem—will surely know
The joy that peace imparts. 　—*Percival.*

HER precious pearl, in sorrow's cup,
　Unmelted at the bottom lay,
To shine again, when, all drunk up,
　The bitterness should pass away.
　　　　　　　　　—*Moore.*

THE little shape, by magic pow'r,
　Grew less and less, contracted to a flow'r;
A flow'r, that first in this sweet garden smiled,
To virgins sacred, and the snowdrop styled.
　　　　　　　　　—*Tickell.*

Snowdrop Tree.

Halesia diptera. NATURAL ORDER: *Styracaceæ—Storax Family.*

HALESIA is a name given in honor of the Rev. Dr. Stephen Hales, an English philosopher and naturalist (1677-1761), to a number of shrubs or small trees found in the rich woodlands that border on the banks of some stream or river. They are found more especially in the Southern States lying adjacent to the Atlantic. The usual height of these trees is from fifteen to twenty feet, though they are occasionally found considerably taller. In the South they bloom from March to May. The flowers, which are white and bell-shaped, make their appearance before the large and ample foliage. It is from a tropical tree of this order that the Storax and Benzoin or Gum Benjamin is obtained. This resinous sap is made to flow by perforating the bark of the stems and branches. It is very fragrant, and is much used in the manufacture of various perfumes. In medicine it is regarded as a stimulant and expectorant.

Exhilaration.

WHAT then remains but well our power to use,
    And keep good humor still, whate'er we lose?
And trust me, dear, good humor can prevail,
When airs, and flights, and screams, and scolding fail;
Beauties in vain their pretty eyes may roll;
Charms strike the sight, but merit wins the soul.
        —*Pope.*

SEE how the day beameth brightly before us!
    Blue is the firmament, green is the earth;
Grief hath no voice in the universe chorus:
    Nature is ringing with music and mirth.

Lift up thy eyes, that are looking in sadness;
    Gaze! and, if beauty can rapture thy soul,
Virtue herself shall allure thee to gladness—
    Gladness! philosophy's guardian and goal.
        —*From the German.*

I'D laugh today, today is brief,
    I would not wait for anything;
I'd use today that cannot last,
Be glad today and sing.
        —*Christina G. Rossetti.*

Southernwood.

Artemisia abrotanum.   NATURAL ORDER: *Compositæ—Aster Family.*

RATHER dense of growth, and of a height of from three to five feet, the Southernwood is a well-known shrubby plant quite frequently found in old fashioned gardens. The leaves are much divided, and the flowers are yellow, while a pleasant, bitter, aromatic odor pervades the whole plant. It is frequently called Old Man, and sometimes Boys' Love. The botanical name of the genus is derived from Artemis, the Greek appellation of the chaste huntress and goddess, Diana; and the specific title abrotanum, which denotes the Southernwood proper as distinguished from other varieties of the Artemisia, is of uncertain derivation. This plant is possessed of tonic, narcotic and other medicinal properties, and is frequently used in domestic medicine, particularly in places remote from a pharmaceutist or physician.

Jesting.

PERHAPS the jest that charm'd the sprightly crowd,
   And made the jovial table laugh so loud,
     To some false notion owed its poor pretense.   *Prior.*

TRUE wit is nature to advantage dress'd
  What oft was thought, but ne'er so well express'd;
Something, whose truth convinced at sight, we find;
That gives us back the image of our mind.

As shades more sweetly recommend the light,
So modest plainness sets off sprightly wit; [good,
For works may have more wit than does them
As bodies perish through excess of blood.
                    —*Pope.*

AS in smooth oil the razor best is whet,
  So wit is by politeness sharpest set;
Their want of edge from their offense is seen;
Both pain us least when exquisitely keen.
            —*Young.*

HE cannot try to speak with gravity,
  But one perceives he wags an idle tongue;
He cannot try to look demure, but spite
Of all he does, he shows a laughter's cheek;

He cannot e'en essay to walk sedate,
But in his very gait one sees a jest,
That's ready to break out in spite of all
His seeming.   —*Knowles.*

Speedwell.

Veronica arvensis. NATURAL ORDER: *Scrophulariaceæ—Figwort Family.*

VERONICA ARVENSIS, or Field Veronica, is found chiefly in dry fields throughout the Northern and Middle States. It is a small plant, from two to six inches high, with pale green foliage, and flowers that are blue in color. There are some native species of this plant that flourish only in the black and heavy soil of wet ditches. A variety called Spiked Speedwell, a native of Europe and Asia, with beautiful blue or pink flowers, is now cultivated for the adornment of our gardens. It is supposed by some authorities that this plant was named in honor of St. Veronica. The common Speedwell is used by the poorer classes in Sweden as a substitute for tea, the true Chinese herb being probably saved for special occasions. Medicinally, it is reputed to possess properties that are sudorific, diuretic, tonic and expectorant.

Female Fidelity.

OH! the tender ties,
  Close twisted with the fibers of the heart!
Which broken, break them, and drain off the soul
Of human joy, and make it pain to live.
—*Young.*

AND at last he wakened from his swoon,
  And found his dear bride propping his head,
And chafing his pale hands, and calling to him;
And felt the warm tears falling on his face:
And said to his own heart, "She weeps for me!"
  And yet lay still, and feigned himself as dead,
That he might prove her to the uttermost,
And say to his own heart, "She weeps for me."
—*Tennyson.*

SHE is as constant as the stars
  That never vary, and more chaste than they.
—*Procter.*

SHOULD I change my allegiance for rancor,
  If fortune changes her side?
Or should I, like a vessel at anchor,
  Turn with the turn of the tide?

Lift, O lift, thou lowering sky,
  An thou wilt thy gloom forego!
An thou wilt not, he and I
  Need not part for drifts of snow.
—*Jean Ingelow.*

Spiderwort.

Tradescantia Virginica.   NATURAL ORDER: *Commelynaceæ — Spiderwort Family.*

NAMED after John Tradescant, a favorite gardener of Charles I. of England, and after his son of the same name, both distinguished botanists and travelers, this plant is familiarly known as the Spiderwort. It is a common plant, with coarse, grass-like leaves, and pretty purple or rose-colored flowers of a delicate texture. It is almost impossible to prepare a perfect specimen for the herbarium, as the least pressure discolors and withers its petals beyond recognition. The stem when broken discovers a viscous juice, that spins out like a spider's silken thread as the parts are separated, thus giving it its common appellation. The Cleome pungens has also been sometimes called Spiderwort, or Spiderflower, but belongs to the Caper Family, and is a tall, showy, biennial plant. The flowers, which bloom in racemes, are separately rather curious in structure. The petals are mounted on threadlike claws, and extending above them, about twice their length, are the six stamens, like so many legs of a spider. *Cleome*, from the Greek, means something closed; and *pungens*, from the Latin, signifies piercing.

Transient Happiness.

BUT I forgot the parting words she said,
So much they thrilled the all-attentive soul;
For one short moment human heart and head
May bear such bliss — its present is the whole;
I had that present, till in whispers fell
With parting gesture her subdued farewell.
— *Jean Ingelow.*

BLESSED, thrice blessed days! but ah! how short!
Bless'd as the pleasing charms of holy men,
But fugitive, like those, and quickly gone.
O slippery state of things! What sudden turns,
What strange vicissitudes, in the first leaf
Of man's sad history! today most happy;
And, ere tomorrow's sun has set, most abject!
How scant the space between these vast extremes!
— *Blair.*

THE spider's most attenuated thread
Is cord — is cable — to man's tender tie
On earthly bliss; it breaks at every breeze. — *Young.*

Spikenard.

Aralia racemosa.   NATURAL ORDER: *Araliaceæ—Ginseng Family.*

FOUND chiefly in the woods of the Northern States and Canada, this plant has a pleasant, aromatic root, which is sometimes used medicinally, and as an ingredient in some manufactured beverages. It is not to be understood, however, that this is the true Spikenard (sometimes called Nard) so highly spoken of in Scripture, which is supposed to belong to India, as only an inferior kind is found in Palestine. It has an aromatic smell, and is a favorite article of perfume in Thibet and Nepaul. It is said to grow in large tufts, rising upward like grass, and forms an article of considerable traffic in Egypt and Turkey. It is from this plant that the highly-precious, odoriferous ointment is made, and a box containing a pound, in the time of our Saviour, was valued at more than three hundred pence, or denarii, a Roman coin, which, at fifteen cents each, amounted to about forty-five dollars.

Benefits.

HE that neglects a blessing, though he want
  A present knowledge how to use it,
Neglects himself.   —*Beaumont and Fletcher.*

AND 'tis not sure so full a benefit,
  Freely to give as freely to require;
A bounteous act hath glory following it,
They cause the glory that the act desire.
          —*Lady Carew.*

TO brag of benefits one hath bestown,
  Doth make the best seem less, and most seem
So oftentimes the greatest courtesy   [none;
Is by the doer made an injury.
          —*Brome.*

TO meditate, to plan, resolve, perform,
  Which in itself is good—as surely brings
Reward of good, no matter what be done.
          —*Pollock.*

MIND despatch'd upon the busy toil,
  Should range where Providence has bless'd the
Visiting every flow'r with labor meet,   [soil;
And gathering all her treasures sweet by sweet,

She should imbue the tongue with what she sips,
And shed the balmy blessing on the lips,
That good diffus'd may more abundant grow,
And speech may praise the pow'r that bids it flow.
          —*Cowper.*

Spruce.

Abies nigra. NATURAL ORDER: *Coniferæ—Pine Family.*

SPRUCE is the name applied by Linnæus to all of the species comprehended under the genus Abies, but later botanists make a somewhat different classification. Spruces, firs, pines, balsams and hemlocks are all closely allied. This variety of Spruce is an inhabitant of the northern part of the United States, where it attains the altitude of seventy and sometimes eighty feet, rearing upward a towering, pyramidal head. Some of the mountain forests in the colder latitudes are almost wholly composed of it. The trunk is straight; the wood is light, yet strong and elastic, and is employed many ways in architecture, but is not as valuable as the White Spruce. The essence is produced by boiling the tops of the Abies nigra in water, then concentrating by evaporation.

Farewell.

FAREWELL, then, thou loved one—O, loved but too well,
Too deeply, too blindly for language to tell!
—Charles Fenno Hoffman.

FAREWELL, my home, my home no longer now,
  Witness of many a calm and happy day;
And thou, fair eminence, upon whose brow
  Dwells the last sunshine of the evening ray,
Farewell! Mine eyes no longer shall pursue
The westering sun beyond the utmost height,
When slowly he forsakes the fields of light.
—Southey.

AND now farewell, farewell! I dare not lengthen
  These sweet moments out; to gaze on thee
Is bliss indeed, yet it but serves to strengthen
  The love that now amounts to agony;
This is our last farewell.
—Mrs. Welby.

Farewell, thou canst not teach me to forget.
—Shakespeare.

FAREWELL! I will omit no opportunity
That may convey my greetings, love, to thee.
—Shakespeare.

WITH that wringing my hand he turns away;
  And tho' his tears would hardly let him look,
Yet such a look did through his tears make way
As show'd how sad a farewell there he took.
—Daniel.

THEN came the parting hour, and what arise
When lovers part—expressive looks, and eyes
Tender and tearful—many a fond adieu,
And many a call the sorrow to renew.
—Crabbe.

Stapelia.

Stapelia bufonia. NATURAL ORDER: *Asclepiadaceæ — Milkweed Family.*

JOHN BODÆUS STAPEL, a renowned physician of Amsterdam, has the posthumous honor of being remembered in this plant. The Stapelia has the appearance of a species of cactus, although it belongs to another family of plants. It is fleshy and branching, without foliage, and the flowers are among the most curious. Before bursting, the bud is somewhat similar in appearance to a large button with five sides, and is attached to a short stem. It is of a bronzed or reddish green hue, but when fully open the calyx spreads out its five points in the shape of a star about two inches broad, and forms part of the flower, having the appearance of being lined with a dappled maroon and velvety surface full of fine wrinkles. In the center stands the corolla, like a ring, short and fleshy, and of the same color. It has a rather unpleasant odor, which is not perceptible unless inhaled intentionally. The several varieties are natives of South Africa: and bufonia, from the Latin *bufo*, a toad, distinguishes this variety, because of its resemblance to that reptile.

Offense.

ALL'S not offense that indiscretion finds,
  And dotage terms so.   —*Shakespeare.*

IF my offense be of such mortal kind,
  That neither service past, nor present sorrows,
Nor purpos'd merit in futurity,
Can ransom me into his love again,

But to know so must be my benefit;
  So shall I clothe me in a forced content,
And shut myself up in some other course
To fortune's alms.   —*Shakespeare.*

I WISH I could say, "Dear friend,
  Tell me, what have I done?
Forgive me, let it be now at an end."
     —*Wm. W. Story.*

WHAT is my offense?
  Where is the evidence that doth accuse me?
What lawful quest have given their verdict up
Unto the frowning judge?
     —*Shakespeare.*

BE not too ready to condemn
  The wrongs thy brothers may have done;
Ere ye too harshly censure them
For human faults, ask, "Have I none?"
     —*Eliza Cook.*

Star Flower.

Sabbatia brachiata.   NATURAL ORDER: *Gentianaceæ—Gentian Family.*

OF the Sabbatias (so called in honor of the Italian botanist Sabbati) there are several varieties, and although but few have found their way into cultivation, yet they deserve to be classified among our most beautiful native plants. The Star Flower, one of the species, is found quite abundantly on dry prairies in several of our Western and Southern States. The stem is about a foot high, with lance-linear leaves. The blossoms are varied in different individual plants. Sabbatia brachiata has flowers of a delicate rose-purple, with a yellow star, which is bordered with green; and Sabbatia stellaria is rose-color, the star of which is bordered with red. It is to this family that the plants belong from which the medical remedy known as gentian is obtained, the properties being both tonic and febrifugal.

Reciprocity.

LET us love now in this our fairest youth,
  When love can find a full and fond return.
—Percival.

AND many hours we talked in joy,
  Yet too much blessed for laughter:
I was a happy man that day,
  And happy ever after.   —*Mrs. Hewitt.*

BE thine the more refined delights,
  Of love, that banishes control,
When the fond heart with heart unites,
  And soul in unison with soul.
—Cartwright.

AND canst thou not accord thy heart
  In unison with mine
Whose language thou alone hast heard.
  Thou only canst divine?   —*Rufus Dawes.*

WHICH is that this of all men on earth
  Doth love me well enough to count me great—
To think my soul and his of equal girth?
  O liberal estimate!

And yet it is so; he is bound to me.
  For human love makes aliens near of kin;
By it I rise, there is equality;
  I rise to thee, my twin.   —*Jean Ingelow.*

WHERE heart meets heart reciprocally soft.
  Each other's pillow to repose divine.
—Young.

Star of Bethlehem.

Ornithogalum umbellatum.   NATURAL ORDER: *Liliaceæ — Lily Family.*

MENTIONED by Pliny, author of a Natural History, who flourished A. D. 77, the Ornithogalum has given rise to much comment as to the origin of its name. It is derived from two Greek words, *ornithos*, a bird, and *gala*, milk — a most singular combination, surely; and we cannot help suggesting the following theory: The Greeks had a pretty and poetic conceit, that in spring a certain wind blew, and with it brought the birds of passage to gladden their bowers with song, and this wind they named *ornithias*, or bird-wind. Now the Star of Bethlehem blooms in April and May, about the time of the birds' return, thus poetically is seen a flower greeting the birds: a flower, too, which is of an opaque white, or milk color. The English name is from the shape of the blossom. The bulbs frequently attain a great size.

Reconciliation.

NOR did he doubt her more,
  But rested in her fealty, till he crowned
A happy life with a fair death.   *Tennyson.*

WHOM but Maud should I meet —
  And she touched my hand with a smile so sweet
She made me divine amends
For a courtesy not return'd.   *— Tennyson.*

WELL do vanish'd frowns enhance
  The charms of every brighten'd glance,
And dearer seems each dawning smile
For having lost its light awhile.   *— Moore.*

I WOULD have my love
  Angry sometimes, to sweeten off the rest
Of her behavior.   *Ben Jonson.*

"AND didst *thou* weep,
  And *I* did not console?
Look up, and be no longer sad!"

She called me by my name:
Our spirits rushed together, glad
And swift as flame to flame.
  Dora Greenwell.

Strawberry.

Fragaria vesca. NATURAL ORDER: *Rosaceæ — Rose Family.*

EVER welcome to our tables, the Strawberry is one of the earliest, most abundant and best known of our fruits, and requires but little description or commentary. We have many varieties of this plant growing wild in meadows and on the hillsides throughout the United States and British America. The Alpine or English Strawberry is found chiefly in cultivation. The fruit is conical, scarlet, and fragrant, and gleams brightly amidst its triple leaves. We are indebted to this order of plants for a great variety of our fruits, namely, the peach, pear, apricot, apple and cherry, as well as the blackberry and various raspberries. The Strawberry is peculiar, in having its seeds on the outside of the fruit, instead of being surrounded by the pulp.

Perfect Goodness.

THY purpose firm is equal to the deed;
  Who does the best his circumstance allow
Does well, acts nobly; angels could do no more.
                – *Young.*

HOWE'ER it be, it seems to me
  'Tis only noble to be good,
Kind hearts are more than coronets,
  And simple faith than Norman blood.
           – *Tennyson.*

THE words which thou hast utter'd
  Are of thy soul a part;
And the good seed thou hast scatter'd
  Is springing in my heart.
           – *Whittier.*

HE was too good to be
  Where ill men were; and was best of all
Amongst the rarest of good ones. *Shakespeare.*

THEN preach'd the humble Strawberry. Behold
  The lowliest and least adorn'd of flowers
Lies at thy feet; yet lift my leafy fold,
And fruit is there unfound in gaudier bowers.

So plain be thou and meek,
  And when vain man shall seek,
Unveil the blooming fruit of solitary hours.
           – *Evans.*

My heart
Contains of good, wise, just, the perfect shape.
       Milton.

Sumach.

Rhus aromatica.   NATURAL ORDER: *Anacardiaceæ—Sumach Family.*

KNOWN familiarly as Sumach, the Rhus aromatica is a pretty shrub from two to six feet high, growing on open lands in Canada and the United States, sometimes covering acres of ground if left unmolested. The flowers are yellowish, and are rather unattractive in comparison with the berries when ripened, which look like so many crimson plumes waving in the air. They possess an acid taste, and are not poisonous. The Venetian Sumach is said by Nuttall to grow plentifully in Arkansas. The Italians use it in preparing leather. Among other species of the Sumach are the Rhus glabra, the bark of which may be used in tanning, and the berries to create a dye; the Rhus typhina, the wood of which is aromatic, and produces a yellow dye; and the Poison Sumach, the appearance of which is similar to the above, except that it is perhaps larger and inhabits swampy places. It is intensely poisonous, even to the touch, and sometimes imparts its pernicious influence to the surrounding atmosphere.

Splendor.

FLORAL apostles! that in dewy splendor
    Weep without sin and blush without a crime,
O, may I deeply learn and ne'er surrender
    Your love sublime!
        —*Horace Smith.*

THE bright sun compacts the precious stone,
    Imparting radiant luster like his own;
He tinctures rubies with their rosy hue,
And on the sapphire spreads a heavenly blue.
       —*Sir R. Blackmore.*

BRIGHT and glorious is that revelation
    Writ all over this great world of ours
Making evident our own creation,
    In these stars of earth, these golden flowers.
       —*Longfellow.*

AND wide a splendor streamed through all the sky;
    O'er sea and land one soft, delicious blush,
That touched the gray rocks lightly, tenderly;
    A transitory flush.
       Celia Thaxter.

Summer Savory.

Satureja hortensis. NATURAL ORDER: *Labiatæ — Mint Family.*

ITALY is the native seat of the Satureja. It belongs to a family of highly aromatic, pungent herbs, most members of which are very useful to mankind for their tonic and febrifugal properties. Several of them — as the thyme, sage, the marjoram and the Summer Savory — are cultivated as herbs, and are used for seasoning soups, or for dressing of fowls and other meats. There is a species sometimes found native in the Western States, but it is considered a rare plant, and is perhaps the Satureja run wild. The name savors of the Satyrs, a class of beings in Greek mythology that apparently represented the luxuriant vital powers of nature.

Success.

APPLAUSE waits on success; the fickle multitude,
   Like the light straw that floats along the stream,
Glide with the current still, and follow fortune.
                      —*Franklin.*

DWELLS within the soul of every artist
   More than all his efforts can express,
And he knows the best remains unuttered,
   Sighing at what we call success.
          —*Adelaide A. Procter.*

IT is success that colors all in life. [honest,
   Success makes fools admired, makes villains
All the proud virtue of this vaunting world
Fawns on success and power, howe'er acquired.
            —*Thompson.*

"TIS not in mortals to command success,
   But we'll do more, Sempronius, we'll deserve it.
            —*Addison.*

SUCCESS, the mark no mortal wit,
   Or surest hand, can always hit;
For, whatsoe'er we perpetrate,
We do but row, we're steer'd by fate.
          —*Butler.*

VIRTUE without success
   Is a fair picture shown by an ill light;
But lucky men are favorites of heaven;
All own the chief when fortune owns the cause.
         —*Dryden.*

SMILE and we smile, the lords of many lands;
   Frown and we smile, the lords of our own hands;
For man is man and master of his fate.
         —*Tennyson.*

Sunflower.

Helianthus annuus. NATURAL ORDER: *Composite — Aster Family.*

LITERALLY, Helianthus, from two Greek words, *helios*, the sun, and *anthos*, a flower, denotes Sunflower. The common variety is a native of South America, and is probably the largest of the species, for it towers sometimes to the height of fifteen feet, with a stalk as large as a man's wrist. This growth depends on the character of the soil, as a poor soil dwarfs and diminishes its stature. The flowers are yellow, and are frequently the size of a large dinner plate. The seeds are very rich and oily, and are sometimes used like almonds for preparing soothing emulsions. In Europe a sort of bouillon is made of them for infants, and in Portugal they are ground into meal for bread, and are sometimes used in the same way by our own American Indians. They are also said to be used as a substitute for coffee. The oil is nearly equal to olive oil, and the stems are useful as food for cattle and also for fuel. It has been asserted that if the seeds are planted around a dwelling the plants act as a preventive of fevers, by absorbing the malaria.

Lofty Thoughts.

PRIDE of the garden, the beauteous, the regal,
    The crown'd with a diadem burning in gold;
Sultan of flowers, as the strong pinioned eagle
    And lord of the forest their wide empire hold.

THERE is a region loftier far
    Than sages know or poets sing —
Brighter than summer's beauties are,
    And softer than the tints of spring.

There is a world with blessings blest,
    Beyond what prophet's e'er foretold;
Nor might the tongue of angel guest
    A picture of that world unfold.

LOOK past yon hills, whose crest bright sunned is
    With the last fond glance that the dead day gives;
Up! let the voice of thy *De Profundis*
    Thrill to those courts where no sorrow lives!

—*Barton Grey.*

Sweet Flag.

Acorus calamus. NATURAL ORDER: *Araceæ — Arum Family.*

NEARLY everywhere in low, wet soils throughout the United States, the Sweet Flag, or Calamus Root, as it is sometimes called, may be found, the grouping of its swordlike leaves adding variety to the surrounding landscape. The root is thick and branching, creeping along through the watery soil like so many reaching fingers. It is highly aromatic to the taste, and is often used medicinally as a mild stimulant and tonic, being highly spoken of by some physicians as a valuable ingredient in ague remedies. The name Acorus is thought to be derived from the Greek *kore*, pupil of the eye, because of supposed value as an eye-salve; and the Latin word *calamus* means a reed. Among the Turks, who are said to consume immense quantities of all kinds of sweetmeats, it is very popular as a confection, it being prepared by a coating of sugar.

Stillness.

On hanging cobwebs shone the dew,
   And thick the wayside clovers grew;
The feeding bee had much to do,
   So fast did honey drops exude:
She sucked and murmured, and was gone,
And lit on other blooms anon.
The while I learned a lesson on
   The source and sense of quietude.
                —*Jean Ingelow.*

A CLOUD lay cradled near the setting sun.
   A gleam of crimson tinged its braided snow;
Long had I watched the glory moving on
   O'er the still radiance of the lake below.
Tranquil its spirit seemed, and floated slow!
   Even in its very motion there was rest;
While every breath of eve that chanced to blow
   Wafted the traveler to the beauteous west.
Emblem, methought, of the departed soul!
   To whose white robe the gleam of bliss is given,
And by the breath of mercy made to roll
   Right onward to the golden gates of heaven,
Where to the eye of faith it peaceful lies,
And tells to man his glorious destinies.
                —*John Wilson.*

Sweet Potato.

Batatas edulis. NATURAL ORDER: *Convolvulaceæ—Convolvulus Family.*

BATATAS, or Sweet Potato, is native to both the East and West Indies, and only within a recent period has the cultivation of the tubers been attempted save in tropical countries or the more remote, warm parts of our Southern States. Latterly, however, they have been introduced into the Middle States, where they have been successfully grown by first starting the plants in hotbeds, and then transplanting them to the soil in which they are to grow. The potatoes are protected in dry sand during winter. The tubers are pointed, sweet and nourishing. The stem is prostrate and creeping, producing purple or white flowers, campanulate in shape, and sometimes quite showy. For mere pleasure it can be grown in the house by placing a tuber in a vessel partly filled with water, when it will reward the cultivator with several quite pretty and lengthy vines. If the first should decay before sprouting, it could easily be replaced until success crowned perseverance.

Hidden Qualities.

THOUGH gay as mirth, as curious thoughts sedate;
   As elegance polite, as power elate;
Profound as reason, and as justice clear;
Soft as compassion, yet as truth severe.   —*Savage.*

I CANNOT soar into the heights you show,
   Nor dive among the deeps that you reveal;
But it is much that high things are to know,
   That deep things are to feel.

SHE was the pride
   Of her familiar sphere—the daily joy
Of all who on her gracefulness might gaze,
And in the light and music of her way
Have a companion's portion.   —*Willis.*

'Tis yours, not mine, to pluck out of your breast
   Some human truth, whose workings recondite
Were unattired in words, and manifest,
   And hold it forth to light.
              —*Jean Ingelow.*

STAND free and fast,
   And judge him by no more than what you know
Ingeniously, and by the right laid line
Of truth, he truly will all styles deserve
Of wise, good, just; a man both soul and nerve.
              —*Shirley.*

Sweet Sultan.

Amberboa moschata. NATURAL ORDER: *Composite—Aster Family.*

QUEER, quaint and isolated, but sunny Persia, is the native land of this plant, while others of the same species are natives of the countries bordering on the Mediterranean. They are all handsome annuals, of easy cultivation, producing purple, white, or yellow flowers, which are endowed with a slight odor of musk. They are about a foot and a half high, and are most excellent for planting in mixed borders, yielding flowers during the whole summer, which reward the cultivator with their perfume, and an abundant supply for bouquets and decorations.

Felicity.

AND may the stream of thy maturing life
Forever flow, in blissful sunlight through
A fairy scene with gladsome beauty rife,
As ever greeted the enraptur'd view!
—*A. W. Noncy.*

OH! happy pair, to every blessing born!
For you may life's calm stream unruffled run!
For you its roses bloom without a thorn,
And bright as morning shine its evening sun!
—*R. T. Paine.*

MY life has been like summer skies
When they are fair to view,
But there never yet were hearts or skies,
Clouds might not wander through.
—*Mrs. L. P. Smith.*

MAY hope not too deceptive prove;
May sweet contentment round you throw
Such bliss as may be found below!
—*T. T. Watson.*

AND I was glad that night.
With no reason ready,
To give my own heart for its deep delight,
That flowed like some tidal eddy,
Or shone like a star that was rising bright
With comforting radiance steady.
—*Jean Ingelow.*

THERE is a spell in every flower—
A sweetness in each spray;
And every simple bird has power
To please me with its lay!
—*Anne Peyre Dinnies.*

Sweet William.

Dianthus barbatus.   NATURAL ORDER: *Caryophyllaceæ — Pink Family.*

CALLED Dianthus, or flower of Jove, by the Greeks, the Sweet William still stands preëminent among the flowers which deck the garden. Although it be surrounded by the modern pinks and carnations, flaunting their beauty with high-sounding names, it deserves cherishing as an antique plant, as well as for its sportive variety. Many species of the Dianthus are natives of Oriental countries, and their colors are superb, attesting the warmth of the Eastern climates, where nature is brilliant in her tints. This species, sometimes familiarly called Bunch Pink, and some other varieties, are natives of Europe.

Stratagem.

AND mar your plot? No; I'm too bold for that;
   I threw him off the scent, and ran with speed
To warn you, señor, how to take the man.
— George H. Boker.

WITH bended bow and quiver full of arrows,
   Hovered about the enemy, and marked
The road he took, then hastened to my friends,
Whom, with a troop of fifty chosen men,
I met advancing. The pursuit I led,
Till we o'ertook the spoil encumbered foe.
We fought and conquered. Ere a sword was drawn
An arrow from my bow had pierced their chief,
Who wore that day the arms which now I wear.
— John Home.

THE maid shakes her head, on her lips lays her fingers,
   Steals up from her seat — longs to go, and yet lingers;
A frightened glance turns to her drowsy grandmother,
Puts one foot on the stool, spins the wheel with the other.
Lazily, easily, swings now the wheel round;
Slowly and lowly is heard now the reel's sound;
Noiseless and light to the lattice above her
The maid steps — then leaps to the arms of her lover.
Slower — and slower — and slower the wheel swings;
Lower — and lower — and lower the reel rings;
Ere the reel and the wheel stop their ringing and moving,
Through the grove the young lovers by moonlight are roving.
— John Francis Waller.

Sycamore,

Platanus occidentalis. NATURAL ORDER: *Platanaceæ — Plane-Tree Family.*

ONE of the largest trees in American forests is the Sycamore or Buttonwood tree, which grows to a prodigious size. It is found most frequently on the banks of some of the large western rivers and on the margins of many of the smaller streams, where the trunk attains a not unusual circumference of fifty feet. Along the entire course of the Mississippi and Missouri rivers, extensive forests of it abound, and no sooner does a bar of sand or an island make itself seen above the surface of the fickle tide, than it is covered as if by magic with a growth of Sycamore saplings that in a few years develop into mighty trees. Its rapid growth is its chief recommendation, as its wood is soft and of no great utility. Its ample foliage makes a very desirable shade, and it thrives under circumstances to which many other trees succumb.

Woodland Beauty.

SYCAMORE with eglantine was spread,
A hedge about the sides, a covering overhead.
—*Dryden.*

I KNOW a forest vast and old—
A shade so deep, so darkly green,
That morning sends her shaft of gold
In vain to pierce its leafy screen:

I know a brake where sleeps the fawn,
The soft-eyed fawn, thro' noon's repose;
For noon with all the calm of dawn
Lies hushed beneath those dewy boughs.
—*Edith May.*

THE rich, deep masses of the sycamore
Hang heavy with the fullness of their prime.
—*Hemans.*

NOISELESSLY around,
From perch to perch, the solitary bird
Passes; and yon clear spring that, midst its herbs,
Wells softly forth and wandering steeps the roots
Of half the mighty forest, tells no tale

Of all the good it does. Thou hast not left
Thyself without a witness, in these shades,
Of thy perfections. Grandeur, strength and grace
Are here to speak of thee.
—*William Cullen Bryant.*

Syringa.

Philadelphus coronarius.   NATURAL ORDER: *Saxifragaceæ—Saxifrage Family.*

THIS showy shrub is one of several bearing the same cognomen, the classic name of which was bestowed in honor of Ptolemæus Philadelphus, an ancient king of Egypt, and the founder of the celebrated Alexandrian library. In early summer it is a handsome object, and is an addition to any landscape when covered by the creamy-white flowers that adorn its stems and burden the air with their honeyed fragrance, the odor of which is similar to the orange blossom, whence it is sometimes called Mock-Orange. It is a native of Europe, but has been very many years naturalized in America. Cultivated on the lawn, its branches sway in graceful luxuriance; but if space is an object, it will allow itself to be trained against a wall, and withhold not its abundant bloom. Another variety, called Philadelphus grandiflorus, is very similar in appearance, but the flowers are odorless.

Memory.

OH! friends regretted, scenes forever dear,
  Remembrance hails you with her warmest tear!
Drooping she bends o'er pensive Fancy's urn,
To trace the hours which never can return.
  — *Byron.*

WE will revive those times, and in our memories
  Preserve, and still keep fresh, like flowers in water,
Those happier days; when at our eyes our souls
Kindled their mutual fires, their equal beams
Shot and return'd, till, link'd and twin'd in one,
They chain'd our hearts together. *Denham.*

I CANNOT but remember such things were
  That were most precious to me.   *Shakespeare.*

FULL'D in the countless chambers of the brain,
  Our thoughts are link'd by many a hidden chain;
Awake but one, and lo! what myriads rise!
Each stamps its image as the other flies!
  — *Rogers.*

STILL o'er these scenes my memory wakes,
  And fondly broods with wiser care;
Time but the impression deeper makes,
  As streams their channels deeper wear.
  — *Burns.*

Tansy.

Tanacetum vulgare. NATURAL ORDER: *Compositæ—Aster Family.*

REMOTELY derived, perhaps, from the Greek *athanasia*, immortal, because of its durable flowers, the common Tansy is an old-fashioned plant of European origin, which has become naturalized from its many years' residence. It has a peculiar affinity for old fence corners near the habitation of man, where once placed it grows without further care or attention. The leaves are beautifully divided and subdivided. The flowers are yellow. The whole plant is pervaded by an aroma which is intensely bitter. The young and tender leaves are used for flavoring some articles of food, such as cakes, puddings and, for epicures, the omelet. In some parts of England it is customary, after the Good Friday service, for the clerk of the parish to carry to every house white tansy cakes as an Easter offering, for which each householder gives him a gratuity. The leaves are also used as a disinfectant, and among Finlanders to produce a green dye. The essential oil is very poisonous.

Resistance.

SHAME on those breasts of stone, that cannot melt
In soft adoption of another's sorrow! —*Aaron Hill.*

SHE was a careless, fearless girl,
  And made her answer plain;
Outspoken she to earl or churl,
  Kindhearted in the main,
But somewhat heedless with her tongue,
  And apt at causing pain.

A mirthful maiden she, and young,
  Most fair for bliss or bane;
O long ago I told you so,
  I tell you so today;
Go you your way, and let me go
  Just my own free way.
—*Christina G. Rossetti.*

HE read their thoughts—they were his own—
  "What! while our arms can wield these blades,
Shall we die tamely? die alone?
  Without one victim to our shades,
One Moslem heart where, buried deep,
The saber from its toil may sleep?" —*Moore.*

Teasel.

Dipsacus fullonum. NATURAL ORDER; *Dipsaceæ—Teasel Family.*

ALL the plants of this class except the **Fuller's Teasel** are devoid of interest, possessing no useful properties; but in Europe clothiers use the heads of that variety to raise the nap of woolen cloth. They are armed with hard, hooked scales, which, being attached for this purpose to a revolving cylinder, brush against the surface of the cloth. The common wild Teasel found by roadsides and hedges is a naturalized plant from Europe. It flowers in large, oval heads, mounted on a stalk from three to four feet high, and the stalks and dry heads may often be seen, in winter, with their spiny cones decorated with sleet or frost, showing prismatic colors in the sun. It is cultivated in Europe in large fields, a rich soil being necessary. The plants are thinned to about a foot apart, and the heads are cut for sale the second year.

Misanthropy.

THERE'S not a day, but, to the man of thought,
  Betrays some secret that throws new reproach
On life, and makes him sick of seeing more.
— Young.

I CAN ne'er forgive the thoughts I bore
'Gainst thee, and 'gainst the race of man entire
For I have stood at bay before the world,
Facing the wolves that well nigh pulled me down,
Until I deemed mankind a hungry pack,
Eager to suck their wounded brothers' blood.
But thou hast come to purge me of my gall,
To heal my wounded heart, to dry my tears,
And plant within my soul a love of man,
Which, by heaven's grace, wrong never shall uproot.
—George H. Boker.

SEARED, shunned, belied, ere youth had lost her force,
  He hated men too much to feel remorse,
And thought the voice of wrath a sacred call,
  To pay the injuries of some on all.
— Byron.

THEY have lived too long, who find
  Their treasury of hope is spent;
They gaze upon the human kind
Like letters on a monument,
  Repeating to the vacant air,
That dust and hollowness are there!
—Anonymous.

Thistle.

Cirsium arvense. NATURAL ORDER: *Composite — Aster Family.*

FIELD CIRSIUM (from the old Greek name), or the True Thistle, is the name of this variety, while the general word Thistle is a common name for various prickly plants which are widely dispersed and very annoying weeds. The most common of these is the Canada Thistle, which is the curse of any land where once established, as every seed is furnished with an airy balloon of its own, to bear it to some new, unoccupied district. It also spreads by its creeping root. The flowers are arranged in small purple heads. There is also a yellow variety. When the leaves are a short distance above the ground in spring, they are sometimes used as a salad, and the stems may be used as a boiled vegetable, if they are first stripped of their skins and soaked a short time in water to extract some of the bitterness pervading them. The following is the tradition of the adoption of the Thistle as the national emblem of Scotland: A body of Danes or Norsemen waiting to attack the Scots during the silent watches of the night, sent out a few spies to reconnoitre; these tramped upon some thistles, and, being wounded thereby, uttered such furious maledictions as to arouse the Scots, who were thus saved from disaster.

Austerity.

HIS breadth of brow, and Roman shape of chin,
Squared well with the firm man that reigned within.
— *Campbell.*

I SHUT the door to face the naked truth,
I stood alone — I faced the truth alone,
Stripped bare of self-regard, or form, or ruth,
Till first and last were shown.

I took the perfect balances and weighed;
No shaking of my hand disturbed the poise;
Weighed, found it wanting — not a word I said,
But silent made my choice.
— *Christina G. Rossetti.*

HIS square turned joints and strength of limb
Showed him no carpet knight so trim,
But in close fight a champion grim,
In camps a leader sage.
— *Sir Walter Scott.*

TRUST the frown thy features wear.
Ere long into a smile will turn.
I would not that a face as fair
As thine, beloved, should look so stern.
— *Wm. Leggett.*

Thorn.

Cratægus coccinea. NATURAL ORDER: *Rosaceæ — Rose Family.*

GROWING usually in dense thickets on the borders of a woodland, or beside some creek or stream, may be found the various species of the Thorn, there being numerous varieties indigenous to the American continent. In height the trees or shrubs are from eight to twenty-five feet, and add much to the glory of the woods when they are covered by their abundant bloom in early summer. The flowers are white, and appear in generous clusters. The fruit, when ripe, in autumn, is mostly scarlet in color, though sometimes yellowish, and in a few individual kinds is both pleasant flavored and edible. The branches are provided with many thorns, from which the common synonym is derived. In some parts of the country the lower-growing ones are used as hedges, but not so noticeably as in England, where many fields are protected by them. The wood is strong and durable.

Difficulty.

BEWARE of desperate steps! the darkest day,
   Live till to-morrow, will have passed away.
— Cowper.

AS one who, journeying, checks the rein in haste,
   Because a chasm doth yawn across his way,
Too wide for leaping, and too steeply faced
   For climber to essay —
As such a one, being brought to sudden stand,
   Doubts all his foregone path if 't were true,
And turns to this and then to the other hand
   As knowing not what to do.
— Jean Ingelow.

FAIN would I stop to remove from thy way
   Stones that have bruised me, and thorns that have grieved;
Set up my errors for waymarks, to say,
   Here I was wounded, ensnared, or deceived.
— Dora Greenwell.

WHICH way? which way? — his eyes grew dim
  With the dizzying whirl, — which way to swim?
The thunderous downshoot deafened him;
Half choked in the lashing spray;
Life is sweet, and the grave is grim, —
Which way? which way?
— Christina G. Rossetti.

Thorn Apple.

Datura stramonium.   NATURAL ORDER: *Solanaceæ—Nightshade Family.*

DATURA is a formation from the Arabic name, and the fruit of the plant is called by botanists Thorn Apple, which should not be confounded with the berries or apples of the thorn tree. The varied properties of this order of plants are highly important, for, although the most of them are dangerously poisonous, yet they form both food and medicine for man. The fruits of the egg-plant, tomato, and the tuber of the potato, are excellent and wholesome food, while the hyoscyamus, atropa and Datura are invaluable in medicine. Every part of the Thorn Apple, or Datura, is a deadly poison. It is used in asthmatic affections, but should be administered only by a careful physician. The flowers, which are trumpet-shaped, are white, slightly tinged with purple. The common name is Jimson or Jamestown Weed, and as such it is found wild on the commons. There are, however, several handsome varieties for garden culture, from foreign countries, that are worthy of attention.

Deceitful Charms.

I SHOULD not like the glass were past,
   Yet want it not entirely new,
But bright and strong enough to last
   About—suppose a week or two.   *Moore.*

BEAUTY is but a vain and doubtful good,
   A shining gloss that tadeth suddenly,
A flower that dies when first it 'gins to bud,
A brittle glass that's broken presently;
A doubtful good, a gloss, a glass, a flower,
Lost, faded, broken, dead within an hour.
          — *Shakspeare.*

LO! when the buds expand the leaves are green,
   Then the first opening of the flower is seen;
Then comes the honeyed breath and rosy smile,
That with their sweets the willing sense beguile;
But as we look, and love, and taste, and praise,
And the fruit grows, the charming flower decays.
          — *Crabbe.*

SHE spoke, and lo! her loveliness
   Methought she damaged with her tongue;
And every sentence made it less,
So false they rung.   *From Ingelow.*

Thrift.

Armeria vulgaris. NATURAL ORDER: *Plumbaginaceæ — Leadwort Family.*

VULGARIS (that is, common) Armeria, or Thrift, is one of a small order of plants that mostly prefer a location near the sea coast or salt, marshy land, whence this variety, which grows wild on the shores of Europe, is sometimes called Armeria maritima, or Maritime Thrift. It has a turf-like appearance, being about a foot high, and pretty in shape, with flowers of a rose-color, clustered in close heads, and blooms during midsummer. There are two or three varieties cultivated as rock plants, some of them being natives of Portugal. Plants of this species need renewing every two or three years. They are very easily propagated, as very small slips vegetate with ease in moist spring weather. All are quite pretty and desirable.

Sympathy.

OH! there is need that on men's hearts should fall
A spirit that can sympathize with all.
— *Phœbe Cary.*

LIKE the sweet melody which faintly lingers
Upon the wind-harp's strings at close of day,
When gently touched by evening's dewy fingers,
It breathes a low and melancholy lay.

So the calm voice of sympathy me seemeth,
And while its magic spell is round me cast,
My spirit in its cloistered silence dreameth,
And vaguely blends the future with the past.
— *Mrs. Embury.*

BUT thou shalt use my heart
As a poor mansion, over which thou rulest;
If so, thou will'st call in thy dearest friends;
They shall be welcome, though they're all mankind.
— *George H. Boker.*

THE soul of music slumbers in a shell
Till waked and kindled by the master's spell;
And feeling hearts, touch them but rightly, pour
A thousand melodies unheard before.
— *Rogers.*

OH! who the exquisite delights can tell
The joy which mutual confidence imparts?
Or who can paint the charm unspeakable
Which links in tender bands two faithful hearts.
— *Mrs. Tighe.*

Tiger Flower.

Cigridia pavonia. NATURAL ORDER: *Iridaceæ — Iris Family.*

HERE is a bulbous plant that is a great favorite for garden culture. The bulbs are placed in the ground in May or June, and grow without further care. The soil should cover them lightly, from an inch and a half to two inches deep. The leaves are sword-shaped, and about a foot long, with lengthwise veins. The flowers are often more than five inches across, though generally about four. They are superbly brilliant in their colors, and, though lasting but a few hours, new ones appear daily for a considerable length of time. The stalk on which they are borne is about a foot and a half high. The Tigridia pavonia (peacock-like) is a rich scarlet, spotted with yellow. There are one or two other varieties with flowers equally desirable, being very rich in their markings. The bulbs should be lifted in the fall, and be kept dry and free from frost, to be planted again in the spring.

Pride Befriend Me!

STERN and erect his brow was rais'd;
  Whate'er the grief his soul avow'd,
He would not shrink before the crowd.
              — *Byron.*

I'LL offer, and I'll suffer, no abuse,
  Because I'm proud; pride is of mighty use.
The affectation of a pompous name,
Has oft set wits and heroes in a flame;
Volumes, and buildings, and dominions wide,
Are of the noble monuments of pride.
              — *Crown.*

SPITE of all the tools that pride has made,
  'Tis not on man a useless burthen laid;
Pride has ennobled some, and some disgraced.
It hurts not in itself, but as 'tis placed.
When right, its views know none but virtue's bound;
When wrong, it scarcely looks one inch around.
              — *Stillingfleet.*

I WILL from henceforth rather be myself,
  Mighty, and to be fear'd, than my condition,
Which hath been smooth as oil, soft as young down,
And therefore lost that title of respect
Which the proud soul ne'er pays but to the proud.
              — *Shakespeare.*

Trumpet Flower.

Tecoma radicans. NATURAL ORDER: *Bignoniaceae — Bignonia Family.*

SCARCELY anyone who has resided or traveled in the Southern States during midsummer could fail to observe the flowers of this handsome and vigorous creeper. Its brilliant scarlet blossoms project their large trumpets from every hedge and bramble where the luxuriant vine has spread itself. In woodlands, particularly near water-courses, it may be seen decorating the stalwart trunks of upright trees, where it has extended its climbing branches from seventy to eighty feet, and where its superabundant growth trails from every branch, and the flowers glow like coals of fire in the midst of the surrounding leafage. It is an admirable permanent climber for outside walls, or for covering trees that have died, where shade is needed. There are some two or three fine plants from the Cape of Good Hope and China, suitable for the greenhouse, and four or five adapted for the hothouse, all having pink and white flowers, which are said to be very desirable.

Fame.

WITH fame, in just proportion, envy grows;
  The man that makes a character, makes foes.
        — *Young.*

WITH echoing feet he threaded
  The secret walks of fame:
The viewless arrows of his thoughts were headed
And winged with flame.
        — *Tennyson.*

WHAT so foolish as the chase of fame?
  How vain the prize! how impotent our aim!
For what are men who grasp at praise sublime,
But bubbles on the rapid stream of time?
        — *Young.*

UNBLEMISHED let me live, or die unknown —
  Oh! grant me *honest fame*, or grant me none!
        — *Pope.*

THE fame that man wins himself is best;
  That he may call his own; honors put on him
Make him no more a man than his clothes do.

Which are soon ta'en off; for in the warmth
The heat comes from the body, not the weeds;
So man's true fame must strike from his own deeds.
        — *Middleton.*

Tuberose.

Polianthes tuberosa.   NATURAL ORDER: *Amaryllidaceæ — Amaryllis Family.*

POLIANTHES, denoting city-flower in the original Greek, is a fine and odoriferous plant, and a native of some of the islands of the Indian Ocean, or perhaps of Mexico, as some think, but it has been cultivated in England for upward of two hundred years, whence in all probability we received it. The flowers are tubular in shape, and have the appearance of sculptured marble, especially the double ones. They are very fragrant, and are borne on a slender stalk about three feet high, which rises from the center of the group of sword-shaped leaves at the base. The root is bulbous or tuberous (whence the common name, which, therefore, is not "tube-rose"), and blooms but once. The young offshoots bloom when two years old. The bulbs, old enough to bloom, are very cheap, and can be ordered from any seedsman. They should be started in a hotbed, and placed in the garden when all danger of frost is over. In very northern latitudes they should be retained in the pot, so as to finish their bloom in the house.

Voluptuousness.

SO sleek her skin, so faultless was her make,
E'en Juno did unwilling pleasure take
To see so fair a rival.
—*Dryden.*

EACH sound, too, here to languishment inclin'd,
Lull'd the weak bosom and induced ease.
Aerial music in the warbling wind,
At distance rising oft, by small degrees
Nearer and nearer came, till o'er the trees
It hung, and breath'd such soul-dissolving airs,
As did, alas! with soft perdition please;
Entangled deep in its enchanting snares,
The list'ning heart forgot all duties and all cares.
—*Thompson.*

THEN stole I up, and trancédly
Gazed on the Persian girl alone,
Serene with argent-lidded eyes,
Amorous, and lashes like to rays
Of darkness, and a brow of pearl
Tressed with redolent ebony

In many a dark, delicious curl,
Flowing beneath her rose-hued zone;
The sweetest lady of the time,
Well worthy of the golden prime
Of good Haroun Alraschid.
—*Tennyson.*

Tulip.

Tulipa Gesneriana. NATURAL ORDER: *Liliaceæ — Lily Family.*

ZURICH was the birthplace, and March 26, 1516, the birthday, of the celebrated Swiss naturalist, botanist and scholar, Conrad Gesner, from whom this variety of the Tulip derives its distinctive name. It is a purely oriental flower; its texture, its depth of color, and even its shape, suggest to the mind the glories of the far-off eastern climes whence it has its birth. It is of Persian origin, and the native name, *dulband*, from whence its synonym in our language is derived, signifies a turban, after their own peculiar national head-dress. The Tulip was introduced into Europe by Gesner, since whose time its cultivation has received the most indefatigable attention. Under European taste, skill and care, the number of varieties has grown to over seven hundred; and the colors into which it has sported are many and magnificent. In old records it is found that in the year 1637 one hundred and twenty Tulips were sold at public auction for nine thousand guilders — equal to thirty-six hundred dollars. There is a species of wild Tulip quite common in the woods and vineyards of Germany. In Siberia the bulbs are used as food, although bitter and acrid.

Declaration of Love.

HELEN, I love thee; by my life I do;
   I swear by that which I will lose for thee
To prove him false that says I love thee not.
—*Shakespeare.*

I AM filled with such amaze.
   So far transported with desire and love,
My slippery soul flies to you while I speak.
—*Rochester.*

DEAR art thou to me now as in that hour
   When first love's wave of feeling, spraylike, broke
Into bright utterance, and we said we lov'd.
—*Bailey.*

I DARE not linger near thee as a brother,
   I feel my burning heart would still be thine.
How could I hope my passionate thoughts to smother,
When yielding all the sweetness to another
   Which should be mine. —*Amelia B. Welby.*

Tussilago.

Nardosmia palmata. NATURAL ORDER: *Composite — Aster Family.*

IN swamps or moist lowlands may be found the few plants known as Tussilago, or Coltsfoot. In the Tussilago farfara, we have the most common species. It is to be found chiefly on clayey soil in the Northern and Middle States. The flower appears singly, and is a many-rayed yellow head, borne on a scaly stalk about five or six inches high, and blossoming before the leaves make their appearance. Another variety called Tussilago by Aiton is now known as Nardosmia, from the two Greek words, *nardos*, meaning spikenard, and *osme*, smell, which plant it resembles in its fragrance. The flowers, which appear in May, are used in the manufacture of perfumery. The leaves are coarse, large and palmate, having a fancied resemblance to a colt's foot, whence the common name. The scientific name is from the Latin *tussis*, a cough, because of its long-recognized value as a cough remedy. Its aromatic properties were only discovered during the present century.

Justice to You.

THE gods grow angry with your patience! 'Tis their care,
And must be yours, that guilty men escape not;
As crimes do grow, justice should rouse itself. —*Jonson.*

IMPARTIAL justice holds her equal scales,
Till stronger virtue does the weight incline;
If over thee thy glorious foe prevails,
He now defends the cause that once was thine.
—*Prior.*

IF but one virtue did adorn a king,
It would be justice; many great defects
Are vail'd thereby —whereas each virtuous thing
In one who is not just, the world suspects.
—*Earl of Sterling.*

YOU are right, justice, and you weigh this well;
Therefore still bear the balance and the sword:
And I do wish your honors may increase,
Till you do live to see a son of mine
Offend you and obey you, as I did,
So shall I live to speak my father's words:—

Happy am I, that have a man so bold,
That dares do justice on my proper son;
And no less happy, having such a son
That would deliver up his greatness so
Into the hands of justice.
—*Shakespeare.*

Valerian.

Valeriana sylvatica. NATURAL ORDER: *Valerianeceæ — Valerian Family.*

JUST why this plant has been called Valerian — whether in honor of the Roman emperor of that name, or of some unknown Valerius, or (which is perhaps the most probable view) from the Latin *valere*, to be well, — seems to be uncertain. It is to be found in nearly all temperate climates. In the United States there are several indigenous varieties, found mostly in lowlands near wooded districts, or in swamps. The leaves of some are composed of several small leaflets arranged opposite each other along a central stem which is terminated by one a little superior in size, in others the foliage is entire. The flowers of the wild species are mostly purple, white or rose. The root of the Valeriana edulis is said to be cooked and eaten by the Indians. It is from the Valeriana officinalis that the extract used in medicine is obtained. It is useful chiefly in nervous affections, though possessing tonic, febrifugal and anti-spasmodic properties.

Obliging Disposition.

DEVOTED, anxious, generous, void of guile,
  And with her whole heart's welcome in her smile.
—*Mrs. Norton.*

THERE are some hearts like wells, green-mossed and deep
  As ever summer saw;
And cool their water is — yea, cool and sweet;
  But you must come to draw.
They hoard not, yet they rest in calm content,
  And not unsought will give.
They can be quiet with their wealth unspent,
  So self-contained they live.

And there are some like springs, that bubbling burst
  To follow dusty ways,
And run with offered cup to quench his thirst
  Where the tired traveler strays.
That never ask the meadows if they want
  What is their joy to give;
Unasked, their lives to other life they grant,
  So self-bestowed they live.
—*Caroline Spencer.*

CAN I yield you blessings? says the friendly heart;
  Fear not I am poorer, though I much impart.
Wherefore should you thank me? giving is my need;
Love that wrought none comfort, sorrow were indeed.
—*Lucy Larcom.*

Venus's Flytrap.

Dionæa muscipula. NATURAL ORDER: *Droseraceæ—Sundew Family.*

KNOWN as a denizen of warm latitudes, and consequently not often found in colder climates, except in hothouse culture, this perennial plant is rather delicate, but can be raised without difficulty if repotted each year and kept standing in a saucer of water. The leaves have a peculiar retractile power, closing whenever an insect lights on the surface, thereby holding it a prisoner within its embrace, only relaxing its hold when it has entirely withdrawn the nourishing properties from its victim. The flowers are white, being grouped in an umbel of from eight to ten on a stalk about a foot high. It is called Dionæa from Dione, the mother of Venus; and muscipula, from the Latin, denotes fly-gates.

Deceit.

WE sail along a rocky shore—the cliffs are gray and green,
   While in the sunlit depths below as lofty cliffs are seen.
We float upon the waves of Life, with Death at either hand,
And what is false and what is true we may not understand.
— *L. Bruce Moore.*

FALSE wave of the desert, thou art less beguiling
   Than false beauty over the lighted hall shed;
What but the smiles that have practic'd their smiling,
Or honey words measured, and reckon'd as said.
— *Miss London.*

WHY, I can smile, and murder while I smile;
   And cry content to that which grieves my
And wet my cheek with artificial tears; [heart;
And frame my face to all occasions.
— *Shakespeare.*

HE seem'd for dignity compos'd, and high exploit,
   But all was false and hollow — *Milton.*

YOU'RE wrong; he was the mildest mannered
   That ever scuttled ship or cut a throat! [man
With such true breeding of a gentleman,
You never could divine his real thought.
— *Byron.*

THEIR friendship is a lurking snare,
   Their honor but an idle breath;
Their smile, the smile that traitors wear;
   Their love is hate, their life is death.
— *Simms.*

Venus's Looking-glass.

Specularia speculum. NATURAL ORDER: *Campanulaceæ—Bellwort Family.*

LOOKING-GLASSES and beauty have always been considered to have a special affinity for each other; hence this plant, the flowers of which have been likened to a "concave mirror," has been dedicated to the goddess of beauty, and called her looking-glass. It belongs to the delightful family of the Campanulas, all of which are attractive, and some very beautiful. It is a small plant about six inches high, and is a native of Southern Europe. The stem branches freely, and it is a pretty little thing for the borders of beds and walks. The flowers are blue, closing at night and opening in the morning. There is an annual variety, with white blossoms, that blooms in August.

Flattery.

NO flattery my boy! an honest man can't live by 't:
It is a little sneaking art, which knaves
Use to cajole and soften tools withal. —*Otway.*

O THOU world, great nurse of flattery,
Why dost thou tip men's tongues with golden words,
And poise their deeds with weight of heavy lead,
That fair performance cannot follow promise?

O that man might hold the heart's close book,
And choke the lavish tongue when it doth utter
The breath of falsehood, not character'd there.

OF all wild beasts, preserve me from the tyrant;
And of all tame—a flatterer. —*Jonson.*

I WOULD give worlds, could I believe
One half that is professed me;
Affection! could I think it thee,
When flattery has caressed me? —*Miss Landon.*

PRAISE too dearly lov'd, or warmly sought,
Enfeebles all internal strength of thought;
And the weak soul within itself unblest
Leans for all pleasure on another's breast.
  —*Goldsmith.*

PERNICIOUS flatt'ry! thy malignant seeds,
In an ill hour and by a fatal hand
Sadly diffused o'er virtue's gleby land,
With rising pride amidst the corn appear,
And choke the hopes and harvest of the year.
  —*Prior.*

Verbena.

Verbena Aubletia. NATURAL ORDER: *Verbenaceæ — Vervain Family.*

BROUGHT into general circulation but a few years since, this beautiful flower is unsurpassed for splendor of color. It is a native of the South, and is a delicate, trailing plant, blooming freely. A few plants will cover a large bed if their branches are pinned down so that they can root at the joints, which they do readily. Among the Romans, the Verbenæ, whence the name of this plant, were sacred boughs, whether of the laurel, olive or myrtle. This particular variety has been designated Aubletia in honor of the French botanist, John Baptist Christopher Fusee Aublet, who flourished in the middle of the last century, dying in 1778.

Sensibility.

SHE smiled; but he could see arise
  Her soul from far adown her eyes,
Prepared as if for sacrifice.
— Mrs. Browning.

YET what is wit, and what the poet's art?
  Can genius shield the vulnerable heart?
Ah! no. Where bright imagination reigns,
The fine-wrought spirit feels acuter pains;
Where glow exalted sense and taste refin'd,
There keener anguish rankles in the mind;
There feeling is diffus'd through every part,
Thrills in each nerve, and lives in all the heart;
And those whose gen'rous souls each tear would keep
From others' eyes, are born themselves to weep.
— Hannah More.

A KINDLY speech; a cordial voice;
  A smile so quick, so warm, so bright,
It speaks a nature full of light.
— Kate J. Hill.

DEARLY bought, the hidden treasure
  Finer feelings can bestow!
Chords that vibrate sweetest pleasure,
  Thrill the deepest notes of woe.
— Burns.

SHE gazed, and in the tender flush
  That made her face like roses blown,
And in the radiance and the hush,
  Her thought was shown.
— Jean Ingelow.

A NEW creation-bloom that rounds
  The old creation, and expounds
His Beautiful in tuneful sounds.
— Mrs. Browning.

Violet.

Viola odorata. NATURAL ORDER: *Violaceæ — Violet Family.*

MANY and various are the Violet species, which are natives of all lands within the temperate zone. Some of them may be found in the fields and woods during spring and early summer, with their delicate little flowers hidden amid their clustered leaves. The Viola odorata is a European Violet. The flowers, though small, are redolent with perfume, and for this quality the plant has been styled *odorata* (odorous), and is to be found in general cultivation abroad. Another Violet (the Viola tricolor), more frequently called Pansy, or Heartsease, we are very familiar with, and through our admiration give it a warm place in our hearts and a cool place in our borders. What magnificence in color! what gorgeous velvet can surpass the bloom of these modest little flowers, lying so close upon Nature's bosom? Says Shakespeare:

"Her looks do argue her replete with modesty."

Modesty.

IN the modesty of fearful duty,
  I read as much as from the rattling tongue
Of saucy and audacious eloquence. — *Shakespeare.*

BEAUTIFUL are you in your lowliness;
  Bright in your hues, delicious in your scent;
Lovely your modest blossoms, downward bent,
As shrinking from your gaze, yet prompt to bless
The passer by with fragrance, and express
  How gracefully, though mutely eloquent,
Are unobtrusive worth and meek content,
Rejoicing in their own obscure recess.
— *Barton.*

HE saw her charming, but he saw not half
  The charms her downcast modesty conceal'd.
— *Thompson.*

THE violet droops its soft and bashful brow,
  But from its heart, sweet incense fills the air;
So rich within — so pure without — art thou,
With modest mien and soul of virtue rare.
— *Mrs. Osgood.*

MODESTY 'S the charm
  That coldest hearts can quickest warm;
Which all our best affections gains,
And, gaining, ever still retains. — *Paulding.*

Virgin's Bower.

Clematis Virginiana. NATURAL ORDER: *Ranunculaceæ—Crowfoot Family.*

THERE are many species of the Clematis or Virgin's Bower, the most of which are grown as coverings to arbors and trellises. The name comes from the Greek word *klema*, signifying a vine or climbing plant. Loudon calls Clematis vitalba, very common in England and France, with its white flowers blooming in August, the Traveler's Joy. Our native species are found wild in the Southern States, clambering over fences and bushes in the most unrestrained manner. Many of them would do admirably well if transplanted to the garden, where they would adorn some otherwise neglected nook. There are several adapted for greenhouse culture, nearly all of them being from warm or tropical climates. The flowers of the varied kinds are white, yellow and purple. They are all worthy of attention.

Filial Affection.

>THOSE tones of dear delight,
> The morning welcome, and the sweet good night!
> —*Charles Sprague*

OH! sweet are the tones of affection sincere,
 When they come from the depth of the heart;
And sweet are the words that banish each care,
 And bid sorrow forever depart!

'TWERE sweet to kiss thy tears away,
 If tears those eyes must know,
But sweeter still to hear thee say,
 Thou never hadst them flow.
 —*Bulwer.*

THERE is in life no blessing like affection;
 It soothes, it hallows, elevates, subdues,
And bringeth down to earth its native heaven;
Life has naught else that may supply its place.
 —*Miss L. E. Landon.*

'TWAS the earliest link in love's warm chain—
 'Tis the only one that will long remain;
And as year by year, and day by day,
Some friend still trusted drops away,
Mother! dear mother! oh! dost thou see
How the shortened chain brings me nearer thee?
 —*Willis.*

Wallflower.

Cheiranthus cheiri. NATURAL ORDER: *Cruciferæ — Mustard Family.*

WALLFLOWER is a low, semi-shrubby, perennial plant, growing from one to two and a half feet in height, and comes from the south of Europe. It is a great favorite on that continent among all classes. Robert Herrick, an English poet of the seventeenth century, has a pretty little poetical legend, to the effect that a young girl much in love, but restrained of her liberty, desired to fly to the arms of her lover, for which purpose she clambered out on a high wall, to which she had tied a silken sash or rope. In descending, the knot untied, and she fell, "bruised, and bleeding, and died;" and Love, in pity, changed her to this plant, to be called forever the "Flower of the Wall." It does not bloom until the second year from seed, and in northern climates should be removed to a light cellar for protection from frost in winter. Cheiri is the Arabic name, and Cheiranthus a formation therefrom by adding the Greek word *anthos*, a flower.

Fidelity in Misfortune.

OH! if there be an elysium on earth, it is this:
　When two that are linked in one heavenly tie,
Love on through all ills, and love on till they die.
　　　　　　　　　　—*Moore.*

YE wallflowers, shed your tints of golden dye,
　On which the morning sunbeams love to rest—
On which, when glory fills the glowing west,
　The parting splendors of the day's decline,
With fascination to the heart address'd,
　So tender and beautifully shine,
As if reluctant still to leave that hoary shrine.
　　　　　　　　　　—*Evans.*

CERTAIN my resolution is to die;
　How can I live without thee, how forego
Thy sweet converse and love, so dearly join'd?
　　　　　　　　　　—*Milton.*

RICH is the pink, the lily gay,
　The rose is summer's guest;
Bland are thy charms when these decay,
　Of flowers, first, last, and best!
There may be gaudier on the bower,
　And statelier on the tree;
But wallflower, loved wallflower,
　Thou art the flower for me. —*Moir.*

Walnut.

Juglans nigra. NATURAL ORDER: *Juglandaceæ — Walnut Family.*

ZEUS PATER (Father Zeus), through the first syllable of the Latin equivalent Jupiter, enters into the formation of the botanical name of this valuable tree, Juglans meaning Jove's acorn; and the walnut is certainly not unworthy of the distinction. In growth it is a majestic forest tree, rising very frequently to the height of eighty feet, and is always a pleasing object to the eye. The wood of the Black Walnut is very extensively used in cabinet work and in building. It is very close grained and heavy, and when freshly sawed it is of a deep violet color. It takes a very good polish, and assumes a brownish tone after being dressed, and looks not incongruous either when upholstered in the richest of fabrics or placed amid the commonest surroundings. The nuts are of a rather flattened globose shape, and the removal of the outward husk exposes the inner shell, which is very rough on the surface.

Intellect.

FORERUN thy peers, thy time, and let
 Thy feet, milleniums hence, be set
In midst of knowledge dreamed not yet.
— *Tennyson.*

RETIR'D thoughts enjoy their own delights,
 As beauty doth in self-beholding eye;
Man's mind a mirror is of heavenly sights,
A brief wherein all miracles scumm'd lie,
Of fairest forms and sweetest shapes the store,
Most graceful all, yet thought may grace them more.
— *Southwell.*

THE mind of man is this world's true dimension;
 And knowledge is the measure of the mind:
And as the mind in her vast comprehension
Contains more worlds than all the world can find,
So knowledge doth itself far more extend
Than all the minds of man can comprehend.
— *Lord Brooke.*

ARISE, my drowsing soul!
 Gird on thy blazing arms of intellect!
One struggle more to master coming time;
And if thy earthly walls then fall consumed,
We'll scale those heights where conquering time is not.
— *George H. Boker.*

Water Lily.

Nymphæa odorata. NATURAL ORDER: *Nymphæaceæ*— *Water Lily Family.*

QUITE inadequate is language, we may say, to the description of this beautiful flower. One might exhaust the whole vocabulary, and yet fall short of expressing that sense of beauty and loveliness that it itself expresses as it rests upon the bosom of the placid stream. Tantalizing, too, is it, like all beauty, seemingly so near, yet only to be possessed by the venturesome few, for "only the brave deserve the fair," and yet only waiting to be plucked by the hand that would clasp it lovingly in its embrace. This lily is shaped like a large rosette. It is composed of numerous pointed petals that curve upward toward the center. They are usually a pure opaque white, though sometimes purplish. In the midst of this exquisite cluster of petals there are innumerable fringelike filaments of the most delicate yellow, that tremble with the least agitation. The leaves are large and rounded, being many times nearly a foot in breadth, and float on the surface of the water around their radiant queen like so many handmaids. The flower is very fragrant, and may well be called, as it sometimes is, the "Naiad, or Bride of the Waters," which is but a free translation of its botanic name.

Eloquence.

MEN are more eloquent than women made,
But women are more powerful to persuade.
— *Randolph.*

POW'R above pow'rs! O heavenly eloquence!
That with the strong rein of commanding words
Dost manage, guide and master th' eminence
Of men's affections, more than all their swords!
Shall we not offer to thy excellence
The richest treasure that our wit affords?

Thou that canst do much more with one pen
Than all the powers of princes can effect;
And draw, divert, dispose and fashion men
Better than force or rigor can direct!
Should we this ornament of glory then,
As th' immaterial fruits of shades neglect?
— *Daniel.*

WHEN he spoke, what tender words he us'd,
So softly, that, like flakes of feather'd snow,
They melted as they fell.   — *Dryden.*

Weeping Willow.

Salix Babylonica. NATURAL ORDER: *Salicaceæ—Willow Family.*

NOT unlike a mass of fringe, it might be fancied, is a clump of Willows as seen against the sky, the small pointed foliage and slender twigs producing that hazy, indistinct effect. It is a pleasing tree either when single or in groups, often indulging in strange and grotesque contortions in its trunk and branches, which are most agreeable to an artist's eye, especially when surrounded by trees of more prim and dignified bearing. Nearly all the varieties have an affinity for locations near streams and ponds, or for low, wet meadow-lands, where they flourish in the abundant moisture. They do not disdain, however, to grow in other and dryer localities, as the many promising shade trees will testify. Being easily propagated, it is probably one of the most desirable trees for speedy growth. The Weeping Willow differs from the common species merely in having long, pendulous branches, from which it receives its name, and in memory of the Israelitish assemblage mentioned in Psalm cxxxvii., that hung their harps upon the Willows and wept by the waters of Babylon.

Melancholy.

AS the drain'd fountain, fill'd with autumn leaves,
The field swept naked of its garner'd sheaves;
So wastes at noon the promise of our dawn,
The springs all choking, and the harvest gone.
— *O. W. Holmes.*

COME, rouse thee, dearest! 'tis not well
    To let the spirit brood
Thus darkly o'er the cares that swell'
    Life's current to a flood.
As brooks and torrents, rivers, all
Increase the gulf in which they fall,
Such thoughts, by gathering up the rills
Of lesser griefs, spread real ills;
And with their gloomy shades conceal
The landmarks Hope would else reveal.
— *Mrs. Dinnies.*

BUT hail! thou goddess, sage and holy!
    Hail! divinest melancholy!
Whose saintly visage is too bright
To hit the sense of human sight,
And therefore to our weaker view,
O'erlaid with black, staid wisdom's hue.
— *Milton.*

Wheat.

Triticum vulgare.   NATURAL ORDER: *Gramineæ*—*Grass Family*.

UNSURPASSED in value, and of a beauty based upon its intrinsic merits, the Wheat plant is decidedly the most useful, widely dispersed, and most essential plant in cultivation. No other product forms so entirely the support of man, and none other is more prolific in its yield under favorable circumstances. The growing grain is a pleasing sight from the time it first spreads its mantle of green over the fields till it stands in golden beauty, bending the stalks with their wealth, and culminates in a ripened and bountiful harvest. Wheat is supposed to have originated in Asia, on the high table lands of Thibet, where it still grows in its primitive state, an humble and grasslike plant, with very small seeds. Ceres is called the goddess of the harvest, and the mythological writers say that before her time the earth was rough, and covered with briers and unprofitable plants.

"Ceres was she who first our furrows plough'd,
Who gave sweet fruits and easy food allow'd;
Ceres first tamed us with her gentle laws,
From her kind hand the world subsistence draws."

Riches.

RICHES, like insects, while concealed they lie,
Wait but for wings, and in their seasons fly.
—*Pope.*

ABUNDANCE is a blessing to the wise;
The use of riches in discretion lies;
Learn this, ye men of wealth—a heavy purse
In a fool's pocket is a heavy curse.
— *Cumberland.*

EXTOL not riches then, the toil of fools,
The wise man's cumbrance, if not snare, more
To slacken virtue, and abate her edge, apt
Than prompt her to do aught may merit praise.
—*Milton.*

THERE is no comfort but in outward showing
In all the servile homage paid to dross;
Better to heart and soul the silent knowing
Our little store has not been gained by loss.
—*John Boyle O'Reilly.*

White Walnut.

Juglans cinerea. NATURAL ORDER: *Juglandaceæ — Walnut Family.*

EVERYWHERE throughout our country, but more especially in the Northern and Middle States, the White Walnut, perhaps more commonly known as the Butternut, is to be found. The former is the more proper designation, as it belongs among the true Walnuts. The trunk is usually rather short, but large in girth. The branches spread horizontally, giving it a large, rounded head, sometimes thirty or forty feet high. The foliage has a plumy appearance, each leaf being composed of several leaflets arranged in pairs along a stem, with a single one to terminate the point. The nut is elongated in shape, and encased in a husk or sheath that is inseparable from it, and in that respect differing from other Walnuts. The kernel is very sweet, pleasant-flavored, and rich in oil, which gives it its most familiar synonym. The wood is useful in some of the arts. The bark is used in medicine as a cathartic, and by dyers to produce a brown dye.

Understanding.

YET I doubt not through the ages one increasing purpose runs,
And the thoughts of men are widened with the process of the suns.
Tennyson.

TIME has small pow'r
  O'er features the mind molds. Roses, where
They once have bloom'd, a fragrance leave behind;
And harmony will linger on the wind;
And suns continue to light up the air,
When set; and music from the broken shrine
Breathes, it is said, around whose altar-stone
His flower the votary has ceased to twine—
Types of the beauty that, when youth is gone, [e'line.
Breathes from the soul whose brightness mocks de-
George Hill.

WITH mind her mantling cheek must glow.
  Her voice, her beaming eye, must show
An all-inspiring soul,
Levi Frisbie.

MIND, despatch'd upon the busy toil,   [soil;
  Should range where Providence has blessed the
Visiting every flow'r with labor meet,
And gathering all her treasures sweet by sweet.
She should imbue the tongue with what she sips,
And shed the balmy blessings on the lips,
That good diffused may more abundant grow,
And speech may praise the pow'r that bids it flow.
Cowper.

Winter Cherry.

Physalis Alkekengi.   NATURAL ORDER: *Solanaceæ—Nightshade Family.*

OF all plants this is perhaps the most variously named, being called indifferently Ground Cherry, Winter Cherry, and Strawberry Tomato. The first name is applicable to several of the same genus, because of their habit, being merely straggling, herbaceous plants of low stature. It belongs to what is classed as the Nightshade family, which embraces plants not only producing flowers to gratify the eye, but fruits for the sustenance of man and the pleasing of his palate—as the tomato, potato, and egg plant. The Winter Cherry is found in gardens and cultivated fields, growing as if indigenous to the soil, though in some instances care is given it, which of course improves its quality. The fruit is about the size of a strawberry or cherry, being yellowish in color, and remains on the plant during winter, which explains its second synonym, while the third is sufficiently apparent. The berry is surrounded by a bladder-like calyx, which hides as well as protects it, whence the name Physalis, from the Greek, denoting a bladder.

Deception.

YOU vow, and swear, and super-praise my parts,
When I am sure you hate me in your hearts.
— *Shakespeare.*

AH! many hearts have changed since we two parted,
And many grown apart as time hath sped—
'Till we have almost deem'd that the true-hearted
Abided only with the faithful dead.

And some we trusted with a fond believing,
Have turn'd and stung us to the bosom's core;
And life hath seem'd but as a vain deceiving,
From which we turn aside, heart-sick and sore.
— *Mrs. C. M. Chandler.*

AN open foe may prove a curse,
But a pretended friend is worse.
— *Gay.*

WHAT man so wise, what earthly wit so ware,
As to descry the crafty, cunning train
By which deceit doth mask in visor fair,
And cast her colors, dyed deep in grain,
To seem like truth, whose shape she well can feign,
And fitting gestures to her purpose frame,
The guiltless man with guile to entertain?
— *Spenser.*

Witch Hazel.

Hamamelis Virginiana.   NATURAL ORDER: *Hamamelaceæ—Witch Hazel Family.*

CANADA and various parts of the United States produce this large shrub about as commonly as Virginia, from which it derives its distinctive qualification; its name, the Greek appellative of the medlar, has been misapplied by a mistake which it is now hard to rectify. The small branches were formerly used to discover veins of water and precious metals; and there are those who have inherited sufficient superstition to still have faith in their efficiency. We have seen wells said to have been so located, but how an unconscious piece of hazel should be more wise than man, is more than can be divined. A recent theory is, that it may be through some law of electricity not yet understood. The mode of procedure is in this manner: A branch that is forked is held, one branch in each hand, the main end pointing upward; the moment that it passes over water, it turns around and points to the earth. It is said, however, not to turn in the hands of everyone.

Witchery.

> I HAVE led a life too stirring for those vague beliefs
> That superstition builds in solitude.   —*Miss Landon.*

OUR witches are no longer old
  And wrinkled beldames, Satan-sold,
But young and gay and laughing creatures,
With the heart's sunshine on their features;
Their sorcery—the light which dances

When the raised lid unvails its glances,
And the low-breathed and gentle tone
Faintly responding unto ours,
Soft, dreamlike as a fairy's moan,
Above its nightly closing flowers.
   —*Whittier.*

> WHAT are these, so wither'd and so wild in their attire,
> That look not like the inhabitants o' the earth,
> And yet are on 't?   —*Shakespeare.*

BUT the witch-hazel's flower
  Of golden velvet, opening when the storm
Comes on the wings of winter to deform, [hour.
Charms with contrasting bloom while ruin rules the
   —*Alfred B. Street.*

I KNOW—whereon the sirens sit—
  An island in a dark-green sea.
Oft at the wind's own will past it
  I sail my boat delightedly.
   —*James Maurice Thompson.*

Wormwood.

Artemisia absinthium. NATURAL ORDER: *Compositæ — Aster Family.*

ARTEMISIA (so called in honor of the goddess Artemis, the Greek equivalent of the Roman Diana), or, in our vernacular, Wormwood, is an intensely bitter plant, and has very powerful medicinal properties. Its flowers are yellow, and it is to some extent naturalized in the mountainous districts of our Northern States. Columella, the Latin writer on agriculture of the first century of our era, mentions both the plant and absinthites, or Wormwood wine; and the celebrated Greek medical and botanical writer, Dioscorides, also speaks of it perhaps a century later. The Roman Wormwood is the kind usually found in our gardens, and is a native of Austria and other parts of Europe.

Absence.

YE flowers that droop, forsaken by the spring;
  Ye birds that, left by summer, cease to sing;
Ye trees that fade when autumn heats remove;
Say, is not absence death to those who love?   —*Pope.*

LIKE as the culver on the bared bough,
  Sits mourning for the absence of her mate,
And in her songs sends many a wishful vow
For his return that seems to linger late:

So I, alone now left, disconsolate,
  Mourn to myself the absence of my love;
And, wandering here and there all desolate, [dove,
  Seek, with my plaints, to match that mournful
    —*Spenser.*

SHORT absence hurt him more.
  And made his wound far greater than before;
Absence not long enough to root out quite
All love, increases love at second sight.
    Thomas May.

OH Absence! by thy stern decree
  How many a heart, once light and free,
Is fill'd with doubts and fears!
Thy days like tedious weeks do seem,
Thy weeks slow-moving months we deem,
Thy months long-lingering years.
    J. T. Watson.

WHAT tender strains of passion can impart
  The pangs of absence to an amorous heart?
Far, far too faint the powers of language prove—
Language, that slow interpreter of love!
Souls paired like ours, like ours to union wrought,
Converse by silent sympathy of thought.
    —*Pottison.*

Yarrow.

Achillea millefolium. NATURAL ORDER: *Composite—Aster Family.*

PASTURES and old fields throughout the Northern States are the favorite haunts of the Yarrow. The stem is about a foot high. The foliage is cut or parted into numerous divisions, thereby giving it the name of Milfoil, from the Latin *mille folia*, signifying a thousand leaves. Achilles was said to have discovered its medicinal properties while studying botany under Chiron the centaur, from which circumstance it has been honored with his name. The flowers are white or rose-colored, and bloom in flat-topped corymbs from June to autumn. The whole plant has a pungent taste and aromatic odor. A. ptarmica (from the Greek *ptairein*, to sneeze), or Sneezewort, is another variety, run wild in many places, but also sometimes cultivated in gardens.

War.

IS death more cruel from a private dagger
   Than in the field, from murdering swords of thousands?
Or does the number slain make slaughter glorious?
                                   —*Cibber.*

TWO troops in fair array one moment show'd,
  The next, a field with fallen bodies strow'd:
Not half the number in their seats are found,
But men and steeds lie groveling on the ground.
The points of spears are stuck within the shield.
The steeds without their riders scour the field.
The knights unhorsed, on foot renew the fight;
The glittering falchions cast a gleaming light,
Hauberks and helms are hew'd with many a wound,
Out spins the streaming blood, and dyes the ground.
                                   —*Dryden.*

'TWAS blow for blow, disputing inch by inch,
   For one would not retreat, nor t' other flinch.
                                   —*Byron.*

      War, my lord,
Is of eternal use to human kind;
For ever and anon, when you have pass'd
A few dull years in peace and propagation.
The world is overstock'd with fools, and wants
A pestilence, at least, if not a hero.   —*Jeffery.*

HE is unwise that to a market goes,
   Where there is nothing to be sold but blows.
                                   —*Abyn.*

Yew.

Taxus baccata.   NATURAL ORDER: *Taxaceæ — Yew Family.*

WITH a trunk of large girth, and broad-speading branches, the European Yew is a tree of low stature. Associated, as it nearly always is, with the burial places of the dead, it has among all nations become an acknowledged emblem of sorrow. Either through the nourishment of the soil becoming wholly exhausted, or because of the shadow cast by its foliage, little if anything grows beneath its shade; and an old idea is, that to sleep beneath its branches benumbs or stupefies the brain. The Latin synonym is derived from the original Greek name *taxus*. On account of its pernicious qualities the ancient poets, as Ovid, Silius and Lucanus, considered it the "tree of the infernal regions." There are some fifty species scattered throughout the temperate zone, several of them being mere shrubs. The Dwarf Yew, or Ground Hemlock, is found in Canada and our Northern States, inhabiting a rocky soil and shady, cool places, where it grows to a height of about three feet. It produces a small, red, waxy-looking berry, open at the top, which surrounds a single black seed.

Sorrow.

PAST sorrows, let us mod'rately lament them;
For those to come, seek wisely to prevent them.
— *Webster.*

ONE fire burns out another's burning;
One pain is lessen'd by another's anguish;
Turn giddy, and be help'd by backward turning;
One desp'rate grief cure with another's languish;
Take thou some new infection to the eye,
And the rank poison of the old will die.
— *Shakespeare.*

IT breathes no sigh, it sheds no tear,
Yet it consumes the heart.
— *Sheridan.*

AMAZ'D he stands, nor voice nor body stirs;
Words had no passage, tears no issue found;
For sorrow shut up words, wrath kept in tears;
Confused effects each other do confound;
Oppress'd with grief, his passion had no bound;
Striving to tell his woes, words would not come;
For light cares speak when mighty griefs are dumb.
— *Daniel.*

THE good are better made by ill;
And odors crushed are sweeter still!
— *Rogers.*

Yucca.

Yucca filamentosa. NATURAL ORDER: *Liliaceæ — Lily Family.*

BEAR-GRASS is a common synonym for Yucca, the aboriginal name of this plant, which compares not unfavorably with the Aloe among foliage plants. The leaves are stiff and sharp-pointed, forming a mass some two or three feet broad, and even more in old plants. There are six or seven species or individual plants, differing somewhat in their style of foliage, yet with a strong similarity noticeable in them all. They do not bloom until quite large, when a tall stem rises from the center, from three to four feet high, sometimes producing from "two to four hundred bell-shaped florets." All the species are natives of the Southern States, and each and all make a fine and imposing appearance in the garden or on the lawn. The Yucca filamentosa has long threads trailing from the margins of the sharp-pointed leaves, whence it is sometimes called Adam and Eve's Needle and Thread.

Authority.

A MAN in authority is but as
   A candle in the wind, sooner wasted
Or blown out than under a bushel.
—*Beaumont and Fletcher.*

NOT from gray hairs authority doth flow,
   Nor from bald heads, nor from a wrinkled brow;
But our past life, when virtuously spent,
Must to our age those happy fruits present.
—*Denham.*

HE doth not nicely prank
   In clinquant pomp, as some of meanest rank,
But armed in steel; that bright habiliment
Is his rich valor's sole rich ornament.
—*Joshua Sylvester.*

HENCEFORTH in my name
   Take courage, O thou woman! man, take hope!
Your graves shall be as smooth as Eden's sward,
Beneath the steps of your prospective thoughts;
And one step past them, a new Eden gate
Shall open on a hinge of harmony,

And let you through to mercy. Ye shall fall
No more, within that Eden, nor pass out
Any more from it. Live and love,—
Doing both nobly, because lowlily!
Live and work,—strongly, because patiently!
—*Mrs. Browning.*

Zinnia.

Zinnia elegans. NATURAL ORDER: *Compositæ—Aster Family.*

ZINNIA was named in honor of John Godfrey Zinn, a German botanist who flourished in 1757, when the science was in its infancy. In the cultivated plant of today can hardly be recognized the primitive flower found in the fields and roadsides of the Southern States, which, even in its simplest form, has been considered handsome. Formerly the blossom was only scarlet, and single; but care in propagation has doubled it to the center, and it has sported into hues many, rich and varied. The flower perishes slowly without closing its petals, losing its bright tints and assuming more sobriety as its days are numbered. On this account it is sometimes called Youth and Old Age.

Thoughts in Absence.

LOVE reckons hours for months, and days for years;
And every little absence is an age. —*Dryden.*

WHAT shall I do with all the days and hours
That must be counted ere I see thy face?
How shall I charm the interval that lowers
Between this time and that sweet time of grace?
—*Frances Anne Kemble.*

O TELL him I have sat these three long hours
Counting the weary beatings of the clock,
Which slowly portion'd out the promis'd time
That brought him not to bless me with his sight!
—*Joanna Baillie.*

I WEPT thy absence, o'er and o'er again,
Thinking of thee, still thee, till thought grew pain.
And memory, like a drop that night and day
Falls cold and ceaseless, wore my heart away!
—*Moore.*

CALL thou me home! from thee apart
Faintly and low my pulses beat,
As if the life-blood of my heart
Within thine own heart holds its seat,
And floweth only where thou art.
—*Mrs. E. Oaks Smith.*

THERE'S not an hour
Of day or dreaming night but I am with thee;
There's not a wind but whispers of thy name,
And not a flower that sleeps beneath the moon
But in its hues or fragrance tells a tale
Of thee. —*Procter.*

PART II.

Cultivation and Analysis of Plants.

Practical Floriculture.

HE hand that made such bountiful provision for the body, was not unmindful of the æsthetical cravings of the higher nature of man, so He hath filled the air with bird-music for the delight of the ear, and hath planted the fields and hung the boughs with blossoms that paint themselves in a multiplicity of hues for the gratification of the eye. The two latter we gather around us in our homes, and the songsters sing their sweetest strains regardless of the prison bars, while the flowers, during their short lives, yield both beauty and fragrance from their fragile bells as a reward to the hand that careth for and cherisheth them. All the world love flowers, and are all the better for that love, for the soul is refreshed while the eye is pleased with their contemplation. Children delight in them; by them young men and maidens interchange compliments; and to the aged they speak of a beautiful home beyond the tomb. The wealthy pride themselves on their conservatories and flower-bedecked lawns; people in the middle walks of life like to have a few in their windows or on a stand devoted to the purpose; and even the dingy cottages of the poor are not infrequently adorned with at least a single plant, often the only link apparently that binds the inmates to the beautiful.

Having devoted a very considerable space to the Language and Poetry of Flowers, the author has thought that some practical information, drawn mainly from her own experience, in relation to the care and cultivation of plants, would prove a useful addition to the work. For however one may admire flowers, through a mere natural impulse or instinct, the cultivation of them requires taste, tact, patience and much painstaking attention. And even these qualities, to be only measurably successful, demand a solid substructure of information in regard to the wants, peculiarities and habits of plants. It will, however, be remembered by every thoughtful reader that there are but few things in this world worth knowing that do not require much patient attention; and the amateur culturist must therefore not be discouraged. Few studies will better repay one than floriculture, in the charms of the gentle, peaceful influence which it throws around the human soul. In the language of the poet Wordsworth,

> He is happiest who hath power
> To gather wisdom from a flower,
> And wake his heart in every hour
> To pleasant gratitude.

Leaving poetry and the fascinations of flowers, we now propose to descend to the more material and coarser elements that underlie the growth of plants; and "to begin with the beginning," or where the flowers begin, it becomes our duty to unfold what is required, in the way of soil, water, etc., for the practical culture of flowers.

SOILS.

FIRST comes **Loam**, which plays so important a part in all vegetation, and which is described as a mixture of sand, clay and carbonate of lime, with the oxide of iron, magnesia and various salts, also decayed vegetable and animal matter. It varies in different localities in regard to depth as well as quality. In some places it is brown, and in others nearly or quite black, particularly in the West, where in the bottom lands of the Missouri it is sometimes found more than thirty feet deep, as wells of that depth have failed to reach its bottom. If it is stiff and heavy, the clay predominates; in which case for flower-beds, and indeed for farming purposes also, it would be improved if a moderate proportion of sand or stable-manure were well worked through it to make it more porous and, as gardeners say, warmer; for, if the soil is too cold and retentive of water, plants do not thrive.

Sand is a very useful material in plant-growing, especially in greenhouse and window culture; and, while it contains no nutriment, it is sometimes used to grow some kinds of bulbs, to start slips, and, as has been said, to make soil more porous. Its uses are to make lighter the soil with which it is mixed, so that the delicate roots can feel their way through it; to draw the heat from the atmosphere; and to act as drainage, so that the soil will not sour. Silver sand is the most recommended, as it is a little coarser and sharper, as well as cleaner; but as this is only found in certain localities, other or common sand can be used as a substitute. It should be rather coarse, and from the surface when possible, if for immediate use, as it will then have been improved by the action of the air. It is also benefited by washing, which can be done by putting a quantity in a tub, pouring water upon it, stirring with a stick, and then pouring off the water. The admixture with loam is sometimes one part sand to three or five of the other, according to the plants grown.

Leaf-Mold is one of the most delightful soils for many plants, and it is very highly prized by all who occupy themselves with their cultivation. Leaves are frequently gathered into pits after they fall by the action of frost, and left until they decay; but the mold is found more abundantly in the woods, particularly in hollows where the winter's wind has drifted the leaves, and where they lie in the damp and perish. Only think of gathering into a flower-pot, to nourish a new plant, what has been the shade of perhaps a hundred years, with all its vanished glories of crimson and gold!

Turf, or grass-sods, is another article much recommended for potting plants, and should be cut about three inches thick. This of course must have time given it to rot before it is fit for use. Spring or summer is the best time for cutting, when the grass is growing, as there is more nutriment in it. The sods should be packed in a heap, the grassy surfaces toward each other. In this state fermentation commences, and the vegetable portions decay. When this process begins, the heap should be turned and stirred repeatedly with a fork, until it finally becomes a pulverized or crumbled mass. It may then be mixed with about an equal proportion of manure and of leaf-mold, when it is fit for growing most kinds of plants.

Peat is a soil of vegetable origin, found mostly in low lands, especially in swamps or what are known as bogs. It is a black mold consisting of roots, wood and kindred substances in an entirely decomposed condition, or undergoing the process of decay, and is more or less saturated with water. Some few plants, like the Venus's Flytrap, Pitcher Plant, Heath, and many varieties of Ferns and young Azaleas, require this soil in its normal condition or slightly mixed with sand; or, what is still better, as well as more definite, a soil composed of four parts peat, two of sand, one of garden-loam, and one of leaf-mold. In the greenhouse and hothouse it is mixed in smaller proportions for numerous plants.

MANURES.

Manure should be entirely decomposed, and from two to three years old, and if still older it will be all the better. Cow-manure is far superior for most uses, as it is finer and a more gentle stimulant. The coarser manure from the stables answers well for covering flower-beds in fall and putting around shrubs to keep them from frost, roses rejoicing particularly in its great strength. In using any solid manure for the stimulation of plant growth, especial care should be taken to incorporate it thoroughly with the various other elements of the prepared soil. Manure-water is prepared by placing the manure in a tub or other vessel and pouring boiling water thereon. After letting it stand until it cools, it can be drawn off for use, reducing its strength by the admixture of two parts pure water to one of manure-water; it is better to apply it "weak and often." Manure-water, or liquid manure, may be made from most of the domestic manures or cattle-droppings, as well as from guano, phosphate of lime, etc. Sheep-droppings also produce excellent liquid manure for many plants.

It may seem troublesome to think of using so many ingredients for the cultivation of flowers, but they are necessary to form the different requisites for various plants if one proposes to keep many. Country amateurs can find most of them close at hand; and persons living in the city, if they keep only a few plants, will find it more convenient to go to some florist and purchase a sufficient quantity already prepared, always naming the plants they wish to raise. The florist's experience is of great value to the amateur.

FLOWER-BEDS.

CONSIDERABLE care should be exercised in the preparation of flower-beds, after which they will give less trouble, and will last for many years with a little addition of manure every fall or spring. They may be various in shape—either round, triangular, palm-leaf or stars—or several of one shape with grass or paths between, grouped or massed together. They should be dug to the depth of at least a foot, and deeper if the natural soil is stiff or heavy. If the soil is poor, it would be advisable to remove it entirely and supply its place with better. If the drainage is bad—a wet soil, for instance—the surface earth that has been loosened for the bed should be thrown aside, and two or three inches of gravel, coal cinders or what is still better, some long straw manure or brush, be placed in the bottom, the soil thrown in again, manured if necessary, the lumps well beaten out, and the bed raked fine and even. After this it will require only to be well stirred with a digging-fork every spring to loosen it up a little. It is better in low situations that the beds should lie a little above the surrounding surface; but in high, dry lawns exposed to the wind, it is well to have them a little lower, the edges being trimmed as frequently as may be required; or, if surrounded by gravel walks, a border of close-cut grass is very neat as marking the outlines of the bed. In some parts of California flower-beds are well rolled down, to pack the surface, so as to give off less evaporation during the months of drouth. The terra cotta manufactured for the purpose, as well as tiles, bricks standing on end and touching sides, or thin, flat stones set in the same manner, are sometimes used to preserve beds from the encroachments of grass.

FLOWER-BEDS IN RELATION TO SYMMETRY AND COLOR.

In arranging flower-beds, some attention should be paid to the effect different plants will produce when brought together. The taller ones should go to the center, and the lower growing and prostrate ones toward the margins, so that one will not hide another. The same rule applies to straight borders of walks, the taller ones going back against the grass. This is usually easy to do, as in most cases the heights of plants are given on seed packets. For a fine display, too much forethought cannot be given to the various colors that are to be brought in contact, as some colors, though handsome in themselves, utterly destroy the beauty of each other. For instance, scarlet and purple and some shades of blue do not affiliate at all, and are what are called antagonistic colors. We will fill an imaginary bed with Verbenas of inharmonious tints if put together wrongfully, but very pleasing and harmonious if rightly placed. Our stock consists of a dozen plants each of scarlet, purple, pink or rose color, and white. Placing the scarlet at one angle of the bed, we arrange next to it the pure white, that harmonizes everything in color and reconciles natural antagonism; adjoining it we plant our purples, and then our rose-tint—and how happily the two latter combine! The pale tints of all colors are more easy of assimilation than the deep ones, but what richness and depth of tone there is in some of the darker ones! For display-beds cut in the lawn or grass-plats, masses of one color for each bed, or at most two complementary colors, produce the finest effect.

In order to determine in a ready and simple way which colors will be best alongside of each other, either in beds of flowers or in bouquets, place a sheet of white paper so that the eye can be suddenly cast upon it; then gaze steadily upon the flower or leaves that it may be wished to plant or arrange so as to harmonize or form a good juxtaposition; after gazing two or three minutes, suddenly cast the eye on the white paper, and the color will be seen that will be best to place near whatever has been looked at.

DEFORMITIES CONCEALED.

About many neat and even handsome homes there are oftentimes dilapidated buildings, sheds or fences that may be hidden out of sight and transformed into things of beauty, at least during the summer season, by the use of some perennial climbing plants. The Ampelopsis quinquefolia, Celastrus scandens, Clematis virginiana, Tecoma radicans and others of the same character (see Climbing Plants, p. 393), will serve this purpose.

Many of the annual climbers can also be used to good advantage. The Echinocystis lobata, or Wild Cucumber, is a rapid and luxuriant grower, and has the further advantage, not common among climbers, of long racemes of sweet-scented flowers. A single plant will sometimes cover a good-sized building in a season. The Ricinus communis, or Castor-oil Plant, though not a climber, is often used for this purpose in ornamental grounds, its large and abundant peltate foliage forming an excellent screen. The Helianthus annuus, or common Sunflower, and the allied species, Helianthus tuberosus, or Jerusalem Artichoke, will also serve the same useful purpose in an effective manner.

PROPAGATING PLANTS.

NATURALLY some amateur culturists will have occasion to use one or more of the simpler methods of propagating plants, which are on that account here subjoined.

SOWING SEEDS.

In sowing seeds, some thought should be had for their size and construction. Small ones, as the Portulaca and Petunia, it is quite sufficient to scatter on the ground, and, rubbing the hand gently over the surface, mix them with the soil. For others it is well to mix them with some finely pulverized earth, and sow both together. Larger seeds, like Sweet Peas, Four-o'clocks, Beans, and various others, require planting, a process which is different from sowing, inasmuch as the seeds are placed in the earth, in proportion to their size, from one to two or more inches apart; and none should be embedded deeper than five times its own diameter. The outer or whitish shell of the Nasturtium, and of some others that have a double shell, should be removed with the thumb-nail or a knife. Some flat seeds, like the Cobæa, should be put in the ground edgewise, to prevent decay. The cottony substance around the Globe Amaranth seeds should be picked off for the same reason. Very hard seeds, like the Acacia and Sweet Peas, should be soaked in hot water, as also the Cypress Vine and Verbena seeds. Verbena seed should be pushed lengthwise into the soil, a little more than its own length. Evening or just before a shower is the best time for sowing seed; a heavy rain would be apt to wash small ones away. As soon as the seeds are sown, a piece of old carpet or other heavy cloth spread over them, secured from blowing away, is a necessity for successful raising, to insure uniform temperature and moisture; and this covering should be retained until the seeds have sprouted. After the plants are up, or when the carpet is removed, they must be shaded with thin muslin or white paper. They should be sprinkled with a watering-pot that has a fine rose-spout, or, in the absence of such an article, a small clothes-broom dipped in water answers the purpose very well.

As some small seeds produce plants disproportionately large — as, for instance, Mignonette, Sweet Alyssum, Petunia, Portulaca and numberless others — they should be thinned out as soon as the plants are sufficiently established, leaving always the best. If it is desired to transplant any of them to another place, it will be well if some earth be taken up with them. Certain plants transplant badly, and should be sown where they are to grow; and we believe that where such directions are found on seed packets, it is an indication of their delicacy on that point.

CUTTINGS OR SLIPS.

Slips or cuttings, as the latter name indicates, are pieces cut from the branches of growing plants, and should rarely have less than three joints. The old and careful manner of cutting immediately under a joint, is the best, though many plants will succeed where this precaution is neglected. The leaves adhering to the joints are generally shortened, that is, cut short, to save unnecessary waste of vital force. Cuttings may be inserted in clean, coarse sand, powdered charcoal, coarse brickdust, or clear sawdust, and in pots, boxes or beds, in or out of doors in summer, but within doors only and in a warm, moist atmosphere, in winter.

Some cuttings, as most of the Geranium Family, as well as the fleshy and succulent plants, as the Cactuses, will strike readily in almost anything out of doors, from May to September. Soft-wooded cuttings of Oleander will strike in bottles of water; and similar cuttings of Verbenas, Heliotropes, Petunias and many others, will take root in dishes of sand and water, care being taken not to allow the sand to become entirely dry.

Rose cuttings should be made of shoots that are about half ripe, that is, half way between soft vegetable matter and hard wood, cut into lengths of three joints or leaves, entirely removing the lower leaf. An even temperature and a warm, moist situation are demanded by rose cuttings, while careful shading from excessive heat is equally indispensable. Leaves of Begonias, Hoyas and some other plants, will strike root and form new growths if rightly cared for.

In transplanting cuttings after they have rooted, the particles of matter that adhere to the rootlets should be flirted, filliped or washed off before placing them in their new homes.

LAYERING.

As a rule this process of propagation is mostly had recourse to early in August, and is accomplished thus: A shoot of the current year's growth should be taken and cut about half through near a joint, when it should be laid down in the soil and covered over with moss, manure or other substance that will retain moisture around the incision; and the head or end of the shoot should be left uncovered. Many ornamental shrubs, such as Snowballs, Tree Cranberries and the like, can be raised only in this manner or from seeds.

OFFSHOOTS.

These form a natural kind of layering, where the plant sends forth a horizontal, underground stem or shoot, which needs but to be cut off from the parent stem at the proper season, to constitute an entirely distinct plant. They are nearly similar in character and appearance to the familiar above-ground runners of the strawberry and many other like plants.

BULBS.

Bulbs are mostly increased by offsets or bulblets formed on the sides of the previous growth, and generally require two or more years before they bloom. All bulbs require a peculiarly rich, deep soil, and plenty of liquid manure while in a growing state. They are best kept in a bed or box by themselves to facilitate the extra attention necessary to develop a strong, healthy growth.

POTTING PLANTS.

MANY persons dread the performance of this simple part of floriculture, which is not at all difficult unless the plant is too heavy or unwieldy. First, there should be in readiness some broken potsherds, bits of charcoal, or the like, for drainage, and the extra soil for the larger pot to which the transfer is to be made. This soil should be thoroughly damp—not wet and muddy, but so as to sift nicely from the hand. The articles for drainage should be placed in the bottom of the pot to the depth of about half an inch, with an additional half inch of moss if convenient, after which the whole should be covered over with a layer of the earth prepared as above. The plant to be transferred is supposed to have been watered some hours before, so that the earth will not crumble away from and tear the roots. The right hand, with the palm downward, should be placed over the surface of the ball of earth surrounding the plant, so that two fingers will be on each side of the stem; then pot and plant should be lifted bottom upward with the left hand, and the pot gently struck against the edge of a table, when it will ordinarily come off nicely. Should it, however, prove rootbound (that is, with the roots so crowded as to adhere to the sides of the pot), a few stronger blows will cause it to relinquish its hold. The young rootlets, if fresh and healthy, should not be disturbed; if dead—as will sometimes be the case from having been either too wet or too dry—they should be cut off, as they would be an unwholesome element in the pot, and would have a tendency to prevent the growth of new and healthy ones. The large or broken roots necessary to be removed should be cut smoothly with a sharp knife.

CULTIVATION AND ANALYSIS OF PLANTS.

With very large plants that are too weighty to lift in the hands, by putting a thick bandage around their stems or trunks to keep the bark from being bruised, a rope can be attached with a loop or loops through which a stout stick can be slipped, when it can be lifted, and the ends of the stick be rested on something of sufficient height, and the pot or tub driven off. This process generally requires assistance; but if alone, and we can at all raise the plant, and the spirit moves us then and there to make the change, we frequently settle the matter by a few energetic blows with a hammer, which leaves us with a broken pot and our plant free for its new home. In repotting such, care should be used in straightening out the roots as far as possible in various directions, to prevent matting, supporting the plant during the operation, and sifting the soil in carefully and evenly. If the plant has matted its roots, it is sometimes best to cut off clean with a sharp knife the ball of earth and such rootlets as it may contain, about an inch or more from the bottom. If the ball is found very dry, it will be advisable to soak it in a pail of water until it becomes thoroughly saturated, when it should be laid aside for a few minutes to drain before being repotted.

The plant thus removed, with its ball of earth, should be gently set down in its new receptacle; and, if found to stand too high or too low, earth must be removed or added, until the surface is within about an inch of the edge of the pot, and carefully pressed down around the plant to secure it in its place, in an erect position. It should then be watered and set back a little from the light, and again watered about the second or third day, or sooner if it begins to wilt, but sparingly at first. If the soil keeps moist after the first watering, the plant should have its leaves carefully damped two or three times each day, but on no account should water be put on the soil until it gets partially dry. This delay is to allow new roots a chance to start. If a plant is slow to start, it should be placed on a board, under which a hot brick, or a pan of boiling water, changed two or three times daily, has been set. Plants should be guarded against drying winds and the heat of the sun for a few days, until the roots shall have established themselves in their new quarters.

After removal the foliage will generally fall, but only to be replaced by such as will be healthier and more pleasing to the eye. Sometimes our greatest expectations will provokingly disappoint us, but a true lover of flowers will not be discouraged thereby.

Sometimes plants have to undergo the process of being potted backward, as it is called. This is when they are weak, diseased, or refuse to bloom when they have too much rootroom. In this case the plant is removed as before, and the ball nicely and evenly trimmed and pressed into a smaller pot.

When soil is exhausted, or becomes filled with vermin, it many times benefits a plant to wash the earth entirely from the roots, which should be done gently so as not to injure the young and tender rootlets.

We have frequently had admirable and unexpected success with hothouse plants in our ordinary living room, where there was no moisture except what evaporated from the earth in the pots, with an occasional pan of water set upon the stove in winter. One or more pans of water, according to the size of the collection, placed near the plants in a hot, dry room, will facilitate the growth; but ordinarily, damping the leaves and keeping them clean will prove sufficient; and this much at least should always be done. We mention this, as many think the raising of a plant from the hothouse an impossibility.

Hothouses are usually built low, so as to be kept at a higher temperature, and water is used so freely that there is a great deal of moisture in the atmosphere, which helps the plants to a growth something approaching what they would have in their tropical homes. When we enter these low-built houses, the plants are so seductive, either through their gorgeous blossoms or ample and variegated foliage, that we can rarely resist the temptation of carrying away one or two trophies, while knowing that we cannot expect them to thrive quite so well when reduced from their high diet, as it were; but yet we find they do well enough not to entirely discourage us. A few failures make more lasting impressions than constant and complete success; and if we study out the causes of those failures, the lessons will not be too dearly bought.

WATERING PLANTS.

GOOD culture is secured as much by care in watering plants as by anything else; for if too much water is given, it is worse than giving too little. Many inexperienced cultivators have an idea that to be told to give a plant plenty of moisture means to keep it wet and cold all the time. For an intelligent discrimination in this regard, it is of the first necessity to understand the native seat and habits of the plant. The Fuchsia, for instance, is a native of Brazil on its mountain slopes, and is accustomed to a moist atmosphere that never becomes stagnant. Like conditions must as nearly as possible be artificially secured in our latitudes; it must therefore have plenty of moisture and be guarded from strong sunlight. The Calla Lily needs a large quantity of water (in fact, will grow in water) up to the time of flowering; after which it is better to put it in a bed or border to get a season's rest, depending upon the clouds for its supplies. Begonias and Ferns need plenty of moisture, but abhor stagnation; and it is better to syringe water over the leaves than to be constantly drenching the soil around the roots.

A good thing for the plants is to let them occasionally go dry at the roots. This is nature's remedy, for even in the wettest climates there are some dry periods. No plant should be allowed to drop its leaves for want of water; a watchful eye can do more than set rules in the proper watering of plants. If the leaves droop, unless in newly potted plants, water is called for, and should be applied to root and leaf. The ear can also be utilized: a knock on the side of a pot will disclose the need of water by the hollow sound emitted, while a dull, heavy tone shows there is already water enough.

If the soil remains wet a long time in a pot or box, which is technically styled "water-logging," some means to dry it should be devised, as boring holes in the box, placing the pot on a warm stove, or on its side to drain, or the like. The smaller the pot or box, the more watering the plant requires, all things else being equal.

All succulent or thick-leaved plants, after they have made their season's growth, may be put away for rest, and be left without injury, and even to advantage, for many months, deprived of water, in a dry place, which, however, should be kept free from frost.

PRUNING PLANTS.

UNDER the three terms, Pruning, Cutting Back and Pinching, are understood only different degrees or forms of the same process. The pinching is simply a milder pruning with the finger and thumb; and the cutting back is mainly applied to the pruning off of all dead wood back to the quick, or the restoring of a plant or shrub to its proper shape when it has grown misshapen by neglect. Pruning is best done in the late fall or early spring, while the sap is at rest; it consists in removing the useless, thin, poor shoots of the previous growth. But little pruning would be needed in amateur culture if the finger and thumb, under the guidance of a watchful eye, were used freely in removing, by what is technically called pinching, all poor growths while the shoots are soft and green.

INSECTS.

THESE pests, the bugbear of amateurs, as a rule settle only on plants that are in a slow state of growth, or that are suffered to become dirty. Besides their destructiveness, they render plants untidy and soiled; and where they become epidemic, as it were, they render them disgusting. It is only idleness or ignorance that allows insects to injure plants; and those having only a few in pots have no excuse for being troubled with them. Cleanliness is nature's great remedy. When they make their first appearance, the whole plant should be washed with soapy water, and afterward dipped two or three times into a tub or pail of clean water. This simple process, repeated whenever necessary, will keep a large majority of plants free from the insect nuisance.

FOLIAGE INSECTS.

Aphis Rosæ.—This insect, known also as the green-fly, is one of the most common of plant insects, and is so named by reason of its fondness for the tender shoots of all species of roses. Still it is not at all particular as to diet, and feeds promiscuously on almost any plant upon which it finds lodgment, except perhaps such strongly scented ones as some kinds of the Geranium. Taken singly, it is not at all repulsive, being in color the most delicate, transparent green, and frequently with beautiful gossamer wings, and has, for such a small creature, a firm and stately walk. Collectively their destruction is great, as all the juice of the plant is absorbed to satisfy their insatiable appetite. With watchfulness this plague may be kept down in small collections. Fumigation is the best remedy for them, and this operation may be performed either in a room, close box or barrel, by placing damp tobacco-stems or leaves on some coals, in some kind of fire-proof vessel, and care being taken that they do not blaze. Most rough-leaved plants cannot endure fumigations, and are, in greenhouses, put under the staging when this work is going on.

Thrips.—These are small, spotted flies related to the *aphide*, and found on the backs of the leaves, though they will attach themselves to any portion of a neglected or unhealthy plant. They are not quite so easily got rid of as the green-fly, but washing the plant in tobacco-water, and afterward in clean water, will drive them off. The best remedy is a solution of Gishurst's Compound, a kind of soap sold by first-class seedsmen. This will not only destroy these insects, but most others. The scaly bugs cannot withstand it, and angleworms will die if it drops upon them. It also acts as a stimulant to plants, and is not enough known to amateurs in this country.

Red Spider, so called, known by its classic name as Acarus, is an insidious enemy to plants. It is a minute insect, but capable of producing considerable destruction, as it feeds on the most delicate parts of the leaves, causing them to soon perish. It is about the size of the eye of a fine cambric needle. The body is usually red, though sometimes brown. They congregate on the under sides of the leaves in great numbers, where they feed like a herd of cattle on a broad plain.

When a plant is suspected of being infested, or if the leaves perish and no other cause is known, a leaf may be turned over on the finger, and held so until the warmth passes through it, when, if there are any, they will be seen like mere specks of dust beginning to show powers of locomotion. The fine webs created by this small, insignificant creature, clog and impair the functions of the foliage, which are really the lungs of the plant. Dryness of the atmosphere is very favorable to the existence of this insect, and, as it has a repugnance to water, sprinkling, syringing or pinning wet cloths or papers around individual plants at night, is the remedy. A very good preventive is to keep a pan of water on the stove in winter, as it gives off a vapor to the atmosphere. A little flour of sulphur sprinkled on a heated brick or flat-iron, placed where the fumes can rise up among the leaves of the plants, is also an excellent remedy.

Mealy Bug.—This is an entirely innocent looking insect, but yet at times exceedingly troublesome where plants are kept at a high temperature, and is consequently found more frequently in a hothouse, from whence it is many times transferred to the greenhouse. It is a small, oval insect about an eighth of an inch in length, with a slightly rounded back that is covered over with a short, white plush; the body underneath is brownish in color, and from the sides articulate several tiny legs. It more often rests at the axils of the leaves, yet many times underneath them. Where they accumulate to a great extent, whale-oil soapsuds is efficacious, or they can be brushed off with a small brush.

We have never had them to any great extent, and our method is to lift them off with a needle, as bruising them on the plant is said to be injurious on account of the juice that escapes. The eggs are deposited in little, white, webby knots, and left by the parent on various parts of the plant. Under the microscope, when torn asunder with two pins or needles, so as not to crush them, there are revealed several brown eggs—some half a dozen, or less.

Coccus.—There are several kinds of insects known under this Latin name, that in our vernacular are called *scales*, being in color either brown or white. They are a rounded oval, their encasement being a glossy, tough skin or shell. They adhere closely to the leaves or stem on which they feed, and are not easy to dislodge. As far as our own experience and observation go, we find the young to be migratory, but probably not for any great length of time, as we find them fixed when quite small, in which condition they feed and grow. The eggs are hatched under the parent, and in lifting a large one with a needle it is no unusual thing to see the litter of young run about in a hurried manner at the unwelcome disturbance.

Washing with strong soapsuds is a remedy for this annoyance. If picked off by hand, washing should not be neglected, as it destroys the young; fumigation will not answer so well. We remove them by running a needle through the crown of the shell, and washing afterward. The white ones are very partial to Oleanders. They are also fond of Olives, Camellias, Acacias, Calla Lilies, Oranges and various evergreen trees.

Verbena Mite.—This is a microscopic insect that destroys the plant for which it is named, as also the Heliotrope and other rough-leaved plants, causing the foliage to turn brown. It is difficult to dislodge it, as it cares but little for water, fumigations or ordinary methods. To promote a vigorous, healthy growth of the plant is the best remedy.

Roller Caterpillar.—This insect, perhaps more commonly known as the Rose Slug, is the larva of a moth, that makes its appearance early in May and lays its eggs on the under side of rose leaves. These hatch out in a few days, producing the small, green caterpillars, which at once begin to eat the leaves on the under side. Toward evening they creep on the upper side of the leaves, where, if not disturbed, they will eat all night, and leave the foliage as if it had been burned. With watchfulness at the proper time they are easily got rid of by being carefully picked off and killed, and the first lot disposed of is generally the last of them for the season. Hellebore powder or Paris green sprinkled on the leaves when they are damp or wet will destroy them; but the safest thing to dust upon roses is soot from soft coal, for when it washes off it acts as a useful stimulant. In fact, soot mixed with guano, in about equal quantities, and boiling water poured upon them, make an excellent liquid manure for all kinds of flowers; which, when diluted in the ratio of one part to three of clean water, may be poured over the heads of plants, keeping them free from insects and at the same time contributing to a healthy growth. It is not advisable to use poisonous remedies against insects; it is far better for the plant as well as its care-taker if the latter use only the eye, the hand and the great natural cleanser, pure water, with an occasional admixture of soap.

Rose Beetle.—This small insect derives its special name from its partiality to rose leaves, being seldom found on any other plant. It is not very destructive or numerous, and can be easily disposed of by keeping the plants clean and in good order. Thousands of Roses are made unsightly or destroyed every season by insects which a little precaution on the part of the cultivators, in the timely application of common remedies, might readily have prevented.

Tobacco Worm.—This is a worm which attacks other plants besides tobacco, especially creepers, and has a special liking for the Ampelopsis or Virginia Creeper. If not disturbed it will soon make its presence known by eating off the leaves, and even the tender shoots, straight before it. It generally appears in June, and under various colors, according to what it feeds upon. It grows to a monstrous size, being sometimes from four to six inches long, with a formidable looking horn; and often shows fight when disturbed. Being large, there are never very many on one vine; and they are taken off one by one and killed. They are the larva of what is commonly known as the death's-head moth.

ROOT WORMS.

The enemies to plants are not those alone that are classified as foliage insects which feed upon stem, leaf and flower, but there are others that infest the soil and burrow among the roots. These are the most dangerous, as they often remain hidden until the mischief is done. They can, however, be detected by the watchful cultivator, through certain symptoms, such as stunted or retarded growth, or continued weakness of the plant without any apparent cause. A good general precaution is, while raking or sifting the soil, to cast aside grubs, chrysalides and all traces of insect life.

Angleworm.—This worm, also known as the earth-worm, does far more damage by the displacing of the earth than from any actual injury. In tunneling through the soil, in search of nutriment, it swallows a portion of it, and this is brought to the surface and forms what is called a worm-cast. The best way to be rid of these is to turn the ball out on the hand, and where any are seen, seize them before they have a chance to withdraw, and pull gently until they come out entire. Another method is to pour some weak lime-water on the soil, when the worms will rush to the surface, where they can be destroyed. An application of a teaspoonful of liquid ammonia in a pint of water will also force them out.

Milleped.—This is a small, glossy worm, not infrequently found in leaf-mold, decaying vegetation, and occasionally also upon the collar or crown of a diseased plant. It has a hardened or shelly covering composed of concentric rings, numerous fringe-like feet which move in an undulatory manner, and two delicate antennæ, and when touched curls in a ring with the head inward. They are very fond of moisture, and by laying a piece of damp moss or a folded piece of damp paper or cloth on the soil, they will congregate under it so that they can be taken off in great numbers. Where there are many in a pot, they granulate the soil to such an extent that plants cease to thrive. Watering with lime-water is useful in destroying them, but a little soot mixed in the soil is still more effective.

Cut-worm.—This is a black-gray slug which generally feeds on soft, young plants in early spring, and cuts them off about the collar, just beneath the surface of the ground. There is no remedy for this slug but to catch and kill it. To guard a plant from its approach, pieces of coarse cardboard, or of tin, bent into a cylinder, and embedded about an inch in the soil, encircling the stem of the plant, constitutes a serviceable protection. Another good way is to trap them under sods of grass turned downward; they delight to creep under such covers, where they may be picked up every other day or so, and killed. The cut-worm is the larvæ of a fly not unlike the mosquito in shape, but with a body about an inch in length, and having long, awkward looking legs. The females have thicker bodies than the males, and should be destroyed on sight. This pest is so numerous some years that it destroys whole acres of herbaceous plants. Once on the coast of Galway, in Ireland, the trees and shrubs in an area of many square miles dropped their leaves through its having eaten all the young roots; but the law of nature's compensations was made manifest in the increased prosperity of hogs and chickens.

Wire-worm.—This is a reptile mostly met with near sloughs or damp places. It lives upon the roots of plants, more especially of Wallflowers and Stocks, and is easily driven out of pots or from the roots by applying a weak dilution of *aqua ammoniæ*—say a tablespoonful to a gallon of water—or by a slight admixture of soot in the soil.

DISEASES OF PLANTS.

DISEASE seldom takes hold of plants while surrounded by such circumstances as are favorable to their full development; ordinarily it springs from neglect, but occasionally from accidental causes, such as deterioration of soil, overpowering by dust and dirt, overcrowding, and the like. The leaves, being the lungs of the plants, must be sedulously guarded from becoming clogged with dust, deranged by insects, or scorched by exceeding heat, all which are prolific sources of disease. Everything about the roots and rootlets should be sweet — that is, free from offensive odors — and composed of substances that are easily dissolved by rain or water; for the rootlets, being the mouths, will refuse unwholesome food, and the plant will soon sicken.

Mildew.— This is a fine, minute, white, fungus growth, not peculiar to plants, but affecting them as well as other things where the conditions are favorable. It generally arises in plants where an unequal temperature or distribution of moisture prevails in the different parts, as when any one portion is too dry, too wet or too cold. It is most easily removed by applying through a common pepper-box a *very light* dusting of flour of sulphur on the parts affected, and prevented by maintaining equal conditions in the various parts of the plant.

Blackrust.— This is a black, moist, fungus growth that is produced mostly by excessive moisture and the absence of the necessary amount of warmth. The remedy is the same as for mildew, with the addition of securing greater heat.

Damping Off.— This disease is mostly caused by want of air, changes of temperature, or excessive moisture; and therefore most frequently occurs among plants, cuttings and seedlings that are overcrowded. A little powdered, dry charcoal, or dry sand, sprinkled in among the plants, will help to keep it down, when the diseased ones should be carefully removed; and, if still too crowded, even healthy ones must be sacrificed.

PRACTICAL PRECEPTS.

1. Syringe the leaves of plants, unless in extremely cold weather, at least once a day, with water at the temperature of the place where they are growing; when syringing or sprinkling in the hot sun, the plant should be shaded, otherwise the leaves will become spotted.

2. Give plants fresh air by letting down the windows when the outside temperature is sufficiently high; at other times by opening the doors into other rooms.

3. Shield the rootlets of plants from a too close contact with the rays of the sun; as by encircling the pot in a larger one, or by protecting the box with a detached board or sheet of paper at some little distance, to intercept the direct heat.

4. Protect all plants from extreme changes of temperature, from drafts and puffs of cold air.

5. Remember to give plants their needed season of rest after they have finished flowering, by withdrawing them, with the exception of a few creepers and the like, into the shade and withholding the wonted supply of water.

6. Relieve plants by cutting off all dead flowers, leaves and branches; this will serve to lengthen the season of bloom; but care should be taken not to allow the refuse to accumulate on or around the pots or beds. Keep plants that tend to a straggling or spindling growth, shapely and compact by cutting off all weak and misplaced shoots.

7. Relieve plants from insects as soon as detected; do not wait till tomorrow, for by tomorrow you may have no plant worth speaking of. To keep your collection free, examine and, if necessary, purify all new acquisitions.

8. Keep a few cups of water among house plants, to evaporate; where saucers filled with water are used for certain plants, these cups are unnecessary.

9. Where a plant is grown with a saucer of water underneath, raise the pot above the water by little wooden blocks or stones.

10. Keep the soil sweet by occasionally letting it go a little dry, or stirring it up gently with a fork; a table fork will do for house plants.

11. Never throw away soot; mix it in the soil, which it will help to fertilize, while it is very effective in driving away insects; it will also heighten and beautify the color of all red and blue flowers.

12. Never waste soapsuds; it can be applied with advantage to all kinds of growing shrubs and plants. Even in winter it can be utilized by being poured upon a manure or compost heap, or where plants are to grow the ensuing season.

13. Use moss freely as a topping for the soil in pots and boxes; if put on neatly it is ornamental, besides being useful in retaining moisture and protecting the upper rootlets until the leafage is sufficiently developed to discharge that function. Sponges may be placed among plants and watered for the like purpose of maintaining moisture, being also susceptible of ornamentation by sowing in them the common garden cress or canary grass.

14. Mix well all soils for plants; making of the several ingredients one homogeneous mass, carefully throwing out all the lumps, half-rotted bits of wood, and other refuse.

15. Protect plants against heavy drippings from houses, trees, and the like; none will thrive under such an infliction.

16. To insure a pleasing succession of flowers in plants of the same species, select different varieties, or set those of the same variety at different times; indeed, nature will, unaided, secure a partial continuity, as scarcely any two will bloom at the same time.

17. Throughout the flowering season, apply alternately plenty of water and weak liquid manure to all bulbous and free-blooming plants. Where plants grow too fast, the temperature should be reduced.

18. In watering house plants some discretion should be used to save carpets from the drippings; several ingenious contrivances have been devised, and they are purchasable at seedstores; but most persons can extemporize their own.

19. Do not cut off the withering leaves of bulbous plants, but let them die or decay naturally and fall off in due season, as while the leaves decline the sap goes back into the bulb, replenishing its store of strength for the ensuing season.

20. Steep new pots to close the pores, but allow them to drain off before using; thoroughly wash old ones, and scald them to kill fungus.

21. In raising plants, sow the seeds unsparingly; it is easy to weed out the poor and weakly seedlings, leaving of the strongest as many as may be desired for vigorous growth.

If it is preferred to use home-raised seed, always select from the best-shaped and prettiest-marked flowers, designating them while yet in bloom by a system of letters or other marks, which will indicate their character and color, written upon proper labels.

22. Accustom plants to plenty of air before permanently removing them out of doors; or, when taken out, temporarily protect them from cold spells by frames or otherwise.

23. Do not pull up slips or cuttings to ascertain if they have rooted; this fact may be learned without prejudice to the rooting process, by probing at their sides; and, ordinarily, by noticing the character of the leaves — vigorous or otherwise — they shoot upward.

24. Do not paint the receptacles or surroundings of plants a green color, as it makes the foliage look pale by contrast; and, being themselves green, any other color whatever will produce a better effect; drab, lemon, slate or white forms a good contrast.

25. Before using tobacco-water to destroy insects on plants, ascertain its strength by experiment on a single leaf; if too strong it will discolor the leaves and hurt the plant.

26. Put small plants in small pots, transplanting to larger ones as they increase in size; too much room gives too much moisture, and thereby retards the healthy action of the rootlets, which naturally seek the outside of the ball of earth to get air.

27. Turn window plants around to the light once or twice each day; otherwise they will grow one-sided.

28. Utilize tulip-beds and the like, after the plants have finished flowering for the season, by sowing therein the seeds of annuals, or transplanting thither some bedding-out plants, as Verbenas and others.

29. On the approach of a frosty night, prolong the freshness of window plants by drawing them away from the window, or interposing some shield between them and it.

30. To protect outdoor plants and lengthen their period of blooming, on the approach of frost use heavy coverings, as old carpets, quilts, or good, stout wrapping papers.

31. Use common clay pots for immediate contact with plants; if the glazed kinds are desired for ornamental purposes, they should be procured large enough to admit placing the common kinds within them.

32. Wash salt-water sand free of salt before using it around plants.

33. Keep plant soil as nearly level as possible, to insure uniformity in watering and in applying liquid manure; the practice of piling up the soil around the stems is both injurious and unsightly in house plants.

34. If plants need support, set the stakes firm in the soil, burning the ends slightly where there is danger of sprouting.

35. To ripen the wood of plants, place them, after the season of flowering, on beds of coal ashes, as a protection against worms.

36. In taking up plants in the fall, cut around the plant so as to mark out a ball a little smaller than the intended receptacle. This should be done with a sharp knife or spade, without reference to the rootlets that may be cut away. Thus circumscribed, it should be allowed to remain a week or ten days before removing, keeping the ball wet meantime, and be then transferred on something broad enough to sustain the whole ball.

37. Do not take up plants from the open ground too late in the fall for winter growing; it is better to sacrifice two or three weeks of their beauty in their old location outside than to have miserable looking plants half the winter indoors.

38. Give fresh air freely to plants newly brought into the house, opening windows and doors in pleasant weather for the first four or five days; the change is great to them, and if they are neglected in this respect their leaves will turn yellow and die.

39. Remember that liquid manure is to be applied only when plants are growing; and that it is safest to administer it weak and often.

40. Buy plants always from neighbors or well known growers: for the first are near to remonstrate with and receive explanations from if anything is wrong; while the latter will, through care for their own reputation, if for no higher reason, be likely to do you justice.

41. Do not waste time and money on poor plants or cheap seeds; good ones will occupy no more room, and will give much more satisfaction.

42. In house plants, pot the cuttings, slips or shoots, before the roots have grown too large; even a single root, half an inch or an inch in length, will be sufficient to insure success.

43. If in doubt about the treatment of a plant, study its nature, habits, and wants, as described elsewhere.

44. In cultivating plants, be mindful of the old adage, "a stitch in time saves nine"; and be assured that continual watchfulness is the price of the highest success.

> "What landscapes I read in the primrose's looks,
>   And what pictures of pebbled and minnowy brooks,
>   In the vetches that tangled the shore!
>   Earth's cultureless buds, to my heart ye were dear,
>   Ere the fever of passions, or ague of fear,
>   Had scathed my existence's bloom;
>   Once I welcome you more, in life's passionless stage,
>   With the visions of youth to re-visit my age,
>   And I wish you to grow on my tomb."

Culture of Favorite Plants.

ABUTILON.

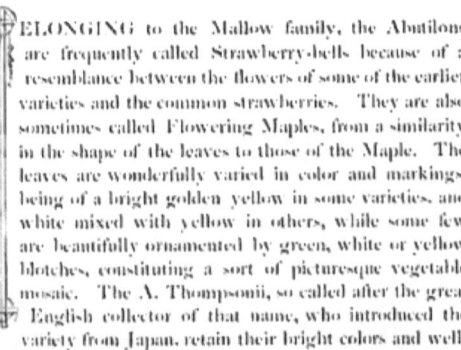

BELONGING to the Mallow family, the Abutilons are frequently called Strawberry-bells because of a resemblance between the flowers of some of the earlier varieties and the common strawberries. They are also sometimes called Flowering Maples, from a similarity in the shape of the leaves to those of the Maple. The leaves are wonderfully varied in color and markings, being of a bright golden yellow in some varieties, and white mixed with yellow in others, while some few are beautifully ornamented by green, white or yellow blotches, constituting a sort of picturesque vegetable mosaic. The A. Thompsonii, so called after the great English collector of that name, who introduced the variety from Japan, retain their bright colors and well-defined markings during even the hottest weather. They are especially adapted to our Southern States, where they attain immense proportions, growing from ten to fifteen feet high and spreading laterally to a corresponding extent. They are also not inappropriate to northern culture, through their accommodating habit, as they may be kept in an ordinary cellar over winter, with occasional waterings to prevent the soil from becoming entirely dry. The stems are slender, and those of the smaller ones can be trained to form a pretty window-screen, or to assume an umbrella-like or other fancy shape to suit the taste of the cultivator. They should be grown in a rich, sandy soil; and, as has been intimated, they will thrive in or out of doors, though all will be the better for a partial shading when planted outside. This can be the most easily secured by setting them to the north of a fence, an evergreen or a shrub somewhat higher than themselves. They make an abundance of small roots near the stem, and, being what gardeners term gross feeders, they should have plenty of liquid manure during their season of growth and bloom. They flower freely during the winter and spring months in about sixty degrees of heat, and some varieties continue to flower all summer when properly cared for. In removing Abutilons indoors on the approach of winter, from the beds or borders where they have been resting, it is best to anticipate a little, that they may have time to make a few rootlets in their new abode before the cold weather is fairly upon them.

ACHYRANTHUS.

CHAFF-FLOWER is the significance of this name, which is derived from the Greek, and has been given to this plant because of the chaff-like appearance of its blossoms. The plant is one of the most attractive of the well known Amaranth family, and is beginning to be perhaps better known as the Iresine. Under whatever name, it is in all its varieties a very pretty, desirable and easily cultivated garden or house plant. The beauty of its varied foliage will enhance the attractiveness of the best collection. It will grow in any common garden soil, in an atmosphere ranging from fifty to seventy-five degrees, the latter grade being absolutely necessary for a rapid growth. A few of the bright-colored varieties, as the A. Lindenii, with its long, pointed leaves, are always conspicuous among a collection of window-plants, the bright red foliage contrasting admirably with the surroundings, and producing almost the effect of flowers among the green leaves of the other plants. The varieties known as Gilsonii and Aureus Reticulatus have rounded leaves, the latter being also conspicuous for their gold and crimson web-like markings; while the former are generally an intense crimson, but with weakening shades down to a salmon color. They form an effective ornament when introduced among Rose Geraniums or other like green foliage plants; and can be planted so as to assume any shape to suit the taste of the cultivator, as a circle around other plants, a cross or heart in the midst of others, and the like. They can be easily kept from straggling by pinching back with the finger and thumb, and thus maintained for a whole season in the shape it was originally designed they should present. For winter plants, a few cuttings should be taken in July, and put aside in a shady place, either in sand or common soil, where, if well watered, they will strike root in from ten days to two weeks, when they can be potted for use. These new plants will prove far superior to the old ones.

AGAPANTHUS.

ONE among the Liliaceous plants, to which order it belongs, is more picturesquely beautiful, perhaps, than this pretty azure-blossomed flower. The name signifies, in the original Greek, a love-flower, and the plant is sometimes called in our vernacular the African blue lily. It is a very ornamental plant for the parlor, the outdoor pedestal or tree-stump, and, indeed, will show itself to advantage anywhere. Its long, graceful leaves, curving to either side of the bulb, make it attractive even when not in bloom. From among the leaves it shoots upward, to a height of from eighteen inches to three feet, one or two stout flower-stalks, which are crowned with a mass of azure flowers, springing from and surrounding a common center like an umbrella, whence the epithet umbellatus. The bulbs are among the class known as Cape bulbs, because originally introduced from the Cape of Good Hope. They require a liberal allowance of pot room, as they send out very large rootlets, which will sometimes break a pot if not removed in time to a larger one. They grow well in a good, sandy loam, which should be well packed in among the rootlets. It is sometimes of advantage in transplanting to give them an entirely new soil, care being taken not to hurt the live roots, and dead ones being cut out with a sharp knife or scissors. The Agapanthus is among the few plants that grow more valuable with age. Even the leaves can be kept green, if desired, from year to year without apparent detriment; one or two will perhaps fall off in a season, but these will be replaced by others. It is slow to evince any sign of disease, and should therefore be all the more carefully tended. Its enemies are most frequently the scales, and occasionally the mealy bugs. The season of blooming varies from spring to fall in different plants, mainly according to treatment, and not infrequently they will flower twice in the same season. After flowering they should be given a season of rest by being supplied with less water for one or two months, whereupon they will perhaps again show signs of new growth, when they should receive a more liberal allowance of water. While blooming, they require a free use of liquid manure. Being natives of a warm climate, they delight in a moderate heat, and will not thrive at a lower range than fifty-five degrees.

ALTERNANTHERAS.

UNDER this name, formed probably from the changing habit of the leaves in respect to color, is introduced a pretty, low-growing or dwarfish plant of the Amaranth family. It delights in a rich, sandy soil and in an abundance of water, when freely growing in a warm atmosphere, in or out of doors. Under the sun's heat, the leaves assume in succession many different colors, as green, brown, pink, carmine, orange, and yellow, frequently rivaling the various shades of our forest leaves in autumn, or the beauties of the rainbow, whence it is sometimes called Rainbow Plant. Being small and easily kept under control with the knife, scissors, or even the fingers, they are much used for number, name or phrase work in fancy parterres; and the outline of such words, phrases or numbers can be easily maintained through an entire season by clipping, as they not only are not injured thereby, but receive the added advantage of a more compact growth. They will endure a greater degree of heat than almost any other plant, and their colors become deeper and more beautiful in the full glare of the sunlight. Though but of recent introduction, they have already sported into many handsome varieties. Of these the best known are: A. tricolor, which derives its distinctive appellation from the three most frequently-recurring colors, a rose ground with yellow bands and purple veins. A. magnifica, because larger, stronger, and more magnificent in every respect, including color. A. spatulata, from the spatulate, that is, obovate, oblong, or battledore-like form of the leaves, which are commonly a bright crimson and green. A. grandis, among the most recent varieties, is so called because of its still stronger habit of growth, and superior effectiveness in combination, the leaves being bronze with rich magenta tips.

AMARYLLIS.

THE Amaryllis, through all its various species, produces the most brilliant flowers, blooming generally in the winter and early spring. This family of plants has been much divided of late years, and the many known to the masses under the above name have other appellatives as well. They delight in a rich soil made up in about equal parts of well-rotted manure (sweetened by exposure to the air), leaf-mold or spent hops and good loam, with a slight admixture of sand. To rest and ripen the bulbs for future use, after the flowering season, the pots are embedded in the soil in the open air until the approach of winter, when they should be taken where they are to grow and bloom. Our own experience is practical, so we will give it. We purchased five bulbs, two with persistent foliage, and three that would keep it only a part of the year. These last we planted in pots, having the promise that they would bloom that summer; but they only grew leaves, and filled their pots with thick, white roots as large as a pen-holder. In due time they lost their leaves and went to sleep, and we intended keeping them dry, as directed. By some means, two got enough moisture to retain their long roots, and they bloomed the following spring; the third spent its strength in forming roots again. Of course, under proper circumstances, they should blossom every year. Abundance of water and occasional applications of manure-water are required during the season of leafage. They should be set in not less than seven-inch pots, with about half the bulb bedded in the soil.

ASTER.

WHEN in their course the spring and summer flowers have passed away, and the months come on that ripen the fruits and finish the harvests, we find ourselves dependent upon such flowers as the Asters and Chrysanthemums for the beauty of our flower-beds, the first named furnishing an almost infinite variety, both in shades of color and styles of flower. Some of the dwarf kinds appear like a gathered bouquet, so closely are the flowers crowded together. Whatever the style of flower, they all require the same treatment. The seeds should be started in a bed or box prepared for the purpose, and from there transplanted to where they are to bloom, before they begin to grow or start their flower-stalks. They can be placed a foot apart, in rows, if it is desired, or set singly for specimen plants. Water should be supplied them until well established, and in August a dressing of manure, with occasional supplies of manure-water. This treatment will give an increase of flowers, as well as improve their quality. Any favorite may be potted before frost, to finish its bloom in the house. In saving seeds, the outside rows would be the best developed and ripest. A friend who is eminently successful in Aster culture pulls the plants from which seeds are desired before frost, and hangs them up by the roots, so that the sap will go into the ripening seeds as they dry.

AZALEA.

RARELY cultivated as window plants, the Azaleas are in great demand for exhibition purposes, and for cut flowers in winter and spring. There is, however, no reason why they may not, with reasonable attention, be successfully cultivated as house plants. The soil for very young plants should be nearly all peat, or leaf-mold, where peat cannot be procured; but for older ones, three parts peat and one part each of loam, leaf-mold and sand. The time for repotting is after the blooming season, except the plants are large and have appropriate sized tubs or boxes, when they will not need it for several years, requiring only that the soil be enriched with liquid manures. The plant belongs to the heath family, and, like most of that tribe, have roots somewhat resembling the fern, which should never be allowed to become entirely dry, care being taken not to go to the other extreme and drench it so that the soil would sour and the roots decay. The average temperature required is between fifty and sixty degrees, and plenty of air, provided it be not under that temperature, should be always admitted. They bloom from February to May, and the larger ones produce hundreds of flowers, at once delighting the beholder with the munificence as well as the magnificence of their adornment. The flowers of some varieties are white, while others run through all the various shades of red, from rose to bright carmine, often beautifully marked, like the carnation.

BALSAM.

HOWEVER much these plants are valued, they seldom receive the attention which they deserve. It is true that the miserable manner in which they are many times sown and left to take care of themselves may partly account for this, for under such circumstances they are far from attractive, as the flowers are apt to partake of the quality of the plants. Rightly grown, however, they form most magnificent specimens for garden or conservatory decoration. For early plants the seeds should be sown in a hotbed. As soon as they develop two leaves besides the two thick seed-leaves, they should be removed into pots or boxes, and these be plunged again in the bed. During growth they should be allowed plenty of air, and ample room for their branches to extend; and by supplying a richly-manured soil they may be made to grow to a great size.

The Balsam delights in a moist, well-manured situation, and is among the handsomest annuals cultivated. The plants should frequently have waterings of manure-water; and, as their stalks are succulent, they should never be allowed to suffer from drouth. While most plants suffer from intense heat, these seem to clothe themselves with greater beauty in the very height of summer. When the main or central stem is of sufficient height, the pinching out of the tip has a tendency to increase the side branches.

In the garden they should be set about a foot and a half apart, with the same care for their nourishment as in the conservatory, stakes being supplied them to prevent their being overturned by the wind. The flowers are rich in quality and in colors, being either plain, spotted, splashed or streaked, and in the double varieties they fully equal the Camellia. For bouquets and decorative purposes fine thread-wire is drawn through them in the same manner as for the Camellia, and the ends brought together, thus leaving the flower in a loop, and forming a manageable stem. A little damp moss or cotton-batting being then placed at the base of the blossoms, keeps them fresh for some time. The flowers of this plant occasionally bloom double without the aid of the cultivator.

BEGONIA.

MAINLY cultivated in the hothouse until a comparatively recent period, Begonias are now kept principally in the greenhouse, except when it is wished to stimulate them to an extraordinary growth, for which purpose the hot, steamy air of the former is more suitable. Of the Begonias there are several kinds, differing in both leaf and flower. The first and probably most cultivated are those popularly known as the Elephant's Ear, with large leaves, oblique and rounded at the base, and sharply pointed at the apex, with the upper lobe, or half, much more developed than the lower. They are richly colored, being changeable in tints from bronze to green, with large silver bands in some, and irregular spots in others, the underside being of a reddish-purple tint. The upright or bushy varieties have transparent stems, many of them with glossy, irregular, waxy leaves, while the flowers are of various colors, from white to bright carmine. The broad-leaved kind should be watered freely during summer; the other species when in bloom, and at other times just sufficiently to keep them in fair condition. There are also some with tuberous roots, which can be laid away during their season of rest, in any place that is free from frost, the roots only being sparingly moistened. Begonias should be only sprayed, that is, lightly syringed, as the water bears the leaves down to such an extent that they do not spring upright as readily as other plants. The soil used is one part peat, one of loam, and one of decomposed manure. The large ones are easily propagated from the leaves, thus: Take a leaf, cut the stem off rather close, lay it on a surface of wet sand in a pot or box that can be covered with glass; pin the leaf down with broom splints, then with a knife cut across the large veins in numerous places, and at each cutting roots will start, from which young plants will spring. These should be potted as soon as the leaves get to be from half an inch to an inch long. Many of these plants accommodate themselves readily to the family sitting-room, only they must be kept free from frost. We have some of the large-leaved ones that have for several years hung just back from the windows, where they get about an hour of sunshine daily, and this in a small, ordinary parlor, requiring no great care except hanging farther in on extra-cold nights, the ordinary watering daily, or less frequently in winter, and dusting the leaves with a small feather-duster.

BOUVARDIA.

FIRST brought to notice about a century ago, being introduced from Mexico, it was named in honor of Dr. Bouvard, director of the *Jardin des Plantes*, at Paris; and is one of the most attractive of the Madders, freely blooming through the winter. The flowers appear in trusses on each new shoot, and are of various colors, from a bright carmine through all the shades of red to almost a pure white. They are waxy in texture and of a compact growth, forming a very striking bunch of flowers not unlike the cluster of the Lilac; and for purposes of floral decoration they are very general favorites. A rich loam, with a slight admixture of sand, forms the best soil for their cultivation; and they are best grown outdoors in summer, where they will bloom through August and September. They can be made shapely lawn shrubs by careful pruning of all straggling shoots. They are very desirable indoor plants for winter blooming, and should not be allowed to catch the slightest nip of the early frost, but be removed in season, as they cannot thrive in an atmosphere that falls under fifty degrees. Even when not vitally injured, they are slow to recover from the effects of cold; and, though more easily hurt by too much than too little water, the soil must not be permitted to become "dust-dry." The Bouvardias are seldom propagated from regular shoots or cuttings, but mainly from pieces of the roots laid horizontally in sand, and covered to the depth of about an inch. These require a uniform heat of from seventy to seventy-five degrees in the bed or box where they are set; and sometimes will not show growth for four or five weeks, but must not on that account be disturbed.

CACTUS.

GREAT arid plains and rocky, infertile wastes, where other vegetation is sparse and water scarce, are the native homes of these peculiar plants. The curious and varied manner of their growth amazes us at first, and finally fascinates us, making the charm complete when we behold the superb blossoms of some of the species. They are divided into several classes, according to their manner of growth, many of them being foreign plants. Of the Cereus there are several kinds, among which the Cereus flagelliformis, or Whip Cactus, and the Cereus grandiflorus, or Night-blooming Cactus, are the best representatives. The first grows in long, branching stems, having ten angles, and needs support to keep it upright. The flowers are of a ruddy pink, lasting for several days. The latter has stems of only five angles, and at night produces its flowers, which fade before the morning. They are very large, varying from seven to twelve inches in diameter, the petals being white, and the calyx yellow within and brown without. The genus Opuntia, of which the Prickly Pear is a specimen, are hardy plants, with yellow flowers, indigenous on the sandy shores of Lake Michigan. The genus Echinocactus have many deep angles, with curious swellings with each set of spines; the Epiphyllums have flat leaves without spines, producing flowers at their margins; Melocactus is the genus familiarly called Turk's Cap; and the Mamillarias are distinguished by their numerous tubercles or small, rounded projections.

All the Cactaceæ will grow in any soil where there is no stagnant moisture nor actual frost, but for the best results they should have a soil composed of loam, leaf-mold and sand, with abundant drainage. A group of any of these plants forms a very attractive object in a window. They are very free from insects, causing little or no anxiety in that respect, though some beetles will feed upon the young tips. Like all succulents, they need comparatively little water; if shriveled, however, the roots and enveloping earth should be soaked in a pail of water for two or three hours. While growing, they need water about three times a week, and every day if in very small pots. Slips may be taken from the parent plant, and inserted about an inch deep in comparatively dry sand. Some genera, as the Echinocactus, Melocactus and Mamillaria, are also propagated from the tubercles or offshoots, and from seeds.

The Staphelias are Cactus-like plants that require the same treatment. Young plants are potted about once a year; large ones, when in good sized pots, only once in three or four years. These plants are all fond of heat and a dry atmosphere.

CALADIUM.

KNOWN to florists and many amateur culturists as a suborder of the handsome-leaved Arum family of plants, the Caladium is itself subdivided into almost innumerable species and varieties. Of these perhaps the most conspicuous are the C. esculentum and the C. odoratum, both of which are cultivated mainly for the size and beauty of the leaves. These often measure, under fair cultivation, thirty-six inches in length by twenty-four in breadth. Both of these species present a majestic appearance scattered singly through a lawn, on the bank of a rivulet or pond, or collected in groups at convenient distances, their shield-like leaves making them a somewhat conspicuous ornament among other foliage. They delight in abundance of water, and grow best where it is close at hand; but if planted on higher grounds the roots should be thoroughly drenched with water at least once a day in warm weather; they can hardly have too much. A depth of eighteen to twenty-four inches of good, rich soil must underlie them.

The approach of frost should be anticipated in preserving these plants for future growth, as they are very sensitive to cold. Leaves, stems and roots should not be plucked off, but should be allowed to dry back to the tuber, which can be then kept in a warm place, embedded in sand, until needed for the next season. Smaller specimens can be kept growing through the winter, as parlor plants, by giving them plenty of water and warmth. In spring they should get a start for two or three weeks indoors before being put out, as they thrive much better afterward for that preliminary indulgence. The roots of the small, fancy ones should be kept in their pots and have just a little moisture, else the tubers are apt to perish from "dry rot," and be entirely lost. The smaller varieties are among the prettiest marked foliage plants at our command, and are almost innumerable. Many of them are so difficult to cultivate that few people can grow them successfully unless under specially favorable circumstances. There are, however, two or three pretty varieties that will succeed well as common house plants, and they can be pointed out by most florists.

CAMELLIA.

OFTEN used as a pretty natural ornament for the hair of some stately queen of society or less pretentious belle, the Camellia has been very generally admired for the rich, waxy appearance of its charming, rose-like flowers. It is not very general in house cultivation, as the idea seems to prevail that it is difficult for it to accommodate itself to the circumstances surrounding other house plants. True, it does not thrive in a dry atmosphere, as there its thick, green leaves are liable to the attack of insects, but a little watchfulness would keep these away. It does not require a high temperature, the average running from fifty to sixty degrees, the lowest being at night. The best soil to use is good loam or peat. All coarse manures are obnoxious to it. The plants are sometimes repotted just before the young growth begins — say in February or March; though the best time is immediately after the flowering season. The buds of the Camellia are apt to be so crowded that some must fall to make room for others to bloom; and, as the stems are so short as to endanger the cluster if it should be attempted to pinch out the superfluous ones with the finger, a good method is to take a sharp knife or pair of scissors and clip off the upper half of the buds to be removed, or otherwise wound them, leaving the remaining half-buds, which become sickly from the wound, and drop of their own accord. Growers of large flowers only leave one or two to the branch. When in the bud they must not suffer either from too much or too little water, as buds drop from both causes; deprivation of water for two hours after it is due, or making the soil soaking wet, is equally disastrous to the buds, and of course cuts off all hope of flowers. The leaves and branches should be frequently sponged or washed, but syringing is not recommended, as the foliage easily becomes spotted; the soil and roots should be watered regularly once a day while the leaves and buds are forming; and a little more water is needed when the buds are opening into flowers. They require light, but should not be exposed to the direct rays of the sun, as in their native woods they enjoy a natural shade through the surrounding trees. They should be removed indoors early, as the slightest frost will nip the buds. After they have flowered all winter they should be moved out in spring to some shady nook where the strong sunlight will not strike them; a few hours of the morning sun, however, will not prove injurious. From the seeds they bloom in three years. These plants can be also budded, grafted and inarched with different varieties in the same manner as other shrubs.

CANNA.

LANDSCAPES famous for gorgeous beauty have always abounded in India, and of these there are but few in which the Canna (on this account called Indica) does not form an indispensable contributor to the loveliness of the prospect. This has become so universal a favorite, that it is cultivated in all civilized countries; and helps to give a semi-tropical appearance to many northern conservatories and gardens. As ornaments for the parlor they are also very fine, and may be kept in good condition the year round by proper care and attention. The genus belongs to the Arrowroot family, but is not cultivated in this country for any nutritious properties, the beauty of the foliage and the flowers having engrossed the whole attention of cultivators. It might, however, be made a valuable food product. Of late years florists have produced a large number of new varieties, all of them pretty and desirable. To grow Cannas large, they should have plenty of room in a good, rich, deep soil, a loose, sandy loam being the very best for the purpose. Soapsuds or other liquid manure applied freely, say twice a week during warm weather, will be very acceptable to the plants and reward the care-taker with a greater wealth of leaf and flower. Those not wanted indoors for winter decoration can be lifted, with as much soil around the roots as possible, and allowed to dry in that condition; when the drying process is completed the tubers can be stowed away in any frost-free receptacle; they will bear a considerable degree of cold, but contact with actual frost is ruinous. For winter decoration it is best to use one or two side shoots of the old tuber, as they are just about to sprout; they should be taken off in August and placed in a four-inch pot, changing them to larger ones as they need more room. These plants grow from one to twelve or fifteen feet in height, and vary in colors of foliage from the lightest shade of green to a very dark bronze. The flowers are also of a great variety of shades.

CARNATION.

ALL through the ages much attention must have been paid to this plant, or at least to the family to which it belongs, as we find that the Pink, the primitive source of countless varieties, was known to the Ancient Greeks as Dianthus, or Flower of Jove. And to this day the varieties have been incessantly multiplied, the plant being easy of culture and thriving in almost any fertile soil. The flowers are an acquisition to bouquet makers, not only on account of their beauty, but for their clove-like or spicy odor. They can be propagated from the seeds, but such are more uncertain in quality of flower than those propagated from an old plant. Cuttings or slips can be taken freely from the old plants, and should be cut at the joint so as in breaking to leave a rounded end, or else be severed just below the joint. The slips should be set in a crock, near the edge, as close together as desired, the sand being well pressed to cause slow evaporation, and the pot being covered with a glass while striking root. The layering process may also be used. The mode of procedure is to select strong, low-growing shoots around the plant, cut off the lower leaves and diminish the length of the upper ones, and then with a sharp knife make a clean, slanting cut on the lower side of the stem, penetrating about half through it, terminating it near the next joint above the edge of the blade. The earth is then loosened an inch or so deep, and the layer pegged down, the end being slightly tilted to keep the wound open, and covered with fresh soil well pressed down. In this way the old plant feeds her nurslings through the half-dissevered bark until the slips take root. The Remontants, or Monthly Carnations, are much cultivated as house plants, their frequent flowering making them very popular, although the "monthly" blooms are confined to tropical and subtropical climes, and the summer months in other latitudes. The best kinds are imported from Germany and Italy, where their cultivation has been made a special industry for two or three hundred years.

COLEUS.

VERY few plants had so effectually escaped the march of hybridizing improvements and experiments as this simple flower, so long the delight of the humble cottagers of Great Britain under the familiar name of French Nettle. It, however, fell under the observation of that prince of experimenters, Verschaffelt, of Paris, who gave the first impetus to the production of varieties, which have since been multiplied indefinitely by many others. It has now become indispensable to large and small collections, being a universal favorite with rich and poor. The slight blotch of bronze that ornamented the original nettle-like leaf of the simple Coleus has been made to assume, under the skillful manipulations of the scientific hybridizers, nearly all the shades of the three primitive colors, red, blue and yellow; and various combinations of these and their many shadings. So conspicuous is the tendency to change in the markings by this process that one variety has been styled the Chameleon. The number of varieties in actual cultivation is very considerable and continually growing larger. They will grow in almost any soil, but do best in a compost of leaf-mold and good loam, requiring, however, plenty of moisture in whatever soil during their season of growth. They are very sensitive to cold, being in fact as good as thermometers down to the freezing point, the leaves presenting different appearances at different degrees under fifty. In the upper ranges they will recover with proper attention and increased warmth within seventy-five degrees, but if touched by actual frost they are doomed to perish. For winter culture, cuttings should be taken in August and set in any shady situation in any soil or in sand, when they will strike root by simply watering them every evening in hot, dry weather. When sufficiently rooted, they should be potted and taken indoors before the approach of early frost. It is useless to attempt their cultivation where the temperature falls below fifty-five degrees.

CRAPE MYRTLE.

WHEREVER there exists a true love of flowers, this member of the Loosestrife family is necessarily popular. Its bright, deep-green, glossy leaves, like those of the Myrtle, give rise to the second part of the name, though there is no relationship between the two families. It is called Crape from a loose resemblance between the blossoms, when seen at a distance, and a bunch of red or white crape. These flowers grow in large clusters or panicles, of which there are sometimes several hundred to a plant, and continue in bloom until nipped by the early frost, the first bloom varying with the latitude in which grown, from May to August. Each individual blossom presents a singular appearance, the many long, silken stamens standing apart from the rest of the flower, and the multitude of these flowers, when seen against the background of the leaves and sky, give the semblance, as has been said, of masses of crape thrown loosely over the plant. The branches are thin and soft when growing, and may easily be kept in place by pinching off the straggling shoots, thus securing a compact, tidy and symmetrical bush. Smaller specimens can be grown indoors for blooming in early winter, if placed in good, open sunlight. The plants intended for this purpose should be allowed to rest during the previous summer in some shady place, with only enough water supplied to keep them from dying. In northern latitudes the outdoor specimens should be transferred to some dry cellar or dark corner of any spare room, which in ordinary winters is all the protection they need. They are all the better to withstand the frost if the wood has been well ripened by withholding moisture for two or three weeks before frost, upon the first appearance of which they should be immediately housed. A rich loam, lightened with leaf-mold, or rather with peat, is the most favorable soil, which, during the season of growth, ought to be further enriched by plentiful supplies of liquid manure. It is propagated by new shoots, like the Abutilon.

CROCUS.

EASILY cultivated, as it grows freely in any soil not positively soggy, the Crocus is an admirable little bulb to bloom in early spring. After planting, the bulbs will take care of themselves if supplied with an annual dressing of manure. They should be set deeply, some three or four inches, either in groups or rows, as desired; and should not be disturbed except they appear on the surface, as sometimes happens, the cause always being the formation of the new bulb on the top of the old one. The bulbs are very cheap, and might be set abundantly. Their most appropriate use in the garden is for bordering beds of other bulbs, or they may be used with great effect in forming letters or other simple designs on the lawn. Except when a bed is wanted for other purposes, they may be planted about an inch apart; but where that is the case they can be set at a greater distance, and after the leaves disappear the place may be sown with annuals. For the house they may be planted in pans of sand or in any of the pretty designs manufactured for them out of terra cotta or pottery ware, and set away until they show growth. They can be put in the ground anywhere, with their accompanying pots, but should be covered up with ashes to protect them from rats and mice, as well as from the frost; or they may be stored indoors in a dark cellar or closet, being protected in the same way. About midwinter they can be removed at intervals, to insure a succession of flowering, into the house or conservatory, where they are intended to bloom. They must always be kept at low temperature until near the blooming period, for too great heat lengthens and weakens the stem. They also bloom in water, in small glasses adapted to them, made on the same principle as Hyacinth glasses. Bulbs should be set in the fall. They can be raised from seeds, blooming in three years, that being the average for most kinds of bulbs. All Crocus bulbs should be set about the last of October, or early in November.

CYCLAMEN.

PERHAPS there are but few plants for fall, winter and spring cultivation that will afford more pleasure to the industrious and watchful amateur than this attractive little plant. It never grows more than six or eight inches high, but it has beautiful mottled leaves, and the flowers, which are borne on single stems, have a velvety center encircled by rays of a purplish red; and in some varieties lilac and white, while in a few they approach a maroon. These ray-like petals turn down, as in the Dodecatheon Meadia or Shooting Star, sometimes called the Prairie Pointer. The bulbs should be obtained as early as possible in the autumn, so that they can be planted at intervals to promote an orderly succession in their periods of blooming; or, they may be planted all at once, but treated with different degrees of heat, water, and other attentions, to hasten or retard their development. The plumper ones should be preferred; but if shriveled ones only can be had, they may be freshened by being enveloped in damp moss or cotton batting for one or more days. They delight in a good, rich soil, in which they are planted so as to leave about one-fourth of an inch of their substance above the surface. The soil should receive a little water, and the pot be put away in a sheltered place with a northern aspect, or under a tree, until they begin to grow, giving a little moisture as required. When the leaves begin to start, the plants can be brought forward to the light and given all the air possible every day, with water when necessary, care being taken that they do not decay through being too abundantly supplied. After their blooming season is over, the watering should be gradually reduced as the foliage withers, and finally almost discontinued. They are then put away in a shady, airy situation, free from rain, yet where the soil will not at any time become actually dry; but if there is any danger of such a contingency, a little water around the bulb might be given, as it must on no account be allowed to decline from its plump condition. In the fall they should have the soil shaken from them, and be placed in a fresh, rich compost. The larger bulbs often produce as many as two hundred flowers. The withered flowers should be clipped off, unless seed is desired; of those left for seed the stem will curl until the seed vessel is drawn down into the soil, where they ripen. Propagation otherwise than by seed is ordinarily impracticable with this bulb, as its solid nature almost precludes its division, and only the skilled practitioner can hope for success. When grown from seed it takes three years to bloom, unless specially petted and fostered by some skillful hand, and therefore most amateurs prefer to purchase blooming bulbs. Their chief enemies are mice and excessive moisture.

DAISY.

DAISY, from the Saxon, denoting day's eye, because of its habit of opening early in the morning, is a great favorite, as indeed it has been for ages. Whether growing by the roadside, a neglected beauty, or petted and cared for by some flower-loving cottager, its praises have long been sung by the greatest among European poets. In this country the Bellis perennis, or common double European Daisy, is extensively cultivated as a choice exotic; while the whole-leaved species, or B. integrifolia, is indigenous from Kentucky southward to the Gulf of Mexico. A heavy clay soil seems to be the natural choice of these simple beauties, but they will grow in almost any soil if supplied freely with water. In shaded nooks they will retain their flowers a long time, but the direct rays of the sun cause them to prematurely drop both flowers and leaves. The flower of the Daisy in the natural state is single, and borne on the top of a long, slender flower-stalk; but by cultivation it has become double, and has even sported into several curious and beautiful multiplex varieties. They have, however, seen their greatest popularity in this country. They can be cultivated in and out of doors, but as house plants must have all the light possible in the winter months. They are easily propagated by divisions of the plant, early in September in northern latitudes, the parts thus separated being set two or three inches apart in a sandy loam, with an eastern aspect. They should be protected from a too heavy drenching by rain or otherwise, and for this purpose a gentle, eastward slope is the best site. On the approach of regular frosty weather, they should be covered with a layer of leaves to about six inches in depth, protected by branches of trees from being blown away. When the weather is mild, this covering should be raked off for half a day, and restored before the approach of the night chill, a few times through the winter. Many are kept in garden frames, with only one inch of leaves.

As has been intimated, there are several varieties in cultivation, a favorite one being known as the Hen and Chickens (scientifically B. prolifera), because of a number of miniature flowers growing around and under the protection of the larger flower. Upon the whole, in the hot, dry climate of this country, the Daisy, in the estimation of some intelligent amateurs, is very unsatisfactory for outdoor cultivation.

DICENTRA.

SHOWY Dicentra, scientifically known as Dicentra spectabilis, has been with many other pretty plants imported within the last thirty or more years, by indefatigable collectors, from Japan and northern China, to enrich the Flora of Europe and America. It belongs to the Fumitory family, and is very hardy, being able to endure the frosts of the severest winters of our Northern States. It will, however, be grateful for a slight covering of leaves or other protection, and will repay its benefactor by a growth of greater vigor the ensuing season. Low, damp situations do not suit it, as it likes a dry, airy location, with plenty of room and a rich soil to grow in. It is a very fine ornamental plant when standing alone, and, like rare exceptions in the human family, it assumes a milder and more mellow beauty with advancing years. The long racemes of heart-shaped flowers—hence the popular name of Bleeding Heart—curving away from the center of the plant give it a peculiarly attractive appearance, while the leaves, resembling some varieties of the Fern family, coöperate to enhance its beauty. Fading early, care should be taken to plant it where the vigorous and abundant foliage of other plants will gracefully cover up its disappearance.

To grow in pots for winter use it is best to cut off a few shoots from the old root in early fall; which, being properly cared for, will gratify the owner by its few but pretty racemes in the early spring. It is best propagated in all cases from divisions of the roots; though it may, but with no slight difficulty, be raised from either seeds or cuttings. The Dicentra has a somewhat peculiar history, having for many years after its introduction been considered a plant exclusively adapted to hothouse culture, and its hardy properties having been discovered merely by the accident of being left out all winter in the flower garden at Cantrell Hall, the seat of the Childers, near Doncaster, England.

DRACÆNA.

COMMONLY called Burning Bush, from the bright-red leaves of some of the varieties, the Dracæna has long been in cultivation, and is very generally admired as one of the most conspicuous of the Liliaceous family. The gum of commerce, called dragon's blood, is a product of this and some allied plants, being obtained by incision of the stems. The characteristic attraction of these plants consists in the graceful habit and enduring properties of their leafage. The Dracæna draco and other varieties are elegant indoor plants, alone or in groups. The palm-like stem, with surmounting tuft, cannot fail to attract attention; while the bright, transparent radiance of the leaves will delight the most indifferent beholder. It is much used for hanging baskets and vases, and when partially shaded among green foliage it is rarely eclipsed by the most brilliant of Flora's gems. Content to grow in almost any soil, it thrives much better in one that is largely composed of peat or bog-earth. Much water is acceptable, and during the season of growth is readily appropriated by this thirsty plant, which also revels in a warm atmosphere. It is usually propagated by florists from sections of the root, as already described under Bouvardia and elsewhere. It may, however, be rooted from small off-shoots that grow on the side of the stem; and also from seeds, but this last method is rarely followed.

ECHEVERIA.

BELONGING to the class of plants known as Houseleeks, which are often carefully grown on the roofs of cottages and stables by many of the peasantry of Europe, under a superstitious belief that they afford protection from lightning and other calamities, the Echeverias are a very ornamental, thick, flesh-leaved tribe of cultivated plants. They are in demand for ornamental plants in houses, on rockwork and on high, sandy ground; as also sometimes for low edgings of beds and walks. Some of them look not unlike old, rusty iron; others have bluish-green leaves; and one variety, called the E. rotundifolia, or round-leaved, makes an elegant vase plant to surmount a pillar or parlor-stand. Being of the very easiest culture, almost anyone can cultivate them in nearly every condition of soil or climate; but an excess of water in cold weather will prove fatal. Some of the species flourish through the winter, sending out spike-like racemes, two or three feet in length, of a very waxy, flesh-colored appearance, which remain a long time on the stems. Other low-growing species have bright yellow flowers, after the manner of the Mossy Sedum or Wall-Pepper. They luxuriate in a loose, sandy soil, containing some leaf-mold, and though not dependent on a rigid regularity in the water supply, they should not be entirely neglected during the growing season. Side-shoots, or even the flower-stems, can be made the means of propagation, being set in clean sand and sparingly watered until rooted.

ERYTHRINA.

RUDDY is the meaning of the botanic name, derived from the Greek, and the plant belongs to the widely-extended Pulse family, having, in common with most of the allied genera, a butterfly-shaped flower. There are several thousand species of the Pulse family — nine thousand, some one has computed — scattered throughout the world, and for the most part they are of the highest utility in the animal economy of the universe. Containing a relatively large proportion of nitrogenous and bone building material, they are extensively used everywhere as food for man and beast, but nowhere as much used by human beings as would be for their well-being. The elegant Erythrina, sometimes called Coral Plant, ought to have a place in every outdoor collection; it is a fine object standing alone in a lawn or garden, its long racemes (often not less than two feet) of thick, waxy, coral-like buds and flowers making its splendors conspicuous at a very considerable distance. The large, trifid leaves and general robust habit of the plant also add their attractions. As a window plant it is a fine ornament, but requires more root-room than can ordinarily be allowed it. A rich, black or yellow loam well stirred up is the best soil for this plant, though it will grow in almost any kind of earth. In the summer months the growing plants must have a fair supply of water; and be taken up before or soon after the first slight frost. If allowed to endure the early frost, they should be previously protected by four or five inches of extra soil around the roots. During the winter they may be kept in any dry cellar, protected from frost, but not wholly deprived of moisture; a covering of moss or damp sand around the dormant roots will meet this requirement. Early in summer, say in May, they may be set out for the season, care being taken to protect them in the colder latitudes from the later frosts, when they will bloom from June to October. They can be propagated from cuttings of small shoots or raised from the seed; but those who want large plants soon will find it most convenient to buy them already in an advanced condition from the florists. Good, large, specimen plants of the E. crista-galli, which is the favorite species, are commonly sold at a very moderate price.

FITTONIA.

FITTONIA is a very ornamental plant of the Bottle-brush tribe, a subdivision of the Myrtle family, and is largely utilized for hanging-baskets, ferneries and Wardian cases, where the atmosphere is moist and still. It can, however, be grown as a single specimen, in a separate pot or among other plants, indoors where any extra shade is provided; but the Wardian case or glass shade seems to be its especial delight. The fine white or purplish-red streaks of the leaves make them an attractive ornamental plant. They require great care in cultivation, and should never be subjected to drafts, hot or cold. A very good soil for them is about equal parts of chopped sphagnum, or bog-moss, peat-earth, potsherds and charcoal, well mixed.

Natives of the bogs or quagmires of the tropics, they require a large amount of heat, as well as moisture, all the year round; they cannot be grown where the atmosphere falls below sixty. In favorable circumstances the Fittonia will spread itself freely, but it can easily be controlled by the usual method of pinching or cutting out when it encroaches where it is not wanted. This plant mixed with some of the Lycopodiums, especially the Selaginellas, constitute very pretty parlor ornaments under glass shades, and will require very little water if the glass is left on, as what they evaporate, being held within the case, condenses and is again absorbed. During the hot weather, however, they should receive an occasional sprinkling or syringing with tepid soft water. In cold weather, when there is risk of the temperature going below sixty degrees, they should be wrapped in paper, flannel, a shawl, or whatever is most convenient. Their worth and beauty will compensate for the extra care they require; but careless amateurs cannot well succeed with these delicate exotics. There are three species, all desirable, in general cultivation.

FUCHSIA.

SWINGING bells and neat, glossy foliage mark the Fuchsia, which has for many years formed one of the most attractive of plants for both greenhouse and parlor culture. Dryness of the atmosphere, one great cause of failure, can be obviated by sprinkling in the summer, and a vessel of water on the stove in winter. Buds drop from several causes, the fault above mentioned being one, and from the two extremes of keeping the roots either too dry or too wet. In summer, when in bloom, it would be advisable to water the plants twice a day if the pot is pretty full of roots and the shrub of fair size. This should be thoroughly done, but on no account should the plant be allowed to stand in a saucer of water. This advice presupposes an open soil and free drainage. After the flowering is over, water should be given more sparingly — about twice a week — as growth at this season (except in the winter-flowering varieties) should not be encouraged. They can be wintered in any common cellar, free from frost. Among the best varieties for indoor blooming in winter are the F. speciosa, the F. serratifolia multiflora and the Rose of Castile. For outdoor blooming they require a partially shaded situation, under trees or arbors or in the vicinity of other bushes; though when planted they will bloom in a sunny place also, but not so well.

Fuchsias are propagated from slips, and when required for large plants should be kept continually growing, shifting into the next size larger pots as soon as the roots touch the sides, until they reach the largest size, when they should be transplanted into boxes or tubs, where they may be left for many years, giving them an annual top-dressing of cow-manure, and frequent applications of liquid manure during the season of growth. They can also be grown from the seed, sometimes giving new varieties. The rule for soil is one part each of loam, leaf-mold and cow-manure; but for a fine specimen plant it should be at least one-half cow-manure.

FUNKIA.

GREAT numbers of people know this species of the Liliaceous family under the more common title of the Day Lily, though it is easily distinguishable from the Hemerocallis, or common Day Lily, both in the leaf and flower. The leaves of the Funkia are obovate, while those of the Hemerocallis are a broadish linear; the flowers of the latter are a light yellow, and those of the Funkia a bluish white, and somewhat smaller, with a tubular shape. Another difference easy to be observed is that the Funkia blooms from July to September, while the other is earlier. The botanic name, given in honor of a German botanist, has not quite universally replaced the older name in popular acceptance, and the delay has occasioned some little confusion in the minds of many amateurs. The Funkia, which is fast becoming recognized as the true Day Lily, is from China and Japan. Its finest species, the F. subcordata, or Japonica of the catalogues, the favorite old white Day Lily of the gardens, is a beautiful border plant and perfectly hardy. The fine heart-shaped leaves of the Funkia are always pretty from their first sprouting until they fall; and the plants are well adapted to fill an unsightly waste place, as their habit is so cosmopolitan that they will grow in any soil, though they are by no means indifferent to a rich one. The rich, pearly and very fragrant trumpet-shaped flower, which survives only for a day, but is promptly followed by its fellows, is a great favorite wherever known, and amply compensates for the little care it requires in cultivation. In hardy and cold-enduring properties the Funkias are excelled by but few plants, enduring the winters of even our northern latitudes without injury. Grown easily out of doors, under trees or in open beds, no collection should be considered complete without them. As house plants the smaller variegated sorts are much used, and under such favorable circumstances these often anticipate their season of flowering. For the embellishment of cemeteries, public parks and other places not receiving close attention, they have been found very acceptable, withstanding privation and neglect better than most cultivated plants. They are usually propagated from divisions of the roots, which grow in large masses, and are easily separated, either while the plant is dormant—that being the best time—or while in bloom. The method is the same as in the Dicentra.

GARDENIA.

HENCE sprang the error that confounds the Gardenia with the Cape Jasmine it is somewhat difficult to conjecture, as they resemble each other only in the odor they emit, and even belong to different families, the Gardenia being a Madder. They have been known in cultivation under this name (given them by Linnæus in honor of his correspondent and friend, Dr. Alexander Garden, of Charleston, South Carolina) at least one hundred and twenty years; how much longer under their former name it is difficult to say. It is a very fine, robust, ornamental shrub, with thickish, glossy leaves of an oblong or elliptical form; and produces large, loose masses of double flowers. The G. camelliflora has a large double flower not unlike a medium sized Camellia, hence the name of the species. All the Gardenias delight in a rich soil, composed, in equal parts, of leaf-mold, old cow-manure and good loam; and, except when dormant, in abundant moisture, which, however, should not be suffered to become stagnant. It is important, and even necessary to their well-being, that they be kept clean; and hence, if syringing be found insufficient, the sponge should be cautiously and gently applied, the hand supporting each leaf while it is being washed. They will give an abundance of white flowers during the winter when properly cared for and supplied with the necessary warmth, which should not be less than sixty-five degrees. In even the coldest sections of our country they can be put out of doors in the summer, and allowed to rest for one or two months, when, if desired, it can be started to grow again by the free application of water. It is propagated by cuttings of the young side-shoots, which should be treated in the usual way already mentioned under Abutilon;

but very rarely from seeds, as it is too slow a process, requiring three or four years to obtain a good specimen. They are easily cultivated as house plants, and are recommended to amateurs as choice beauties, well worthy of their attention.

GERANIUM.

THE Geranium in all its varieties is one of the most satisfactory among house-plants, being admirably adapted for either window, parlor, greenhouse or garden culture. They run through various shades of color. Of the reds, the deep or blood tints are much handsomer than the paler or orange reds, and the pink and white are both delicate and pure. The double ones do not drop their petals like the single ones, yet some of the single ones hold their own well, and bear very broad trusses. The single white are many times very fickle, scarce holding the first flower until the second unclasps, which is very provoking if a full cluster for a bouquet is desired. It is well to make this inquiry when purchasing plants, for where there is a difference the labor might as well be expended on those that will give the most lasting pleasure. We have one plant, a deep cherry color, that holds its blossoms nearly a month, with from thirty to forty florets in a truss. Geraniums are rather herbaceous in growth, their stems being a grayish green, and but slightly woody. When grown in the house during summer they should be given plenty of air to ripen their stalks, as they withstand the cold better. Those that blossomed in summer can be buried in a dry pit and covered with a foot of leaves, or kept in the cellar in an entirely dark place, free from frost, and require little or no water; We say entirely dark, as in a partial light they develop a useless, spindling growth. They can also be wintered at a window, if the space is not wanted for blooming other plants, the watering being governed by their needs. For future outdoor decoration large plants may be pulled up by the roots, the loose soil shaken off, the green wood and leaves trimmed back to the ripe wood, and the green cuts carefully powdered with charcoal and air-slacked lime, when the whole may be hung up in a dark place free from frost. In the spring the plants should be withdrawn from their retreat, trimmed back considerably, repotted if necessary, and given a little special attention, when they will very soon grow.

Geraniums are among the easiest plants to slip. They must have two joints at least, and three would be better, the cutting being just at the third. They are less apt to damp or rot off if laid aside for two or three days in the shade before planting, as by that time the broken end heals over, or forms a scar, which prevents the sap from escaping. They are then ready for planting. Many, however, put them down entirely fresh. Some kinds can also be started in wet sand, and set on the window-sill in the sun, in which case the sand must be kept always sopping wet, like mud, the slips being potted as soon as the roots are assured; but the fleshy, succulent varieties require less water. They can also be rooted in soil. For ourselves, not wanting many at a time, we stick them down in pots of our large plants, close to the side of the pot, where the slope of the crock gives them sufficient drainage, and the heat it draws from the air furnishes all the warmth required. When raised from seed, the long spur attached should be cut off, as it is likely to work the seed out of the ground.

Most of the Geraniums have strong-scented foliage, and are quite free from insects. The Rose Geranium, with its lemon-scented leaves, is, however, an exception, as the aphis or green-fly considers its green shoots a dainty bit. The Apple, Nutmeg and Pennyroyal Geraniums are grown for their fragrant leaves, and are well adapted for hanging-baskets, but are better for pot culture.

Geraniums require a rich, loamy soil. To have them bloom in winter, they must not be allowed to bloom during summer, and should be kept with a scanty supply of water. In early fall repot and trim back well, give more water, and occasionally liquid manure, and the branches will probably give flowers by December.

GLADIOLUS.

DESERVEDLY among the most popular of bulbous plants, the Gladiolus will always repay, by its abundance of flowers, for the care and attention bestowed upon it. In modern times it has been so extensively hybridized that the varieties now number several hundreds, and are in a fair way of being swelled to thousands. By this process, however, they have been made less hardy, and the new specimens require more careful handling than the old. All the varieties will grow in almost any soil, the richer earth, however, in every instance producing the better flowers. The spot selected should be enriched with good manure, which should be thoroughly incorporated with the soil. The bulbs should be planted three to six inches deep, according to size (bulblets only one inch), and four to six inches or more apart, and abundantly watered in dry weather. Supports should be furnished each plant, if in a windy situation, to keep the flower-stalks upright. However small the collection, it will be found most agreeable to have a number of varieties, as by this means a pleasing continuity in the times of blooming is most readily insured. Other plants may be grown in the same beds, provided they are a low-growing kind, as for instance the Mignonette; the shade or protection afforded by the leaves of such seems to be beneficial to the bulbs during the process of growth; and they also help to relieve the scarcity of foliage in the slim, gaunt Gladiolus. As window or house plants they are scarcely desirable, requiring too much root-room, and not possessing any compensating peculiarities of foliage or even of flower. They propagate themselves by forming new bulbs upon the older ones, and a number of bulblets under the new bulb. These bulblets should be planted in beds by themselves, as they have to be grown from two to four years before flowering. They should not be planted, however, until they have been kept eighteen months, as if started sooner very few of them will grow. The bulblets invariably produce the same variety as the parent. When the flower-stalks are dead, or after the first light frost, the bulbs should be lifted, and such as may be unripe allowed to dry in some airy place, when they may all be trimmed of the spent roots and leaves, and stored away where they will not mildew from moisture or suffer from frost. The Gladiolus is the finest cut flower in existence. The spike placed in a vase, after the first flower has expanded, will develop and open every bud, and grow more delicate and beautiful to the last.

HELIOTROPE.

AMONG the favorite plants for window culture, and one of the most desirable for the greenhouse, is the Heliotrope; and this on account of its clusters of vanilla-scented flowers, which are the various shades of lavender or purple, and are in great request for cut-flower decorations and bouquets. If we might be allowed the expression we should call it one of the most quick-tempered of plants, pouting and petulant, to be led coyly along as if not being led, or else given its own way, when it will grow gloriously. It is quite susceptible to a change of atmosphere. A plant brought from the greenhouse should be watched that it get not too dry in the soil, which will be when it looks very dry on the surface, or else the leaves will begin to turn yellow or brown, and in a few days will drop. We have sometimes turned the balls of earth out on our hand, and found the fine rootlets, that should be like white silk and full of life, one brown, decaying mass, rendered so by the withholden cup of water on the one hand, and on the other by the porousness of the pot, that had withdrawn what moisture they derived from the soil. All this dead substance should be picked off gently, and the plant replaced in the pot; when, with a little more attention, it will begin to grow again, having become accustomed to its surroundings.

When placed in the ground in summer the Heliotrope grows finely, but is very impatient of removal, as the lifting disturbs the roots too much. Those who wish a choice specimen saved should secure slips from it first, and get them rooted; then they will not be entirely helpless in case of failure in removing the plant. In taking up a large plant the following directions may be observed: Cut the roots all round the plant, so that the ball of soil will be a little less than the pot or box it is intended to grow in; let the cutting be done with a very sharp knife or spade, and after the cutting let the plant remain in the ground for six or eight days. When ready to transfer, lift the plant as gently as possible from the ground with something broad enough not to disturb the roots, and place it in the pot; put this in an entirely dark place for a few days, giving no water at first (as the soil should be in a condition not to require it), watching to see when it begins to revive, then gradually move it to the light and trim it back. The foliage will probably fall, but if successful it will start again.

The Heliotrope, to be a fine plant, should be allowed to grow large, and then it would be nearly always covered with flowers. A tub or box is the best place for this plant. For a window, one the size of a butter firkin answers. Indeed, a firkin itself could be used by washing it free from grease, and then soaking out the salt which it has absorbed from the brine. A few holes bored in the bottom would let out all the surplus water, and a coat of stone color, drab or white paint would make its exterior presentable. No one growing the Heliotrope only in small pots can know the pleasure of growing it as a large bush, and pruning it when too rampant. In summer a plant so grown could be placed out of doors to adorn the yard or lawn. The soil recommended is three parts loam, and one part each of leaf-mold, sand and manure. If kept constantly growing it blooms the whole year, its wood becoming quite hard and shrubby. Arrived at this condition, it can be kept for many years in a productive state, by an annual top-dressing, and liberal weekly supplies of liquid manure. It has been known to live for twenty years undisturbed in a sunny corner of a conservatory; it requires warmth in winter, as it cannot stand any frost. The pale varieties develop a larger growth of flowers and are more fragrant than the dark ones. A good way to propagate Heliotropes is to take two-inch cuttings of new shoots, pinching off the bottom leaf, when the slips are inserted in pans of sand and water, and kept abundantly moistened until they show new rootlets or begin to grow. This process is most successfully carried out in summer, or in a temperature of at least seventy degrees; if the heat rise above eighty or fall below fifty the slips will usually fail to strike root.

HIBISCUS.

UNDER this name are included many lovely species of the Mallow family, and all of them are general favorites with both amateur and professional culturists, for house or garden purposes. Their popularity is not of yesterday, but dates far back into the olden times, being known to Pliny (who recommended the Hibiscus for certain medicinal properties in healing ulcers), and bids fair to survive throughout all time. Apart from all useful qualities, medicinal or other, it commends itself for the large, rose-like and very showy flowers, sometimes four or five inches in diameter, which it produces in rather compact clusters on slender and graceful stems. The beautiful, brilliant red of the flowers make the plant conspicuous at a considerable distance, and cannot fail to attract the attention of the most casual beholder. The leaves, which are large, long and somewhat egg-shaped, but sharp-pointed, are always pretty, more especially the variegated kinds, as they hang gracefully drooping around the upright stems. It is familiarly called the Rose of China, but is really indigenous in several other countries, including the United States. Easy of cultivation, it can be kept in good shape by pinching, and its more compact growth will remunerate the cultivator. A soil composed of equal parts of leaf-mold, loam and manure is the best adapted for it; and, like the Abutilon, being a gross feeder, it should receive during the growing season an abundant supply of water and liquid manure. It is mainly propagated from cuttings of the young shoots, and but rarely from seeds. In the summer months it should be plunged, with or without its pot, in some spare bed or border, to take the necessary rest; though it can be made to grow and bloom all the year round by an extra allowance of stimulating liquid manure and free watering.

HOYA.

OF the Hoyas, or Wax-plants, there are three or four common species, all of them very beautiful. They are mostly woody vines of a scandent or climbing nature, with waxy, ovate leaves; and, though properly belonging to the hothouse, can be grown with the greatest ease as parlor plants, always with the understanding that warmth must be supplied in winter, and that they be kept free from frost. Of course, the blossoms must not be expected to appear as abundantly as when placed in a higher and moister temperature, but, should they utterly refuse to bloom, the beauty of the foliage would amply compensate for the little care they require. They can, however, be almost always made to bloom by withholding the usual water supply, and suffering them to become partially dry for several weeks. The flowers are most exquisitely beautiful, the clusters being composed of from fifteen to twenty florets arranged in the form of a simple umbel. Each floret is in the shape of a five-pointed star, with the points slightly recurved. The texture is like wax, with a rather plushy surface. The buds open always in the evening, and all at one time, as if by electricity, so sudden is the transition from bud to blossom. When plants are well established they grow freely and rapidly, if not neglected in the matter of a judicious application of water to leaf and root. One in our own collection (the Hoya carnosa), in a twelve-inch pot, makes each season vines about eight feet long, and blooms very freely in a common sitting-room with a southern aspect.

We would advise our readers, however, to secure good-sized plants in the first place, those with old flower stems or buds, if possible; for, though growing readily from slips, they are many times very perverse in starting runners, often remaining stationary for a provokingly long time. The flower or bud stems come from the axils of the leaves, generally at every alternate joint of the young growth, forming one year and blooming the next, and from that on, season after season, though sometimes skipping. Occasionally buds come from the old wood of the vines as well. These dark or woody flower-stems should never be cut off, as there is always a central or live tip for future bloom, and the apparent unsightliness is amply compensated for by their superior flowers.

The best soil is said to be three parts loam, two parts leaf-mold, and one part sand, with a little broken charcoal. It should be light and open, with good drainage. The repotting should be done in spring, just as soon as the plant begins to grow, and the plant thoroughly watered; after which water should be withheld a week or more until new roots begin to form. When in a large pot they need not be disturbed every year. In summer they should be watered when the earth is dry on the surface; in winter, once a week, or less often, will do. During the growing season the plant should have a watering of liquid manure, not very strong, once or twice a week.

In propagating, the slips should be laid aside a day or two, until the sap closes the wound. The cuttings should then be placed near the sides of the crock, and started, if possible, in a gentle heat. The leaves also answer as slips. The only insect we have seen on them is the *mealy bug*, which with a little care is easily kept under. In sitting rooms the foliage and stems will require washing occasionally to remove the dust.

Placing these plants out of doors retards or destroys the bloom, unless properly shaded, as the strong sun sears and turns the leaves yellow, from which they never recover; even in the house a thin shade is of service at midday if near the glass. We think, except in tropical climates, that they should not go out at all, as they can be given all the necessary air from open windows.

HYACINTH.

HYACINTHS are among the first plants to make their appearance out of doors in spring, and gladden the earth with their bright bloom. In preparing a bed or box for the bulbs, special care should be exercised, as their fleshy substance renders them an easy prey to disease, and subjects them to the attacks of rats, mice and other enemies. The best soil for them is a very sandy loam well mixed with good leaf-mold and old cow-manure. They should be set in rows, a few inches apart each way, and then covered three or four inches deep with the soil. A handful of sand placed under each bulb will help to prevent decay. The season of planting is from the middle of October to the same time in November. After they have ceased to bloom, and their leaves have decayed or died down to the surface, the bulbs should be taken up and placed in some shady spot to dry, when they should be stored away in an airy situation until again required for planting. These plants are also adapted to pot culture, and can be grown singly, or two or three of different colors, in a crock five or six inches wide. A piece of broken crockery or the like is placed over the hole for drainage; a little old cow-manure is laid thereon, and then the pot is filled, within an inch of the top, with the soil above indicated as best for Hyacinths. Finally the bulb is placed in the soil, with about one-half uncovered. The usual treatment for bulbous plants, as already given under Crocus, is then followed. Hyacinths can be grown in sand, and also in water. In sand they are placed in a proper receptacle and set away as above, the sand being kept merely moist. When the rootlets have got a good start, the leaves will begin to appear, showing that it is time to bring them forward to the light. In regular Hyacinth glasses there is generally a rim or shallow cup for the bulb to rest in. The glass is then filled with rainwater so as almost to touch the base of the bulb. The water should be kept pure by inserting a piece of charcoal and by being changed weekly. The glasses should be put away for about a month in some cool dark place, when they will have rooted sufficiently to be brought forward into the light to finish growth. The single-flowered varieties are the best for glass culture. Hyacinths that have flowered in pots or glasses are afterward fit only for planting in beds or borders. The Hollanders make a specialty of raising Hyacinth bulbs, and have produced and named two thousand distinct varieties, which they supply in immense quantities to the markets of the world. It may be imagined how gorgeous an appearance is often presented in the Netherlands by a twenty-acre lot, or more, wholly planted in Hyacinths; and the fragrance is said to have been noticed fifty miles at sea.

CULTURE OF FAVORITE PLANTS.

LIBONIA.

NEAT and modest in flower, and not without some claim to a subdued magnificence, this lovely member of the Figwort family is of comparatively recent introduction from Japan. The favorite species is denominated L. floribunda, from its free flowering habit, often almost hiding its foliage under the wealth of its blossoms. The color, which is most frequently an orange or pure yellow on the under side, but shading upward to a scarlet or deep, velvety crimson on the upper side of the flower, contrasts finely with the light green foliage of the plant. It is a slender-branched plant and of a tidy, compact growth; it can be formed into the resemblance of a ball encircling and entirely hiding the pot in which it grows, making it a very desirable house ornament. The soil in which it can be best grown would comprise, in about equal parts, sand, leaf-mold, loam and manure. The Libonia delights in plenty of pot-room, water and liquid manure in the growing and flowering season, but abhors stagnant moisture, and therefore should receive its supplies in limited but repeated quantities. It blooms from December to May, after which time it should be placed out of doors in some partially shaded situation. It is most frequently propagated from cuttings about an inch long taken from the young shoots. It can be raised from seed if sown early, and will flower the season following.

In those sections of our country where there is little or no frost, it makes a very fine ornamental plant for outdoor cultivation, either to stand alone or to be grown as a border plant. It is not quite hardy enough to withstand our northern winters, though it will bear considerable cold, and blooms well in about sixty degrees of heat. The beauty of the plant in flower, and the ease with which it may be cultivated, should render it a more general favorite than it has yet become.

LILY.

FOR outdoor culture these bulbs require a good, sandy loam, which should be dug to a depth say of eighteen inches, and well worked; the Japanese, Chinese, and a few other species do best in a clay loam. The bulbs ought to be set five or six inches deep and left undisturbed for several years, as they thrive much better and give more bloom. Stable manure, until thoroughly decayed, or any other fermenting material, is obnoxious to them, but leaf-mold or plenty of good, old cow-manure would be a wholesome enrichment. In removing, it is best to keep them out of the ground as short a time as possible; and if bulbs received from seedsmen are in a shriveled state, a wrapping of moss, or cotton slightly dampened, for two or three days before planting, would freshen them unless past redemption. Many of the choicer variety of Lilies are grown as house plants in cities by those who have no gardens. A good soil for their growth comprises equal parts of loam and peat, or leaf-mold, with which should be incorporated a small quantity of coarse, clean sand. The bulbs are placed a little below the surface of the soil, which should be pressed firmly around them. They are then stored in a cool, shady place where there is no wet, and only enough water given them to slightly moisten the earth until they begin to show growth, when they should receive a liberal supply. The stalks grow from two to three feet, and occasionally much higher, requiring to be propped up with stakes. When in bloom they thrive best in a dry, airy place, as they are liable to contract spots from dampness. After the growing season is over, the quantity of water must be diminished until the stalk dies down, when the bulb should be taken from the old earth and repotted directly in fresh soil, as they thus give finer bloom the next season. Several plants can be put in an extra-sized pot, but for a single bulb a six-inch one is the size.

LILY OF THE VALLEY.

MUCH esteemed for both beauty and fragrance, though in size but an insignificant plant, this lovely genus of the Lily family is extensively grown, more especially in the vicinity of all great cities, for bouquets, baskets, and all manner of ornamental purposes. So great is the demand that the Hollanders have built up an immense trade in the tubers, or rhizomas, which they grow with more success than any other nation, and ship by tens of thousands to all parts of the civilized world. They grow wild in the valleys of the Alleghenies and in the mountainous sections of our Southern States, as well as in similar localities throughout Great Britain and Ireland. But however abundant naturally, those used for cultivation are nearly all the product of the Haarlem beds, imported and sold by the seedsmen at a price so low that it does not pay to attempt the domestication of the wild ones. For house decoration the rhizomas should be planted in four or five-inch pots, in August, and the pots plunged to the rim in a cool, shady place, where they may be left until cold weather. Then they should be set in a shed or other convenient place, sheltered from the sun, and allowed to freeze hard. After all this, they are to be placed in a cool, dark room, where the temperature is above frost, from whence they may be brought forward, a few at a time, and at intervals during the winter, to insure a succession in flowering. For outdoor cultivation the tubers are usually planted in the fall, and covered to a depth of one or two inches, with an upper covering of fallen leaves of about the same depth. To exhibit their attractions to the best advantage, they should be planted in a shady situation; they will, however, grow more rapidly in the full blaze of the sun, but also perish more rapidly there. The soil best adapted to their growth comprises two parts in five of leaf-mold, one of good cow-manure, one of sand and one of loam. Outdoors they can be left to nature's supplies in the matter of watering, but indoors neither the roots nor even the leaves should be allowed to become entirely dry, much less to remain so for any length of time.

LINARIA.

LINARIA cymbalaria, or cymbal-like Toad-flax, is a low-trailing plant of the Figwort family, with Ivy-like leaves, much used for hanging baskets, rockwork and pot culture. It is commonly called Kenilworth Ivy, because of the great quantities to be found amid the ruins of the famous castle of that name near Warwick, England, immortalized by Sir Walter Scott. It is a very easy plant to cultivate, in or out of doors, as it will grow in almost any soil; though like all plants it has a preference, and will grow best in a light soil composed of about equal parts of leaf-mold, loam and sand, with a slight admixture of manure. But whatever the soil, it must have abundant moisture, and it will not disdain an occasional feast of liquid manure. It also delights in a moderate shade, which can easily be provided by planting it among taller-growing plants, in some shady recess, or on the north side of a house, fence or tree. As its free growing habit gives it a tendency to straggle, if space be limited it must of course be kept in place by frequent clippings or pegging back. It will also crowd out small plants if not kept within bounds, but with plenty of room it may be allowed free scope, under which conditions it presents a beautiful, compact mass of foliage, interspersed with numerous small, bluish flowers, not unlike those of the Snapdragon, to which it is related. It is easily propagated by divisions of the roots. Another species, known as the L. vulgaris, or familiarly as the Butter-and-Eggs, is well worthy of a nook in any garden, being hardy and easy of cultivation, and also quite pretty with its wealth of beautiful; yellow flowers. This has underground stems or rhizomas, and propagates itself by what may be termed natural layering, sending in various directions its offshoots, any one of which can be made the germ of a new plant.

MAHERNIA.

KNOWN to science as a member of the Sterculia family, which very closely resembles the Mallows in mucilaginous properties, the Mahernia is a pretty little shrub growing from eighteen to twenty-four inches in height. It is a native of the Cape of Good Hope, and with careful cultivation and a fair share of sunshine it will produce an abundance of sweet-scented, yellow, cup-like flowers during the whole winter and spring. The branches are slender and the leaves laciniate, or lightly slashed, and small, making a pretty mass of foliage if well kept in by pinching or tying back. It delights in a free exposure to the atmosphere, provided this is not excessively cold, and its favorite normal temperature would be somewhere from sixty to seventy degrees, though it will not suffer from the heat unless this ascend to the nineties. It should not, therefore, be crowded out or even shadowed by other plants, but be given plenty of room for roots and branches. The best soil for the Mahernia is, two parts of leaf-mold, one of common earth, one of cow-manure, and one of sand. Cold moisture is pernicious to its roots, as is lime-water also; pure rainwater, "little and often," is the best prescription, as the leaves of the plant will curl up and become sickly if overdosed. It strikes root easily through small cuttings, say an inch long, from young shoots, bedded in clean sand about half their length, the leaves being carefully removed from the embedded part. After they have ceased flowering in the house they should be removed in the spring, for their season of rest, to the north of a fence or some low evergreen, as in that condition they delight in a partial shade. The species generally recommended to amateur culturists is the M. odorata, which is the most sweetly scented, as its name implies; but there are several other varieties also well worthy of attention. The Hector has orange, and the Diana pink, flowers; and both are pretty, highly ornamental and easily manageable shrubs, which will give good satisfaction, though not so fragrant as the M. odorata.

OLEANDER.

GREATLY admired for the beauty of its bloom, this plant is scientifically termed Nerium, from the Greek *neros*, humid, because of its love of moisture. The familiar name Oleander is a corruption, as is generally supposed, of the word Rhododendron, or Rose-tree, from the similarity between its flowers and the smaller Roses. It enjoys a very peculiar protection apparently against the sun's rays, in a triple coat of mail or three-fold epidermis, which is common to but very few other plants. A native of the Levant, it is found on the banks of the sacred Jordan, as well as along other water-courses and muddy bottom-lands, where there is a considerable accumulation of decayed vegetable matter. This, by the usual rule of making artificial conditions approach as nearly as may be to natural surroundings, suggests the value of peat-earth, leaf-mold, turfy loam or similar soils for their successful cultivation. Water in abundance, and unstinted supplies of liquid manure, as a substitute for the wet and decaying vegetable wreck to which they are naturally accustomed, are also implied, and experimentally ascertained, to be necessary to their fullest development. In early summer they should be moved outdoors in northern latitudes, and placed in some bed or border made up of the compost indicated, and freely manured, when they will bloom abundantly, and better reward the cultivator than if kept after the usual old-fashioned method in tubs or boxes. Toward the close of summer, in order to ripen the wood of the Oleanders, the supply of water should be considerably curtailed, but not so as to allow the soil to go entirely dust-dry. Great care should be taken in this respect, as these plants are slow to show injury, on account of the extra epidermis, and therefore nothing should be left to chance. Oleanders are propagated freely from slips or cuttings in the usual way, or by cuttings thrust into bottles or other convenient vessels containing weak soapsuds or even common rainwater. In making these cuttings, which ought to be from two to four inches long, the adhering leaves should be shortened or cut back one-half. Layering can also be used, though it is not found so convenient; and they can of course be raised from the seed, flowering the second season.

PANSY.

VIOLA tricolor, from the triple color of the blossoms, is the scientific name of the Pansy, which itself seems to have been derived from the French *pensée*, a thought, from its habit of hanging its head as if in a pensive or thoughtful attitude. They are among our earliest spring flowers, and are sometimes forced in hotbeds for market long before the grass makes its appearance. They are sold in pots to decorate window boxes, but in the house they do well only for a short time, as their juicy leaves soon become feasting fields for the green-fly, which is very hard to subdue on these dwarf plants. To be at all successful they must have all the air that can be admitted, and not too much sun. To propagate from seed for spring blooming, they should be sown late in August or early in September; for midsummer and fall blooming, they should be sown in spring. To produce large flowers they require a rich soil and a partially shaded situation where they will escape the noonday heat and receive a few hours of the morning or afternoon rays. They may be increased or propagated by cuttings, layers, or divisions of the root. Cuttings are taken about the second spring or fall month. These are much better than the older plants, which are usually woody and hollow, and are best rooted in light, sandy soil in a shady place, being covered with a bell-glass or oiled paper. They should be set an inch or more deep, with the earth firmly placed around them. The varieties are numerous, amounting to several hundred. Seeds should be sown soon after gathering, as they deteriorate in keeping. Layering is done as described elsewhere.

PELARGONIUM.

PELARGONIUMS (from the Greek *pelargos*, a stork, because of the resemblance of the beaked seed to a stork's bill) are plants allied to the Geraniums, constituting a genus of that family and embracing three hundred species, and are occasionally called Fancy Geraniums, of which one of the most popular is known as the Lady Washington. All the Pelargoniums are shrubby or hard-wooded, except the shoots that bear the blossoms. The flowers, which appear in trusses, are variously marked, either darkly veined, or with the upper petals differing from the lower, or shaded from a deep tone to a lighter, as from almost black to scarlet, and so on through cherry, crimson, lilac, white and pink. They are among our handsomest, most delicate and showy flowers. So singularly picturesque are the markings in different varieties of the Pelargoniums that they have been named Clown, Pantaloon and Harlequin, the flowers resembling the typical costumes of these well-known, popular characters. They never thrive so well when placed in the garden, except when retained in the pots in which they are grown, and plunged in the ground; for, if the roots get too much room, the plant grows almost entirely to foliage.

The Pelargoniums are natives of the Cape of Good Hope, and, like other floral importations from that region, are almost hardy enough to endure our severe northern winters. Though they are easy of cultivation, it is better to secure good, tree-like plants, with thick and stout young shoots. After the flowering season is over, ripen the young wood by withholding the water supply; and in the fall prune back to the ripe wood, leaving only two or three eyes to each branch, always preserving the symmetry of the bush. At a window they need turning, as do all plants, to keep them from being one-sided. They should be repotted once or more, according to circumstances, every season in very rich earth, and given larger pots as the plants increase; and the larger and more bushy they are, the better and the more flowers they have. They are most acceptable for groupings and combinations of all kinds, the richness and variety of coloring lending them a peculiar attractiveness as house and conservatory plants, furnishing material for bouquets that cannot be surpassed in richness and beauty. Though, like so many other favorite flowers, they have probably passed beyond their period of greatest popularity, they can never fail entirely to be cherished by the lovers of choice plants.

The method of propagation is to take side-shoots about three joints in length, the bottom joint being fully ripened, and cut clean and smooth underneath, while a portion of each leaf should also be trimmed off. They can be wintered in a cellar, the roots being kept nearly dry.

PEPEROMIA.

SUPERB among the Reseda family for the beautiful markings of the leaves, together with its magnificent habit of growth, the Peperomia is worthy of a place in every collection, whether within doors or out. It delights to grow in a still, warm atmosphere with abundance of moisture, as in a Wardian case, or in some shady nook of the house or garden. There are several varieties that have attained a well-deserved popularity as ornamental plants because of their foliage. They are natives of Brazil, and require semi-tropical surroundings, or a heat of at least sixty-five degrees. A compost made of two parts peat, or bog-earth, one of loam and one of sand, mixed with bits of charcoal or potsherds, forms a congenial soil for their growth. The Peperomias are low-trailing plants, spreading out laterally and striking fresh roots at each joint of their side-shoots. They can easily be propagated by cuttings of these shoots, as they are already provided with rootlets. Combined with Selaginellas, they produce a nice effect by the contrast of their broad, ovate leaves with the narrow, pinnate leaves of the other, an effect which is much enhanced by their peculiar markings. In some these consist of beautiful, grayish-white streaks along the lines of the nerves; in others these streaks are of a reddish tint; while in a few the streaks are replaced by silvery blotches of irregular shapes. These plants should always be watered with tepid rainwater, and by sprinkling or syringing only, and never by pouring, as they insist upon a faithful imitation of the natural process.

CULTURE OF FAVORITE PLANTS.

PETUNIA.

EASILY cultivated from seed, the Petunias are half-hardy perennial plants, blooming the first season, and therefore usually grown as summer annuals. They run through many shades and markings, being mottled, striped, clouded, feathered and in plain colors. The seeds are very small, and should be sown on the surface and rubbed in with the hand or be lightly covered. After the plants are up, they should be thinned out liberally, as each individual plant becomes quite large, and blooms the better for having plenty of room. If the tip of the main branch is taken off, the side branches will be more numerous, thereby giving a more liberal supply of flowers. The double ones are more often grown from cuttings or slips than from seeds. The seeds of double flowers in these plants are obtained by fructifying the pistils with the pollen from a single or semi-double flower; occasionally, however, this process will yield single flowering plants. Petunias are grown in windows and conservatories as well as gardens, especially the double varieties. A good soil for their growth may be made up of equal parts of loam, leaf-mold, good manure and sand. Petunias seed freely, and are largely self-propagating; but a few of the superior hybrids are liable to prove defective in this respect; and, to insure success in raising these fancy kinds, the simplest and best method is to invest a small amount in the seeds raised by some specialist. They will appear early in spring, but all the sooner if the beds be cleared of old flower-stems and other rubbish. A few Petunia plants will in a short time cover an area of several square yards, and therefore furnish a cheap and easy way of floral ornamentation. In thinning out, the strongest specimens should of course be retained, and left not less than six inches apart. They bloom in the open air, in even northern latitudes, from June to frost; and in warmer climes, or raised in hotbeds or under cold-frames, the season of bloom is proportionably prolonged, being virtually all the year round.

PHLOX.

BRILLIANT red or flame color, is the significance of the scientific name of this genus of plants, which belongs to the Polemonium family. The Phlox is a native American plant of many species, all of them pretty, but perhaps none so desirable in every respect as the P. Drummondii, so named in honor of the distinguished Scottish collector, Drummond, who discovered it in Texas, in 1835. Much transformed and improved by cultivation, it has been reintroduced into its native America, and is yearly becoming more popular, one well-known florist cultivating from five to ten acres every year with this plant alone. There are several varieties, and the number is yearly increasing, with flowers varying in color from the deepest crimson to the purest white; and the colored petals are symmetrically arranged around a common center, which itself invariably differs in color from them. The various markings make these flowers to rank with the most beautiful treasures of the floral kingdom, while they are by no means deficient in fragrance.

As a low-spreading plant, the P. Drummondii is no contemptible rival to the far-famed and longer-known Verbena. It even possesses some attractions that give it a decided advantage over that popular flower; for instance, it is less subject to insects and not so dependent on moisture, though it is by no means indifferent to attention in this respect. As a plant for bedding out in large or small quantities, it can scarcely be surpassed, as it blooms early and continuously through the whole summer and fall until frost. In large masses it makes the most brilliant and at the same time the most delicate of flower-beds, while the ease with which it may be cultivated should make it everybody's flower.

For early blooming it is best to sow the seed in a shallow box only two or three inches deep, placed where the seedlings can have some protection from the occasional inclemency of the weather in early spring. It is, however, hardy, and accommodating enough to dispense with such attentions, absolutely requiring only to have its seed sown in any garden soil, but the less attention the later the flowers. It will propagate itself freely by scattering its own seed when fully ripe. To collect the seed of the P. Drummondii, it is necessary to gather the pods when a little more than half ripe, or when they have begun to turn a yellowish brown. They should then be spread out for four or five days in some dry, airy place, to complete the ripening process. Where they are allowed to sow themselves, the ground should not be disturbed in spring, requiring only to be raked free of rubbish and overlaid with a mixture of half common earth and half manure, to the depth of about an inch. This will save considerable trouble in the matter of digging, but will be attended by some extra labor in thinning out. For those, however, who wish to make the most of the Phloxes, the best method is to sow the seed, as already recommended, every year, and dig the soil, where they are to bloom, to a spade's depth, enriching it at the same time with the best manure at hand. As house plants they are not desirable, as they show best in open beds or borders.

PHYSIANTHUS.

DENOMINATED Physianthus from two Greek words signifying nature-flower, it is difficult to determine in what respect this plant is more entitled to that name than a hundred others. The species most in cultivation is denominated P. albicans, from the Latin *albico*, I make white, because of its abundance of white flowers. It belongs to the Nightshade family, and is much grown as a house ornament. The white flowers, which are about an inch in diameter, grow in thick clusters in all the axils, and emit a pleasant fragrance. They are much used on public occasions, as at births, marriages and funerals, in baptismal bouquets, bridal wreaths, and mortuary chaplets. The Physianthus is a good climber, covering a window-frame in a short time, yielding itself to the owner's wishes, and readily assuming such shape as may be desired. Outdoors in warm latitudes the plants bloom freely throughout the summer, growing into large bushes with moderate care. They delight in a rich soil composed of one part cow-manure, one loam, one leaf-mold and one sand. They also delight in abundance of water during warm weather, and plenty of room for the great masses of roots which they form. They are most usually propagated by slips of young wood, but not infrequently by layering. This layering is of course peculiar, as these are pot plants in northern latitudes, and the process is thus: Shoots from the parent plant should be pegged down, near to a joint, in an adjoining pot full of the proper soil, but in which nothing is growing; a little damp moss, or, wanting this, a little cotton-batting kept moist and placed over the joint, will hasten the operation of rooting. They require but little rest, and will take it indifferently at any season; their accommodating habit should not, however, deprive them of due attention in this respect, as they will be all the better for one or two months' rest. They will not flourish in less than fifty-five degrees, and frost will entirely kill them. As they are liable to be infested by mealy bugs and scales, they should be syringed at least once a day in the growing season.

PRIMROSE.

THE Primroses are very attractive flowers in all the varieties, but those most frequent in amateur indoor cultivation are of the species distinguished as the Chinese. These bloom most freely during the latter part of winter and through the spring, and even often into the summer. The leaves are soft and downy, sometimes nearly round, and in other plants so deeply dentate as to be called fern-leaved. The flowers are like delicate porcelain, and appear in upright clusters, each being circular, with a plain or fringed margin. The colors are white, rose, and varying shades through to crimson, with a greenish-yellow eye in the center. They can be grown from the side-shoots (used as cuttings or slips), which, when low down on the plant, start the rudiments of roots even before removal. The great trouble is that they are apt to damp off or decay at the base before rooting. The following method we have found successful. We take the cutting as soon as severed and dust the end with powdered charcoal; we then press it against the soil, taking care not to embed it too deeply, and often prop it to keep it upright; the next process is to cover it with a bell-glass or other glass shade, which is tilted slightly so as to admit fresh air. We administer a spoonful of water about every two days. These Primrose cuttings require a moist, still atmosphere when taking root, but should they show signs of damping off, or becoming sickly, which is evidenced by the leaves becoming yellow, a little dry sand, charcoal or brickdust supplied around the base will help them. They do not thrive if too damp, as a softness or rot attacks the stalk, a fine plant often looking quite healthy at the top when it is gone past redemption just above the root. The leaves, when torn and faded, should be broken off only halfway up the stem, as otherwise the disease mentioned is sometimes produced. They should be kept in a shady situation, and not watered much in summer, as that is their dormant season. When the central stalk becomes bare of leaves, the plant may be turned out of its pot and some of the lower earth removed, the plant replaced and more soil added on the surface. When grown from seeds, these should be sown on a soil of leaf-mold and manure, the surface being rather rough; a paper is then to be tied over the pot or box, and this paper only to be kept dampened. They begin to germinate in about three weeks. When they have developed two or three of their downy leaves, they may be given small pots to themselves, being transferred to larger ones as they grow. For fall blooming they should be sown in March or April; for later flowering, during midsummer. It is better to carefully sow the seeds some distance apart, so that in transplanting each can have soil around its root.

ROSE.

BEYOND all cavil, the Rose is entitled to the preëminence it has ever held as Queen of Flowers. The purity of her blossoms, the exquisite texture of the satin or velvet petals, with their rich hues and delicate tints, the half-pouting buds just untying their green ribbons, the perpetual incense that arises from their opening lips, charm and enchant us, subdue and conquer us, and we become most humble servitors at her throne. There are two grand divisions of Roses recognized by florists and amateurs, known as the Summer and the Perpetual Roses. The former bloom once in summer, whence the name; and under this class are included what are familiarly called June Roses, June Moss Roses and June Climbers, all of which, together with sundry allied varieties, are hardy and easy of culture. The second division are the Perpetual or Remontant Roses, under which are included Bengal, China, Tea-scented, Bourbon, and Noisette Roses. All of these flower several times in the season, and should be well trimmed back wherever they make a weak, spindling growth; the strong, healthy shoots may also with advantage be cut back one-fifth of their length.

According to their habit of growth, Roses may be described as Climbers, Half-climbers, Intermediates and Dwarfs; and these are found in each division of the Rose family. The Climbers throw out long main branches, well supplied with shorter side branches that produce the flowers, in which respect they are different from the others only in the matter of length; the Half-climbers, roughly estimating, reach about one-half, the Intermediates one-fourth, and the Dwarfs one-eighth, as high as the Climbers.

The planting of roses requires special care, and should be trusted to no slovenly hand. They will grow in any ordinary soil, but the richer it is, the finer will be the bushes and the more prolific the blossoms. The place where the plants are to be grown should be dug to the depth of a foot and a half or more, the soil turned to one side, and a good layer of broken brick, stone or coarse gravel placed in the bottom, overtopped by sods with the grassy side turned downward, to secure drainage, where such precaution is necessary; for while the rose likes plenty of water during its growing season, it much dislikes to have its roots standing in a pool, which soon shows its effects on foliage and flower. Good garden loam should be mixed with well rotted manure until thoroughly incorporated, when the compound should be placed on top of the drainage ready for receiving the plant, the roots of which should be firmly embedded by pressing the earth about them. If the soil is very light, it will be necessary to add clay or strong clay-loam to render it more retentive of moisture. A liberal dressing of marl or blue-clay benefits all Roses. The first few rain storms should be carefully watched to see if the soil settles, as it doubtless will do somewhat into the rubbish placed for drainage, and where it does, the shrinkage should be made good by adding more loam. Top-dressing every year, and the application of liquid manure about twice a week, during summer, are beneficial.

It is only by rich feeding that the so-called Perpetual Roses will bloom more than once a season in this our dry climate. These varieties should be pruned twice a year—once in June, and again late in the fall; yet of course the pruning depends somewhat on the latitude in which they are grown. The old wood should be kept well cut out at all times, especially in house roses. Pruning in spring hastens the starting of the buds, and should not be done too early, as a sudden frost would at once destroy all prospect of bloom.

Large trees absorb a great deal of nourishment from the soil, and consequently roses should not be planted too close to them if perfection is expected. They like fresh soil very much, and it frequently benefits pot Roses to wash the soil from their roots, giving them a new supply; but not when budded and blooming, as of course they should not be then disturbed. Roses demand deep, rich soil and plenty of sun and air, to keep them free from disease. If Roses are budded or grafted on other roots than their own, as for instance the brier, or strong-growing wild ones, all canes coming up from the roots should be destroyed as soon as they are observed, as they would absorb much of the nutriment necessary to the well-being of the fairer plant.

The Climbers and Half-climbers are generally propagated by layers, and the other sorts by cuttings. These cuttings should have three or four joints of half-ripened wood, and may be made to strike root in some shady corner outdoors during summer. The Tea and China Roses, which are the most usually cultivated as house-plants, strike root well if placed along the sides of pots where other plants are growing, as in such situations they enjoy the required shade and heat. The blind shoots, that is, such as produce no flowers, are the best for cuttings in all kinds of Rose plants, as they root well and send forth strong, vigorous flower-bearing stems. If cultivated outside, the Summer Roses can be planted in spring or autumn. In extreme latitudes the plants should be drawn together and bound with straw or matting, and the climbers be laid on the ground and covered with sod, sand or manure. When laying down for winter protection, a few handfuls of soot thrown in among the shoots or on the crown is an excellent preventive against the destructiveness of rats and mice. The small Tea Roses are the ones most frequently found in window culture. The success in cultivation is varied, the heat of dry rooms making them likely to be devoured by insects unless considerable care is exercised. They suffer much if their roots become dry, and die outright if kept too wet. A good way to avoid either extreme is, in potting to put some broken potsherds or charcoal in the bottom, filling in around the roots with rich soil; then place the pot into one a couple of sizes larger, and fill the space between with moss or cotton-batting. This intermediate padding should be kept always damp, thus affording the necessary moisture without excess.

SAXIFRAGE.

AMONG the rather extensive family of Saxifrages, perhaps the most commonly cultivated as a house plant is the S. sarmentosa, popularly known as the Beefsteak Saxifrage, and sometimes as the Strawberry Geranium. Originally introduced from China or Japan, its hardy character adapts it to all places and all conditions of the atmosphere above the freezing point. Its leaves are very nearly heart-shaped, or approaching the kidney shape; and are thickish, slightly hairy, of a bright green on the upper surface, and a flesh or purplish-red color underneath, not unlike the Begonias. The leaves resemble a small inverted saucer in shape and size, and are often variegated along the edges, or reticulated throughout with peculiar salmon-colored markings, mixed with a yellowish-white. One of the varieties derives its distinguishing name from this feature, being called tricolor. Most varieties of the Saxifrage are liable to run back, as florists say, to the condition of the primitive plant, a plain green on the upper surface of the leaves. It is much cultivated as a parlor ornament in a hanging-basket in combination with others, or grown by itself as a specimen plant, sending over the sides long strings of stems and leaves, which can be easily trained to completely cover the pot. The method of propagation is ordinarily by the little tufts or bunches of miniature plants that grow upon the strings or runners, or upon the sides of the old plant. These will strike root readily in any damp soil or sand, and indeed are often provided with rootlets before being separated from a parent plant. They can also be raised from seeds. These plants require an abundance of moisture, and a temperature of not less than sixty degrees. They can be easily kept green all the year round, if thought desirable, by giving them water and a shady situation in a good, rich soil, although they will accommodate themselves to a very poor one.

SCILLA.

OHIO and the States west and south thereof produce a species of indigenous Scilla scientifically known as the S. Fraseri, and popularly as Wild Hyacinth. The Scilla is a member of the Liliaceous family, and has been long noted for its medicinal properties under the familiar product of syrup of squills, which, however, is chiefly produced from the allied genus, Urginea Scilla. As an indoor or outdoor plant there are few bulbs that give more satisfaction in proportion to the care and time bestowed. For a small plant it is highly ornamental, and is much used for edgings of boxes or stands in parlors, or beds and borders outdoors, being very hardy and requiring little or no protection. Its pretty racemes of fine azure-blue flowers, half an inch to an inch in diameter, are very attractive, as they form a good contrast with the surrounding foliage. Among the earliest of plants to bloom outdoors, they gladden their owners at the first disappearance of frost, being often seen piercing through the late-lying snow. They like a good, rich soil, but will not disdain to grow in even a poor one, though of course with some prejudice to the strength and beauty of leaf and flower. The more moisture the better, provided only that it be not stagnant. In outdoor growth they may be left undisturbed for years; and such annuals as Mignonettes, Petunias and the like, may be sown in the same beds while the Scillas are having their season of rest throughout the whole summer. They are self-propagating by the outgrowth of their tubers, or by their ripened seeds, if the soil be not too much disturbed; and can of course be propagated by the cultivator in the same way. The effect of a mass of their flowers blooming in the early spring amidst the belated snow is picturesquely beautiful; they will bloom all the earlier for having been planted in some quiet, sheltered nook. The bulbs can be taken up and cared for as in the Crocus, but it is really of no advantage, as they will take care of themselves and do better if left undisturbed.

SEDUM.

COMMONLY known by the name of Wall-pepper, or Pepper-moss, the Sedum acre is a low-growing, thick-leaved plant of the Orpine family. The Sedum Sieboldii is another species of a higher growth, brought from Japan by the eminent traveler and Japanese explorer, Dr. P. F. Von Siebold. Both are favorite rock plants, and extensively cultivated in windows as well as for rock work, being of a hardy habit and requiring but little care. The S. acre is much used for edgings or borders, and withstands the frost of even our northern latitudes. Spreading broadly along the ground, and rising to a height of from one to two inches, it resembles a carpeting of moss, but surpasses these plants in bearing a very considerable number of bright-yellow flowers during the season of bloom. Some rocky, barren districts in Europe are rendered quite picturesque by the large masses of the Sedum that grow in the fissures and on the ledges. The S. Sieboldii is a prettier as well as a larger plant than the S. acre, and its peculiar growth in pot culture renders it a more universal favorite. Its stems gracefully droop over the edge of the pot to a length of from nine to fifteen inches, sending out a cluster of three roundish leaves at intervals about an inch apart along the whole length, and producing a terminal cluster of greenish-white flowers to each stem. There are some varieties with very prettily variegated leaves, and some with the leaves almost entirely white and having a purplish fringe along the outer edge. Being thick and fleshy, they present an appearance of wax leaves. Any sandy soil will grow the Sedums well, and they require no manure, liquid or otherwise. The S. Sieboldii will be the better for a season of rest for two or three months; and can be propagated from cuttings of about two inches in length, after the manner of the Cactus; while the S. acre is generally best propagated by divisions of the old plant. A later and more hardy variety is the S. macrophyllum, or large-leaved, which is rapidly rising into favor. Being easy of cultivation, and generally of a variegated foliage, it commends itself as a special favorite for indoor or outdoor ornamentation.

SELAGINELLA.

WOLF'S FOOT is the significance of the name Lycopodium, the scientific title of the family to which this genus Selaginella belongs. The family is commonly called Club Moss, and this genus West-India Moss, the finest specimens having been imported into Europe from those regions. Though scientifically ranked with the Mosses, they are in reality a sort of intervening group or connecting link between the Mosses and the Ferns. Many of the species rise to no inconsiderable height and look much more like Ferns than mosses; ranging all the way from an inch to two feet. The S. densa, which is among the low-growing species, forms a dense mass of minute Fern-like foliage resembling a thickly-wooded forest in miniature. There are at least twenty species in common indoor cultivation, and easy to be procured from the florists. The chief use made of the Selaginellas is in Wardian cases, or as forming a pleasant topping for hanging-baskets, boxes and the like. They delight in abundant moisture and a high temperature, and will grow well in a common sitting-room in some shady nook, where the atmosphere is generally still and moist. They are propagated by cuttings or divisions, but more easily by the latter method. One part chopped moss, one peat-earth, and one sandy loam, with a few pieces of charcoal, will form an excellent compost for their growth. They are easily kept green all the year round by a little extra attention in the matter of watering.

SMILAX.

RARELY has any climbing vine taken such hold of the popular heart for decorative purposes as has this delicate, twining, bright-leaved beauty. Thousands of yards are used every year for decorations on all occasions, both joyous and sad. It is a native of the Cape of Good Hope, and constitutes an independent order of plants nearly allied to the Lilies. The root is formed by numerous tubers united in a crown, from which the vines spring. A fertile sandy soil is the best adapted for its culture, and while in an active or growing state it should have a copious supply of water, which might be occasionally interchanged with liquid manure. The vine itself resembles a fine cord following a zig-zag course like a shallow herring-bone stitch, at each angle or joint of which there is a glossy leaf of oval shape, with veins running lengthwise, the effect of which is to give it a rather unique appearance. After it has started, small twine must be supplied for a support, except it be left to fall as it pleases. The flowers, which in this plant are a secondary consideration, are a greenish-white, and fragrant. The vines are used in making floral arches in the house, or in the garden in a sheltered nook, for forming festoons and wreathing around baskets. They are propagated by division of the roots and from seeds. For parlor culture it is best to secure good, healthy plants that are just about to start into leaf; as, if too far advanced in growth when removed, they are very liable to suffer from the change of situation unless in the hands of some one thoroughly skilled in their management. They are much helped by a daily syringing of the leaves, or, if inaccessible, the free use of a feather duster is a partial substitute. When raising the Smilax from the seed, the amateur must wait at least two years for his plant, though skilled cultivators have developed it in one year. The time for planting is in October, though greenhouse-men manage to keep two sets — one for summer and one for winter growth, planting a second time in midwinter. It does not require a very sunny place, and when at rest should have but little water until the vines begin to start. It needs frequent syringings to repel the red spider, its most formidable and destructive enemy.

STEPHANOTIS.

MADAGASCAR is the native home of the Stephanotis floribunda, a lovely plant of the Milkweed family. It is called Stephanotis from two Greek words denoting crown and ear, because of the resemblance in the shape of the anther, the crown of the stamen, to the human ear; and floribunda, from the wealth of its bloom. Most of the Milkweed family are not climbers, but the Stephanotis, the Hoya and some others, are exceptions. The flowers are from one to two inches long, with a waxen, pearly appearance, and grow in clusters around the stems of the axils, and being also very fragrant and of rather a handsome shape, they are of course much used for bouquets and floral decorations. The leaves are thick, fleshy and waxy, with a dark-green midrib, and are themselves a source of much beauty. The Stephanotis, though commonly ranked with hothouse plants, is easily cultivated in a parlor, and will flourish well throughout the winter if kept clean, supplied with liquid manure and tepid rainwater, and kept in an atmosphere not less than sixty-five degrees. About the beginning of summer it should be moved outdoors and placed, with or without its pot, in some partially-shaded bed or border, to enjoy a needed rest, and be moved back late in August or early in September to where it is designed to bloom. It can be propagated from leaves in the manner described under Hoyas, the stem end being inserted in sand to the depth of about half an inch. The plants of this genus are subject to scales and what are called cotton-bugs, which should be wiped off with a sponge in open places, and rubbed off with a half-worn tooth brush in the axils; but the regular syringing will ordinarily prevent their appearance. Although natives of a hot climate, they are liable to be scorched by intense heat through glass, and hence should be withdrawn from the glare of the sun. Perhaps, because being by nature clingers to something larger than themselves, a protecting shadow has become indispensable. The soil used is common peat earth, with a slight admixture of manure and sand to insure the necessary freedom from stagnant moisture.

TRITOMA.

FIRE-POKER plant is the familiar name of what is scientifically known as the Tritoma uvaria. Tritoma signifies thrice-cut, in the original Greek, and is supposed to represent the three sharp edges of the leaf, namely, the two margins and the keel; and uvaria, from the Latin, denotes the not very close resemblance of its raceme of flowers to a bunch of grapes. At a distance, the spike-like raceme looks more like a red-hot poker (whence its very expressive nickname), and, with its supporting stalk rises to a height of from two to four feet, nearly one-half being covered with the bloom. The flowers at their first appearance are a bright red, and change through all the shades of that color down to a light yellow, in which they continue the best part of the season. They are conspicuous at quite a distance, and never fail to attract attention by their peculiar manner of growth; near at hand they are no less striking by the offensiveness of their smell. The leaves, unlike those of most of the other Liliaceous plants, are narrow and grass-like, looking very much like a large tuft of dark-green pampas-grass; but they make up in numbers for what they lack in width. The Tritomas are often set out as ornamental plants in landscapes, lawns and gardens; but are scarcely ever introduced into the parlor or displayed in the window. This is another of those Cape of Good Hope bulbs that contribute so largely to the diversification of our Flora; and by its hardy habit is easily cared for even in our colder northern latitudes. Placed in a box, with a slight covering of earth to protect the roots, and an equally light covering of hay or straw for the head, it will survive any ordinary winter in a common cellar; and can be again planted early in spring as soon as all danger of the heavier frosts has disappeared. The Tritoma will flourish with the same soil and treatment as other Liliaceous plants; and may be propagated in the manner described under the head "Lily."

TROPÆOLUM.

NASTURTIUM, from the Latin, meaning nose-twisted, is perhaps a more significant name for this genus of plants than the one given it in science. It was probably intended to express by that word the pungent odor; while the scientific name Tropæolum, from the Greek *tropæon*, a trophy, seems to have no special application, unless it be because of the shield-like shape of the leaves; and perhaps an observable, though not very striking, resemblance between the flower and an inverted helmet. In ancient Greece, trophies raised on the field of battle were composed largely of captured shields and helmets. It is nicknamed Indian Cress on account of its sharp, pungent taste and its occasional use as a salad. The beauty of the flowers and leaves make it an excellent adornment for fences and rock work, while the fresh leaves may be used as a table vegetable, possessing marked anti-scorbutic properties. The T. Lobbianum, so called after Mr.

Lobb, a distinguished English collector, and the T. peregrinum, named from its rambling propensities, are perhaps the choicest and most popular species for conservatory, parlor or window culture. In greenhouses they are grown abundantly, being trained along the rafters, where their brilliant blossoms illuminate the whole house, giving an abundant supply of floral gems for bouquets and decorative purposes. The Tom Thumb or dwarf bushy species are perhaps the best for hanging-baskets. The varieties in color are quite numerous, and the velvety texture of the flowers is charming, while the odor somewhat resembles the aromatic Cinnamon. When grown in quantities the seeds are gathered for pickles, and are used the same as capers. There are several very delicate tuberous varieties, differing in blossom from the ordinary kind, and only retaining their foliage a part of the year. They are adapted to pot culture, and bloom during April and May, afterward requiring plenty of sun or heat to ripen the roots; as the vines begin to die away, water should be gradually withheld. The pots should be turned on their sides, and kept dry until autumn, when they begin to start vines again. Among the choice species are the Tropæolum azureum, with an azure-colored flower; T. Jarrattii, yellow and scarlet, blooming abundantly; T. speciosum, scarlet; T. tricolorum, scarlet, yellow and black; and several others. All the Tropæolums, to grow well, must have plenty of moisture, a soil rather poor than otherwise, and frequent sprinklings to keep off the red spider.

TUBEROSE.

UNDER this name is included a genus of herbaceous plants not at all allied to the Roses, as is often supposed merely because of the identity of the final syllable. The name really springs from the tuberous character of the roots; and the scientific name, Polianthus, is also rather confusing, as it lacks distinctive expression, meaning 'City-flower.' It belongs to the Amaryllis family, and is chiefly cultivated for its fragrant flowers, which are of a pale sulphury-white color. The tubers of this odoriferous plant may be kept dormant for a long time in any dry, airy, cool place, but must be protected from frost. For early blooming they can be planted from January to March indoors; for later growth, at any time until June. Whenever the tubers show signs of growth, they should be planted at once in pot, box or bed where they are to bloom. Of course it will be necessary in winter to give them shelter in conservatory, greenhouse or elsewhere, with plenty of warmth and light. Neither as tuber or plant can they be touched by frost with impunity. In planting, as in all similar cases, the small tubers are best taken off and set in separate places. These will bloom in about two years if not neglected. A rich, loamy soil having been provided, a few pieces of broken crockery are placed over the hole of a six-inch pot, with the addition of a little moss if at hand, and the earth filled in to within about half an inch of the top, so as to cover the tuber about two thirds of its own length. When all danger of frost is over, they can be turned out of their pots into the border, or with them placed in the soil, to be brought into the house later if desired, when in bloom.

When the stalks begin to run up, stakes or rods should be driven into the ground near them, and the plants secured against the wind. In or out of doors they require an average heat of about sixty degrees, and should therefore be housed early enough not to be touched with frost. In their season of rest the temperature may be reduced to forty, but they are all the better for fifty degrees of heat and no stagnant moisture. Being evergreen in the native state, it is conjectured by some that the Tuberose could be sufficiently rested without allowing its leaves to die; and some florists have them in flower nearly all the year round.

TULIP.

GREAT favorites in former times, when their cultivation fairly amounted to a mania, the Tulips have enjoyed the distinction of having immense sums freely spent in the endeavor to procure some new variety. Those times, already far in the past, will return to them no more; yet they will never entirely lose their popularity, as their gorgeous blossoms brighten the earth simultaneously with the Hyacinth and Crocus, or about as soon as the grasses begin to clothe her in a mantle of green. Tulips are grown abroad much more than in this country, though they are as easy of culture here as there. There are special exhibitions of Tulips held in many countries of Europe every year, which circumstance naturally gives a great impetus to their cultivation, and is itself a survival of the old mania. They construct canvas tents for their Tulip beds, which they hasten to throw up on the approach of every storm, and in many ways manifest a special concern about this favored plant. These show-flowers are known under the names of Bazaar, Flamed, Feathered and Self-colored Tulips. The latter are often watched for years, if well marked, to note their transformation into one of the other divisions. If the event transpires favorably, and a remarkably unique specimen is produced, it is seldom sold for less than one hundred dollars.

Tulips will grow in almost any soil unless there is too much moisture. The bulbs should be planted about six inches apart and covered up to the depth of four inches. The best season for planting is in October. As a protection against severe frost, a layer of leaves about six inches deep, with a foot of stable manure added, will be effective. This covering should of course be removed early in spring. In planting, the usual underlying handful of sand will be found, as a protection against rot, as serviceable to Tulip bulbs as to any others. After the flowers and leaves have died down, the bulbs should be taken up and stored away in some place not subject to damp. There are principally three species in cultivation, viz.: the Dutch, or Van Thol, the Oriental, and the Parrot. To secure a pleasing continuity of flowers, the readiest method is to set bulbs of each of these. The Van Thols bloom in March and April, the Parrots later, and the Orientals last, terminating with June. The Van Thols or Dwarf Tulips are usually planted for window or greenhouse culture; the others are not so well adapted to such purposes.

CULTURE OF FAVORITE PLANTS.

VERBENA.

VERBENA is a flower to which we are perhaps more indebted for the gaiety of our gardens than to any other; and is a simple, procumbent plant from Buenos Ayres. For large beds nothing can equal it, as with judicious training a few plants can be made to cover considerable surface. The beds appear to the best advantage when cut directly in the lawn or grass, as the surrounding green heightens the effect of the brilliant colors by the strong contrast. Although the Verbena will grow in almost any soil, to thrive well it should have that most congenial to it, which is about two parts loam, the same quantity of leaf-mold or manure, and one part good sand. Having secured plants of such colors as will harmonize well, let there be made a cavity the size of the pot they are in, the ball be placed within it, and the soil pressed close around, the plants being arranged two feet apart each way. The branches are then to be laid entirely flat to the ground, and pinned down, so that they will root at the joints, for which purpose broom-splints doubled, forked sticks, or, what would be still better, the common wire hairpin, could be used, this treatment to be continued as long as the branches extend themselves. It would be an advantage to pinch off the early buds until the plants are well established, the future bloom being sufficient compensation. Watering freely at first, secures good leafage, which affords much protection in case of drouth. Seedlings, although they can be started in the open air with ease, give earlier bloom if sown in a box in the house or hotbed.

These plants are also most excellent for window boxes and verandas having a sunny exposure. In pot culture, for success, they must be kept in a growing state continually to insure health and thrift. Cuttings make better plants than the old ones, and should comprise about three joints of the young growth. They can be rooted in wet sand, and even in water; in either case they should be potted as soon as rooting is assured.

VIOLET.

LARGELY used for bouquets and floral decorations, Violets, as distinguished from the favorite species called Pansy (already spoken of), are generally cultivated in four or five varieties, such as the Neapolitan or Italian, the English, the Russian, etc., and are highly valued by florists for winter decorations. For window culture they are best grown in a box, though with extra attention in the way of water and cleanliness they will grow well in pots. They all require a rich, sandy loam, and a shady situation. In moist climates they are much used in borders or for the edgings of walks. The flowers are small and simple, and not at all to be compared with the Pansy, though they have a very fine odor of their own, which makes them very acceptable in the absence of that transcendent favorite.

In the early summer the plants, which grow in bunches, should be set out, about a foot apart, in some quiet, sheltered place, the weeds and grass kept well subdued, and a liberal supply of water given when required. It will be of great advantage to mulch them with leaf-mold, sawdust or manure, according to circumstances, filling up the interstices between the plants, and completely covering the soil to the depth of two or three inches. As soon as frost makes its appearance, frames should be set over the beds and covered with glazed sashes, and in cold latitudes these frames should be banked with stable manure. In extremely cold weather the sashes will require to be covered with mats or shutters, which should be made close-fitting and weatherproof. Thus protected, they will bloom early in spring, otherwise the flowers will come later, or not at all. The extra labor and expense will be recompensed by the earlier flowering of these plants; and the frames, sashes, mats and shutters can be used for many other less hardy plants after having done service for the Violets. In warm climates these precautions are of course unnecessary, as there they will bloom all the year round if desired. Indoors, the flowers begin to appear in autumn, and continue to bloom through the winter and spring.

WEIGELA.

HANDSOME, hardy and accommodating, the Weigela, so called in honor of the German botanist, Weigel, is a desirable shrub of the Bignonia family. The original species, introduced from China, was designated W. rosea, because of its rose-colored flowers. It is one of the prettiest of the shrubs that have, through the zeal of collectors within the last fifty years, been made to enrich the Flora of Europe and America. The large, trumpet-shaped flowers, appearing generally in pairs at the axils on almost every stem, add much to the beauty of the plants, while the foliage admirably supports by its density and abundance the graceful effect. One new variety, called the W. variegata, will often have some leaves entirely white, others green, and still others mixed, all in the same plant. Another variety, the W. amabilis, will flower from May to October, surpassing the variegata and rosea, whose blooming is confined to the earlier months, May and June; it also is superior to them in size of leaf. Small specimens of any of the Weigelas may be grown in the parlor, and being hardier than most house plants, are easily taken care of. They should have a season of rest, by withholding water, for one or two months in the early fall, to ripen their wood before being transferred to the house for winter blooming. The same course can be adopted to advantage with those which are to be left out all winter, for if watered freely to the close of the season, the frost would find many green shoots, through which it would seriously damage the whole plant. Being hearty feeders, they luxuriate in abundance of rich, liquid manure during the flowering season, in or out of doors; and the soil in which they grow can scarcely be made too rich. During hot, dry weather, they demand a free use of the watering pot. They can be best propagated by layering or side-shoots; by cuttings, also, if taken while the shoots are fresh and green, but these require to be carefully watered and protected from the winds.

Neglected Beauties.

MECHANICAL imitation of our predecessors in the choice and culture of favorite plants, for the most part borrowed from abroad, is not worthy of our age or country. Powers of independent observation should be cultivated by amateur culturists, as nothing contributes so much to their enjoyment as what they discover for themselves. More especially is this applicable to the study of indigenous plants, so frequently neglected by persons who pride themselves upon their knowledge of the common exotics. Every climate is especially adapted to the growth of certain kinds of plants, which propagate themselves naturally in their proper habitat, with little or no effort or labor on the part of the cultivator. A knowledge of these circumstances will render easy the covering up of blemishes in the landscape, or unsightly patches in a yard, lawn or garden. It is a fact not creditable to our exercise of independent judgment or natural taste, that very many of the native American wild flowers find a cordial welcome in the gardens of the European aristocracy, while denied the smallest attention in their own home, republican America. This is entirely wrong, as many desolate-looking homesteads could be made quite cheerful by the presence of these neglected beauties. With very little trouble, expense or attention, these wild flowers could in many instances be made to rival or eclipse the imported favorites. Many species of wild native shrubs and plants are being pushed out of existence by the agricultural needs or heedless unconcern of our advancing civilization, and like their human antitypes and cotemporaries, the Indians, bid fair to be entirely overwhelmed and rooted out, before many generations, if not rescued by timely interference. Possessing an indigenous Flora of great intrinsic beauty, no specimen that survives former neglect should be allowed to perish by the more enlightened flower-lovers of today. Nor should this work of preservation be left to directors of botanical gardens, professional florists and enterprising seedsmen; but all lovers of their country who cherish a friendly interest for plants should labor in this neglected vineyard, assured of a pleasant, if not an enriching, reward. Wild flowers are nature's jewels in emerald settings.

CHOICE NATIVE WILD FLOWERS.

Among the most widely-spread and attractive of native wild flowers are the following, selected from an almost innumerable multitude of like beauties.

Anemone nemorosa, or Wind-flower of the Woods, is a pretty, low-growing plant, adapted to any shady border or neglected corner in a garden, or where most other plants will refuse to grow. It is an early bloomer, shooting up its pinkish-white flower before the frost is fairly out of the ground. There are six species of the Anemone indigenous to the United States, and some imported ones are also cultivated. (See A. coronaria, p. 18.)

Uvularia, or Bellwort, is one of the prettiest of the native Lilies, and blooms about as early as the Anemone. It comprises four well-known species, viz.: U. grandiflora, U. perfoliata, U. sessiliflora and U. flava, any of which is worthy of a place in the choicest indoor or outdoor collection.

Erythronium, or Dogtooth Violet—which, by the way, is not a Violet, but a Lily—is also a very pretty low-growing wild flower, which blooms about the same time as the foregoing; it has blotched leaves, and its lily-like flowers gracefully droop and recurve their petals, as in the Fuchsia, but in open sunlight become wheel-shaped. There are four species of this plant which are indigenous in our American woods, all pretty, and destined to become general favorites for parlor or garden, as they already are in Europe.

Dodecatheon Meadia, or Shooting Star—sometimes called the American Cowslip, and not unfrequently in Illinois the Prairie Pointer—is one of our neglected prairie-flowers worthy of a better fate. Flowering quite early, and needing but a damp place in any common soil in or out of doors, it fully equals the Cyclamen in the color, form and fragrance of its blossoms.

Tradescantia Virginica, or Spiderwort, is already described (p. 281), to which may be added that it will flourish with little attention, in any soil, in or out of doors, requiring only plenty of sunlight and water.

Coreopsis, or Tickseed, already described (p. 94), is as easily grown as any of the foregoing wild flowers, but requires plenty of room to develop its best specimens.

Asclepias tuberosa, or Butterfly Weed—sometimes called Pleurisy Root—is a very fine ornamental plant that grows wild on most sandy or gravely soils throughout the country, awaiting the notice of floriculturists. In a few instances it has been transferred to gardens with good effect, and will no doubt one day be extensively cultivated in and out of doors, as its perennial roots, besides its native attractiveness, will specially recommend it.

Cassia Chamæcrista, literally signifying Dwarf-crested Cassia, is familiarly called Partridge Pea, because of an alleged partiality of the partridge for its seed. When not in flower it so closely resembles the Mimosa, or Sensitive Plant, as to be sometimes mistaken for it; and as it evinces a degree of sensitiveness, by closing on the approach of rain or night, this mistake is not inexcusable. But they are essentially different, as the Cassia has a very bright, showy, large, yellow flower, while the flower of the Mimosa is very insignificant. The Cassia has already been introduced into the seedsmen's catalogues, and is of course forevermore rescued from oblivion. It is adapted to indoor or outdoor purposes, and those who have experimented with it prefer to raise the seedlings under glass.

Liatris, or Blazing Star of our western prairies, is a very fine, showy plant for outdoor cultivation. There are at least ten species indigenous to the United States, all of them pretty, desirable, and easily cultivated. Their bright, purple-red flower-spikes constitute their chief attraction.

Gentiana crinita, or Fringed Gentian, so graphically described by our great American poet, William Cullen Bryant, is deserving of all the effort and expense that may be necessary to introduce it into cultivation. It now grows naturally in moist, sandy places, and those who seek to cultivate it should endeavor to prepare similar surroundings. There is quite a number of other species of the Gentian, all of them hardy, interesting and worthy of attention. Many of these will undoubtedly prove to be very acceptable house plants, as well as garden ornaments, at no very distant day.

Asters, or Starworts, are a numerous family of extremely pretty plants, there being no less than sixty native American species, all of which are very admirable for the abundance and beauty of their flowers.

Sometimes a single plant will attract great attention on account of the dense masses of flowers with which it is covered. The most common and perhaps the most desirable species are the A. multiflorus, just alluded to, generally abounding in white flowers; the A. grandiflorus, where the flowers are somewhat larger and usually purple, with a yellow eye; and the A. cyaneus, with lanceolate leaves and large blue flowers; this last is perhaps the handsomest of all the Asters. It is clear that these plants may be easily cultivated here in their native habitat, when so many have been cultivated in Europe as exotics. They will grow in any soil, providing it is artificially or naturally kept moist. Some species grow too large for indoor culture, but the smallest plants of the A. multiflora would certainly prove very delightful house plants, as their mild fragrance, abundant bloom, and comparative indifference to attention could not fail to give satisfaction.

The wild plants here selected will constitute a nice collection in themselves, and have been chosen because of their general excellence, and also because they will supply a continuous bloom, in about the order in which they have been named, from early spring until early frost. But time and space would fail us to enumerate half the beautiful wild plants that adorn our woods, prairies, mountain slopes and shaded valleys, and the little that has been said is rather by way of suggestion than elaborate treatment.

CLIMBING PLANTS.

FOR house decoration nothing is finer than a good climber, and the number of varieties that can be grown around a window frame or doorway, over a mantelpiece, or to entwine a picture, is so great that it is difficult to make a choice. And even in our northern latitudes anybody who is rich enough to afford a fire during the night may indulge in a choice climbing plant. The investment of a few cents in such seeds will furnish, with little care, a beautiful framework of foliage and flowers for a whole winter. The wealthy may indulge in an endless variety of pretty climbers, native and exotic, but every one may have one or more of the native kinds, which scarcely fall behind the more expensive imported beauties. Some are cultivated for the richness and abundance of their foliage, which is, moreover, in a few varieties, remarkably variegated; others for their curiously-shaped flowers — like a bell, finger, or trumpet — which are also often strikingly marked in various colors.

There is a pleasure in daily watching a plant climb, creep, or twine itself around the things near it. The rapid growth of many of them is truly wonderful, some making no less than six inches in a single day. The seeming intelligence with which they appear to feel and reach out for supports is one of the most striking phenomena of plant life. The adjusted proportion with which they push out a flower here and a bunch of leaves there, is truly artistic, being carried on under the guidance of that greatest of all artists, Mother Nature.

The whole collection here loosely designated Climbing Plants, may more properly be divided into Climbing, Twining, Creeping and Trailing Plants, from each of which classes a few choice examples are subjoined.

CLIMBERS.

Climbers proper are such as send out coiled tendrils, an inch or more in length, by which they lay hold of either projection or crevice, to sustain themselves as they climb. They, however, sometimes dispense with these tendrils when a natural support for the main stems has been already attained; as, for instance, when a long shoot has reached the summit of a house, tree, or other horizontal or nearly horizontal surface. Among them the most deservedly popular are perhaps the following:

Passiflora Fordii. Ford's Passion-flower, so called in honor of a celebrated English florist of that name, is one of the prettiest and every way most desirable of the true climbers, being larger than the older type, P. cœrulea (p. 233), and more easily cultivated. It is preëminently a parlor plant, surpassing anything of the kind that has been introduced for years; it will, however, like most climbers, do well outdoors from early summer until frost. The very remarkable shape and appearance of the blossom, from which the generic name Passion-flower is derived, is still more conspicuously beautiful and well-marked in this variety, which has most probably been hybridized from the old P. cœrulea and the later P. trifasciata.

Clematis virginiana. The common Wild Virgin's Bower is known scientifically by this name, and it is among the finest of outdoor climbers, being well adapted to conceal unsightly objects in a lawn, yard or garden. (See "Deformities Concealed," page 333.) It is covered with large clusters of white flowers in July and August, which are followed by a crop of the large, plumose, grayish tufts that envelop the seeds, making the plant appear as if short wool-clippings had been spread all over it, thus constituting a very singular object in a collection.

Clematis Sieboldii, originating in Japan and introduced thence by the well-known traveler whose name it bears, has very large blossoms of an azure-blue color, not unlike those of the Passion-flower. It is a rapid grower, and flowers constantly indoors, and, in tropical climates, out of doors.

Clematis Jackmanni, so called from a florist of that name, is a hybrid from the C. Sieboldii and some other species of Clematis. It has a very large flower of a purplish-blue color, often five or six inches in width. The flowers have unusually long foot-stalks; hence they stand away from the stems and leaves, giving the plant quite a graceful and unique appearance.

Clematis John Gould Veitch, or "Double Blue Clematis," is perhaps the climax of beauty and grace in the Clematis tribe. The flowers are not only double and of a fine azure-blue, but they last longer than the others, often remaining for several weeks; and a well-grown plant sometimes gives the appearance of a string of blue balls, reaching from the base to the summit.

There are perhaps not less than forty other species or varieties of the beautiful Clematises, all in cultivation, which may be procured from any first-class florist.

Cobœa scandens, or Climbing Cobœa, is an extremely handsome climbing plant, with large, pinnate leaves, producing a dark-purple flower not unlike that of the Foxglove in shape, and blooms all summer out of doors. Indoors it will bloom throughout the winter. There is a variegated sort which has the added attraction of varying colors in the leafage, sometimes the leaflets on one leaf-stalk being entirely white, while those on the next will be the usual green.

Eccremocarpus scaber, literally Rough Hanging-fruit, is a very beautiful climber; its leaves resemble some of the Ferns or the Meadow Rue, and it has a flower which is a dull red on the top and a light yellow at the bottom. The plant grows rapidly in a warm atmosphere, in or out of doors.

Cucurbitaceæ, or Gourd Family, comprise many beautiful climbers (see Lagenaria vulgaris, p. 147; Echinocystis lobata, p. 333). They are highly ornamental both in fruit and foliage, and admirably adapted to hiding unsightly places.

TWINERS.

Under this term are included such plants as do not shoot out tendrils like the climbers proper, but wind or twine their stems or leaves around supports as they mount upward.

Ipomœa, or Morning Glory, is perhaps the best known of twining plants, and is entirely worthy of its great popularity. Its habit of growth is very peculiar: At first it sends forth two curiously-shaped seed-leaves, quite different from the aftergrowth. Between these two leaves springs a shoot with a small, heart-shaped leaf, which grows to a relatively large size; for when first noticed it is like a pin's head, and in a few days it reaches a diameter of three or four inches. The shoot mounts higher, throwing these broad leaves to either side, and twines around any projection that offers, as if gifted with intelligence. In time a trumpet-shaped flower appears at the axil, opening most generally in early morning, whence its common name; and, perishing before night, is not infrequently replaced by other flowers, sometimes to the number of eight or ten, continuously, on the same axil.

Quamoclit vulgaris, or Cypress Vine, is already described, page 171.

Calystegia sepium, or Bracted Bindweed of the Hedges, is a twining plant often found by the road-sides of our country, east and south of the Mississippi, and is a very fine plant, well adapted to house culture. A double variety of it is much used by the florists for hanging-baskets and for training into window-frames in or out of doors. The roots being perennial, it can be kept from year to year undisturbed in the same place, to yield its annual wealth of leaves and flowers as a cheap embellishment to our homes. The ease with which it may be secured, as well as cultivated, should not be allowed to depreciate its value in the estimation of lovers of flowers. Should the vine at any time become unsightly, the whole may be pruned down to the ground, when it will make a new, healthy start, if in a warm atmosphere and duly refreshed alternately with liquid manure and water.

Boussingaultia baselloides, or Madeira Vine. This is another cheap and easily procurable twiner, requiring but little care in the development of its beauties. It will grow thirty feet long, and spread laterally as much more, in one season, under favorable circumstances. As the plants grow larger they need more root-room, and therefore require not infrequently to be transferred to larger pots several times in a season. It will do no harm to begin with a larger pot than they need, provided that the soil is not too much watered.

Mikania scandens, or Parlor Ivy (perhaps more familiarly known as German Ivy), is a rapid-growing substitute for the slower and more valuable English Ivy, this rapidity of leafing constituting its principal recommendation.

Lonicera, or Honeysuckle, of which there are several highly-prized species in cultivation, is a well and favorably known genus of twining plants. The most popular species is perhaps the L. sempervirens or Trumpet Honeysuckle. It flowers all the season out of doors, and makes a good parlor plant when rightly cared for, blooming all the year round in skillful hands, whence it is called *sempervirens*, always green or flourishing. It is unnecessary to describe or even to name the different species or varieties of the Honeysuckle; they are all pretty and desirable twiners, easily procured and as easily cultivated, and most of them are very hardy.

Celastrus scandens, or Climbing Bittersweet, is a native twiner with beautiful, glossy leaves, and waxy, red berries which hang on the plant until late in the fall, and often through the winter.

Aristolochia sipho, or Dutchman's Pipe, is already described on page 35.

Lathyrus odoratus, or Sweet Pea, is another old favorite because of its abundant butterfly-shaped flowers, and the sweet fragrance (whence its specific name), which may be replaced but not surpassed by new claimants for popular esteem. The different varieties have differently-colored flowers, and from a single seed-packet one may sometimes have half a dozen variations in color.

Maurandia, in three choice varieties, mostly with a pale-purple or bluish flower, is an acceptable, low-growing twiner, adapted to hanging-baskets and window-screens.

Thunbergia, also in three varieties, somewhat resembles the Morning Glory, but the tube of the corolla is closer, and the flower is more flattened on the top, resembling a miniature table. The color is orange, yellow or white, with a black eye in the center of each flower. They are very subject to Red Spider, and therefore not desirable for house plants.

Menispermum Canadense, or Canadian Moonseed, is among the favorite twiners, but is not so generally known among amateur culturists as it deserves to be. The small, yellow flowers grow in drupes in the axils, and the fruit, which is a small, dark berry, grows in a thyrsus, resembling a bunch of grapes. Another species, the M. palmatum, is much grown in Mozambique and other parts of the east for its commercial value, yielding the well-known tonic and antiseptic drug, calumba. The M. Canadense possesses the same properties, but in an inferior degree. It is, however, grown in this country mainly for its ornamental flowers, fruit and leaf.

Wistaria Sinensis, or Chinese Wistaria, is a rapid-growing twiner of superb appearance in leaf and flower. The flowers come in long racemes like the Lupine inverted, but larger and more waxy in texture, while in color they resemble the Lilac, which, however, they surpass in the delicate tintings, often progressing through the various shades from a deep blue to a pearly white. There are many varieties of the Wistaria, but none superior to the W. Sinensis. Their size forbids their adoption as indoor plants unless in large conservatories.

Phaseolus multiflorus, or Scarlet Runner — sometimes called Spanish Bean — though most frequently cultivated as a vegetable, for the pod and the inclosed bean, is not to be despised as an ornamental indoor or outdoor twiner. It sends out long racemes of bright scarlet, butterfly-shaped flowers, which, contrasting with the green foliage around, produces a very pleasing effect. Many people grow it because of its artistic beauties, elevating it from the kitchen garden to the parlor window.

Adlumia cirrhosa, or Fringed Adlumia, is one of the most beautiful and hardy of twining plants. It climbs by its leafstalks, which serve the purpose of tendrils, and grows to a height of ten or twelve feet in a season. The flowers come in delicate flesh-colored panicles, and succeed each other all summer.

Jasminum officinale, or White Jasmine, is already described, page 175.

Humulus lupulus, or common Hop, page 162.

Periploca Græca, (literally Greek twiner), or Silk Vine, is a hardy, ornamental twiner, common throughout our northern States and worthy of attention.

CREEPERS.

This class of plants is distinguished by the property of clinging by the rootlet-like shoots, or sucker-like attachments, which it sends out at convenient distances, for catching hold of the wall or other surface or support along which it creeps.

Hedera Helix, or English Ivy, is perhaps the choicest of all creeping plants, and has been immortalized in prose and verse, Charles Dickens's almost unique contribution to poetic literature, "The Ivy Green," being forevermore associated with its beauties. The permanency as well as the deep, glossy, green color of the leaves makes it a universal favorite. Its hardy qualities render it fit for cultivation almost everywhere; and it needs more protection from heat than it does from cold. It thrives best in the United States when planted to the north of a house, fence, or other shade. A good way to save outdoor Ivies in winter is to lay them down carefully along the ground, and cover with sods in their natural position, grass upward. Indoors, the English Ivy should be kept clean and shielded from an excessively dry heat. In ordinary living rooms, a daily damping of the leaves will prove sufficient. (See p. 174.)

Ampelopsis Veitchii, or Veitch's Creeper, a distinct species introduced from Japan by the florist Veitch of London, is of the same genus with the A. quinquefolia, the common American or Virginia Creeper, but differs much in the manner of growth, the structure of the leaves, and other peculiarities. Its young shoots are of a rich, brown purple, and its leaves are rounded and simple, while the flower is inconspicuous. A peculiarity of the Veitch's Creeper that should strongly recommend it to a more general acceptance, is its habit of attaching itself, without aid from its owner or mechanical contrivance of any kind, to whatever object is near; the young stems send out sucker-like attachments by which they cling to wood, stone, or indeed to any substance, however smooth. Another attractive feature of this Creeper is the crimson-purple coloring of its rather persistent foliage, which clings to the branches often until midwinter in sheltered places, presenting an appearance almost as bright and beautiful as if the leaves were so many flowers.

Ampelopsis quinquefolia, already alluded to, has five leaflets with serrate edges on a common stalk, curling gracefully downward, and is so familiar, under the name of Virginia Creeper, as to need no further explanation.

Tecoma radicans, or Trumpet-flower, has been described, page 304.

Ficus repens, or Creeping Fig, originally introduced from China, is now a very popular delicate creeper, which holds itself firmly by its rootlets to any uneven surface, and is much used in conservatories, but not out of doors. In parlors it should be planted among other plants, as it requires shade and moisture. The leaves are small and firm, resembling green parchment, and will endure much neglect without being destroyed.

TRAILERS.

The epithet "trailing" is sufficiently indicative of the habit of these plants, which might be said to hug the ground, so low is their growth.

Epigæa Repens, or Trailing Arbutus — sometimes called Mayflower — has been put forward in some quarters as suitable to be adopted as the national flower of the United States, and is described on page 23.

Tradescantia zebrina, or Wandering Jew, is a low-spreading, trailing plant, differing from the more erect Tradescantias in that respect, and striped in brown and green, zebra-like, whence its specific name. There is another species — the T. alba, or white-flowered. Both are much used for hanging-baskets and for rock work, or to cover old stumps or other deformities. They demand copious moisture, but are almost indifferent to soil conditions. They are of the same genus as the T. Virginica, page 281.

Several Trailing Plants have been described elsewhere, as follows: Mentzelia Lindleyi, or Golden Bartonia, p. 42. Stellaria media, or Chickweed, p. 81. Mesembryanthemum crystallinum, or Ice-plant, p. 164. Portulaca grandiflora, or Great-flowered Portulaca, p. 249. Potentilla formosa, or Handsome Five-finger, p. 250. Trifolium repens, or Shamrock, p. 274. Fragaria vesca, or Wood Strawberry, p. 287. Verbena Aubletia, p. 311. Nepeta Glechoma, or Ground Ivy, p. 148. Vinca, or Periwinkle, p. 237.

These are but a few of the many plants of the four classes — Climbers, Twiners, Creepers, Trailers — that might be mentioned, and are chosen because they are all easily cultivated, needing but little care when once established, and because they are, in foliage, flower and fruit, the most beautiful of their respective kinds. Moreover, they all may be easily propagated from cuttings or slips, by layering, and from divisions of the roots, as well as from seeds.

The best general rule for cuttings would be perhaps to make them in the early spring before the plants begin to sprout, burying them about two inches, or a third of their length, in the ground. In the hands of a skilled workman these cuttings can also be taken in the fall, the same method being followed. Green shoots two or three inches long, severed from the parent stem, with a little of the old bark attached, will generally make good plants if placed to strike root in a box of moist sand, and protected from drying winds as well as excessive heat.

A light, rich soil is congenial to most if not all the climbing plants of the foregoing classes; and a good artificial soil will comprise two parts leaf-mold, one cow-manure, one loam and one sand. They are, however, not especially dependent on soil conditions, but require, as essentials to a thrifty growth, abundance of water for leaf and root; and an occasional application of liquid manure, if one wishes to take the trouble, will insure a more vigorous growth and an increased loveliness of foliage. Their chief enemies are the red spider, scales and caterpillars, which can easily be kept down by daily syringing and other careful attentions.

If it be desired to test the full capacity of the common climbing plants, the soil should be dug to the depth of about a foot, and on each available side to a distance of three feet, when the earth thus disturbed should be freely mixed with manure and leaf-mold in about equal parts, and plenty of root-room allowed to each plant, especially for the first season.

FERNS.

KNOWN to science as Filices, from the Latin, these flowerless plants possess a characteristic charm in their peculiar leafage or fronds. The many pretty forms of these leaves, and the various shades and tints of color, from a pure bright green to a golden yellow, are among nature's loveliest products. They constitute a remarkable family of the class designated Acrogenous, from two Greek words that signify increasing in growth from the extremity, which is one of the most conspicuous classes of the Cryptogamous or Flowerless series. The whole Fern family, or Order of Filices, is divided into eight suborders, six of which are represented in the United States. It is only within a comparatively recent period that these lovely members of the vegetable kingdom have been thought worthy of a place in collections of plants. Lacking the common element of conspicuous flowers, with their accompanying attractions of brilliant coloring and fascinating fragrance, the Ferns had long failed to elicit the admiration they deserve. But a more refined taste has learned to fully appreciate their merits, and specimens are now brought together from nearly every quarter of the world to adorn gardens, conservatories and parlors. In fact many wealthy admirers build greenhouses for their exclusive cultivation. Some Ferns from tropical and subtropical climes often have a tree-like appearance, while others from colder regions are so dwarfish that they have frequently been mistaken for mosses by those not possessed of a thorough and discriminating botanical knowledge. Many of them succeed well as common house-plants when kept out of drying winds or currents of cold air, care being taken to dampen their fronds daily. Some are hardy enough to endure excessive heat as well as ordinary winds, with the simple provision of supplying enough of moisture at the roots. The Lomeria Gibbii will even grow best in a strong sunshine; also the Scolopendrium vulgare, the Polypodium vulgare, and the Adiantum capillis-veneris will grow well in an exposed situation. Some Ferns, as the Adiantum cuneatum, A. trapeziforme, A. Farleyense, Lygodium palmatum, and many others, will only grow well in moist, still situations, as in a Wardian case or in a quiet nook sheltered by other plants.

As a generally good, manufactured soil for most Ferns, chopped sphagnum, or gray bog-moss, common loam, broken charcoal or potsherds, and sharp, silver sand, all well mixed in about equal parts, cannot be surpassed.

Ferns are often found growing on inaccessible rocks near mountain streams, or in the valleys, in the woods or on the prairies, varying in size and form. One that most delights in rocky places, is a curiosity of its kind, and is familiarly known as the Traveling Fern. Its leaves bend over until the tips touch the earth, where they readily strike root and form new plants. These doing likewise, the whole constitute a network of Ferns often covering several square yards. All the foregoing species of Ferns are evergreens, and every house or yard may be beautifully decorated at little or no expense by a collection of native Ferns, the many and various members of which may be picked up in country rambles. A good guide to their successful cultivation would be to note the soil and location where they naturally flourish best, and endeavor to reproduce in their new home the same conditions and surroundings, as nearly as circumstances will permit. When Ferns, or indeed any plants, are collected at a distance, they should be wrapped in a closely-woven wet cloth, both roots and fronds, and the bundle wrapped in another but dryer cloth, for transportation. Two common handkerchiefs, one wet and the other dry, will serve the purpose very well. In this way they can be safely carried long journeys, while for shorter distances, paper wrappings will suffice.

GRASSES.

THIS order of plants, scientifically designated, from the Latin, Gramineæ, is one of the most useful of nature's products for the support of animal life, and is coëxtensive with the animal kingdom, being found almost everywhere. In tropical and subtropical climates, some of the grasses assume a tree-like appearance, as the Bamboo, Sugar Cane, and Indian Corn. Wheat, Oat, Barley, Rye, Rice and some others furnish the staple food for the great majority of mankind; and most domestic as well as many wild animals derive their sustenance from these and other members of the Grass family. And as the human family depends largely upon these animals for food and clothing, it is not easy to conceive, much less to estimate how much the world owes to the two hundred and ninety-one genera and three thousand eight hundred species of the grass family. In this large array there is but one species that is not nutritious; this is known as Lolium temulentum, or poisonous Darnel Grass, which fortunately is not very plentiful. Where found, its rough exterior and bitter taste are repulsive to animals, and therefore its destructive powers are but little felt. Our home surroundings are often beautified by the short-cropped lawn Grasses, making a delightful natural carpet for children's play, as well as a pleasing object for the eye to rest upon. Though far removed from the gaudy and brilliant colorings of the Tulip, and for the most part but simple, unpretending plants, the Grasses possess a modest beauty all their own, or shared only with the Ferns. The florists and collectors have been busy for some time in bringing together the Grasses from distant parts of the world, and an admirer might now collect in his yard or window enough of specimen Grasses to effectively aid his children in their geography lessons, on the well-known principle of association of ideas. For instance, he might say this Grass in our southwest corner is from New Zealand; that in the southeast is from Australia; that other in the extreme east is from Japan; the next to the west is from China. And thus he might form the circuit of the whole world, pointing consecutively to the Grasses of India, Persia, Turkey, Greece, Italy, Spain, Portugal, Azores, West Indies and America. Many of the Grasses are well adapted for indoor culture, and all for outdoor, in their proper climatic surroundings. Among the very choicest of the former are Panicum variegatum, which presents transformations of color equally singular and beautiful; the Isolepsis gracilis, with its bright-green, wiry leaves, adapted to borders in shaded nooks; Festuca cæca, which is a fine ornamental grass for pots or vases, and contrasts well with the Holcus lanatus, or Velvet-Grass, which is of a silvery appearance and not unlike the common ribbon-grass of our gardens, but of finer texture. These four Grasses which we have singled out form a neat little collection for indoor culture when grown together, even without any admixture with other plants. A generally acceptable soil for the growth of nearly all Grasses, is made up of equal parts of cow-manure, leaf-mold, loam and sand well mixed; and all Grasses like water, but not stagnant moisture.

HEATHS.

WELL known to our Anglo-Saxon literature, because indigenous and widely spread in the countries where that literature had its rise, the Heaths have been but little cultivated in the United States, although it is now recognized that twenty-six of the genera are natives of this country. The order is scientifically called Ericaceæ, from Erica, the Heath proper, the accepted type of the family. There are five or more suborders, perhaps seventy genera, and about eleven hundred species, besides uncounted varieties. Erica carnea, fleshy Heath, so called on account of its flesh-colored bloom, and Erica Mediterranea, or Heath of the Mediterranean, whose bloom is of a somewhat darker flesh-color, are cultivated by our florists and others, and are much valued as exotics. They make desirable window plants if plentifully supplied with moisture and protected from excessive heat, whether artificial or natural. The more common indigenous sorts are the Kalmia, or Sheep Laurel; the Azalea arborescens (Tree-like Azalea), or False Honeysuckle; the Rhododendron, or Rosebay; the Rhodora Canadensis, or Canadian Rhodora; the Ledum latifolium, or Broad-leaved Labrador Tea; the Andromeda in several species; the Vaccinium in a large number of species, known in the vernacular as Blueberry, Cranberry, etc.; Gaylussacia, or Huckleberry; and the Pyrola, or False Wintergreen.

All these members of the Ericaceæ family are of easy culture, but, being originally natives of bogs, downs and sheltered mountain dells, they grow best on northern slopes, behind fences or evergreens, or otherwise protected from the noonday sun as well as from drying winds. Like the Begonias, they delight in a steady supply of uniform moisture. The fibrous rootlets are very fine, and extremely sensitive to deleterious substances, such as clods of half-rotted manure, lumps of clayey, uncongenial soils, and the like.

The best compost for their growth is three parts leaf-mold, one of sharp sand, one of common earth, and one of well-rotted manure. Commonly growing upon a substratum of freestone, a limestone or other calcareous subsoil is hurtful, and the application of lime-water is accordingly found to be pernicious; hence rainwater should alone be used. An occasional dose of liquid manure will prove acceptable to these plants when in flower or when making a new growth. The Ledums, Kalmias, the small plants of the best varieties of the Rhododendron, the Azalea nudiflora, and other dwarf members of the family, besides the two imported species already mentioned, make pretty house plants,

In a south-looking window the young leaves require careful protection from the sun's rays, as they may easily be scorched beyond recovery.

Though exposed to the open air, and at a rather low temperature, in their native homes, these plants are less hardy than would be supposed, and therefore should be carefully shielded from strong, drying winds, whether hot or cold.

The most common plant of the whole order is the Calluna vulgaris, which covers extensive tracts of waste moors throughout Great Britain and Ireland, and which is also found sparsely in Canada and our New England States. This is more hardy than any of the other species, and will flourish in almost any soil with a temperature under fifty; but in more southern latitudes it requires to be shaded in hot weather.

MOSSES.

MUSCI, or Mosses, which comprise three orders and thirty-six genera of cryptogamous plants, are among the lower forms of vegetable life. In the economy of nature they come next to the Lichenes, or Lichens, serving by their decay to form a suitable soil for the more beautiful and more useful plants. They grow in such dense, compact masses — often a hundred to a square inch — that their remains constitute a bed in which plants of a higher order may strike root. They are to be found in all climates and on all soils, requiring as absolutely essential only a constant, gentle moisture. The Mosses cover with a coat of emerald green the trunks of trees, the sides and summits of barren rocks, the moldering walls of old ruins, the margins of running brooks, the crevices of damp, subterranean caves and the like. The Sphagnum palustre, or Gray Bog-moss, is much used in Lapland and other countries of North Europe for bedding and coverlets. When flattened out by use, they can be renovated so as to assume their original elasticity by being soaked in water and again dried. The tenacity of life in the Mosses is truly wonderful; they have been known to have rooted and grown afresh after having lain pressed in a herbarium for thirty years.

In collections of plants, it is found worth while to cultivate them as toppings for the stands, pots or boxes in which ornamental plants are grown. They prevent a too rapid evaporation of the moisture, where it is desirable to retain it, besides adding a neatness which the uncovered soil does not present. Some amateurs make a specialty of growing a patch of Mosses for the yard or house, because of their intrinsic beauty, and the refreshing greenness of the dense, compact mass in which they grow. They can be studied to advantage only with the aid of a microscope, and are by that means found to present the appearance of miniature trees and various other curious forms. The Tortulas resemble small, fine screws, whence their name. The Hypnums, or Feather Mosses, are probably the most numerous, and are often exceedingly pretty, resembling miniature ferns, feathers, or trees.

Structure of Plants.

ANIMATED nature includes, besides animals, all plants, by which are meant in this connection the living organisms that constitute the vegetable kingdom, such as trees, shrubs, herbs, vegetables, grasses, ferns, etc. It will be recollected that there are three great "kingdoms" in nature — the mineral, the vegetable and the animal; and of these the one we are at present concerned with holds the middle place. Plants are living things, and the superior vegetables approach so nearly to what are generally considered inferior classes of the animal kingdom, that scientists are at a loss to determine the exact dividing line. On the other hand, it is well known that certain minerals are remains of former vegetation. Hence, in nature one kingdom merges into another by gradations so fine that where one begins and the other ends remains a sort of mysterious secret eluding the analytical powers of man. Vegetable life, like animal life, is a continued succession of renewal and decay, of assimilation and elimination. Growth may therefore be said to be the result of the assimilating processes in excess; maturity, of a balance of the assimilating and eliminating; and decay, of an excess of the eliminating processes. Vegetables derive their support from the atmosphere, as well as from the soil, and, like animals, contain a far greater proportion of water than of anything else. The other ingredients are carbon, derived from the carbonic acid gas imbibed from the air; often a little nitrogen; and generally a small quantity of mineral substances absorbed in liquid form through the roots.

CHEMISTRY OF PLANTS.

Plants are now generally recognized as containing about eighteen of the sixty-five primary elements known in nature, and these are all contributed by the vegetable kingdom to the support of animal life. It is equally pleasing and instructive to learn, through the scientific principles of the chemistry of plants, how and of what materials the beautiful forms that we see around us are made, as well as what useful properties they possess. Thereby we obtain an unerring guide to the most wholesome food for ourselves and our domestic animals; and a discriminating sense of the proportion in which the different kinds should be used. Hence we know that it is unwise to partake of the same plants too continuously, frequent changes being a fixed law of their healthful action on the human system. By a knowledge of the chemical components of the human frame on the one hand, and those of the useful plants on the other, man is enabled to select the materials proper to be used in accordance with his varying needs. It is easy to eat too much of plants that contain sulphur, lime, phosphorous, fatty, carbonaceous matter, or any other of the chemical ingredients of plants, when the system may really demand the use of those endowed with quite different properties; hence the value of this knowledge.

It is truly wonderful that an order of plants, containing perhaps several hundred genera and many thousand species, will maintain, throughout all their variety of form and color, a predominance of one or more chemical elements. For instance, the Cruciferæ, or Mustard family, one of great utility to man, every member of which affords nutritious and medicinal benefits, principally anti-scorbutic, or scurvy-destroying, in character. They all contain nitrogen and sulphur more largely than other plants, which accounts for their yielding ammonia when undergoing decay, as well as for their blood-purifying properties. Many of our familiar table condiments, as mustard, horseradish, cress, etc., belong to this order. The Cruciferæ are natives of the temperate zone, and are a natural antidote for the excessive use of fat-producing matters, so common in those regions.

The order Leguminosæ is perhaps the largest of all, and is remarkable for containing lime, albumen and starch. Its value in the animal economy is great, as it furnishes the bone and sinew, which constitute the essential framework of the animal structure. Like the other useful plants, they are found everywhere, to meet the necessities of universal animal life, while the poisonous or dangerous plants are confined to a very limited range. The Leguminosæ are also possessed of many well-known medicinal properties, whose value can scarcely be overestimated. Plants yield about thirty-four different products, such as resin, oil, wax, gluten, starch, sugar, etc.; and at least eight well-known acids, viz.: oxalic in rhubarb, tartaric in grapes, citric in lemons, malic in apples, gallic in oak, benzoic in balsam, prussic or hydrocyanic in almonds, and phosphoric in oats.

Vegetable chemistry, as may be conjectured from the remarks already made, is much too extensive a subject to receive proper attention in a subsidiary paragraph of a popular work devoted mainly to the poetry and cultivation of flowers; but this much it has been thought desirable to insert as a slight hint on an important subject, and a stimulus to further investigation.

For the more easy comprehension of the general principles of botany by the unscientific lover of flowers, it is now proposed to consider the individual plant under the various relations of its internal structure, and its component parts viewed externally, together with the more important subdivisions of these, in a natural sequence, and in as few words as possible. What plants are composed of becomes then the next subject for consideration.

TISSUES.

Plants are made up of innumerable minute sacs, called cells, and generally of a lot of tubes or vessels, which were also originally rows of these cells, the whole constituting the material substance of plants, or what is technically known as tissue. The nourishment of plants passes from cell to cell through the thin membranes that constitute the cell walls. These cells are of a definite structure, as found by microscopic observation, and the tissues are of different kinds according to the structure and arrangement of the cells and tubes.

Cellular tissue, which composes the whole structure of some of the lower orders, as mosses, seaweeds and the like, is where the whole mass is made up of these minute oval sacs crowded close together. Peculiarly flattened, they compose the outer layer known as the skin or epidermis.

Wood tissue consists of long tubes, tapering and closed at the ends, placed side by side, which form in woody plants what is known as wood proper.

Bast tissue consists of long, flexible tubes, closed at both ends, and is mostly found in the *liber* or inner bark, constituting in hemp and flax the portion of those plants used in the manufacture of linen, ropes, etc.

Vascular tissue consists of long tubes or vessels, formed of superposed cells the partitions between which have been absorbed, and comprises what are variously called dotted ducts, spiral vessels, annular bands, etc.

The chief organs of plants are four, viz.: 1, Root; 2, Stem; 3, Leaf; 4, Flower. Each of these is subdivided under different aspects and relations.

ROOTS.

ROOTS are the parts by which the plant draws nourishment from the soil, and are sometimes supplied with *rootlets*, holding about the same relation to them that they do to the plant. Roots are of six kinds: *Fibrous*, when composed of tufts of fibers with pores at their points, as in common grasses (1*); *repent* or *creeping*, as in the Couch-grass (2); *fusiform*, or *spindle-shaped*, as in the Carrot (3); *premorse* (as if bitten off) when the spindle-shape ends quite abruptly, as in the Plantain (4); *tuberous*, as in the Potato, where the root comprises one or more roundish, solid masses, fed by rootlets from the soil (5); *bulbous*, where the root is one round, solid mass, producing buds from the upper surface and rootlets from the lower, as in the Narcissus (6); the bulbous is, however, sometimes a mass of overlapping, fleshy scales, as in the Lily (7), or of concentric coats, as in the Onion.

Collar.—The collar is that portion of the plant where the root merges into the stem, or where they both unite (8).

In respect of duration, roots as well as plants are designated and defined as follows:

Annuals are such as in one season grow from the seeds, blossom, and ripen their seeds for the following year, and then perish. Among the annuals are to be found many of the most charming of the summer flowers, some blooming for short periods of a week or two, and others during the whole season.

Biennials are such as start from the seed one summer, and spend all their strength in establishing their roots and laying up nutriment for the flowerstalks of the following year, when they blossom, ripen seed, and perish, having fulfilled their mission. Some very pleasing flowers are found among this class. In order to have flowers of any of the Biennials every year, seeds must be sown each year, thus calculating a year in advance.

* The figures inclosed in parentheses, pp. 404 to 410, refer to the illustrations on page 408.

Perennials are those that live and bloom year after year, except under extraordinary vicissitudes, many of them blooming the first summer if sown early in the spring. Such plants can be propagated by a division of the roots and cuttings as well as by seeds. Some of these cannot be surpassed for utility and beauty, and are best for permanent beds where circumstances will not permit the steady attention demanded by other classes of flowers.

STEMS.

NEXT to the root is the stem, or that part of the plant which springs from the root, and serves to support the leaves, buds and flowers. It usually seeks the light, appearing above the ground, and is subdivided as follows: *Simple*, when found without branches (8), as in the Parnassia; *compound*, when branched, as in the Chickweed (9); *forked*, when parted into two equal or nearly equal branches, as in the Bouvardia (10); *erect*, when growing upright, *ascending*, when rising obliquely upward—when several stems grow from the same root, the central one is often erect and the others ascending, as in the Violet (11); *prostrate*, or *procumbent*, when it lies flat along the ground, as in the Petunia; *creeping*, or *repent*, when it runs along the ground and sends out roots from its joints—sometimes a plant has an upright stem, and sends out creeping shoots from its base, as in the Strawberry (12); *twining*, or *voluble*, as in the Hop, when they rise by spirally coiling themselves around supports; *climbing*, or *scandent*, when they rise by clinging step by step to other objects, as in the Ivy.

Stems are classified according to certain peculiarities of size and duration, as follows: *Herbaceous*, when they die down to the ground every year, as in Mint or other herbs, whence the epithet; *fruticose*, when living from year to year, and of considerable size, like Lilac or other shrubs; *suffruticose*, when fruticose or shrubby below, and herbaceous above, as the Horseshoe Geranium; *suffrutescent*, when the stem has an appearance of being moderately shrubby, and is only a little woody, as the Pelargonium; *arborescent*, when approaching to a tree-like appearance, as the Oleander; and *arboreous*, when it is the trunk of a tree properly so called, as the Magnolia.

The stem is composed—beginning from the center—of the *pith*, the soft, spongy substance in the center of many plants, consisting of cellular tissue; the *wood*, or material immediately surrounding the pith; the *liber*, or inner bark, which is fibrous; the *cortex*, or outer bark, which consists of cellular tissue only; and the *epidermis*, or skin—a thin, membraneous covering, with pores, that envelops all the rest. The stem, longitudinally considered, comprises the *nodes*, or knots; and *internodes*, or parts between the knots.

It has been already stated that the stem is usually above ground; there are, however, several forms of underground stems, as the *rhizoma*, or rootstalk, a creeping stem growing wholly or partly beneath the soil; the *corm*, which is a very short, fleshy rhizoma; the *bulb*, a shorter stem, usually underground, with excessively crowded and overlapping coats; and the *bulblet*, which is a small excrescence that grows on the older and larger bulb.

Stalks.—The stalks are the off-shoots from the stem, which directly support the leaves, and are variously styled peduncles, pedicels, petioles, meaning respectively flowerstalks, footstalks and leafstalks.

Axil.—The axil is the angle formed on the upper surface, between the stem and leaf, where the buds, called on that account axillary, spring from the stem (13).

LEAVES.

UNDERSTOOD to be expansions or elongations from the stem, leaves consist of a network of fibers or nerves in two distinct sets, one to each surface. The purposes they serve are mainly three: to expose a broader surface to the action of the light and heat, to aid evaporation, and to facilitate the absorption of carbonic acid from the air. They discharge the function fulfilled by the lungs in the animal kingdom. They are called *radical*, when they spring around the root, as in the Dandelion; *alternate*, when only one appears on each joint of the stem, as in the Toad-flax (13); *opposite*, when in pairs opposite each other, as in the Mint (14); *whorled*, when in a circle around the stem, as in the Purple Eupatorium (15); and *tufted*, when they appear in bunches or tufts at the top, as in the Eryngo (16), or as in the Palm.

Leaves are further distinguished as *sessile*, when they sit, as it were, on the stem, without intervening stalks, as in the Eryngo (16); *deciduous*, if they fall annually, as in most trees and shrubs; and *persistent*, if they survive the season, as in the evergreens.

A leaf is *simple*, when composed of one piece only, as in the Round-leaved Bell-flower (17); *binate*, *ternate*, *quaternate* or *quinate*, according as it has, on a common stalk, respectively, two leaflets, as in the Listera; three, as in the Clover (18); four, as in the exceptional four-leaved Clover; or five, as in the Ampelopsis (19); *pinnate*, when a number of leaves are arranged feather-like along the stalk, as in the Pea (20). A simple leaf is sometimes wavy along the edge, as in the China Primrose (21), or has three lobes, as in the Hypatica, five, as in the Castor-oil Plant, or seven, as in the Lady's Mantle (22).

Leaves are *digitate*, when they all spring, like so many fingers, from the tip of the leaf-stalk, as in the Virginia Creeper (23); *palmate*, when the leaflets leave a space at their common center, not unlike the palm of the hand, as in the Horse-chestnut (24); *pedate*, or foot-like, as in the Chenopodiums, or when a palmate or other leaf has an additional cleft in the edge, not as deep as the digitate, and hence called pedate, as in the Mandrake (25); *peltate*, or shield-like, when the stalk is attached at or near the center, as in the Nasturtium (26); *perfoliate*, when the stalk passes through the leaf (27), as in the Bone-set; *connate*, when two leaves are joined at their bases, the stalk passing through at the junction, as in the Lychnis (28).

Again, by reason of peculiarities of the edges, leaves are called *entire*, when there is an unbroken, gradual curvature of the margin, as in the Silene (29); *crenate*, *crenelled* or *scollopped*, when it is notched like a scollop shell, as in the Ground Ivy (30); *serrate*, or *saw-edged*, as in the Rose (31); *pectinate*, or *comb-like*, an expression sometimes used where the edges are a deeply-cut dentate; *dentate*, or *toothed*, as in the common Hoarhound (32); *incised*, or *cut*, also called *laciniate*, when slashed or cut more irregular than in the dentate, as in the Fennel; *undulate*, or *wavy*, as in the Beech; *sinuate*, or *sinuous*, that is, of larger scope than the wavy, but of the same general outline, as in the White-oak; *lobed*, when cut in sections, with the incisions reaching about halfway to the midrib, and these may be *two-lobed*, *three-lobed*, etc., according to their number, as already described; *cleft*, when cut still more deeply, half way down or more toward the midrib—the Latin equivalent *fid*, as a suffix, from *findo*, I cleave, with a qualifying prefix, is very much used in this connection, as *pinnatifid*, *multifid*, *bifid*, etc., denoting respectively *cleft like a feather, many-cleft, two-cleft*, etc.—*parted*, when almost reaching the midrib; and *divided*, or *bisected, trisected*, etc., when incised quite to the midrib.

In addition to the foregoing divisions, leaves are distinguished, as to form or general shape, by epithets that are sufficiently clear in themselves, or may be readily comprehended by reference to the engraving on page 328, viz.: *Linear*, as in grass; *oblong*, as in the Chickweed (33); *hairlike*, as in the Schizanthus (34); *strap-shaped*, as in the Heath (35); *elliptical*, as in the Rose (31); *oval*, or *egg-shaped*, as in the Apple (36); *obovate*, or *inversely oval*, as in the Juneberry (37); *rounded*, as in the Round-leaved Violet (38); *heart-shaped*, as in the Dog Violet (39); *inversely heart-shaped*, as in the Clover (18); *kidney-shaped*, as in the common Water-cress (40); *arrow-shaped*, as in the Sagittaria (41); *angular*, as in the Hypatica (42); and *sword-shaped*, as in the Gladiolus (43).

Stipules are two winglike appendages that are often found at the base of the leafstalk (united with or distinct therefrom), sometimes *oblong*, as in the Evening Primrose, and at others *arrow-shaped*, as in the Rose (44).

Bracts.—These are the small leaves that are sometimes found immediately below the flower-cluster, on its stalk or *peduncle*, as in the Pentstemon (45, 46), generally green, but occasionally picturesquely colored, as in the Poinsettia. When they appear on the *pedicel*, they are called *bracteoles*, as in the Cardamine (47); and when these grow in a circle, or whorl, they are called an *involucre*, as in the Thistle (48).

Buds are the germs of the branches, as the seed is of the whole plant, and sprout from the stem as this does from the root; hence the branches might be regarded as secondary stems, or even as individual plants springing from the buds. These buds are called *terminal* when they appear at the end of the stem, and *lateral* when they appear at the sides; the most important of the lateral are the *axillary* already mentioned—the others being *accessory* or *supernumerary* when two or more supplement the axillary, and *adventitious* when they appear elsewhere than at the axils.

Æstivation, or *præfloration*, is the arrangement of the parts of the future flower in the bud before blooming; and is called *open*, when the calyx and corolla are not closed over the other parts of the flower; *valvate*, when the several parts meet each other exactly by the edges without overlapping; *induplicate*, if the edges are turned in; *reduplicate*, if turned out; *contorted*, when the edges are twisted; *imbricated*, when they overlap; *quincuncial*, if two parts are inside, two outside and one intermediate; *vexillary*, if one petal inwraps the other parts; *plicate*, if the tubular corolla or calyx is folded lengthwise; and *supervolute*, if the folds are wrapped around each other in one direction.

FLOWERS.

LOOKING at flowers from the technical, scientific standpoint, they are the whole aggregate of the organs of reproduction; æsthetically they are the crowning glory of the plant; and familiarly, the bloom or blossom, the part for which alone most plants are cultivated. The chief parts of the flower are the Calyx, Corolla, Stamen, Pistil, Pericarp, Seed, Receptacle and Nectary.

Calyx, from the Greek through the Latin, denoting a cup, is the outer covering or leaf-like envelope of the flower, mostly green, but at times colored; it enfolds the bud before it is fully in bloom, and afterward generally surrounds the blossom loosely. Its chief use apparently is to support and protect the fine inner parts by its greater consistency; it was considered by Linnæus to be the continuation of the outer bark, performing the same service to the bud as the bark does to the stem. The calyx varies much; it is sometimes double, as in the Flax (49), and at others is a mere ring which afterward becomes the down, as in the Teasel (50).

Corolla, an abbreviated form of the Latin *coronilla*, a little crown, comprises the leaves of the flower proper, or blossom, within the calyx. These leaves are called petals, and are usually as many as the sepals of the calyx. When the petals are all of the same size and shape, the corolla is called *regular*, as in the Silene (51); and this regular corolla may be *salver-shaped*, as in the Lychnis (52); *funnel-shaped*, as in the Primrose (53); *wheel-shaped*, as in the Holly (54); *bell-shaped*, as in the Bellflower (55); *trumpet-shaped*, as in the Convolvulus (56). Other corollas are termed *irregular*, as when the petal is only one, but divided into lobes; if the lobes are open, it is called *gaping*, as in the Mint (57); if closed, *personate* or *masked*, as in the Snapdragon (58); when there are four petals placed crosswise, the corolla is called *cruciferous*, as in the Radish (59); *papilionaceous*, or *butterfly-shaped*, when there are five rudely resembling a butterfly, as in the Pea (60).

When the calyx and corolla are not readily distinguishable, the whole corresponding part that encircles the stamens and pistils is called *perianth*, from two Greek words: *peri*, around, and *anthos*, a flower. Sometimes this word is used by preference, and said to be *double* when the calyx and corolla are both present and clearly distinguishable. Some flowers have neither calyx nor corolla, as in the Equisetum (61).

Stamen, from the Greek through the Latin, signifying the warp, and this from its standing or upright property, denotes one of the small organs, of which there are generally several, that stand around the center of the perianth, as in the Coreopsis (62), and in most flowers. They comprise the *filament*, or thread-like (sometimes awl-like), upright portion, and the *anther*, or flower proper, which is the part essential to reproduction, and contains the fine white, yellow or black dust called *pollen*, or fertilizing matter. The filaments are sometimes in bundles, as in the St. Johnswort (63), and at others form a hollow tube, as in the Mallows (64); the anthers are sometimes free when standing separately (64), or united into a ring, as in the Dandelion (65).

Pistil, from the Latin denoting a pestle, is the central part and seed-bearing organ of the flower, as in the Anagallis (66); and comprises three parts: the *ovary* (a), the hol-

STRUCTURE OF PLANTS.

low case or pod containing the rudimentary seeds called *ovules;* the *style,* or column (*b*), wanting in certain flowers, which bears aloft the third part, known as the *stigma* (*c*). This is the extreme viscous tip of the flower, and is exposed on all sides for the reception of the impregnating pollen from the encircling stamens. Sometimes an ovary has several styles and stigmas, when the pistil is called *compound,* and each part a *carpel,* as in the Blackberry (67). Some flowers have only stamens, while others of the same plant have only pistils as in the Cucumber (68), and as those alone that have pistils produce seed, they are called *fertile,* while those possessing stamens only are designated *barren.* Again, the pistils and stamens are sometimes to be found only in different plants of the same species, as in the Willow (69). When in different flowers of the same plant, they are called *monœcious,* from two Greek words meaning single-housed, as in the Cucumber; when in different plants, they are termed *diœcious,* or two-housed, as in the Willows. When the ovary is above the base of the perianth, it is termed *superior,* as in the Purslane (70); when below, as in the Roses, it is called *inferior.*

Pericarp (from the Greek *peri,* around, and *karpos,* fruit), or seed-vessel, is the case, pod or covering of the seed or seeds of a plant, the enlarged and ripened ovary, which with the enclosed seeds constitutes the fruit. It presents various forms in different plants, as the *capsule* in the Purslane (71), the *silique* in the common Mustard (72), the *silicle* or *capsella,* a short pod (72), in the Shepherd's Purse, the *legume* or long pod in the Bean (73), the *berry* in the Currant (74), the *nut* in the Hazel (75), the *drupe* in the Hawthorn (76), and the *cone* in the Pine (77). Fruits are *fleshy* when the seeds are encircled by a juicy, pulpy substance, as in the Apple, the Pear, the Melon and many others. *Stone-fruits* is the name given to those in which the pulpy matter incloses the hard, horny substance, or "stone," which covers the seed. They are called *dry-fruits* when the seed-vessel does not become juicy or pulpy, but is a mere husk or dry covering, as in Wheat, the Five-finger, the Ground Cherry, etc.

Seed.—This is the portion destined to reproduce the plant, and is itself the result of the action between the stamens and the pistil, indicated above. The stigma receives the pollen, which is conveyed through the style to the ovary, where it comes in contact with the ovules, producing the seed that in due time arrives at the maturity necessary to reproduce the plant according to its kind. When the *plumule* or embryo plant is enclosed in a seed of two cotyledons, it is styled, from the Greek, *dicotyledonous,* that is, having two lobes, as in the Bean (78), when in one, it is *monocotyledonous,* as in the common Grasses or Sugar-cane; and when there is no apparent nourishing seed-lobe, it is called *acotyledonous,* as in the Ferns.

Receptacle is the top of the stem, or apex of the flowerstalk, from which the organs of the flower spring, and into which they may therefore be conceived as gathered or inserted, whence the name. It is *conical* (79), as in the Obeliscaria, *chaffy* (80), as in the Thistle, or *bristly,* as in the Cactus (81), and is the part on which the other portions of the flower rest, as in the Scabious (82).

Nectary is a term applied to any of the organs which may happen to contain nectar, that is, the sweet secretions from the plants. The nectary of the Crown Imperial comprises a number of cells around the center of the flower, while in the Crowfoot it is a scale at the base of the petals (83).

INFLORESCENCE.

DIFFERENCES in the mode of flowering or in the general arrangement of the blossoms along the stem or branches, mark the various forms of inflorescence. When the flower that terminates the axis opens first, and the others in the order of their nearness to this one, the inflorescence is called *determinate, definite,* or *centrifugal,* as in the Hydrangea. When this order is reversed, and the first flower to bloom is the one farthest from the terminal one, this being the very last, the inflorescence is said to be *indeterminate, indefinite,* or *centripetal,* as in the Gladiolus. In a few genera the inflorescence partakes of both peculiarities, and is called *mixed,* as in the Teasel, and also the Liatris, familiarly designated Blazing Star. Flowers, like buds, are known as *terminal* when they appear at the end of the stem, as in the Parnassia (8); *whorled,* when grouped around the stem in a circle, as in the Mint; and *axillary,* when at the axils, as in the Pentstemon (45).

The flowerstalk, when common to the whole cluster, is called a *peduncle,* the individual stalk of each separate flower being a *pedicel,* as in the Cardamine (47). When the peduncle bears a single flower, the inflorescence is called *simple,* as in the Morning Glory (56). When the peduncle with its flower springs directly from the root of the plant, the inflorescence is called a *scape,* as in the English Primrose (84); and when it has several flowers placed one above another and sessile (that is, without pedicels), it is called a *spike,* as in the Veronica spicata (85), or *spadix,* which is a fleshy variety of the spike, as in the Spiranthus; *raceme,* where each flower of a cluster has its own pedicel arranged along a lengthened axis, as in the Canadian Milk-Vetch (86); *panicle,* or branched cluster, where each pedicel (itself a branch of the peduncle) again branches, as in the Stellaria (87); *corymb,* where the lower flowers are on longer stalks, the intermediate on shorter, and the top ones nearly or quite sessile, as in the Mountain Ash (88); *cyme,* where the stalks are irregularly branched, but the flowers are nearly level at the top, as in the Dogwood (89); a *fascicle* is a cyme with the flowers crowded into a bundle, whence the name, as in the Sweet William; a *glomerule* is a dense, compact cyme resembling a head, as in the Cocklebur; *umbel,* where the flower-stalks spring, like so many umbrella ribs, from a common center, and rise to about the same height, each bearing its flower, as in the Milkweed (90); when, as sometimes happens, there is a smaller umbel on each pedicel, instead of a single flower, the inflorescence is called a *compound umbel,* as in the Carrot (91); when crowded in a dense mass and sessile, it is called a *head,* as in the Button-bush (92); a *catkin,* or *ament,* is a spike enclosed in a deciduous scale, as in the Hazel (93); a *thyrsus* is a compact panicle of pyramidal shape, as a bunch of grapes or the cluster of the Lilac.

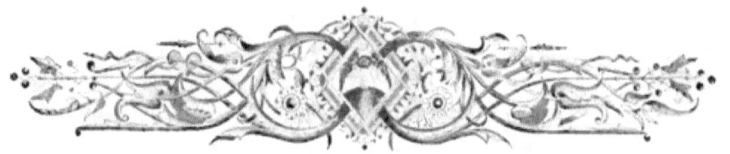

Divisions of the Vegetable Kingdom.

GREAT interest is naturally felt by all amateur culturists in the divisions of the vegetable kingdom. Ages before the knowledge of plants developed into the complete science called botany, certain relationships and affinities were known to exist between many of them; but the formal distribution into the subjoined divisions and subdivisions is a comparatively recent addition, and has been adopted by scholars for the purpose of placing before the mind in a clear and methodical manner the various degrees of relationship that exist between plants. An exhaustive enumeration in the present state of botanical science embraces the following twelve heads: Series or Subkingdom, Class, Subclass, Order or Family, Suborder, Tribe, Subtribe, Genus, Subgenus or Section, Species, Race, and Variety.

To aid the student of floriculture in forming a clearer conception of the arrangement, relationship and subordination of the different members of this distribution, the whole vegetable kingdom might be likened to the available war forces of the United States. The Series would correspond to the military as distinct from the naval, and *vice versa;* Class, to the regular army as distinct from volunteers, or the reverse; Subclass, to the "Army of the Potomac," or the like; Order, to army corps; Suborder to division; Tribe, to a brigade with its full complement of cavalry, artillery and infantry; Subtribe, to the more usual incomplete brigade of two or three regiments; Genus, to a regiment; Subgenus, to a battalion; Species, to a company; Race, to a company of infantry as distinct from one of cavalry; and Variety, to the same company with the shades of difference arising from the variation in numbers, discipline, or any other minor feature — for instance, Company A, as differing from Company B in any one or several of these respects.

In this methodical arrangement it will be noticed that the Variety, a subdivision of the Species, is the lowest term, as the individual plant does not obtain an individual name. The Species is designated by the name of the Genus to which it belongs, with a distinguishing epithet, usually an adjective, added to denote the peculiar characteristic (or what it has been agreed to consider such) of each particular Species. Thus in Rosa moschata, or Musk Rose, Rosa represents the Genus Rose; and moschata, a Latinized version of musk in the adjective form, or musky, denotes the characteristic distinction of the Species. Hence it is not strictly correct to say that such a name corresponds to that of an individual, as Publius Cornelius Scipio; but it would be allowable to compare it with Cornelius Scipio — Cornelius, the gens, or clan, and Scipio, the family name within the clan — if, like the Romans, we lived in a state of society where these constituted a recognized division of the community. The Variety is further distinguished by one or more additional epithets, adjectives or names of persons, subjoined to the name of the Species to which it belongs, as the Fragaria Virginiana Illinoensis — the Illinois Variety of the Species of Strawberry known as the Virginian.

What these various terms imply will now be explained more in detail, taking for this purpose the foregoing divisions, as used by most modern writers on floriculture, and in an inverse order, beginning with the most restricted:

Variety.—By this term is meant such a group within the same Species as is marked in all its individuals by some striking peculiarities, and often so as to create a doubt whether it does not constitute a distinct Species.

Subspecies, or Race.—Where the marks of the Variety are regularly propagated.

Species is an aggregate of such individual plants, or varieties of plants, as agree in common attributes and characteristics, and which are designated by the same distinguishing epithet, as the Rosa moschata, already explained.

The Species of plants have been estimated, and probably within bounds, as high as one hundred and twenty thousand, of which nearly four thousand belong to our own country, east of the Mississippi. The more conservative estimates of earlier botanists, putting the number at about sixty thousand, will therefore have to be abandoned; the more, as new discoveries are being perpetually made.

Subgenus, or Section, is used by some botanists to denote such collections of certain Species as are more nearly allied to each other than the other plants of the same Genus.

Genus.—This embraces all the various Species that bear a strong resemblance to each other, but differ in the shape or general proportion of their parts; thus the various Species of the Roses belong to one Genus.

Tribe and **Subtribe** are subdivisions of the Suborder in some elaborate systems of classification.

Suborder.—For convenience of treatment, and because of important differences, an Order is often subdivided into three or four Suborders, each embracing several Genera, as, for instance, the Order Rosaceæ into the Almond or Plum, the Pear, and the Rose proper.

Order comprehends many Genera broadly resembling one another, as in having their flowers and seeds constructed on the same plan, but with very striking differences in important features. Thus the Order Rosaceæ, or Rose family, embraces not only Roses proper, but Strawberries, Blackberries, Apples, Pears, etc.

Subclass, or Alliance, is a subdivision of the Class, and embraces several Orders.

Class.—This is a still broader grouping or aggregation of plants, comprising various Orders that resemble each other in some few important features.

Series, or Subkingdom, is the first grand division of the vegetable kingdom, and embraces all such classes as are not radically so very different as to refuse to be grouped together because of their most essential properties, such as flowering or not flowering.

Systems of Classification.

WHO it was that first invented a system of classification of plants is uncertain. Since the days when Solomon, king of Israel, "spake of trees from the Cedar tree that is in Lebanon even unto the Hyssop that springeth out of the wall;" or those of Zoroaster, who is said to have taught that the primeval creative power called forth from the blood of the sacred bull 120,000 forms of plants; or earlier still, if the reader wishes, since the time when primitive man began first to observe and wonder at his surroundings, until the present hour, the glory of the vegetable creation has necessarily excited his admiration. The Chaldæan shepherds, who are credited with the discovery of astronomy, through their undisturbed contemplation of the "flowers of heaven," could not have been entirely unmindful of the "stars of earth, the beautiful flowers."

Theophrastus (B. C. 374–286), a Greek philosopher and pupil of Aristotle, wrote a "History of Plants," and a work "On the Causes of Plants," which evince not a little knowledge of the organs and physiology thereof. Pliny the Elder (A. D. 23–79), in his great compilation, the "Thirty-seven Books of Histories of Nature," gives many curious bits of information in reference to about one thousand plants. Dioscorides, who flourished about one hundred years later, described five hundred plants; and his work is remarkable as being the source of much of the terminology still used in our books on floriculture.

Scientific botany, however, owes its rise to the revival of letters in the sixteenth century. Otto Brunfels (1464–1534) is considered the first among the moderns to attempt a classification of plants. Andrea Cesalpino (1519–1603), Italian physician and botanist, was perhaps the first to establish a natural system of classification. Robert Morison (1620–83), a Scottish physician and botanist, separated plants into woody and herbaceous, and divided them into eighteen classes. John Ray (1628–1705), English botanist, separated flowering from flowerless plants, and subdivided the former into monocotyledonous and dicotyledonous plants. A. Q. Rivinus (1652–1723), a Saxon anatomist and botanist, published, in 1690, a system based on the differences of the corolla. J. P. de Tournefort (1656–1708), French botanist, described about eight thousand species in twenty-two classes, the classification being based mainly on the differences in the corolla.

CULTIVATION AND ANALYSIS OF PLANTS.

ARTIFICIAL SYSTEM OF LINNÆUS.

The system of Linnæus (1707-1778), comprised twenty-four classes, distinguished from each other by certain external peculiarities, relating to the stamens and pistils, which were expressed by equivalent Greek compound words, and is therefore called artificial. Though superseded by the natural systems of more recent botanists, it still possesses both interest and value, as much of the terminology of Linnæus has been permanently ingrafted on botanical science. Among other things, he was author of the binomial system of naming plants by the genus and specific characteristic. This system is as follows:

TWENTY-FOUR CLASSES.

PHÆNOGAMOUS ("APPARENT MARRIAGE"): WITH STAMENS AND PISTILS MANIFEST— FLOWERING PLANTS.

1. Monandria, with one stamen.
2. Diandria, with two stamens.
3. Triandria, with three stamens.
4. Tetrandria, with four stamens.
5. Pentandria, with five stamens.
6. Hexandria, with six stamens.
7. Heptandria, with seven stamens.
8. Octandria, with eight stamens.
9. Enneandria, with nine stamens.
10. Decandria, with ten stamens.
11. Dodecandria, eleven to nineteen (literally, twelve) stamens.
12. Icosandria, with twenty or more stamens, adhering to calyx.
13. Polyandria, with twenty or more stamens, adhering to receptacle.

} STAMENS OF EQUAL LENGTH.

14. Didynamia, "two with power;" two long and two short stamens.
15. Tetradynamia, "four with power;" four long and two short stamens.

} STAMENS, UNEQUAL LENGTH.

} STAMENS UNCONNECTED WITH EACH OTHER.

16. Monadelphia, "single brotherhood," that is, with filaments in one bundle.
17. Diadelphia, "double brotherhood," with filaments in two bundles.
18. Polyadelphia, "many brotherhoods," with filaments in more than two bundles.
19. Syngenesia, "together born," united by the anthers.

} STAMENS JOINED WITH EACH OTHER.

} STAMENS SEPARATE FROM THE PISTIL.

20. Gynandria, hermaphrodite.

} STAMENS ADHERING TO THE PISTIL.

} STAMENS AND PISTILS IN THE SAME FLOWER.

21. Monœcia, "single-housed," in the same plant.
22. Diœcia, "double-housed," in two plants.
23. Polygamia, "polygamous," in one, or two, or more than two plants.

} IN SEPARATE FLOWERS.

CRYPTOGAMOUS PLANTS; STAMENS AND PISTILS INDISTINCT— FLOWERLESS PLANTS.

24. Cryptogamia, "concealed marriage."

TWENTY-SIX ORDERS.

The foregoing twenty-four *Classes* were subdivided into twenty-six *Orders*, according to the number of pistils or distinct stigmata, as far as the twelfth order, inclusive; and above that the differences were founded on other peculiarities. It is not to be understood that each Class had twenty-six subdivisions known as Orders, but that this distribution formed a basis for thus distinguishing as many Orders as might be found by actual observation. The Class twelve or thirteen, for instance, might be comprehensive enough to give scope for the elaborate subdivision into twenty-six Orders, while most others would seldom reach beyond five, and many might have only one, two or three. The orders were as follows:

1. Monogynia, with one pistil.
2. Digynia, with two pistils.
3. Trigynia, with three pistils.
4. Tetragynia, with four pistils.
5. Pentagynia, with five pistils.
6. Hexagynia, with six pistils.
7. Heptagynia, with seven pistils.
8. Octogynia, with eight pistils.
9. Enneagynia, with nine pistils.
10. Decagynia, with ten pistils.
11. Dodecagynia, with twelve pistils.
12. Polygynia, with many pistils.
13. Gymnospermia, with naked seeds.
14. Angiospermia, with covered seeds.
15. Siliquosa, with seeds in siliques, or long pods.
16. Siliculosa, with seeds in silicles, or short pods.
17. Monogamia, having some florets with stamens and others with pistils.
18. Polygamia equalis, all florets having stamens and pistils.
19. Polygamia segregata, each floret having a separate calyx.
20. Monœcia, having stamens and pistils on separate flowers of the same plant.
21. Diœcia, having stamens and pistils on two plants.
22. Triœcia, having stamens and pistils on three plants.
23. Filices, Ferns.
24. Musci, Mosses.
25. Hepaticæ, Liverworts.
26. Algæ and Fungi, Seaweeds, Lichens, Funguses.

NATURAL ORDERS OF LINNÆUS.

No one was more sensible of the need of a natural classification of plants than the distinguished author of this artificial system, who declared that a method of classification, based on the true intrinsic differences of plants, was "the first and last desideratum in botany;" and he accordingly busied himself in arranging such a method, leaving as his contribution in that direction the following fifty-eight families:

1. Palmæ — Palms.
2. Piperitæ — Arums.
3. Calamariæ — Sedges.
4. Gramineæ — Grasses.
5. Tripetaloideæ — Rushes.
6. Ensatæ — Sword-leaved, as the Iris.
7. Orchideæ — Orchids.
8. Scitamineæ — Dainty plants, as the Banana.
9. Spathaceæ — Sheathed, as the Narcissus.
10. Coronariæ — Crown-bearing, as the Lily Family.
11. Sarmentaceæ — Runner-bearing, as the Strawberry.
12. Holoraceæ — Whole-rooted, as the Goosefoot.
13. Succulentæ — Succulent, as the Purslane.
14. Gruinales — Crane-bill, as the Geranium.
15. Inundatæ — Pond-weeds, as the Potomageton.
16. Calycifloræ — Where the calyx-tube encloses the ovary, as the Oleaster.
17. Calycanthemæ — With the stamens inserted in the throat of the calyx, as the Melastomas.

CULTIVATION AND ANALYSIS OF PLANTS.

18. Bicornes — Two-horned, where the pollen is discharged by two pores or tubes, as in the Heath and Cranberry.
19. Hesperidæ — Myrtles
20. Rotaceæ — Wheel-form, as the Anagallis.
21. Preciæ — Primroses.
22. Caryophylleæ — Pinks.
23. Trihilatæ — Maples.
24. Corydales — Tufted, as the Fumitory.
25. Putamineæ — Pod-like-fruited, as the Caper.
26. Multisiliquæ — Many-podded, as the Hellebore.
27. Rhœadeæ — Soothing, as the Poppy.
28. Luridæ — Lurid, as the Nightshade.
29. Campanaceæ — Bell-like, as the Bellflower.
30. Contortæ — Twisted back, as the Milkweed.
31. Vepreculæ — Bushy, as the Daphne.
32. Papilionaceæ — Butterfly-shaped, as the Pea
33. Lomentaceæ — With jointed pods, as the Cassia.
34. Cucurbitaceæ — Curved, as the Gourd.
35. Senticosæ — Thorny, as the Rose.
36. Pomaceæ — Apple.
37. Columniferæ — Column-like, as the Mallow.
38. Tricocceæ — Three-kerneled, as the Spurge.
39. Siliquosæ — With long pods, as the Mustard; same as Cruciferæ, or Tetradynamia.
40. Personatæ — Masked, as the Snapdragon; nearly same as Didynamia Angiospermia.
41. Asperifoliæ — Rough-leaved, as the Borage.
42. Verticillatæ — Whorled, as the Holly; nearly equivalent to Didynamia Gymnospermia.
43. Dumosæ — Swelling, as the Viburnum.
44. Sepiariæ — With seeds hedged in, as the Jasmine.
45. Umbellatæ — Umbrella-like, as the Parsley.
46. Hederaceæ — Ivy.
47. Stellatæ — Star-like, as the Madder.
48. Aggregatæ — Scale-like, as the Scabious.
49. Compositæ — With massed flowers, as the Sunflower.
50. Amentaceæ — With catkins, as the Willow.
51. Coniferæ — Cone-bearing, as the Fir.
52. Coadunatæ — United at the base, as the Magnolia.
53. Scabridæ — Rough, as the Nettle.
54. Miscellaneæ — Miscellaneous flowering plants not embraced in the foregoing.
55. Filices — Ferns.
56. Musci — Mosses.
57. Algæ — Seaweeds.
58. Fungi — Funguses.

NATURAL SYSTEMS.

THE more recent botanists have developed various natural systems of classification, based on the internal affinities and essential properties of plants. One of the great advantages derivable from such methods is the bringing together into the same groups the plants that approach nearest to each other in structural characteristics. They are of course more philosophical than the artificial methods, which depended mainly on outward similarities; but the final determination of the numerous divisions and subdivisions of the vegetable kingdom, and the most appropriate nomenclature, has not yet been reached. The investigations of specialists are continually bringing to light new peculiarities, or differences that had escaped the notice of earlier observers. And hence every new writer on botany devises a method which is assumed to be an improvement on what preceded him.

Our distinguished native botanist, Dr. Asa Gray, of Harvard University, whose elementary works on botany have been declared by competent criticism to be "unsurpassed in the language for precision, simplicity, perspicuity and comprehensiveness," has formed a very elaborate system, mainly natural, but with a slight admixture of the artificial method.

The following table, showing a natural system, has been constructed, mainly from the "Genera Plantarum" of the late Austro-Hungarian botanist, Stephen Ladislaus Endlicher:

SYSTEMS OF CLASSIFICATION.

Classes, with their Orders and Genera.				Cohorts.	Sections.	Regions.
Scientific Name.	Translation.	Ord.	Gen.			
Algæ	Sea-weeds	7	122	*Protophyta* (first-born): First in the economy of nature, thriving without soil, deriving their growth from the sea or air.		*Thallophyta:* "Abundantly-sprouting plants," or the classes of plants that grow in the form of a "thallus," and without any well-marked discrimination between leaves, stems and roots — mostly composed of flattened cellular tissue, and growing in a dense mass of green tufts or fronds, which lie along the ground — **Flowerless Plants.**
Lichenes	Lichens	1	87			
Fungi	Funguses	5	474	*Hysterophyta* (late-born): Flourishing upon the soil made for them by the remains of the Protophyta.		
Hepaticæ	Liverworts	1	20	*Anophyta* (upward-born): Of a still higher grade than the foregoing sections, so called because of a tendency to upright growth.		
Musci	Mosses	3	70			
Equiseta	Horse-tails	1	1		*Acrobrya* (from *acron*, top, and *bruein*, to sprout): Stem growing only from the top; the same as Acrogens in other classifications.	
Filices	Ferns	7	70			
Hydropteridæ	Water-wings	2	10			
Selaginæ	Selago family	3	11			
Zamiæ	Hart-stems	1	10			
Rhizantheæ	Root-flowering	1	14			
Piumaceæ	Gramineæ (Grasses)	1	120		*Amphibrya* (from *amphi*, around, and *bruein*, to sprout). With the stem increasing or growing peripherically, or what, in other systems of classification, is known as the Endogenous Plants.	
Enantioblastæ	Cyperaceæ (Sedges)	1	47			
	Oppositely-budding	5	33			
Helobiæ	Marsh-living	2	20			
Coronariæ	Crowned perianth	6	94			
Artorhizæ	Bread-rooted	2	17			
Ensatæ	Sword-like	3	110			
Gynandræ	Hermaphrodite	2	335			
Scitamineæ	Dainty plants	3	18			
Fluviales	River plants (Naiads)	1	6			
Spadiciflóræ	Spadix-flowering	3	51			
Principes	Princely plants (Palms)	1	64			
Coniferæ	Cone-bearing	4	28	*Gymnosperms:* Naked seeds.		
Peperitæ	Pepper-like	1	43			
Aquaticæ	Aquatic	1	10			
Juliferæ	Catkin-flowering	15	72	*Apetalæ:* Without petals.		
Oleraceæ	Potherb-like	4	70			*Cormophyta* "Plants with trunks" or stems, where the root, stem and leaf are well discriminated; with the flowers apparent, and the distinction in the organs of fructification well defined — **Flowering Plants.**
Thymeleæ	Platform-like	9	145			
Serpentariæ	Serpent-like	2	8			
Plumbagines	Leadworts	2	10			
Aggregatæ	Clustered	3	859			
Campanulineæ	Bell-like	5	90	*Gamopetalæ:* With united or united petals; equivalent to monopetalous in other systems.		
Capritoliæ	Climbing-leaved	3	246			
Contortæ	Twisted	8	247			
Nuculiferæ	Small-nut-bearing	8	219			
Tubulifloræ	Tube-flowering	5	90			
Personatæ	Masked	7	318			
Petalanthæ	Petal-flowering	4	76		*Acramphibrya* (from *acron*, *amphi* and *bruein*, as above). With stems growing or increasing from the top and peripherically; or what, in the other systems of classification, are known as the Exogenous Plants.	
Bicornes	Two-horned	2	89			
Discanthæ	Disk-flowering	7	252			
Corniculatæ	Horn-shaped	4	77			
Polycarpicæ	Many-fruited	8	142			
Rhoeadeæ	Rhubarb-like	5	201			
Nelumbiæ	Nelumbo-like	2	10			
Parietales	Wall-plants	13	94			
Poponiferæ	Melon-bearing	3	33			
Opuntiæ	Prickly-pears (Cacti)	1	9			
Caryophyllineæ	Walnut-like-leaved	4	103	*Dialypetalæ:* With separate petals; equivalent to the polypetalous of the other systems.		
Columniferæ	Columnar	4	126			
Guttiferæ	Drop-bearing	9	93			
Hesperides	Evening plants	5	71			
Aceræ	Maples	3	56			
Polygalineæ	Very milky	2	16			
Frangulaceæ	Brittle	2	100			
Tricocceæ	Three-kerneled	7	129			
Terebinthianæ	Turpentine-yielding	10	197			
Gruinales	Cranebill-like	6	22			
Calycifloræ	Calyx-flowered	5	102			
Myrtifloræ	Myrtle-flowered	4	172			
Rosiferæ	Rose-bearing	5	77			
Leguminosæ	Leguminous plants	3	441			

The Influence of Floriculture.

SUCH literary leave-takings as epilogues and *Envoys* have grown into perhaps deserved disuse; for, as Shakespeare says, "A good play needs no epilogue;" yet, before taking final leave of a work that has constituted the delightful labor of many years, and bidding good-bye, as it were, to the thousands of human beings to whom the book will afford an introduction, the author would fain add a parting word to enforce the incalculable moral, intellectual and æsthetic value of floriculture. Science, in any department of knowledge, is of intrinsic worth to the human mind, but floriculture is eminently instructive, useful and agreeable. If all the plants of the world were of one shape, size and color, there would result a monotonous uniformity so burdensome to our imagination as can scarcely be conceived in the presence of the almost infinite variety we now enjoy. Nature, as if enticing us to search for her hidden treasures, has produced many wonderful forms so different from each other that our curiosity is awakened when we first observe some unusual product of her handiwork; and, thus stimulated, we are led to look for fresh peculiarities, and to push our investigations into the innumerable recesses of the vegetable kingdom.

The researches of the botanists have added largely to our list of food-plants, and have given us a sure guide as to which, among the many varieties of edible plants, are best adapted to supply our wants. Indeed, primitive man must have been a botanist in a small way when he first discovered that plants afforded food fit for his use; so that a rude botany must have been the first science cultivated among men. The first step toward civilization was therefore made by each wild tribe when, with some uncouth dibble, or pointed stick, they planted the first seed in the fruitful earth; and the cultivation of plants, though doubtless long confined to the food-plants only, constituted an important factor in the career of humanity as it progressed to refinement. Even now, when man has reached the greatest height yet attained, there is no better test of the civilization of the individual or the nation than the degree in which floriculture has become a fine art. So the amateur culturist may gather confidence from the thought that his favorite pursuit is the first and the last step in the progress of civilization. A knowledge of the healing properties of plants has been found no less useful by physicians. Indeed, for long ages the healing art was entirely confined to their use; and Liebig has said that all ordinary diseases may be cured or averted by a judicious change of the constituents of our plant-food.

THE INFLUENCE OF FLORICULTURE.

An outline study of botany, or (what is sometimes substituted for this) a close observation of nature, is necessary in most of the arts and sciences. The graceful, wavy, curved lines of flowers, leaves and fruits form an important feature in architectural ornamentation, as well as in the minor arts of cabinet-making, engraving, molding and the like. The exquisite blending of colors in the flowers and foliage of plants furnishes the painter with studies which he may imitate but cannot surpass. And the poets have ever been indebted to the vegetable kingdom for some of their happiest flights of brilliant fancy.

A love of flowers will supply a praiseworthy incentive to the merchant, clerk, artisan or laborer to leave behind him the smoke, dust and discomfort of the crowded city, and bask during an hour's or a day's leisure in the invigorating country air, while he enlarges his stock of knowledge by investigations that gently interest but do not overtax his intellectual powers. The moralist will find in the love of plants and flowers a helpful handmaiden to religion and virtue; even the mechanical pursuit of the mere trade of gardener has been conducive to a relatively superior morality, and freedom from crime. Horace Mann found that there were fewer gardeners, in proportion to their numbers, than of any other trade or calling in the poorhouses and prisons of Great Britain. Floriculture has also an advantage over many amateur pursuits in the cheapness and facility with which it can be followed, as every plant may be regarded as an unfolded book, and every flower an attractive object-lesson, while, unlike mechanics, astronomy or chemistry, it needs no expensive working apparatus. Flowers are the most delightful of all teachers.

THE USE OF FLOWERS.

God might have bade the earth bring forth
    Enough for great and small,
The oak-tree and the cedar-tree,
    Without a flower at all.
We might have had enough, enough
    For every want of ours,
For luxury, medicine and toil,
    And yet have had no flowers.

Then wherefore, wherefore were they made,
    All dyed with rainbow light,
All fashioned with supremest grace
    Upspringing day and night:—
Springing in valleys green and low,
    And on the mountains high,
And in the silent wilderness
    Where no man passes by?

Our outward life requires them not;
    Then wherefore had they birth?
To minister delight to man,
    To beautify the earth;
To comfort man—to whisper life,
    Whene'er his faith is dim.
For who so careth for the flowers
    Will care much more for him!

Mary Howitt.

Index of Sentiment.

A BELLE — Orchis, 227.
ABRUPTNESS — Borage, 52.
ABSENCE — Wormwood, 322.
A CONSTANT HEART — Bellflower, 47.
ADULATION — Cacalia, 63.
A GIFT — Eutoca, 130.
AGRICULTURE — Medick, 205.
ALLUREMENT — Quince, 255.
ALWAYS DELIGHTFUL — Cineraria, 80.
AMBITION — Hollyhock, 158.
A MEETING — Musk Plant, 215.
A MESSENGER — Iris, 173.
AMIABILITY — White Jasmine, 175.
AMID NATURE'S BEAUTIES — Persimmon, 238.
ANTICIPATION — Anemone, 18.
ARCHITECTURE — Candytuft, 71.
ARTIFICE — Fennel Flower, 133.
A SOUR DISPOSITION — Berberry, 48.
ASYLUM — Juniper, 176.
A TRIFLING CHARACTER — Bladdernut, 51.
ATTACHMENT — Ipomœa, 171.
AUSTERITY — Thistle, 299.
AUTHORITY — Yucca, 325.
AWAKENING LOVE — Lilac, 188.

BASENESS — Dodder, 115.
BASHFUL MODESTY — Sensitive Plant, 273.
BEAUTY IN RETIREMENT — Rhodora, 258.
BELOVED DAUGHTER — Potentilla, 250.
BENEVOLENCE — Calycanthus, 68.
BENEFITS — Spikenard, 282.
BENEFICENCE — Feverfew, 135.
BEWARE — Oleander, 223.
BLUSHES — Sweet Marjoram, 201.
BLUSHING BEAUTY — Damask Rose, 262.
BOASTING — Hydrangea, 167.
BONDS OF LOVE — Honeysuckle, 161.
BOUND BY FATE — Marsh Andromeda, 17.
BOUNTY — Double China Aster, 83.
BRAVERY — Lion's Heart, 191.

BRILLIANCY — Poinsettia, 246.

CALUMNY — Hellebore, 156.
CAN YOU BEAR POVERTY — Browallia, 57.
CHARMS — Sweet Balm, 38.
CHARMS — Musk Rose, 265.
CHASTITY — Orange, 226.
CHEERFULNESS — Spring Crocus, 101.
CHEERFULNESS IN OLD AGE — Aster, 32.
CHIVALRY — Daffodil, 107.
COLD-HEARTED — Lettuce, 187.
COMPLAINT — Ground Pine, 150.
CONFESSION — Lavender, 184.
CONFIDENCE — Geranium, 144.
CONSOLATION — Snowdrop, 277.
CONQUER YOUR LOVE — Asclepias, 27.
CONTEMPT — Carnation, 75.
COQUETRY — Day Lily, 113.
COUNTRY LIFE — Oats, 222.
COURTESY — Maurandia, 203.
CRUELTY — Marigold, 200.
CURIOSITY — Walking Fern, 134.

DANGER — Dragon's Claw, 117.
DEATH — Deadly Nightshade, 114.
DECEIT — Adder's Tongue, 2.
DECEIT — Venus's Fly-trap, 309.
DECEITFUL CHARMS — Thorn Apple, 301.
DECEPTION — Winter Cherry, 320.
DECEPTIVE APPEARANCES — Chestnut, 80.
DECLARATION OF LOVE — Tulip, 306.
DEFENSE — Privet, 252.
DEFORMITY — Begonia, 46.
DELAY — Eupatorium, 128.
DELIRIUM — Foxglove, 140.
DEPARTURE — Sweet Pea, 234.
DESIGN — Dyer's Weed, 119.
DESPAIR — Almond, 7.
DETRACTION — Clotbur, 89.
DEVOTION — Heliotrope, 155.

INDEX OF SENTIMENT.

DIFFICULTY — Thorn, 30.
DIFFIDENCE — Cyclamen, 105.
DIGNITY — Dahlia, 108.
DISCRETION — Lemon Blossom, 186.
DISTRUST — Buttercup, 61.
DOES HE POSSESS RICHES — Golden Bartonia, 42.
DOMESTIC INDUSTRY — Flax, 137.
DOMESTIC VIRTUE — Sage, 269.
DREAMS — Osmunda, 229.

EARLY FRIENDSHIP — Periwinkle, 237.
ECSTASY — Lophospermum, 195.
ELEGANCE — Birch, 49.
ELOQUENCE — Crape Myrtle, 100.
ELOQUENCE — Water Lily, 316.
EMULATION — Asparagus, 29.
ENERGY — Salvia, 270.
ENJOYMENT — Ground Ivy, 149.
ENTHUSIASM — Gum Tree, 151.
ESTIMATION — Indian Mallow, 170.
ETERNITY — Eternal Flower, 127.
EXCESSIVE SENSIBILITY — Aspen, 30.
EXHILARATION — Snowdrop Tree, 278.
EXPERIENCE — Sarsaparilla, 271.
EXTENT — Gourd, 147.

FALSEHOOD — Apocynum, 20.
FAME — Trumpet Flower, 304.
FANCY — Globe Flower, 146.
FAREWELL — Spruce, 283.
FATE — Hemp, 157.
FAVOR — Sassafras, 272.
FEAR — Arethusa, 24.
FELICITY — Sweet Sultan, 293.
FEMALE FIDELITY — Speedwell, 280.
FEMALE LOVELINESS — Justicia, 177.
FEMININE BEAUTY — Calla Lily, 67.
FESTIVITY — Parsley, 232.
FICKLENESS — Lady's Slipper, 179.
FIDELITY IN MISFORTUNE — Wallflower, 314.
FILIAL AFFECTION — Virgin's Bower, 313.
FITNESS — Sweet Flag, 291.
FLATTERY — Venus's Looking-glass, 310.
FOLLY — Columbine, 93.
FOPPERY — Cockscomb, 92.
FORESIGHT — Holly, 159.
FORGIVENESS — Aloysia, 9.
FORMALITY — Ice Plant, 169.
FORTITUDE — English Moss, 125.
FRANKNESS — Basket Osier, 228.
FRIENDSHIP — Rose Acacia, 1.
FUTURE HAPPINESS — Celandine, 78.

GAIETY — Butterfly Orchis, 62.

GOOD NATURE — Mullein, 214.
GOODNESS — Mallow, 198.
GOOD WISHES — Sweet Basil, 43.
GOSSIP — Cobæa, 91.
GLORIOUS BEAUTY — Clianthus, 88.
GLORY — Laurel, 183.
GRACE — Fuchsia, 142.
GRANDEUR — Ash, 28.
GRATITUDE — Canterbury Bells, 72.
GREATNESS — Cotton Plant, 98.
GRIEF — Aloe, 8.

HAPPY AT ALL TIMES — Coreopsis, 94.
HARDIHOOD — Cranberry, 99.
HEALTH — Fir Balsam, 136.
HEROISM — Nasturtium, 218.
HIDDEN QUALITIES — Sweet Potato, 292.
HIGH BRED — Penstemon, 236.
HOLY LOVE — Passion Flower, 233.
HOME — Eglantine, 121.
HONESTY — Honesty, 160.
HONESTY TRUE NOBILITY — Dogwood, 116.
HONOR — Oak, 221.
HUMILITY — Broom, 55.
HYPOCRISY — Bugloss, 58.

I AM THY PRISONER — Catchfly, 76.
I AM YOUR CAPTIVE — Peach Blossom, 235.
I DIE IF NEGLECTED — Laurestine, 184.
I CHANGE NOT — Globe Amaranth, 12.
I LIVE FOR THEE — Red Cedar, 77.
IMMORTALITY — Amaranth, 11.
IMPATIENCE — Balsamine, 41.
IMPATIENCE — Cuphea, 103.
IMPERIAL POWER — Crown Imperial, 102.
INDECISION — Bulrush, 59.
INDIFFERENCE — Mustard, 216.
INDUSTRY — Clover, 90.
INFATUATION — Cardamine, 73.
INGRATITUDE — Ranunculus, 257.
INJUSTICE — Hop, 162.
INNOCENCE — Dwarf Pink, 118.
INNOCENCE AND BEAUTY — Daisy, 109.
INSPIRATION — Angelica, 19.
INSTINCT — Pitcher Plant, 244.
INTELLECT — Walnut, 315.
INTOXICATION — Baccharis, 35.
INTRINSIC WORTH — Gentian, 143.
INTRUSION — Bouncing Bess, 53.
I REJECT YOU — Black Hoarhound, 50.
I RESPECT THY TEARS — Bayberry, 44.
I WILL THINK OF IT — Single China Aster, 84.

INDEX OF SENTIMENT.

I VALUE YOUR SYMPATHY — Wild Balm, 39.
JEALOUSY — Hyacinth, 166.
JESTING — Southernwood, 279.
JUSTICE — Rudbeckia, 267.
JUSTICE TO YOU — Tussilago, 307.

KEEP YOUR PROMISES — Petunia, 239.
KNIGHT-ERRANTRY — Monkshood, 211.

LABOR — Broom Corn, 56.
LASTING FRIENDSHIP — Ivy, 174.
LET ME HEAL THY GRIEF — Arnica, 26.
LEVITY — Larkspur, 182.
LIGHTNING — Pomegranate, 247.
LIGHT-HEARTEDNESS — Shamrock, 274.
LOFTY THOUGHTS — Sunflower, 290.
LOVE — Myrtle, 217.
LOVELINESS — Austrian Rose, 260.
LOVE OF NATURE — Magnolia, 197.
LOVERS' TRYST — Beech, 45.
LUXURY — Horse Chestnut, 163.

MALEVOLENCE — Lobelia, 193.
MARRIAGE — Citron, 87.
MATRIMONY — American Linden, 16.
MEDICINE — Endive, 124.
MEEKNESS WITH DIGNITY — Plumbago, 245.
MELANCHOLY — Weeping Willow, 317.
MEMORY — Syringa, 296.
MENTAL BEAUTY — Kennedya, 178.
MERCY — Chamomile, 79.
MERIT — Coriander, 95.
MERIT BEFORE BEAUTY — Alyssum, 10.
MIRTH — Pimpernel, 242.
MISANTHROPY — Teasel, 298.
MODESTY — Violet, 312.

NECESSITY — Mermaid Weed, 207.
NIGHT — Ebenaster, 130.
NOBILITY — Queen of the prairie, 254.
NOVELTY — Calceolaria, 66.

OBSTACLES TO BE OVERCOME — Mistletoe, 210.
OFFENSE — Stapelia, 284.
OPINION — Escallonia, 126.
OPPORTUNITY — Phaseolus, 240.
OBLIGING DISPOSITION — Valerian, 308.

PAINTING — Auricula, 33.
PARENTAL AFFECTION — Oxalis, 230.
PATRIOTISM — American Elm, 15.
PEACE — Olive, 225.
PERFECT GOODNESS — Strawberry, 287.
PERFECT LOVELINESS — Camellia, 69.

PERSECUTION — Fritillaria, 141.
PERSEVERANCE — Canary Grass, 70.
PHILANTHROPY — Melilot, 206.
PHILOSOPHY — Pine, 243.
PLEASURE — Loasa, 192.
POLITENESS — Ageratum, 4.
PRAISE — Queen of the Meadow, 253.
PREFERENCE — Apple Blossom, 21.
PREFERMENT — Cardinal Flower, 70.
PRESUMPTION — Snapdragon, 275.
PRIDE — Amaryllis, 13.
PRIDE BEFRIEND ME — Tiger Flower, 303.
PROMPTITUDE — Matthiola, 202.
PRODIGALITY — Aristolochia, 25.
PROSPERITY — Nemophila, 219.
PROVIDENCE — Oleaster, 224.
PROXIMITY UNDESIRABLE — Burdock, 60.
PRUDENT ECONOMY — Chicory, 82.
PURIFICATION — Hyssop, 168.
PURITY — Lily, 189.

QUICK-SIGHTEDNESS — Hawkweed, 152.

READY ARMED — Gladiolus, 145.
RECIPROCITY — Star Flower, 285.
RECONCILIATION — Star of Bethlehem, 286.
REMEMBERED BEYOND THE TOMB — Asphodel, 31.
REMEMBRANCE — Rosemary, 264.
REPENTANCE — Rue, 268.
REPOSE — Morning Glory, 212.
REPROOF — Euphorbia, 129.
RESERVE — Rock Maple, 199.
RESISTANCE — Tansy, 297.
RETIREMENT — Lake-flower, 180.
RETURN OF HAPPINESS — Lily of the Valley, 190.
RICHES — Wheat, 318.
RIGOR — Lantana, 181.
RIVALRY — Rocket, 259.
RUMOR — Mayweed, 204.

SECRECY — White Rose, 266.
SENSIBILITY — Verbena, 311.
SCULPTURE — Hoya, 165.
SHAME — Peony, 231.
SINGLE BLESSEDNESS — Bachelor's Button, 36.
SIMPLICITY — Arbutus, 23.
SLANDER — Nettle, 220.
SLEEP — Opium Poppy, 248.
SLIGHTED AFFECTIONS — Chrysanthemum, 85.
SOLITUDE — Heath, 153.
SORCERY — Enchanter's Nightshade, 123.
SORROW — Cypress, 106.
SORROW — Yew, 324.

423

INDEX OF SENTIMENT.

SORROWFUL REMEMBRANCES — Adonis, 3.
SPLENDOR — Sumach, 288.
STAR OF MY EXISTENCE — Chickweed, 81.
STOICISM — Box, 54.
STRATAGEM — Sweet William, 294.
SUCCESS — Summer Savory, 289.
SUCCESS CROWN YOUR WISHES — Coronilla, 97.
SUSPENSE — Ipomopsis, 172.
SWEETS TO THE SWEET — Daphne, 111.
SYMPATHY — Thrift, 302.
SYMPATHETIC FEELING — Balm of Gilead, 40.

TALKING — Rosebay, 261.
TEARS — Helenium, 154.
TEMPERANCE — Azalea, 34.
TEMPTATION — Apricot, 22.
TIME — Four o'clock, 139.
THANKFULNESS — Agrimony, 5.
THINE TILL DEATH — American Arbor Vitæ, 14.
THOUGHTS IN ABSENCE — Zinnia, 326.
THOUGHTS OF HEAVEN — Snowball, 276.
THREATS — Rose-leaved Rubus, 263.
TRANSIENT HAPPINESS — Spiderwort, 281.
TRANSIENT BEAUTY — Night-blooming Cactus, 64.
TRIFLING BEAUTY — Flower-of-an-Hour, 138.

UNANIMITY — Phlox, 241.
UNDERSTANDING — White Walnut, 319.

UNFORTUNATE ATTACHMENTS — Mourning Bride, 213.
UTILITY — Grass, 148.

VARIETY — Portulaca, 249.
VICE — Darnel, 112.
VICISSITUDE — Locust, 194.
VIRTUE — Mint, 209.
VIVACITY — Houseleek, 164.
VOLUPTUOUSNESS — Tuberose, 305.
VORACIOUSNESS — Lupine, 196.

WAR — Yarrow, 323.
WIT — Ragged Robin, 256.
WITCHERY — Witch Hazel, 321.
WOODLAND BEAUTY — Sycamore, 295.
WORTH ABOVE BEAUTY — Corn Cockle, 96.
WORTHY ALL PRAISE — Fennel, 132.

YOU EXCITE MY CURIOSITY — Molucca Balm, 37.
YOU PLEASE ALL — Currant, 104.
YOUR EYES ARE BEWITCHING — Eyebright, 131.
YOUR QUALITIES SURPASS YOUR CHARMS — Mignonette, 208.
YOU TERRIFY ME — Snake Cactus, 65.
YOUTH — Primrose, 251.
YOUTHFUL RECOLLECTIONS — Dandelion, 110.
ZEAL — Elder, 122.

424

www.ingramcontent.com/pod-product-compliance
Lightning Source LLC
Chambersburg PA
CBHW032137010526
44111CB00035B/597